Supreme Court Decision-Making

SUPREME COURT DECISION-MAKING

New Institutionalist Approaches

EDITED BY
Cornell W. Clayton
and Howard Gillman

THE UNIVERSITY OF CHICAGO PRESS • CHICAGO AND LONDON

CORNELL W. CLAYTON is associate professor and acting chair of the Department of Political Science at Washington State University. For more details, see Contributors.

HOWARD GILLMAN is associate professor of political science at the University of Southern California. For more details, see Contributors.

The University of Chicago Press, Chicago 60637
The University of Chicago Press, Ltd., London
© 1999 by The University of Chicago
All rights reserved. Published 1999
Printed in the United States of America
08 07 06 05 04 03 02 01 00 99   1 2 3 4 5

ISBN: 0-226-10954-2 (cloth)
ISBN: 0-226-10955-0 (paper)

Library of Congress Cataloging-in-Publication Data

Supreme Court decision-making : new institutionalist approaches /
  edited by Cornell W. Clayton and Howard Gillman.
      p. cm.
    Includes bibliographical references and index.
    ISBN 0-226-10954-2 (cloth : alk. paper).—ISBN 0-226-10955-0
  (pbk. : alk. paper)
    1. United States. Supreme Court—Decision-making. 2. Judicial
  process—United States. 3. Law and politics. I. Clayton, Cornell
  W., 1960– . II. Gillman, Howard.
  KF8748.S878 1999
  347.73'26—dc21   98-20662
                                                                  CIP

♾ The paper used in this publication meets the minimum requirements of the American National Standard for Information Sciences—Permanence of Paper for Printed Library Materials, ANSI Z39.48-1992.

CONTENTS

**Part Two: Legal Norms and the Internal Structure
of Supreme Court Decision-Making**

**Part Three: Extra-Judicial Influences on Supreme
Court Decision-Making**

FIGURES AND TABLES

Figures

Tables

ACKNOWLEDGMENTS

First, we are grateful to our contributing authors for their wonderful work and helpful suggestions. We were lucky to work with such a fine group of colleagues, particularly in light of the fact that edited volumes can be a nightmare to manage if one does not have the benefit of talented contributors who are committed to the project. We learned quite a bit from their efforts and we hope that the same will be true for our readers.

Over the years our belief in the importance of adopting more institutional perspectives on Supreme Court decision-making has been fortified and refined by many friends and colleagues, including Mark Graber, Michael McCann, John Brigham, Susan Burgess, Christine Harrington, Bill Haltom, Sandy Levinson, and H. W. Perry. We owe a special debt of gratitude to Rogers Smith, not only for his friendship and support but for his ongoing efforts to encourage public law scholars to explore various camps within the so-called "new institutionalism."

John Tryneski, from the University of Chicago Press, has been a consummate editor and we appreciate the support and guidance he provided at every stage of the project. We also appreciate the efforts of the anonymous reviewers of the manuscript, since their comments helped us work with the authors to further improve the volume.

Institutional support for the preparation of the manuscript came from the Departments of Political Science at the University of Southern California and Washington State University, and we would like to thank our chairpersons, Sheldon Kamieniecki and Lance LeLoup. Sarkis Mahdasian assisted our efforts in assembling the various pieces of the manuscript into a coherent whole, and we appreciate his work.

As always, our families deserve the final nod for their understanding and support when the demands of this work occasionally took us away from more important responsibilities. The Claytons who deserve the credit are Cornell's wife, Wendy, and his children, Katherine and Nicholas. In Los Angeles the essential support staff includes Howard's wife, Ellen, and his children, Arielle and Danny.

Cornell W. Clayton, at Pullman, Washington
Howard Gillman, at Los Angeles, California
December 1997

Beyond Judicial Attitudes: Institutional Approaches to Supreme Court Decision-Making

Howard Gillman and Cornell W. Clayton

The Dominance of the Attitudinal Model of Supreme
Court Decision-Making

For quite some time political scientists studying the Supreme Court treated this institution as little more than a collection of individuals who were pursuing their personal policy preferences. Undoubtedly the main reason for this level of analysis was the eminently defensible observation that the Court's decisions reflected the attitudes or world views of the individual justices. Once it could be shown that justices with different values voted differently, and that the general trajectory of the Court's decisions changed after changes in the Court's personnel (Baum 1988), many onlookers easily concluded that little else needed to be said by way of explanation of the Court's behavior. In the words of the most rigorous and enthusiastic proponents of the so-called "attitudinal model," "The Supreme Court decides disputes in light of the facts of the case vis-à-vis the ideological attitudes and values of the justices. Simply put, Rehnquist votes the way he does because he is extremely conservative; Marshall voted the way he did because he [was] extremely liberal" (Segal and Spaeth 1993:65).

The preoccupation of Supreme Court scholars with the attitudes and policy preferences of individual justices also seems reasonable and sufficient in light of the fact that Supreme Court decision-making is much less affected by conspicuous bureaucratic structures than is the case with either the Congress or the presidency. Even after one has taken into account the ideology of legislators, it is difficult to imagine adequate explanations of the behavior of Congress as an institution without some reference to such things as committee structure, the seniority system, and the formal powers of the House and Senate leadership.

Similarly, while there may be a few presidential scholars who feel as
though one can adequately understand presidential behavior with reference to the personal or psychological characteristics of individual
presidents (Barber 1972, 1992; Kearns 1976; George 1980), in general it
is understood that the presidency is not so much a person as an institution, an institution that is characterized by an even more complicated
and elaborate bureaucratic structure—Cabinet departments and agencies, the Executive Office bureaucracy, and various White House offices—than that which shapes congressional behavior (e.g., Campbell
1986; Hess 1988; Nathan 1983; Pfiffner 1988, 1991; Waterman 1989).

By contrast, while it is true that over the last half-century or so there
has been an increase in the number of offices associated with the Supreme Court, nevertheless the day-to-day work of the justices is almost
completely unaffected by the sorts of battling bureaucracies and clash-
ing committees that shape the presidency and Congress. On the Court,
most of the battles or clashes are interpersonal rather than intrabureau-
cratic. Even when infighting is evident, the standard practice has been
for the justices to proceed on their own, as individuals. This is made
possible by the absence of formal hierarchies among the justices, their
equal access to relevant information, and their ability to participate as
individuals whenever the Court hands down a decision and thereby
formally exercises its power. Thus, in contrast to other political institutions, the Supreme Court has an organizational structure that helps to
authorize the kind of individual level of analysis preferred by supporters of the attitudinal model.

This is not to say that attitudinal theorists have paid no attention to
the institutional features of the Court. Some structural explanations are
usually offered for why the justices are free to pursue their personal
policy preferences. For example, it is common for some behavioralists
to point out that life tenure and control over jurisdiction enables the
justices to act on the basis of a preferred course of conduct (Segal and
Spaeth 1993:69–72, Rohde and Spaeth 1976:72). Still, in many cases
even this modest attention to issues of institutional context is lacking
in behavioralist studies (Baum 1994b:758). The treatment of the Court
as an institution is largely limited to the recognition that justices of the
Supreme Court are expected to perform certain tasks or chores, such
as setting an agenda by granting writs of *certiorari* or casting votes in
cases. Once these institutional chores are identified, the analysis usually reverts back to an examination of how the personal attitudes of
the justices affect the way they approach these chores. Little systematic
effort is made to explore whether institutional norms or contexts have

an independent effect on the justices' attitudes or their ability to advance a preferred course of conduct, possibly because it is assumed that reference to such independent institutional effects is unnecessary given the sufficiency of attitudinal explanations that demonstrate correlations between individual level policy preferences and judicial voting behavior.

Why the Attitudinal Model Is Not Enough

There is no reason to take issue with the observation that Supreme Court justices act in ways that reflect who they are and what they believe. At some level, all political behavior must be explained with some reference to individual values, attitudes, or personalities (Taylor 1985). Still, there are good reasons to think that there may be much to be gained by focusing less on the policy preferences of particular justices and more on the distinctive characteristics of the Court as an institution, its relationship to other institutions in the political system, and how both of these might shape judicial values and attitudes.

Specifically, any attempt to explain behavior with reference to beliefs but not to contexts such as institutional settings will inevitably be incomplete for at least two reasons. First, institutional settings are an omnipresent feature of our attempts to pursue a preferred course of action. It is not possible to imagine political behavior—or, for that matter, any purposeful human behavior—proceeding without some overt or tacit reference to the institutional arrangements and cultural contexts that give it shape, direction, and meaning. Even if political actors come to think that they are free to promote a preferred agenda, it is necessarily the case that this experience is a by-product of a set of favorable institutional conditions and is not evidence of the irrelevance of context. In fact, in such a circumstance one of the most interesting questions that can be explored is whether the experience of unfettered freedom is a function of the tendency of relevant players to pursue only those agendas that do not trigger the potential constraints that are latent in every context.

This is just another way of saying that different contexts make it more or less possible for individuals to act on different sets of beliefs. When participants interpret the experience of freedom or constraint as a set of opportunities and risks they may find themselves engaging in a form of cost-benefit analysis in order to think through what course of conduct seems most rational in light of their goals. A less strategic conception of the constraints imposed by institutional contexts would

suggest that certain settings hold a sense of appropriateness about
what kinds of behaviors or motivations are considered acceptable under certain circumstances. Either way, whether one's orientation to
context is accomplished via calculation or a sensitivity to propriety, it
is still the case that our sense of what can be done flows out of our
encounters with particular contexts, and thus an account of purposeful
human behavior must always be attentive to the relationship between
various courses of conduct and the settings within which they are embedded.

For example, while Supreme Court justices certainly act in accordance with a set of beliefs (on what other basis would they act?), it
may be the case that the justices also believe that certain kinds of attitudes—such as a desire to promote the well-being of political allies—
would be an inappropriate or risky basis for decision-making, either
because the exhibition of such attitudes violates a sense of institutional
propriety or because of a strategic calculation that the justices would
have to pay too high a price for exhibiting these attitudes. The fact that
the justices habitually act in certain ways, promoting some attitudes
or goals and not others, might suggest that every member of the Court
freely chooses to indulge only certain kinds of attitudes and goals over
all other potential agendas (including political patronage) or it might
mean that institutional norms and contexts have some impact on the
particular beliefs that justices seek to promote. Either way, attention
to the institutional settings within which justices operate will put us
in a better position to evaluate the adequacy of attitudinal theories of
Supreme Court politics. Indeed, even the ability of contemporary behavioralists to investigate the attitudes of individual justices has been
facilitated by the collapse in the 1940s of a traditional set of norms that
discouraged justices from writing separate concurring and dissenting
opinions (see O'Brien's essay in this volume). In this respect, attitudinal
theory may itself be viewed as the by-product of a developing and
historically contingent set of institutional practices.

Beyond being able to make sense of individual-level judicial preferences and the ability of institutional settings to affect the individual
justice's capacity to pursue those preferences, there is a second, and
perhaps more important, reason why it is essential for Supreme Court
scholars to attend to institutional contexts and not just judicial attitudes. Individuals who are associated with particular institutions often
come to believe that their position imposes upon them an obligation
to act in accordance with particular expectations and responsibilities.
In other words, institutions not only structure one's ability to act on a

set of beliefs; they are also a source of distinctive political purposes, goals, and preferences. In fact, it is tempting to argue that what makes something a recognizable "institution" is not the hard reality of a building but instead some discrete and discernible habits of thought, including a set of attitudes about the appropriate functions to be performed by people associated with the institution and the relationship between these responsibilities and those performed by other institutions (see Gillman's essay in this volume). James Madison counted on this sort of attachment when he wrote in Federalist No. 51 that in order for a system of checks and balances to work "the interest of the man must be connected with the constitutional rights of the place."

With respect to Supreme Court politics, this means that the justices' behavior might be motivated not only by a calculation about prevailing opportunities and risks but also by a sense of duty or obligation about their responsibilities to the law and the Constitution and by a commitment to act as judges rather than as legislators or executives. If this is true, then the tendency of some attitude theorists to characterize Supreme Court politics in the language of conventional partisan wrangling may result in a misunderstanding of the driving force behind judicial behavior. While a judge's vote may sometimes correlate with the behavior expected of a partisan, the attitude expressed by the vote may not be reducible to goals and purposes that are more commonly associated with other institutions. We can only find out whether a set of distinctive norms and traditions affects a judge's behavior if we are more attentive to the habits of thought that constitute the Court as an institution.

Supreme Court Politics and the "New Institutionalism" in the Social Sciences

Over the past few years we have seen in the social sciences generally a renewed interest in studying how political behavior is given shape, structure, and direction by particular institutional arrangements and relationships (Koelble 1995; March and Olsen 1989; Powell and DiMaggio 1991; Steinmo, Thelen, and Longstreth 1992). This research has also made its mark on public law scholarship (Smith 1988, McCann 1994, and the works cited in the essays in this volume by Clayton; Maltzman, Spriggs, and Wahlbeck; and Gillman). Like traditional, pre-behavioral legal studies, much of the new work takes seriously the effects of judicial norms and legal traditions and attempts to situate the Court in larger political contexts. Some of those who engage in this new work, like more traditional institutional scholars, are less fastidious about maintaining barriers between normative and empirical inquiry than are most behavioralists. After all, approaching the topic of Supreme Court politics as "if politics matters" (Smith 1992) makes it more likely that political analysis can double as a critique of norms and traditions that are believed to have an unfortunate influence on judicial behavior. Moreover, by broadening the scope of inquiry to include features of judicial behavior besides votes on cases—such as the act of constructing an authoritative ideology or strategizing about how to cope with potential opponents—this scholarship holds out the promise of making research more relevant to the issues commonly addressed in classrooms.

One of the challenges of organizing a volume around institutional approaches to judicial decision-making is that there are nearly as many ways to think about institutions as there are practitioners of institutional analyses. In his review of the recent literature on the so-called "new institutionalism" Thomas Koelble (1995) has suggested at least three broad camps. In one camp are those who embrace rational choice or positive theory. Because these scholars assume that political agents share a common interest in maximizing their preferences they focus on how structural arrangements affect the strategic calculations of participants. Those who engage in this work seek to explore how political behavior flows not only from a set of attitudes but from a rational calculation about how best to accomplish one's goals in light of the risks and opportunities presented by particular institutional configurations. By carefully mapping out the costs and benefits of adopting particular courses of conduct in particular settings, these rational-choice institutionalists hope to show how the behavior of judges and other power holders is as much a product of the need to adjust to context as it is a reflection of a set of *a priori* policy preferences.

In the second camp are those whose work seeks to provide historical accounts of institutional development or interpretive characterizations of the actions of judges and other political actors. These scholars argue that one of the failings of rational-choice institutionalism is that it excludes from the analysis the issue of preference formation. Supreme Court scholars engaged in these historical institutional studies tend to assume that judicial behavior is not merely *structured* by institutions but is also *constituted* by them in the sense that the goals and values associated with particular political arrangements give energy and direction to political actors. The work is historical because it is assumed that, over time, as institutions interact with other features of the political system and attempt to cope with a changing society they might transform themselves and develop new norms, traditions, and functions.

A final group of new institutionalists argue that individual conduct is not just the consequence of particular institutional settings but the product of much larger social frameworks. According to these ethnographic or social institutionalists, individuals find themselves embedded in "cultural and organizational 'fields' or 'sectors' which determine the very concept of self-interest and utility." Thus, the conduct of individuals within particular institutions must be understood within the contextual web of attachments, obligations, and affective bonds that constitute the essential grounds for conduct. These would include such broad social and cultural structures as class, race, gender, and religion. The work is ethnographic because it is assumed that the presence or absence of distinctive habits of thought can only be discerned with careful attention to particular institutional practices and the larger cultural or ideological contexts within which institutions develop their identities.

The Outline of this Volume

In his influential essay calling for a new institutional approach to public law, Rogers Smith expressed the hope that a reconciliation of various institutionalist camps would allow scholars to focus more attention on "different types of structures or institutions that, we hypothesize, constitute and empower political actors and their environments in important ways, endowing actors with specifiable constraints or capabilities, or both" (Smith 1988:90). In this collection we cannot promise a reconciliation, but we hope to provide a collection of the best work performed by Supreme Court scholars who are interested in focusing attention on how the institutional characteristics of the Court, as well as the Court's relationship to other features of the political system, are essential to an adequate understanding of Supreme Court decision-making. There are of course many other important aspects of Supreme Court politics, other than how the justices decide cases, that are appropriate subjects for institutional analyses—the Court's impact on social reform, the Court's relationship to public opinion, the Court's ability to encourage or blunt political mobilization, to name only a few. In this volume, however, we focus on the relatively narrow, but important, question of how and why the justices on the U.S. Supreme Court and state courts of last appeal decide cases the way they do.

We begin in part 1 with three essays addressing the preliminary

question of what it means to conceptualize the Court as an institution. Many scholars share a commitment to institutional analysis but sharply disagree about what kind of analysis should flow from this commitment. Represented among these essays are a number of competing and overlapping positions on whether an institutional approach should emphasize: actual or "real" structures, processes, and responsibilities; distinctive habits of thought; the meanings and values the political system attaches to the institution; or the risks and opportunities that are encountered by political actors as they strategize about how to rationally promote their interests.

Cornell Clayton begins this discussion by placing the emergence of new institutional scholarship on courts within the context of the historical development of public law as a distinct field in political science. He draws attention to how the new institutionalism has emerged in response to a growing awareness of certain weaknesses in behavioral approaches—particularly their reliance on instrumental or positivist conceptions of law and politics—and how behavioralism itself emerged as a response to the traditional or "old" institutionalism practiced by scholars such as Edward S. Corwin, Robert E. Cushman, and Charles Grove Haines. Emphasizing the kinship between this "old" and the "new" institutionalisms, Clayton calls for research that rejects instrumental conceptions of law and politics in favor of the "constitutive" conceptions held by these earlier scholars. He concludes his essay with the suggestion that a promising path for future research is to connect such a constitutive conception of law and politics to empirical studies that seek to situate the Court's decisions within the context of broader features of the American political system.

The essay by Forrest Maltzman, James Spriggs II, and Paul Wahlbeck argues the merits of studying judicial decision-making within the framework of a positivist theory of institutions (PTI). Building on Walter Murphy's (1964) early study of strategic justice, scholars using the PTI approach seek to understand particular judicial decisions by mapping out the strategic or institutionalized terrain that conditions the possible set of realizable choices that justices can make. Maltzman, Spriggs, and Wahlbeck suggest that this approach holds the best promise for synthesizing the concerns for law and legal structures of traditional institutionalism with the behavioralist insight that judges define the law according to their underlying political preferences.

In the final essay of part 1, Howard Gillman suggests that while strategic studies may be able to draw attention to certain aspects of Supreme Court politics, they are also burdened by a conception of "institutional politics" that is unnecessarily narrow; thus, he suggests historical and interpretive approaches provide opportunities to explore a broader range of institutional effects. Gillman argues that, from an interpretivist perspective, institutions should be thought of as attempts to routinize particular political purposes or "missions," and that institutional politics should focus on how these distinctive institutional world views or perspectives shape judicial attitudes. Among other things, this means that Court scholars should examine the putative role of the Court in the political system and the extent to which the justices feel a sense of obligation to the performance of this role, as well as to the maintenance of institutional legitimacy and efficacy.

As you read essays in subsequent parts, keep in mind these earlier theoretical discussions. They may help you develop a critical point of view about the strengths and weaknesses of various approaches to Supreme Court politics.

In part 2 we turn to a series of essays that examines the relationship between the justices' decision-making and legal norms as well as the Court's internal norms, structures, and processes. The emphasis in these essays is on how the distinctive features of the Court as an institution shape and direct how and why it exercises its power.

David O'Brien begins this part with a discussion of the changing institutional norms structuring opinion-writing on the Court. Historically, justices placed a premium on "opinions for the Court," that is, "institutional opinions" rationalizing the Court's decision. But in the post–World War II period institutional opinions have become devalued and the number of individual opinions—concurring in, dissenting from, as well as separate opinions in part concurring and dissenting from the Court's ruling—have proliferated. O'Brien describes and offers several explanations for the changing norms governing opinion-writing. Chief among these, O'Brien argues, is the collapse of consensus around constitutional jurisprudence and the resultant disharmony on the Court over how to justify particular decisions.

Charles Sheldon's chapter examines similar trends in the opinion-writing norms of state supreme courts. Noting that justices actually confront conflicting institutional pressures when it comes to deciding whether to write a separate opinion—some supporting dissent and other supporting consensus—Sheldon focuses on the reasons that justices offer for authoring dissenting or concurring opinions. Having surveyed 117 former clerks to justices on the Washington State high bench, Sheldon found that the propensity to dissent is structured by several factors, including such things as the level of jurisprudential harmony

on the court, the existence and function of intermediate appellate
courts, and the existence of certain internal professional norms about
what is the appropriate purpose or goal of a dissenting opinion.

In her chapter on the institutional basis for leadership by the Chief
Justice, Sue Davis reviews the existing literature on Court leadership
and concludes that there is a need to move past studies of opinion
assignment alone and to focus more attention on other areas of Court
leadership. She suggests a number of areas ripe for future studies of
leadership from both rational-choice and historical/interpretive institutional perspectives. Ultimately, however, she concludes that efforts
to reconcile these approaches in order to find a unified institutional
approach are unlikely to succeed because they begin with disparate
assumptions about politics and human behavior. Consequently, Davis
concludes that scholars interested in studying Court leadership should
eschew such a reconciliation in favor of recognizing the value of a diversity in the field.

The two final chapters in part 2 examine the role of "the law" and
judicial doctrine in shaping and constraining the ability of individual
justices to pursue their political policy preferences. Examining "judicial
liberalism and the problem of welfare rights," Elizabeth Bussiere argues that the Court's failure to find positive welfare rights rooted in the
Constitution in such cases as *Shapiro v. Thompson* (1968) and *DeShaney v.
Winnebago* (1989) can be explained only by the Court's adherence to
relatively stable conceptions of the Equal Protection and Due Process
Clauses rather than by the political preferences of individual justices.
Likewise, Ronald Kahn's chapter on the Rehnquist Court argues that
it has been less conservative and more counter-majoritarian than attitudinalists and rational-choice scholars would have predicted. The reason, Kahn suggests, is that the justices hold a constitutive conception of
the law in which "polity" and "rights" principles, and not conventional
political attitudes and policy preferences, guide decision-making.

In part 3 we turn from the law and internal Court norms and practices to the external relationship between the Court as an institution
and other institutions in the political system. After all, like all institutions,
the Supreme Court arose out of, and operates within, a particular political and constitutional system. The Court's ability to persist and even
thrive in this political system is a by-product of an unformalizable combination of considerations, including: the general social patterns of conflict
and consensus that are generated by specific cultural, institutional, and
class frameworks; the relationship between the Court's jurisprudence
and the beliefs, interests, and legal views of other powerful political

actors such as Congress and the President; the ability of interest groups to mobilize support or opposition to the Court and its decisions; and the justices' ability to cope with setbacks, adjust to changing circumstances, and more generally protect the Court's authority and legitimacy.

This final part begins with a chapter by Lawrence Baum. Professor Baum examines how the recruitment and selection process of Supreme Court justices interacts with other institutional characteristics of the Court—such as life tenure, discretionary jurisdiction, and the Court's insulation from direct external control—to affect the goal orientations and motivations of the justices. Baum concludes that together with these other institutional features, the recruitment and selection process has a powerful effect of freeing justices to concentrate on "legal" concerns and legal policy. But this freedom is not a constraint; justices can also act to advance interests other than "legal" positions and goals, including political policy objectives and advancement of personal self-interests.

Lee Epstein and Jack Knight's chapter examines the growing role of *amicus curiae* advocacy before the Supreme Court. They argue that organized interests perform functions for the justices similar to those performed by lobbyists for legislators: these groups provide information about the views and preferences of other political actors. This information is vital to the justices, who, Epstein and Knight argue, must make strategic decisions about how best to advance their individual policy preferences so as not to provoke opposition from other powerful political actors. In other words, just as information about the views of particular groups allows legislators to make strategic decisions about how best to advance a particular policy end through legislation, so too does it enable justices to make decisions that will maximize their policy positions through law.

Jeffrey Segal's chapter, though not a direct response to Epstein and Knight, tests one of the fundamental assumptions of the rational-choice model of Supreme Court decision-making: whether in deciding cases the justices feel constrained by the positions of other political actors such as Congress. In particular, Segal looks at whether there is any empirical support for what he calls the "separation of powers model" (see, e.g., Marks 1988; Spiller and Gely 1992) which assumes that judicial decisions are dependent upon congressional preferences. Examining the Court's statutory decisions in civil liberties and economic cases between its 1946 and 1992 terms, Segal found little support for this assumption. Instead, he concludes that the Court's unique institutional context in fact insulates the justices from most external political constraints and frees them to pursue their individual preferences.

Even if one accepts Segal's claim that there exists little empirical evidence of a significant relationship between the Court's decisions on the merits and the positions of most other external political actors, the question of why the justices are free to simply pursue their policy preferences in such cases still remains. Charles Epp's chapter may provide one answer. Epp argues that the process by which the Court grants *certiorari* both limits the extent to which individual justices can exert direct influence over the types of cases the Court decides and simultaneously accentuates the influence of important external political groups in setting the Court's agenda. Epp argues that the Court's agenda is responsive to what he calls "concentrated external pressures," consisting of changes in the availability of the various resources that facilitate appellate litigation. Hence the Court rarely acts to decide cases in controversial policy areas without the support of other actors such as the legal profession, the Department of Justice, or major interest groups.

In the final chapter of this volume, Melinda Gann Hall and Paul Brace argue for a comparative approach to understanding the institutional determinants of judicial decision-making. Their chapter analyzes how a variety of institutional factors—including recruitment and retention methods, internal operating rules, and the presence of lower appellate courts—work together to shape decision-making on state supreme courts. Examining how various state supreme courts have decided capital punishment cases, Hall and Brace conclude that judicial decision-making is inextricably tied to a court's institutional environment in highly systematic and predictable ways.

More than thirty years ago Glendon Schubert edited a volume entitled *Judicial Decision-Making* (1963). That volume was a collection of essays written by judicial scholars employing the then "new" behavioralist approach to studying courts. In many ways this volume represents a response by a succeeding generation of Supreme Court scholars, who are trained in political behavioralism but who have rediscovered the value and importance of understanding institutional contexts. Each of the chapters seeks to explain a disarmingly simple question: How do institutions influence the way judges make decisions? Each chapter's author(s) provides a different answer to this question. This volume does not, and has not sought, to provide a common answer to this question, but has instead represented the diverse views and array of the new institutional scholarship. To this extent it is the editors' hope that it will serve at once as a valuable introduction to this new research and a catalyst for future debate and discussion about its direction.

PART ONE
Conceptualizing the Supreme Court as an Institution

1

The Supreme Court and Political Jurisprudence: New and Old Institutionalisms

Cornell W. Clayton

For some, the theme of this volume may be puzzling. Each contributor shares the view that institutions influence Supreme Court decision-making. In other words, these authors see formal and informal legal structures—such as constitutions, statutes, judicial doctrines, or shared conceptions of equality or liberty—as independent variables and the justices' decisions as dependent ones. Yet this is hardly a novel idea to most lawyers and judges, who routinely behave as if the law and legal institutions matter greatly. Nor is it a new idea to those familiar with the classic public law scholarship produced by Robert Cushman, Edward Corwin, Charles Grove Haines, and others in political science. Indeed, the average person on the street would think that scholarship which suggests that the law influences judicial decisions is simply belaboring the obvious. So what explains this volume?

To understand what may be new or important about the scholarship in this volume, one must place it into context to see how it differs from other ways of understanding Supreme Court decision-making. The purpose of this chapter then is primarily descriptive and historical. It is to explain how political scientists who study law and courts have come to think about their subjects and methods of inquiry, and to explain why a proposition that seems patently obvious and conventional to legal practitioners and the public at large strikes us as original and fresh. To make these explanations, it is necessary to consider what has become the predominant, behavioralist approach to studying the Supreme Court, the so-called "attitudinal model" (Segal and Spaeth 1993), and to consider how "new institutionalism" departs from that approach as well as from a more traditional or "old institutional" approach to studying courts.

More generally, I hope to say something about what it means to *properly contextualize* judicial decision-making as a political activity. This will lead me to say something about how I think political scientists should conceptualize institutions and the new institutionalism. In particular, I want to suggest the importance of viewing legal institutions as part of the broader political system, as being given their individual meaning by their context within the existing pattern of institutional relationships that make up the political regime. I hope to do this in a way free of the idiom and jargon that often characterizes self-conscious disciplinary work.

Realism, The Legal Academy and the "Old Institutionalism"

The philosophical realism of the early twentieth century profoundly influenced both the nascent social sciences and the legal academy. Within political science scholars such as Lawrence Lowell, Woodrow Wilson, and Charles Beard argued for a less idealized understanding of government institutions and for a more realistic analysis of how they actually functioned and what interests they served. These "old institutionalists" dissented from the then prevailing view "that the state, the economy, and society reflected human nature" and instead insisted that "these were constructed according to historically evolved patterns, which they called institutions, that were themselves open to modification" through reflective judgment and wise legislative choices (Ethington and McDonagh 1995). Chief among these institutions was the state—and by extension the Constitution—which is why these old institutionalists were often described as interested in "state" or "constitutional" studies.

Likewise, within the legal academy Legal Realists such as Oliver Wendell Holmes, Karl Llewellyn, and Jerome Frank dispatched traditional mechanistic and formalistic conceptions of the law, and instead emphasized the creativity found in judging. As with any broad intellectual movement, American Legal Realism had several strands and varieties, but at its heart was the now well known critique that judges did more than simply *find* law, they also *made* law (see Llewellyn 1930). An important consequence of the Realist movement was that law could no longer be understood in isolation but now had to be considered in light of larger political, economic, and social background structures (Posner 1987). Llewellyn recognized this loss of disciplinary autonomy in a frank admission:

Included in the field of law under such an approach is everything currently included, and a vast deal more. . . . Part
of law, in many aspects, is all of society, and all of man in
society. . . . As to the overlapping of the field as thus
sketched with that of other social sciences, I should be sorry
if no overlapping were observable. The social sciences are
not staked out like real estate. Even in law the fines for tres-
pass are not high (1930:465).

Given the loss of disciplinary autonomy, it is not surprising that public law emerged as a distinct subfield within political science as a consequence of the Legal Realist movement. What allowed political scientists
to say something of interest about law that could not be said more
authoritatively by judges and academic lawyers was that the discussion at some level now took place on the terrain of politics, something
over which political science presumably had unique insight. Thus,
from the very outset, the subfield of public law was wedded to a "realistic" or a political understanding of the legal process. Judicial decisions and political values were intimately connected, and law was only
relatively autonomous from broader political and social structures. In this
sense, all post-Realist political science, both in its institutional and behavioral varieties, has been wedded to a "political jurisprudence" (although this term was later used by Martin Shapiro [1964a, 1984, 1989]
to describe a more limited form of inquiry).

Realism had very different consequences for how the legal academy
on the one hand, and political science on the other, came to teach and
think about law and the judicial process. Because the core function of
the legal academy was to train lawyers, judges, and legal practitioners,
the academy proved more impervious to changing conceptions of law
and its new linkage with politics. Although the definition of the traditional "legal model" and the degree of professional adherence to it can
be debated, what cannot is that precedent, *stare decisis*, and formalism
continue to be the way most law students experience law and the way
judges describe what they do in written opinions. With the exception
of the occasional course in jurisprudence and the occasional statement
of "judicial candor," the law school curriculum and judicial opinions
continue to rely on a fairly traditional "legal model" to explain the craft
of law. As Richard Posner notes, long after the ascendance of the Realist
movement in legal scholarship:

[L]aw professors, with only a few exceptions, continued to
believe that the only thing law students needed to study

was authoritative legal texts . . . and the pertinent commentary on them, plus the power of logical discrimination and
argumentation. The only change from Langdell's day . . .
was that law was increasingly recognized to be a purposive
instrument of social control, so one had to know something
about society . . . to improve law. But that "something" was
what any intelligent person with a good general education
and common sense knew (1990:425).

To be sure, elite academic lawyers recognized that Realism undermined the traditional assumptions of American jurisprudence, creating
a crisis in particular for justifying the institution of judicial review
(Fried 1988). The outpouring of constitutional theory, especially after
the activism of the Warren Court, by scholars such as John Hart Ely,
Ronald Dworkin, Bruce Ackerman, and others represents a concerted
effort to reconcile the belief in judicial review and rule of law with
the Realist recognition that judging itself was an exercise of political
power (Seidman and Tushnet 1996). Nevertheless, both these "neo-
traditionalist" efforts to rescue judicial review from Realism (Posner
1990) and the radical critiques of the law offered by post-Realist movements—such as critical legal studies, law and economics, and feminist
jurisprudence—have all remained remarkably compartmentalized
within the legal academy, confined largely to discussions of jurisprudential theory. They are curiously detached from the processes of pro-
fessionalization and practice of the legal craft.[1] Judges rarely rely upon
these theories in their written opinions, and legal training continues to
use rather traditional methods of case study and doctrinal analysis to
teach students how to lawyer. Typical of the legal practitioner view of
the law is Justice Scalia's opinion in *American Trucking Assns. v. Smith*
(1990):

> The very framing of the issue that we purport to decide to-
> day . . . presupposes a view of our decisions as *creating* the
> law, as opposed to *declaring* what the law already is. Such
> a view is contrary to that understanding of the "judicial
> Power," US Const, Art III, Sec 1, cl 1, which is not only the
> common and traditional one, but which is the only one that
> can justify courts in denying force and effect to the uncon-
> stitutional enactments of duly elected legislatures. . . . To
> hold a governmental act to be unconstitutional is not to an-
> nounce that we forbid it, but that the *Constitution* forbids it
> . . . (174).

Justice Scalia and like-minded jurists know well that Realism rendered apolitical theories of law untenable long ago, but they insist that the craft and practice of the law can be separated from its theoretical and academic conceptualization. Indeed, this schizophrenia in the legal profession leads some contemporary students of the judicial process to criticize judges for "disingenuous" or "self-deceptive" behavior (Segal and Spaeth 1993; Bork 1990; Posner 1985). For reasons that should be partially evident now, and to which I shall return, I think these criticisms are wrong if they intend to describe what judges *believe* as opposed to how judges *behave*. The schizophrenia between practitioner-based and academic conceptualizations of law truly exists, and the only debate now is over how—not whether—the "legal model" survives as the *Zeitgeist* for the legal academy and the legal profession. While some see it as a model to explain and predict what decisions judges reach (Segal and Spaeth 1993), others argue that it remains as a prescriptive theory for good judging (Brisbin 1996; Rosenberg 1994; Smith 1994). Still other scholars see it as something in between (Knight 1994; Knight and Epstein 1996b; Songer and Lindquist 1996).

There are undoubtedly several reasons for this schizophrenia. First, many of the leading progressive Legal Realists were co-opted into the judiciary and the reforms they advocated were accomplished via such things as the abandonment of a "liberty to contract" jurisprudence and adoption of the Federal Rules of Civil Procedure. Second, the political consensus in the United States that followed the New Deal and World War II masked the fact that law had become more intimately entwined with politics. During a period where ideological and cultural consensus is strong it is natural to think of law not in political but in technical terms (maybe during such periods the law in fact ceases to *be* political) (Posner 1990:427).[2] Finally and most importantly, law schools by the 1930s had become professional training centers whose primary function was to produce legal practitioners. If lawyers and judges continued to practice and describe their craft on the basis of the traditional legal model (for whatever reasons) it made little sense for law schools to change the way they educated practitioners. Moreover, the traditional legal model has utility because it accurately describes most of what takes place in the practitioner community. Legal Realism suggests that law is indeterminate only at some levels, and the hierarchical structure of the court system means that only a small number of judges and lawyers regularly confront questions at those levels, the so-called "hard cases" in courts of last resort (which is why most Realist analysis focused on the Supreme Court).

Political scientists, on the other hand, always understood that they were not interested in law as such, but only in understanding how law was part of politics. In their history of the public law subfield, Murphy and Tanenhaus note that "the leading scholars in public law during this period, Edward S. Corwin, Robert E. Cushman, Charles Grove Haines, and Thomas Reed Powell, were all Legal Realists" (1972:13). While these political scientists relied upon methods of doctrinal and historical analysis similar to those used by legal educators of their day, their sole goal was to understand how law and individual judicial decisions were related to the broader political contexts that gave them meaning. Indeed, no clearer statement of this political jurisprudence can be found than the preface to Cushman's 1925 textbook, *Leading Constitutional Decisions:* "The Supreme Court does not do its work in a vacuum. Its decisions on important constitutional questions can be understood in their full significance only when viewed against the background of history, politics, economics, and personality surrounding them and out of which they grew" (see also Haines 1944:48).

Murphy and Tanenhaus point out that time and again these doctrinally oriented or "old institutional" scholars recognized the same types of political influences on judicial decision-making that later "behavioral" scholars studied (1972:15). They stressed that "particular litigation before the Court was but a stage in a struggle between contending political forces." They explained that judges acted strategically to avoid adverse "reactions ranging from widespread popular abuse of the Court and even defiance of its rulings to attempts to diminish the Court's authority or tamper with its membership." And they emphasized "the broader systemic consequences of major decisions" (*ibid.*).

Still, these old institutionalists believed that politics entered the judicial process in subtle and complex ways. They did not hold a positivist view about politics or the law, in the sense that they thought policy preferences or individual "interests" determined how judges decided cases. Although they recognized such preferences could affect judicial decisions, they saw politics structuring judicial choice and law in deeper, more constitutive ways (McCann 1996; Brigham and Gordon 1996). Consider Haines' 1922 essay entitled "General Observations on the Effects of Personal, Political, and Economic Influences in the Decisions of Judges":

A complex thing like a judicial decision involves factors, personal and legal, which carry us to the very roots of human nature and human conduct. Political prejudices, the influences of narrow and limited legal training with antiquated legal principles and traditions, or class bias having little or no relation to wealth or property interest, are more likely to affect the decisions of judges than so-called "economic interests" (49).

For these scholars judicial decisions were political acts not because judges were like elected policy makers who consciously advanced policy preferences or constituent interests, but because law itself was a process for constructing political values and legal interpretation was always influenced by deep political forces that shaped judicial attitudes at the affective and cognitive level. These scholars also recognized that this constitutive conception of the relationship between politics and law required linking descriptive analysis of legal doctrines and institutions to normative political analysis. Perhaps the most widely known constitutional scholar of his time, Edward Corwin, devoted his entire work to understanding how the historically situated political purposes and goals of the Constitution ought to give that document meaning. In *The Twilight of the Supreme Court* (1934) Corwin explained why the Court should ensure that "the Constitution of a progressive society keep pace with that society." His writings on presidential power (1940) emphasized the historical contingency of the separation of powers doctrine and the need to understand its meaning in a modern state. His "Higher Law Background of the American Constitution" (1928) and "The Constitution as Instrument and Symbol" (1936) remain perhaps the best explanations of how historically evolving conceptions of progressive justice undergird constitutional authority. And, in his most important statement on the discipline, "The Democratic Dogma and the Future of Political Science," Corwin argued against efforts to transform the discipline into a positivist "natural science." Not only was political behavioralism (or what he called "the new political science") capable of only modest gains in understanding group and individual values, but, why, Corwin asked, "should the political scientist spend his time measuring stereotypes planted in the public mind by other people when he could be planting some of his own?" (1929:590). Rejecting the definition of political science as either a field of "formal description or legalistic philosophy," Corwin approved of "scientific" methods only if they could be used to do "more expertly and more precisely what has always been done: criticism and education regarding the true ends of the state and how best they may be achieved" (*ibid.*).

Thus, public law differed from law school scholarship of its day not in methods but in scope and focus. In short, the *core of the discipline* was precisely that small band of judicial decision makers, usually on the Supreme Court, whose decisions became political choices. While some academic lawyers shared this research interest, it was never at the core of the legal academy or considered essential for understanding the actual practice of law.

These old institutionalists also held a realistic conception of institutions. They sought to describe institutions as they actually existed rather than in idealized form, and they focused on formal or tangible institutions like courts, judicial doctrines, written opinions, statutes, and constitutions. These institutions were the source of historically stable patterns of ideas and behavior, though not always the ones intended by their framers, because they could be used publicly to justify particular ideas and behaviors, and because they had resources attached to them (usually state power or authority) that could ultimately compel individuals to behave in prescribed ways. In this view, judicial attitudes and behavior were structured by historically evolving legal institutions, which were themselves embedded within broader social and political (state) ones. *Reflective judgments,* as opposed to simple attitudes and behavior, however, always retained partial autonomy from these institutional forces, hence the role of normative analysis. Historical and interpretive analysis was thus used to explain both the actual functions of real institutions as well as their goals and purposes, and it could inform reasoned judgments about reform if the one failed to match the other.

Behavioralism and the Limits of the Attitudinal Model

As with other fields in political science, the combination of "real" (formal and tangible) objects of analysis and informal (historical and interpretive) methods provided a foil for the "behavioral revolution" that swept public law during the 1950s and 1960s (Ethington and McDonagh 1995). Of course, too much can be made of shifts in academic paradigms. Even at the height of the behavioral period there were scholars who continued to use historical and interpretive methods of analysis to understand the evolution of judicial doctrines (e.g., Beaney 1955; McCloskey 1960; Mendelson 1963; Shapiro 1964a). But by the time Glendon Schubert published *Judicial Decision-Making* in 1963, the center of the field had clearly shifted, a change captured in the title of Schubert's introductory chapter, "From Public Law to Judicial Behavior." Again, as with any broad academic program, the behavioral movement had many strands, but in general it emphasized positive theory and methods of inquiry over historical and interpretive ones and focused on individual acts or levels of behavior rather than on institutions or patterns of purpose (Ulmer 1961; Murphy and Tanenhaus 1972).

The watershed in the application of the behavioral approach to studying Supreme Court decision-making came with publication of C. Herman Pritchett's *The Roosevelt Court* in 1948. While Pritchett retained the Legal Realist conception of law and the judicial process, he used quantitative techniques to describe the individual behavior or votes of justices and to rank them according to their support for particular policies. Although Pritchett thought judges were primarily "motivated by their own (policy) preferences," like the old institutionalists he also recognized that judicial "preferences" were influenced by conceptions of what it was appropriate for judges to do. Thus, he developed an intervening variable between a justice's policy preferences and a justice's votes in cases which he called "judicial role conception" (Pritchett 1954; see also Brenner and Stier 1995; Gibson 1978; Perry 1991).

By the early 1960s, scholars like Danelski, Jacob, Nagel, Spaeth, and Ulmer were using behavioral approaches to study other aspects of Supreme Court decision-making (Schubert 1963). Most of these works were extensions rather than innovations on the approach pioneered by Pritchett however.

By 1965 two influential books on judicial decision-making were published, and each in its own way captured the past and future development of positivist political science studies of judicial decision-making. The first, Walter Murphy's *The Elements of Judicial Strategy* (1964), retained the behavioralist emphasis on positivist methodology but shifted the focus away from discrete acts or simple vote counting. Like earlier work by Dahl (1957) and Shapiro (1964a), Murphy emphasized how larger structures of political and social power conditioned the ability of individual judges to affect social policy. Judges who wished to see their policy preferences realized had to make strategic calculations about the views of other colleagues on the bench, legislators, administrators, future litigants, interest groups and other political actors. This consideration forced judges to behave or vote in ways they otherwise would not if left unconstrained by their institutional environments.

Personal policy preferences were still assumed to be the goal of judicial behavior, but institutional structures were viewed as obstacles that justices must overcome to realize their goals. As Murphy explained, "The focus of this book is the question: How can a Justice of the Supreme Court most efficiently utilize his resources, official and personal, to achieve a particular set of policy objectives?" (1964:3–4). Eventually this work led to the development of predictive modeling, or what has come to be called the "rational choice" or "strategic approach" to judicial decision-making (see Maltzman, Spriggs, and Wahlbeck in this volume).

The second book, Glendon Schubert's *The Judicial Mind*—published in 1965—moved in the opposite direction. This work also retained positivist methodology but it shifted still further in the direction of examining individual level behavior and its relation to personal attitudes. Drawing on the work of cognitive and empirical psychology, Schubert developed an "attitudinal" approach that led him to "scale" judicial attitudes and the fact stimuli in cases along a continuum of liberal to conservative ideology. This allowed Schubert to model how particular justices would vote in particular types of cases on the basis of their previously held ideological preferences. Building on this model, Rohde and Spaeth (1976) refined the concept of judicial attitude and argued that "each member of the Court has preferences concerning the policy questions faced by the Court, and when the justices make decisions they want the outcomes to approximate as nearly as possible those policy preferences" (72).

The "mature fruits" of this attitudinal approach to Supreme Court decision-making came in Segal and Spaeth's *The Supreme Court and the Attitudinal Model* (1993). Analyzing Supreme Court decisions over a thirty-year period, Segal and Spaeth found that: 1) that justices' votes within particular issue or policy domains approximate a "unidimensional structure" (that is, the justices' voting patterns remained stable over time); and, 2) that justices' voting patterns correspond closely to their *a priori* policy preferences, as defined by the justices' own previous voting records and newspaper accounts of their policy views at the time of confirmation. In short, the data indicated that "Rehnquist votes the way he does because he is extremely conservative; Marshall votes the way he does because he is extremely liberal," and neither vote the way they do because of the law (65).

By contrast, Segal and Spaeth argued that the traditional "legal model" can be employed by justices to support any decisional outcome and thus lacks any predictive and hence "scientific" value. In subsequent work, Segal and Spaeth adapted their empirical approach to test an important aspect of that model, *stare decisis,* and found that it overwhelmingly failed to explain judicial voting patterns (1996).

Segal and Spaeth limited their model to explaining behavior only in the Supreme Court and only to decisions on the merits because they recognized that the Court occupies a unique institutional position; "because the Supreme Court sits atop the judicial hierarchy, and because in the type of cases that reach the Supreme Court legal factors such as text, intent, and precedent are typically ambiguous, justices are free to make decisions based on their personal policy preferences" (1996:973). Despite this important limitation, the attitudinal model has been criticized on several fronts. For example, Baum (1994) criticizes Segal and Spaeth's work for employing the wrong evidence in support of its primary argument that personal policy preferences, not other considerations such as the law, determine vote outcomes. To begin with, newspaper editorials and past voting records provide only indirect measures of the justices' personal policy preferences. Moreover, Segal and Spaeth's evidence that justices consistently vote to support certain policy *positions* does not demonstrate that they do so *because* of personal policy *preferences.* Many other factors can lead to voting pattern consistency. As Baum explains:

> How, then, do Segal and Spaeth get from their limited evidence to their broad conclusions about Supreme Court decision making? They seem to make an intuitive leap, resting on the unstated premise that the structure they find in justices' votes *could have no basis other than the attitudes of justices* about public policy. It is a highly reasonable leap, one that other students of the Court have made, but it is not compelled by the evidence presented (1994a:4 [emphasis added]).

Knight (1994), on the other hand, sees the attitudinal model failing not for deficiencies in what it attempts to explain, but for what it does not. By focusing narrowly on how attitudes correlate with decisions on the merits, the model misses such things as why justices review some cases but conclude that others are "meritless," or why the facts of previous cases affect the attitudinally driven decisions of future cases, or what drives the justices' opinion when the Court upholds (rather than reverses) a statute or a precedent. The model thus fails to explain the most important aspects of the Court's decision-making. As Knight argues:

> [T]he attitudinal model fails to account for factors which complicate the relationship between an individual justice's vote and the effectuation of a particular outcome. If the decisions of justices are to be explained mainly in terms of their desire to affect public policy (an explanation with which I am in general agreement), then such accounts should at a minimum incorporate those factors which influence what is in effect a strategic calculation (1994:6).

But perhaps the most important failing of the attitudinal approach is not the model itself but rather its characterization of alternative ways to understand judicial decision-making. Attitudinalists such as Segal and Spaeth construct a straw person out of the legal model, suggesting that it postulates "that the decisions of the Court are based on the facts of the case in light of the plain meaning of statutes and the Constitution, the intent of the framers, precedent, and a balancing of societal interests" (1993:32). Under such a model "it should not matter in predicting Court behavior whom the President nominates or whether the Senate confirms" because the values of the justices do not matter in deciding cases (125).

Brisbin (1996), among others, rejects this characterization of the legal model altogether. Rather than predicting how justices vote, the model should be seen as a prescriptive theory about good judging, but whose applicability to the Supreme Court is conditioned precisely because of the institutional factors that Segal and Spaeth recognize. Other critics (Rosenberg 1994; Smith 1994) have argued that the legalist model, as it is *properly understood and applied to the Supreme Court*, does not rely upon the simplistic, mechanical, apolitical jurisprudence that attitudinalists like Segal and Spaeth suggest. Rather, it is better understood as a commitment to apply a set of *a priori* "interpretive canons or principles" (some of which are substantively political) in deciding cases. Thus, the distinction is between a "principled" rather than a "result-based" process of decision-making, not between political and apolitical models. And, as Rosenberg explains, because the commitment is to interpretive philosophy it follows "that it matters a great deal who the President nominates to sit on the Court because different interpretive philosophies will produce different outcomes" (1994:7). Thus Smith points out that attitudinalists seeking to provide an empirically grounded alternative to contemporary normative jurisprudence have attacked the wrong targets:

Segal and Spaeth fail utterly to address what is really their most appropriate "legalist" target now: the sophisticated post-realist jurisprudence of legal scholars like Ronald Dworkin and Bruce Ackerman. These authors *reject* the old mechanical legal model and *acknowledge* the impact of judicial values on decisions. To preserve legal credibility, however, they still try to minimize the significance of judicial values . . . (by insisting judges adhere to moral or political principles rather than specific policy preferences or that judges try to synthesize the "texts" of previous constitutional moments). But Segal and Spaeth fail to take on these potent current targets and instead tilt at long abandoned windmills (1984:8).

The debate about the "legal model" is important for understanding the limits of attitudinal and other behavioral approaches to judicial decision-making. That the "legal model" has such different definitions and expectations is in part a legacy of the schizophrenia in the legal profession itself and in part a consequence of biases in the behavioralist methodology preferred by modern political science. Even if reformulated, the legal model may be descriptively inaccurate. Attitudinalists may be right that justices simply vote their policy preferences and use legal principles to mask their true motives. But the only way to know is to return to interpretive and historical approaches that contextualize their decisions into larger fields of meaning and motivation. Counting votes and other positivist methodologies can describe a particular action or behavior, but not the motive, purpose, or meaning of that action or behavior (Gillman 1997; McCann 1996; Smith 1992). This is because the same action has different meanings in different contexts—for example, raising one's hand in a meeting as opposed to raising one's hand in a fight. Thus, the assumption that similar votes in similar cases have similar motives and meanings cannot hold unless the cases are placed in similar historical and contextual space. For instance, a decision to apply a "colorblind" conception of the Equal Protection Clause to state programs had one meaning in 1954 when states were engaged in overt racial discrimination, but quite a different meaning in 1994 when states were using race-conscious programs to undo the effects of past discrimination and to aid under-represented minorities. Certainly it would be wrong to assume that both votes are equal indicators of a justice's "liberal" political preferences. Yet it is precisely these kinds of assumptions that positivist measures of judicial motivation make.[3]

Behavioralism was the opposite of the old institutionalism. Where the old institutionalists used informal historical and interpretive methods to study relatively formal or tangible subjects like statutes and judicial doctrines, behavioralism used formal, positive or "scientific" methods in order to study intangible subjects like attitudes and process (Ethington and McDonagh 1995:88). In terms of studies of judicial decision-making, behavioralists shared the legal realism of earlier public law scholars. By adopting positivist methodology and a reductionist outlook, behavioralism promised greater clarity and rigor in measuring one aspect of this relationship—namely, how individual political attitudes or values influenced judicial decision-making. What was lost in this shift, however, is important. Perhaps inevitably the shift led to a reconceptualization of both law and politics. Rather than the more complex, constitutive conceptualizations of law held by scholars such as Haines and Corwin as well as by contemporary post-Realist academic lawyers such as Dworkin and Ackerman, attitudinalists increasingly viewed the law as simply the instrument by which judges effected individual policy preferences (Segal and Spaeth 1993).

In this shift from a "constitutive" to an "instrumental" conception of law, behavioral approaches (the attitudinal model especially) lose their capacity to understand law as either a constraining or a motivating force in the judicial mind (Gillman 1993; Kahn 1994; McCann 1996; Smith 1994). Political attitudes become the only posited motivation for judicial decision, and judges are characterized as "disingenuous" or "self-deceptive" when their written opinions claim that legal principles and doctrines are the basis for decision. In a rather strange way, then, the core assumption of Legal Realism—that law and politics cannot be separated—is turned on its head. Not only are law and politics conceptually distinct in such approaches but the justices are motivated by political factors alone and judicial appeals to legal criteria for decisions are a cloak to cover real motives. Thus, an important consequence of the behavioralist reduction of the law is the need to draw a thoroughly "non-Realistic" distinction between law and politics, which in turn leads to the mischaracterizations of the so-called "legal model" and the "intuitive leaps" regarding judicial motivations.

Similarly, the behavioralist reduction of politics to individual policy preferences, without an interpretive account of how preferences are constituted by broader, institutionalized patterns of meaning, strips the analysis of normative content (Barber 1989; March and Olson 1984; Smith 1988, 1992). The old institutionalists insisted that politics was a complex and interactive or constitutive phenomenon that could be understood only by paying attention to individual choices against the institutional patterns of meaning or norms within which those choices were embedded. By contrast, behavioralism's focus on individual level actions led to an instrumental or utilitarian conception of politics in which politics is viewed as simply the aggregation of autonomous individual preferences (Barber 1989; Shapiro 1989; Smith 1989). Judicial politics is thus reduced to describing how the *a priori* policy preferences of individual justices produce particular decisional outcomes on the Court. Absent from the analysis is the concern of earlier public law scholars to link descriptions of judicial decisions to a prescriptive and normative jurisprudence (Smith 1988).

The systemic weaknesses in behavioralist methodology were compounded by the failure of political scientists to recognize the emergence of a schizophrenic conception of law within the legal community itself. If legal practitioners continue to think of their craft as guided by traditional "legal" criteria, or at the very least by a commitment to a principled (albeit a normative) political jurisprudence, then no matter how clear and elegant one's model, characterizing judicial decision-making otherwise only reifies the law and the judicial process as lived, real experiences. Consequently, it is not surprising that legal practitioners and educators who read behavioralist accounts of Supreme Court decision-making usually dismiss them out of hand (Griffin 1996). The ultimate irony is that as political science sought more predictive, "scientific" ways of understanding judicial decision-making, it became of less utility and notice to those actually engaged in the practice of law and to those elected officials who appoint judges. Political scientists, who in the days of Corwin and Haines were considered the leading experts on the Supreme Court and the Constitution, have been increasingly pushed to the sidelines by academic lawyers such as Dworkin, Sunstein, Ackerman, and Bork, who describe more accurately how politics influences judicial decisions.

Thus, while it is certainly true that no serious student of judicial behavior can now doubt that attitudes make a difference to judicial decision-making (see Segal in this volume), what one means by "attitudes" and how these are measured is key. As even Segal and Spaeth recognize, "attitudes" have "cognitive, affective, and behavioral components" (1993:69). A preoccupation with the last of these components and with positivist methodology has led much recent political science research to miss the meaningful ways in which the law and politics interrelate and has made purposeful analyses of judicial motivation, or normative inquiry and prescription, nearly impossible. The result has been an increasingly reified form of scholarship, with questionable external validity and only marginal utility to those outside the academic reward structures of the discipline.

The New Institutionalism

Like other human endeavors, change in scholarly tradition transpires generationally as each generation defines itself against the dominant views and attitudes of its predecessors. Within the social sciences there has been a growing awareness of the weaknesses of behavioralist approaches, and a renewed interest in studying how politics and other activities of human meaning can be understood by reemphasizing the importance of institutional relationships (Grafstein 1992; Koelble 1995; March and Olson 1984, 1989; Powell and DiMaggio 1991; Steinmo, Thelen, and Longstreth 1992).

In political science the shift to a "new institutionalism" was marked by James G. March and Johan P. Olsen's "The New Institutionalism: Organizational Factors in Political Life" (1984). At the heart of the new institutionalism is a challenge to the reductionist and instrumentalist conception of politics that characterized behavioralism, and a renewed appreciation for constitutive and normative conceptions of politics and the role that institutions played in the latter. According to March and Olsen:

> For the most part, contemporary theory in political science considers politics and political behavior in instrumental terms. The intent of actions is found in their outcomes, and the organizing principle of a political system is the allocation of scarce resources in the face of conflict of interest . . . the new institutionalism (challenges) this primacy of outcomes. . . . Through politics, individuals develop themselves, their communities, and the public good. In this view, participation in civic life is the highest form of activity for a civilized person. . . . Politics is regarded as education, as a place for discovering, elaborating and expressing meanings, establishing shared (or opposing) conceptions of experience, values, and the nature of existence. It is symbolic, not in the recent sense of symbols as devices of the powerful for confusing the weak, but more in the sense of symbols as instruments of interpretive order (741).

Rogers Smith's "Political Jurisprudence, The 'New Institutionalism,' and the Future of Public Law" suggested how the new institutionalist approach can be applied to the study of law and courts (1988). Specifically, Smith argued that political scientists should recognize the centrality of legal and political institutions as independent forces in the decision-making process of judges. These institutions were themselves created by past human decisions that were to some degree discretionary, and to some degree are alterable by similar future decisions. But they nevertheless have a life of their own and an influence on the self-conception of judges and other actors who occupy roles defined by them in ways that give those persons distinctively "institutional" perspectives and values. Hence, institutions shape the behavior of legal actors that in turn affects them, and thus makes them appropriate units of analysis in their own right (1988:95).

In terms of the past and future of public law, Smith argues that new institutionalism holds the promise of unifying the behavioralist quest for empirical rigor with the more inclusive conception of politics and law that was part of the normative jurisprudence practiced by traditional public law scholars and contemporary elite academic lawyers.[4] To date at least two major variants of new institutionalist work on law and courts have been identified: the positive theory of institutions (PTI), or the "rational choice" variant; and the historical-interpretive variant (Ethington and McDonagh 1995; Smith 1988). In this volume Maltzman, Spriggs, and Wahlbeck as well as Howard Gillman advocate these two approaches respectively.

Building on the work of Murphy (1964), scholars interested in the PTI approach argue that the key to understanding particular judicial decisions is to map out the strategic terrain that conditions the set of realizable choices a judge or justice can make given the interest in maximizing individual power or individual policy preferences.[5] Gillman offers an extensive critique of this approach as ultimately dependent on historical and interpretive analyses (see Gillman in this volume; see also Smith 1992). At bottom, while this approach shares an interest in analyzing the institutional contexts of judicial activity, it continues to rely upon positivist methods and instrumentalist assumptions about politics and law. Institutions are simply the given set of rules within which the game of maximizing self-interest is played (Gillman 1997). Thus, PTI approaches to judicial decision-making retain the positive and anormative character of behavioralism in general. Given this fundamental weakness, it is unlikely that PTI will provide a more complete and compelling alternative to behavioral and attitudinal approaches to judicial decision-making, especially if a goal of new in-

stitutionalism is to re-unite empirically rigorous research with normative jurisprudence.

Although less prominent in mainstream journals, a growing body of
research on judicial decision-making thus embraces the kind of historical institutionalism that Smith ultimately called for in his work
(1988, 1992). Rejecting the instrumental conception of politics and law
that behavioralism and rational choice offer, these new historical-
interpretive institutionalists seek to explain judicial decision-making as
a process in which judicial values and attitudes are shaped by judges'
distinct professional roles, their sense of obligation, and salient institutional perspectives. Central to this approach then is the use of interpretive methodologies to describe the historic evolution of these institutionalized perspectives or patterns of meaningful action (see Burgess
1993; Gillman 1993, 1994b; Kahn 1994; Smith 1985).

This approach shares both the interpretive methodology and the constitutive conception of legal and political institutions that was held by
the old institutionalists. Like their traditional counterparts, those engaged in this new work are also concerned to link the descriptive and
normative aspects of their inquiry (Smith 1988). So, while it is easy to
see how this new interpretive institutionalism differs from behavioral
and PTI approaches to judicial decision-making, it is not so easy to see
how it differs from the old public law. Martin Shapiro, for instance,
asserts that "the new vogue in institutional analysis acclaimed by
Smith is simply a return to 'traditional political science' " (1989:89).

There is truth to this claim, and much is lost if we obscure the kinship
between the "old" and "new" interpretive institutionalisms; nevertheless, there are significant differences which merit more attention than
I can give them here. For present purposes the most important difference is the new acceptance of a more dynamic and porous conception
of institutions and a reduced emphasis on the importance of the state
in political analysis. Rather than viewing political institutions as "real"
or tangible structures of power, authority, and resources—tied in some
way to the state[6]—many new institutionalists are inclined to de-
emphasize the distinction between these formal structures, and informal norms, myths, habits of thought, or background structures and
patterns of meaning (Gillman 1997; Orren 1995a; Skowronek 1995;
Smith 1995). As Smith notes, institutions are "not only fairly concrete
organizations, such as governmental agencies, but also cognitive structures, such as patterns of rhetorical legitimation characteristic of certain
traditions of political discourse or the sorts of associated values found
in popular belief systems" (1988:91). In this sense the more formal and

tangible institutions that old institutionalists saw as causes or motivations for political action are themselves understood by new institutionalists as created within a received framework of culture and the socially constructed mind. Thus, institutions are not merely influenced by, but are inseparable from, the web of social patterns of cognition and evaluation such as ideology, religion, class, race, and gender that situates all social activity (Selznick 1996; Smith 1995). As Smith explains:

> The Lord Baltimore Hotel is a kind of institution; the Social Science History Association is a kind of institution; the State Department is a kind of institution. But none of these institutions will function for a second if there aren't a whole lot of human beings with ideas in their heads defining their roles in relation to those institutions. It is their purposes, their projects that make those institutions go and work. [To say] that in some sense ideas are secondary to institutions or organizations seems incoherent to me. . . . And if ideas are necessary to an institution's existence and functioning, why treat them as separate and secondary? (1995:138).

This more porous conception of institutions is a legacy of Marxist historical analysis and the structural-functional analysis of sociologists like Weber, Parsons, and Merton (Smith 1988:96). In contrast to traditional institutionalism, both of these currents of thought emphasized the need to move beyond analyzing conscious and tangible institutional patterns to examining the deeper functional and cognitive determinants of those formal institutions. This inheritance, then, is both the strength and weakness of the new institutionalism relative to the old. On the one hand, the more dynamic definition of institutions allows analysis to move beyond describing the formal or tangible actions of political institutions to describing the background structures and culturally embedded meanings to which they are attached. This is particularly important to those interested in understanding how formal political institutions can have contingent meaning based on the relative power relationships between different social groups and classes. On the other hand, abandoning a realist conception of institutions, and especially the connection between political institutions and the state, raises important problems.

First, there is a problem of conceptual and analytical clarity. If the distinction between ideas or patterns of cognitive meaning, and "real" structures of authority and resources is blurred too far, then it becomes impossible to talk about particular institutions as either causing or being caused by particular patterns of beliefs or motives. If ideas and institutions are inseparable, if everything is connected to everything else, then it is unclear where new institutional analysis leads (Smith 1995). Institutional analysis will be left simply describing a myriad of institutional interactions, but will offer little or no theoretical and explanatory value (Gates 1991) and have little utility for empirical analysis (Gibson 1986).

While it is certainly true that understanding background ideas and patterns of cognition are necessary for understanding the social meaning of particular political institutions, it is also true that defining a political institution and assessing its impact or meaning in society are separate tasks. As a matter of analytical clarity, removing the distinction between "background structures" and ideas, and formal or real institutions (between dependent and independent variables), makes it difficult to investigate empirically how institutions shape ideas and patterns of belief, or how ideas may in turn shape institutions.

The second problem with making ideas inseparable from institutions is that the analysis may rob itself of normative content. It may turn itself into a simple description of the moral conventions of particular societies as these are embedded in their historically evolving patterns of institutions and ideas, with no way to offer an independent evaluation of those patterns (Barber 1989). Here the legacy of Marxist historicism and structural-functional sociology is clear. The problem with these earlier approaches is that they were deterministic and left little room for individual agency and meaningful choice, hence they could not recognize the significance of politics itself as a norm-generating process. Individual choices and political actions were seen as epiphenomena of larger materialist or structural forces and not as relatively autonomous events that could in turn shape those forces (Smith 1988: 100).

Scholars interested in understanding how political choices are meaningful must emphasize the degree to which individual choices can be creative and relatively autonomous from the institutional contexts and social background structures that individuals are embedded within. But if ideas are themselves parts of institutions or inseparable from specific institutional contexts, then it is impossible to see how individuals could ever exercise the type of reflective autonomy or reasoned judgment about institutions that normative analysis calls for. If ideas were always contingent or relative to their institutional context, it would be impossible to hold an idea about the appropriate role of an institution or institutions in general that was not itself constituted by them. Hence, historical institutional analysis could never evaluate institutional norms and values; it could only describe them.[7]

Of course, not all analysis must be normative, and not all normative analysis must engage in a debate over foundational principles or "grand theory." But if the new historical institutionalism does not allow ideas and judgments ever to have meaningful autonomy from the institutions that shape them, then it is difficult to see how the analysis can ever have real normative content. Consequently, the effort to reconnect empirical political science with normative jurisprudence may falter.

Resurrecting the "Political Systems" Approach

The problems associated with accepting a more dynamic and porous conception of institutions lead me to suggest the advantages of returning to an interpretive institutionalism that retains a "real" conception of political institutions—as patterns of purpose and meaning that are attached to the state or other forms of political power, authority, and resources. The approach I wish to suggest, however, would also build on the work of Supreme Court scholars who engage in the "political systems" analysis of so-called "political jurisprudence." When Shapiro used the term "political jurisprudence" he did not mean to describe all post-Realist jurisprudence, but rather sought to identify a specific approach that viewed law and judicial decisions as the product of constituent group interactions and political power relationships. Grounded in Robert Dahl, Arthur Bentley, and David Truman's theories of interest group pluralism, scholars in this mold largely retained the behavioralist assumptions about the attitudinal motivations of judges, but explained the array of attitudes on the Court at any given time, and hence the pattern of Supreme Court decisions, in reference to the Court's relative power relationships in the broader political system. Dahl's pioneering work "Decision-Making in a Democracy: The Supreme Court as a National Policy-Maker" (1957), for example, argued that the Court rarely exercises the power of judicial review in a way that is contrary to the interests of the governing coalition in the national political system. Under this type of "political systems" analysis the role of the Court, and hence the cumulative content of its decisions, is dependent on such things as party realignments (Adamany 1980; Funston 1975; Lasser 1985; Shapiro 1978, 1981, 1986; Sheingold 1974) or the alignment and interrelation between powerful social forces and groups (Gibson 1978; Goldman 1982; Rohde and Spaeth 1976; Schubert 1974; Tate 1981).

These early studies have been criticized as falling under the "rational choice" or PTI approach in the sense that they explained the role of courts as bounded by their relationship to other political and social institutions and the groups that control their power (Kahn in this volume; Kahn 1994; Smith 1985). In general, they relied upon the premise that within certain institutionalized constraints judicial decisions reflected the instrumental politics of self-interest or preference maximization. In other words, judges moderate their individual policy preferences when deciding cases not out of an authentic commitment to legal principles or a constitutive political decision-making process, but because they are consciously or unconsciously influenced by institutionalized restraints on their power. Indeed, the most prominent PTI research on the Supreme Court to date has used a positive "separation of powers model" to demonstrate how the Court decides cases vis-à-vis other important political institutions like Congress and the President (Epstein and Walker 1995; Eskridge 1991a; Ferejohn and Shipan 1990; Marks 1988; Spiller and Gely 1992).

Although this critique is certainly true of much of the work done under the label of "political jurisprudence" or "political systems" analysis, it nevertheless goes too far. For instance, a justice authentically committed to the underlying purpose of the doctrine of separation of powers, such as Justice Jackson in *Youngstown Sheet and Tube Co. v. Sawyer* (1952), will be sensitive to the preferences of groups dominating Congress and the presidency. This sensitivity, however, may not be a calculated fear of override or a simple acceptance of the policy preferences of the dominant political coalition. Rather it may be a belief that the purpose of the law itself is dependent on *relative institutional relationships* within the political system. In other words, a justice may believe that individual legal institutions are themselves embedded within, and therefore must draw their meaning from, the larger political system and relative relationships in that system. As Jackson explained in his concurring opinion in *Youngstown:*

> The actual art of governing under our Constitution does not and cannot conform to judicial definitions of the power of any of its branches based on isolated clauses or even single Articles torn from context. . . . It enjoins upon its branches separateness but interdependence, autonomy but reciprocity. Presidential powers are not fixed but fluctuate, depending upon their disjunction or conjunction with those of Congress. We may begin (any constitutional analysis) by distinguishing roughly the *legal consequences of this factor of relativity* [emphasis added].

In a constitutional context where legal sovereignty is purposely fragmented between competing institutionalized actors, one would expect
to find most legal institutions, not just the separation of powers doctrine, to be similarly sensitive to contingent and relative system or re-
gime-wide relationships. In modern federalism cases, for example, the
Court has relied upon "political safeguards," or the definition of constitutional boundaries adopted by the political branches, rather than
upon abstract legal principles to define the constitutional relationship
between state and federal governments. Thus, in *Garcia v. San Antonio*
(1985), Justice Blackmun argued that the proper resolution of Tenth
Amendment cases lies in defining state sovereignty by reference to the
"constitutional scheme rather than in predetermined notions of sover-
eign power . . . we have no license to employ freestanding conceptions
of state sovereignty when measuring congressional authority" (but see
United States v. New York 1992). Once again, the Court's motivation in
this case is perhaps better described as a sincere interest in recognizing
the political contingency of constitutional provisions, rather than as
a strategic calculation or fear of override by the political branches or
dominant political coalitions.

Likewise in cases involving individual rights the Court has often
relied upon conceptions of law that require sensitivity to "contemporary standards" of society, the "evolving standards of decency," or
even the values found in the "conscience and traditions" of our people.
Such standards also require judges who wish to give an authentic interpretation of the law to be responsive to the substantive views and relative relationships between important political groups and institutional
actors.

Standards such as those mentioned above suggest that the Court has
tended to view the law as a constitutive political process in which the
relative positions and substantive views of other political actors are
not just barriers to the promotion of particular preferences but are
themselves the basis of appropriate legal outcomes.[8] In this sense, the
Court is engaged in a constitutive dialogue with other branches and
political actors over the meaning of law (see Fisher 1988). Hence, any
understanding of judicial decision-making as responsive to legal institutions would require attention to the pattern of institutional relationships within the existing political regime.

Scholars using this approach to analyze judicial decision-making
would pay attention to the same legal institutions as old institutionalists (judicial doctrines, precedents, statutes, etc.), but also to the political system relationships (the views of law held by interest groups and
electoral coalitions, found in such things as party platforms, public

speeches, and debates around judicial appointments, and the *amicus* briefs filed by the Solicitor General, members of Congress or interest groups) that political systems scholars emphasized. Normative analysis would turn on identifying the underlying purposes of particular legal institutions in contrast to the specific group institutional-power contexts within which they arose. For example, Clayton (1994) has criticized the Supreme Court's adherence to the so-called *Chevron* doctrine, which requires lower courts to defer to "reasonable" agency interpretations of statutory duty during periods of divided government. If the underlying rationale of the Administrative Procedures Act and separation of powers principles upon which that doctrine rests is that nonelected judges should defer to elected policymakers, then it makes some difference whether the political system can be assumed to produce unified or divided democratic control over the administrative state. If administrative officers are interpreting statutes in an effort to give effect to congressional intent, then a high standard of deference makes sense; if, on the other hand, one cannot assume administrative officers are giving statutes the interpretation that Congress intended (which was often the case during the 1980s) then a broad standard of judicial deference is inappropriate. Other scholars have used this approach to develop explanations for such things as the relationship between doctrinal change, electoral coalitional shifts, and the Supreme Court's institutional autonomy from the elected branches (Silverstein and Ginsberg 1987); how patterns of group power, institutional resources, and larger changes in the polity affect the Court's development of individual rights (Epp 1998; Gillman 1994a); and how the Court's exercise of judicial review can be reconciled with majoritarian democracy (Graber 1993).

The "institutional-systems" approach sketched out above is similar to historical institutionalism as advocated by scholars like Smith. Both would reject the PTI and behavioralist view that legal institutions lack constitutive or formative influence over judicial attitudes. And both would call for interpretive and historical analysis of specific legal institutions as a key to understanding judicial decision-making. The effort to understand specific legal institutions as part of the political system, however, does tie the analysis closely to the formal or tangible institutions that are attached to some form of state or political power, thus avoiding the problems of definitional confusion and historical determinism. Moreover, by paying attention to the real institutional (power and resource) contexts of judicial decisionmaking, this type of analysis can accommodate the fact that judges may often hold different motivations for the same action—some connected to the desire to give effect to legal principles, and others connected to strategic calculations about effecting individual policy preferences. This approach might thereby hold the promise of bridging the insights of PTI regarding strategic behavior with the constitutive conception of law favored by historical institutionalists.

Conclusion

New institutionalism holds out the promise of a more complete and dynamic conception of judicial decision-making than either behavioralism or the old institutionalism provided. Still, it is unclear whether this approach will overcome the problems that are the legacy from whence it springs. PTI approaches must find ways to move past the purely instrumentalist conceptions of law and politics. New historical-interpretive approaches, on the other hand, must resolve the dilemma of holding a porous conception of institutions with the need for conceptual clarity that will allow empirical rigor and meaningful normative analysis. Whether this can be done without resorting back to a more real conception of institutions, and hence to a more traditional style of institutionalism, remains to be seen.

Finally, a promising route for future institutional research is to build on the insights of political systems analysis, linking them to constitutive understandings of law and politics. This requires scholars to see judicial choices not as discrete acts, but rather as embedded within a broader institutional system or political regime that gives individual institutional components meaning. What we label such an approach matters less than the recognition that understanding the *political* meaning and significance of judicial decisions requires placing them in the appropriate political contexts.

Notes

1. Posner (1990) argues that these movements have begun to change the legal academy. However, while they have gained much notoriety as intellectual movements there is still little evidence that they have significantly altered law school curricula or judicial opinion-writing.

2. This may also explain why legal scholars in the 1950s and early 1960s such as Hart (1959), Herbert Wechsler (1961), and Edward Levi (1949) had temporary success arguing that a technical, politically neutral "process jurisprudence" was still possible.

3. Attitudinalists recognize this methodological limitation. Schubert assumed that judicial voting patterns accurately measured political attitudes. This, of course, was circular; votes were used to explain political attitudes, and

attitudes were used to explain votes. Criticisms of Schubert's model led Segal and Spaeth to augment the model with a thin layer of interpretive description—newspaper accounts of the justices' political attitudes. Still, newspaper accounts are an indirect measure of attitudes. More importantly, newspaper accounts of a prospective justice's views usually rely upon past voting records in lower courts or the nominee's self-professed agreement or disagreement with past Court decisions. Thus, the problem of circularity has not been removed. Nevertheless, this is an important recognition that positive methods alone cannot provide the basis for a meaningful analysis of motivations, and hence can only be a relatively small part in a fully explanatory political science.

4. Smith makes four specific recommendations: First, scholars studying law and courts should "conceive of their independent variables as relatively enduring structures" or institutional patterns. Second, they should provide "some indication of the origins of the structures or institutions they examine," with particular sensitivity to how those structures may have arisen from past, controversial political choices." Third, analysts, whether using qualitative or quantitative methods, "should identify as fully as possible their dependent variables, the set of 'meaningful acts,' such as judicial decisions, they claim to explain." And finally, public-law studies of the interrelations between legal choices and the 'background' institutions that shape them should at least raise questions about how those choices have in turn affected such institutions, intentionally or unintentionally" (1988:102–03).

5. Most contemporary PTI scholars also draw on the theoretical arguments of Kenneth Shepsle (1979) and William Riker (1980, 1982), who called for a "return to the study of institutions" out of the recognition that institutional configurations can include or exclude the pursuit and realization of particular interests. In other words, institutional configurations can create "structural equilibria," and it is possible for institutions, themselves the product of past individual choices, to have relative autonomy from the immediate interests and preferences of the individuals who inhabit them. If this is true, then it is important to understand what the structural equilibria are (Maltzman, Spriggs, and Wahlbeck in this volume).

6. The insistence on a connection between political purposes and state authority, power, or resources as a condition of political institutionalization is why early efforts to reinvigorate institutional studies by scholars like Theda Skocpol, Karen Orren, and Stephen Skowronek were often referred to as "bringing the state back in" (Evans 1985; Fiorina 1995b).

7. Smith recognizes this deterministic undercurrent in the new institutionalism when he argues that institutional change does not occur as a result of truly autonomous and creative human choices, but rather as the result of "creative reconfiguration" of existing institutional values and norms (1988:100). Here he leans toward accepting Orren and Skowronek's "multiple orders" thesis which explains change in institutions not in reference to creative and reflective choices, but to the fact that all individuals are simultaneously embedded in multiple institutional arrangements and thus can carry the norms and values associated with one institution to the next (Skowronek 1995; Smith 1995:139). This, of course, does not really solve the fundamental normative problems associated with determinism and evaluating change. While it might explain

changes in one institution by reference to the importation of values from another, it doesn't explain why different institutions have different norms and values, why institutions change at all, and, most importantly, why or how some institutional norms are preferable to others. By saying that institutions affect and cause changes in other institutions, the question of change has been moved back, but, no general explanation of change has been offered and no basis for evaluating the desirability of particular changes is made available.

8. My suggestion here shares much with the constitutional jurisprudence sketched out in Bruce Ackerman's *We the People* (1991), which suggests that the Court plays a role of "preserving" the substantive political values forged during the last "constitutional moment" or regime-forming period. It also shares much with Louis Fisher's (1988) argument that constitutional meaning is fixed via an ongoing dialogue between the Court and the political branches.

2

Strategy and Judicial Choice: New Institutionalist Approaches to Supreme Court Decision-Making

Forrest Maltzman, James F. Spriggs II, and Paul J. Wahlbeck

Perhaps the newest theoretical advance in the study of judicial decision-making is the application of a positive theory of institutions. Just as neoinstitutionalism has challenged traditional ways of thinking about legislatures and bureaucracies, so too has a new institutionalism come to challenge legal and attitudinal approaches to the study of the Supreme Court. Indeed, many students of judicial politics now embrace an approach that recognizes the role of both policy preferences and institutional constraints in shaping Court outcomes (Baum 1997; Epstein and Knight 1998; Wahlbeck, Spriggs, and Maltzman 1998). This approach to the study of judicial decision-making has its roots, of course, in an old favorite of judicial process scholars, Walter Murphy's (1964) work on the strategic behavior of Supreme Court justices within institutional constraints.[1] Reviving Murphy's strategic approach of judicial decision-making, these new studies suggest that justices pursue their policy preferences subject to constraints both endogenous and exogenous to the Court.

This strategic approach rejects two notions central to alternative views of Court dynamics: first, that justices are sufficiently constrained by legal precedent that their policy preferences have little influence over their actions on the bench, and second, that justices are "unconstrained" and thus they are free to pursue their policy goals. In contrast, strategic justices, in the words of Lee Epstein and Jack Knight, "realize that their ability to achieve their goals depends on a consideration of the preferences of others, of the choices they expect others to make, and of the institutional context in which they act" (1997:4).

Although elements of the strategic approach can be found in the attitudinal approach embraced by most judicial process scholars since C. Herman Pritchett's work in the 1940s and 1950s, it constitutes a significant break from dominant explanations of Court politics. In this chapter, we articulate how this approach differs from the attitudinal approach, elaborate on the two forms of strategic decision-making that judicial scholars have tended to embrace, and reflect on the strengths and weaknesses of strategic theories of decision-making. Because the articulation and testing of a strategic approach is still in its formative years, we trust that judicial scholars will not view this as the last word on the strategic and institutional dimensions of Court dynamics.[2]

The Behavioralist Legacy: The Attitudinal Approach

As is well known, the behavioral revolution in the first half of the twentieth century radically altered the study of politics. Rather than merely describing historical events and institutions, political scientists sought to identify and understand empirical regularities. The behavioral approach represented a new and radical departure from political science's normative and anecdotal origins (Dahl 1961; Polsby, Dentler, and Smith 1963), placing political scientists who articulated and tested hypotheses with empirical data at the forefront of the discipline. The behavioral revolution, in short, ushered in the scientific study of politics.

The signal distinction between behavioralists and their predecessors was the behavioralists' abandonment of political science's earliest roots: the study of political institutions. In the words of Kenneth Shepsle, "institutions were, in the thinking of many behavioralists, empty shells to be filled by individual roles, statuses and values" (1989:133).[3] Indeed, the leading behavioral studies of the electorate (Berelson, Lazarsfeld, and McPhee 1954; Campbell, Converse, Miller, and Stokes 1960), Congress (Fenno 1962, 1966; Matthews 1960; Manley 1970), and the judiciary (Schubert 1965; Spaeth 1963) almost always embraced sociological or psychological explanations of behavior. Such psychological and sociological theories of human behavior shared two important tenets. First, both portrayed human actions as free from having to make choices. Instead, human action was said to be dictated by sociological or psychological forces beyond the control of any individual. Sociological and psychological explanations, in other words, were deterministic at their core. Second, both approaches viewed individuals as "fundamental building blocks" (Shepsle 1989:133). Under such a rubric, political outcomes were no more than "the aggregation of individual actions" (*ibid.*).

Although some of the earliest works that embraced the attitudinal approach had explicit links to sociological and psychological theories dominant in the 1950s and 1960s (see Nagel 1961, 1962; Schmidhauser 1961; Schubert 1961, 1962b, 1965; Spaeth 1961, 1963; Ulmer 1970a, 1973; Vines 1964), the attitudinal approach took a significant turn in the 1970s with the advent of rational-choice analysis. Political actors were now seen as maximizers of exogenously determined preferences. This new attitudinal perspective suggested that preferences, not roles or backgrounds, shaped behavior. Drawing on this new perspective, Rohde and Spaeth (1976) placed the psychometric attitudinal model within a rational-choice framework. Somewhat similar to Schubert (1965), Rohde and Spaeth maintained that justices cast votes by thinking about the facts of a case—the dominant legal issue and the types of litigants—in light of their attitudes and values. They went on to argue, though, that justices are free to vote their attitudes because of the insulating nature of the Court's institutional features, specifically because of justices' lifetime tenure, lack of ambition for higher office, and control over the Court's agenda. The shift to the rational-choice framework with its emphasis on maximizing policy goals was furthered in Segal and Spaeth (1993). As they characterize the approach, "Simply put, Rehnquist votes the way he does because he is extremely conservative; Marshall voted the way he did because he is extremely liberal" (1993: 65). Attitudinalists, in short, view justices as "decision makers who always vote their unconstrained attitudes" (Epstein and Knight 1995a: 2). Empirical support for the attitudinal model is widespread. As numerous scholars successfully document, justices votes' are consistent with their policy preferences (Hagle and Spaeth 1992, 1993; Segal and Spaeth 1993; Segal et al. 1995; Segal and Cover 1989).

To be sure, the work of Spaeth and his collaborators is a significant break from the sociological and psychological theories that played such an important role in the early years of the behavioral revolution and of the attitudinal approach. Because preferences can be imputed (see Segal and Cover 1989; Segal et al. 1995; Epstein and Mershon 1996) and because preferences vary across justices, the attitudinal approach accounts for the voting patterns that judicial scholars had noted since Pritchett's work in the 1940s (1941, 1945, 1948). Still, although the attitudinal approach articulated by Spaeth and his collaborators builds from a different theoretical base than the earlier versions of the attitudinal approach, it has two very important links to its sociological and psychological roots. First, the attitudinal approach continues to see the actions of justices as shaped by forces (in particular, preferences) outside the strategic context of the Court. Second, the attitudinal approach continues to view individuals as the analytical building blocks and outcomes as the aggregation of individual actions. The attitudinal model forecasts case outcomes as a reflection of the aggregated preferences of a Court majority. In many respects, then, the attitudinal model as articulated since the 1970s represents the culmination of the behavioral revolution as applied to the study of judicial politics.

A Neoinstitutionalist Approach

The intellectual origins of neoinstitutionalism certainly preceded the behavioral revolution, since it found its roots in early political scientists' focus on the history and mechanics of political institutions. The return to an institutional focus after the 1970s, however, can best be seen as a response—indeed, a backlash—against the two tenets of the behavioral tradition: that human behavior is predetermined and that individual action can be aggregated to account for political outcomes. In contrast, the new institutionalists place rational political actors back into their institutional context, arguing that rational calculation entails consideration of the strategic element of the political game. Instead of being simple goal maximizers, rational actors understand that they face a number of constraints, constraints imposed by the actions of other political actors and by the institutional context in which they act. Justices, in short, are strategic actors who take into consideration the constraints they encounter as they attempt to introduce their policy preferences into the law.[4]

These constraints often take the form of formal rules or informal norms that limit the choices available to political actors (Knight 1992; North 1990; March and Olsen 1984, 1989). In the study of legislative behavior, the effects of institutions on the expression and aggregation of preferences are well documented (see Shepsle and Weingast 1987). The rules of debate (Bach and Smith 1988; Smith 1989; Sinclair 1995), the use of committees (Shepsle and Weingast 1987; Weingast and Marshall 1988), voting arrangements (Shepsle 1979; Weingast 1992) all channel and constrain choices. Bureaucratic decision-making is also constrained by internal rules and procedures (Eisner and Meier 1990) and by actors external to the agency (Moe 1985; Weingast and Moran 1984; Wood 1988; Wood and Anderson 1993). Court scholars have also examined the constraining effects of institutions on judicial behavior. For instance, court behavior is affected by the decisions to establish three-judge federal appellate panels (Atkins 1970, 1972), rules for assigning judges to federal appellate panels (Atkins and Zavoina 1974), rules for assigning opinions to judges (Brace and Hall 1990; Hall and Brace 1989, 1992), rules for seniority ordered voting by judges (Brace and Hall 1993), informal norms of adhering to precedent (Knight and Epstein 1996a), rules governing the number of justices required to grant *certiorari* (see Perry 1991), rules for selecting judges (Brace and Hall 1995), and norms of consensus on the Supreme Court (Walker, Epstein, and Dixon 1988).

Although the label "new institutionalism" is often used to characterize this variant of rational-choice analysis, we focus here on strategic behavior on the Court.[5] We define strategic action as interdependent behavior with justices' choices shaped, at least in part, by the preferences and likely actions of other relevant actors. To act strategically, of course, justices must understand the consequences of their own actions and be able to anticipate the responses of others. Institutions facilitate this process and thus mediate between preferences and outcomes by affecting the justices' beliefs about the consequences of their actions. Institutions therefore influence strategic decision makers through two principal mechanisms—by providing information about expected behavior and by signaling sanctions for noncompliance (Knight 1992; North 1990). It is important to note that while we see strategic justices as responding to the anticipated response of others, strategic justices will not necessarily act insincerely. If the political context favors the justice's preferred course of action, a strategic justice's behavior will be the same as it would be without constraints.[6]

For instance, given the institutional requirement that majority opinion authors must generally gain five votes before their opinions speak for the Court, authors recognize that they are not necessarily free to express their most preferred positions in the opinion, but that they must consider the views of other justices too. If they fail to accommodate the views of their colleagues, their opinions may not carry the imprimatur of the Court. This rule may therefore prompt a justice to accommodate a justice in either the first (Spriggs, Wahlbeck, and Maltzman 1997) or subsequent drafts of the majority opinion (Wahlbeck, Spriggs, and Maltzman 1998). Likewise, institutional rules external to the Court also structure decision-making. The most visible set of rules is the Constitution's separation of powers and checks and balances. In this setting, a justice understands that it is possible for elected officials to overturn an opinion, most likely by passing override legislation. Institutions, therefore, create an environment in which a justice's behavior is dependent on the actions of other justices and other organizations.[7]

Among judicial scholars, the intellectual origins of a model of strategic interaction were offered by Murphy in his path-breaking *Elements of Judicial Strategy* (1964). According to Murphy, a strategic justice is constrained by the actions and preferences of his or her brethren, as well as by actors and influences outside of the Court. Murphy did not see each justice acting independently. Nor did he see outcomes as the aggregation of individual preferences. Instead, Murphy argued, justices' behavior was shaped by the actions taken by the other justices and the potential for action by Congress, the President, and the general public. Although Murphy's classic was well read, its effect on judicial research was very modest until the 1990s. Recently, judicial scholars have attempted to build upon Murphy's contributions by devising and testing models that tap the strategic element of judicial decision-making, including both the strategic interactions amongst the justices and the strategic relationships between the judicial, executive, and legislative branches.

Exogenous Constraints: The Separation of Powers Game

Because the Supreme Court is embedded in a political system in which the legislative and executive branches of government have the capacity to overturn, circumvent, or even ignore its decisions, the separation of powers view suggests that the "Supreme Court will anticipate the reaction of Congress and craft its statutory interpretation decisions so that they will not be overturned" (Bawn and Shipan 1997:1–2). Such a view of the Court is consistent with Murphy's belief that strategic justices may find themselves "in a situation in which [their] objectives would be threatened by programs currently being considered seriously in the legislative or executive branches of government. To cope with either eventuality, a Justice would have open to him a broad range of strategic or at least tactical alternatives" (1964:156).

To prevent Congress from overturning the Court, those who subscribe to the separation of powers approach maintain that the Court takes a position that is as close to its ideal point as possible, without being so far from Congress that it is overturned (Ferejohn and Shipan 1990; Gely and Spiller 1990; Spiller and Gely 1992; Bawn and Shipan 1997). Since Congress itself is constrained by the Executive Branch and since institutional features of Congress such as its bicameral structure

(Marks 1988), the committee system (McCubbins, Noll, and Weingast 1989; Ferejohn and Shipan 1990; Gely and Spiller 1990), and even the subcommittee system (Bawn and Shipan 1997), make it difficult for Congress to overturn a Supreme Court decision, legislative constraints provide the judiciary with a great deal of discretion.[8] Because of the difficulty in forecasting electoral returns (Baum 1997) and in anticipating congressional action (Bawn and Shipan 1997; Melnick 1994; Katzmann 1997; Baum 1997) and because of the extensive set of veto points that exists in the legislative policy-making process (Krehbiel 1998; Segal 1997), Supreme Court justices need not always alter their behavior in anticipation of a congressional response.[9]

Although there is obviously a great deal of uncertainty involved in predicting congressional action, it is important to note that congressional response is not random. As Baum (1997) points out, numerous studies identify when a legislative response is likely (Eskridge 1991a, 1991b; Solimine and Walker 1992; Ignagni and Meernik 1994; Meernik and Ignagni 1997; Bawn and Shipan 1997; De Figueiredo and Tiller 1996). Even if justices recognize the difficulty in anticipating congressional response, we would be reluctant to use this finding as grounds for rejecting the strategic approach. Indeed, a strategic justice would take into consideration a legislative response, and then discount it because of uncertainty. Whereas the attitudinal approach emphasizes the unconstrained nature of judicial decision-making, the strategic approach suggests that justices take into account the constraints that may exist. A strategic justice is sophisticated enough to take this into consideration.

Separation of powers models are a clear break from the traditions of the behavioral revolution. Instead of starting with the individual as the unit of analysis, separation of powers models assume that it is institutional structures that are given and that individuals (legislators and justices) act within these structures. Rather than focusing on individual behavior, the separation of powers literature tends to treat the Court (and Congress) as the unit of analysis. Literature looking at the links that exist between the Court and the broader political environment "is almost completely insensitive to the microlevel models of the linkage process" (Gibson 1983:31).

Furthermore, behavior in a separation of powers game is not predetermined. Instead of simply reflecting the preferences of the median justice, justices playing the separation of powers game have to make strategic choices to avoid congressional censure. For example, even if the Court did believe that Congress was likely to overturn its decisions,

it might opt to base its ruling on constitutional grounds and thus significantly raise the costs associated with overturning the Court (Murphy 1964; Spiller and Spitzer 1992; Segal 1997). Furthermore, justices
may seek to exploit their capacity to draft opinions that fall into several
different dimensions so as to avoid a hostile congressional response
(Segal 1997).[10] Although those who have most rigorously articulated
separation of powers models may succeed in identifying the equilibrium point where outcomes are likely to fall, individuals playing a separation of powers game can pursue many different strategies and are
likely to make numerous miscalculations.

Criticism of the separation of powers literature tends to take two
forms. First, some critics argue that the separation of powers game is
based upon so many unrealistic assumptions that justices cannot seriously allow fear of being overturned to influence their decisions (Baum
1997:96–97; Melnick 1994:263–64). Second, some question the extent of
the empirical support for a separation of powers model. Both of these
points are forcefully argued in Segal's contribution to this volume.

In his present essay, Segal shows that the final votes cast by individual justices usually reflect their ideal preferences, rather than a strategic
calculation about what is acceptable to Congress. Segal views this as
grounds for rejecting the notion that justices take into consideration
congressional preferences when making their rulings. Of course, finding that justices do not moderate their voting behavior to comply with
congressional preferences does not mean that justices are unwilling to
play the separation of powers game. Indeed, Segal concludes by arguing that because of the difficulty in overturning court decisions, the
strategic justice may consider and then ignore congressional preferences (see also 1997:42). While Segal's findings raise questions about
the validity of the separation of powers game, it is important to note
that it is only a first step in empirically testing the exogenous strategic
approach. Indeed, it is likely that justices' responses to the political
environment take forms that are not easily observed in final votes on
the merits. First, a strategic justice who perceives that deciding a case
is too costly is likely to deny *certiorari* and thus not decide the case.
Second, we also suspect that if justices are responding to exogenous
forces that they do so by modifying the legal rule, rather than the disposition, to be more in line with the dominant political coalition. Congress, like the justices themselves, is likely to be more concerned with
how the legal rule undergirding an opinion will affect future social,
political, or economic relationships than with who won the case. Third,
it is conceivable that even though many justices are not altering their

behavior because of an anticipated congressional response, the median justice on the Court (assuming one actually exists) may, and thus the Court as a whole responds to Congress.

Although Segal's study of aggregate voting patterns raises questions about the strategic approach, individual case studies have shown that on highly salient issues there is some evidence of justices playing a separation of powers game (see Epstein and Walker 1995; Eskridge 1991b). For example, in their analysis of the *Marbury v. Madison* case (1803), Knight and Epstein (1996b) document that Chief Justice Marshall wrote an opinion that strategically accommodated the political environment of the time. Likewise, Gely and Spiller (1990) maintain that the Court's decisions in *Grove City College v. Bell* (1984) and *Motor Vehicle Manufacturers Association of the United States v. State Farm Mutual Automobile Insurance* (1983) were influenced by anticipated congressional reactions.

Endogenous Constraints: The Collegial Court Game

Institutional rules, procedures, and norms that are internal to the Court constrain justices' capacity to translate their preferences into legal policy outcomes. The capability of a justice to convert his or her policy goals into law is checked by the Court's agenda setting, opinion assignment, and opinion writing / coalition formation norms and policies (Epstein and Knight 1998). As a result of these institutions, justices engage in strategic behavior as they attempt to shape the Court's policy output into conformance with their policy goals. Such models of strategic interaction recognize the importance of policy preferences in influencing judicial behavior, but hold that justices also act within constraints imposed by the Court's institutional context. The intra-court strategic game thus results from the rules, practices, and institutions of the Court arena.

Perhaps the most important institutional feature of the Court is its collegial character. Contrary to a portrait of the Court as nine separate law firms that have little interaction with one another (Segal and Spaeth 1993:297), the strategic approach recognizes that the behavior of individual justices is shaped in part by the actions and preferences of their brethren. As a result, a justice's choices during the selection and consideration of cases will depend in large part on the choices made by the other justices (see Rohde 1972a, 1972b). Decision-making is interdependent because justices' ability to have majority opinions reflect their policy preferences depends in part on the choices made by other justices.

Below we discuss several of the Court's intra-institutional features and the ways in which they promote interdependent decision-making.

The strategic model also injects a dynamic element into explanations of judicial decision-making, providing variation that is untapped by the relatively static attitudinal model.[11] According to the attitudinal approach, changes in justices' votes should reflect changes in their policy preferences, but such preferences tend to be stable, especially in the weeks or months in which it takes to decide a case.[12] The dynamic nature of the collegial court game poses a significant challenge to the attitudinal model, as behavior is no longer simply the expression of preferences and outcomes are not merely the aggregation of individual preferences.

Indeed, the attitudinal model's focus on final votes on the merits itself obscures the microanalytic foundations of Supreme Court decision-making. By focusing on final outcomes, instead of the dynamic, political process by which legal policy is produced, the attitudinal model misses an important element of decisionmaking. The historical-interpretive approach generally focuses on the Court's final output—in the form of the language contained in final opinions—and thus, like the attitudinal model, it also often misses the microfoundations of the law. Judicial outcomes, in short, cannot be fully explained without attention to the political dynamics of the decision-making process on the bench.

The first institutional obstacle for justices attempting to convert their policy goals into the law is getting appropriate cases on the Court's docket. Unlike Congress, where a single member can initiate a policy change by introducing a bill, individual justices interested in achieving their policy goals cannot independently place a case on the Court's agenda.[13] A justice needs the support or acquiescence of at least three other justices before a case is placed on the Court's docket. This is known as the Rule of Four. Since an individual justice is unable to set the Court's agenda, we expect interaction among the justices to play a role in the *certiorari* process. Even though some judicial scholars focus their attention on exogenous determinants of the *certiorari* decision (Tanenhaus et al. 1963; Ulmer 1983, 1984; Caldeira and Wright 1988; McGuire and Caldeira 1993), others explore an intra-court, strategic approach (Cameron, Segal, and Songer 1997; Caldeira, Wright, and Zorn 1996; Perry 1991; Boucher and Segal 1995; Brenner and Krol 1989). This approach to decision-making suggests that policy preferences alone do not dictate a justice's willingness to support a *certiorari* petition. Instead, justices' willingness to grant *certiorari* depends in part upon the actions of their colleagues. Because a court opinion that is inconsistent with a justice's policy preferences may be more detrimental to the justice's policy goals than no opinion, a strategic justice will calculate how other justices will vote on the cases' merits. Schubert (1962b), Brenner (1979), Palmer (1982), Brenner and Krol (1989), Krol and Brenner (1990), Boucher and Segal (1995), Caldeira, Wright, and Zorn (1996), and Epstein and Knight (1998) argue that a justice's willingness to grant *certiorari* depends in part upon his or her perception of the likely outcome of a particular case.[14]

Anticipating a colleague's eventual vote on a case's merits is not the only strategic interaction that occurs during the *certiorari* process. Although Perry (1991) argues that a justice's vote on *certiorari* is primarily, albeit not always, influenced by legal considerations, he discovers that there is a strategic element to the process. After interviewing five U.S. Supreme Court justices, Perry (*ibid.*) discovered that justices regularly threaten to dissent from a denial of *certiorari* as a strategic mechanism to entice other justices to support *certiorari* (see also Epstein and Knight 1998). The existence of what has become known as "Join Three" also represents an indicator of the strategic nature of the *certiorari* process (Perry 1991; Epstein and Knight 1998; O'Brien 1996:238). Although its frequency of use is unclear, justices occasionally state that they will support a motion to grant *certiorari* because three of the other justices support the petition, and a fourth vote is needed to bring up the case. Although Perry rejects the hypothesis that justices "join three" as part of an explicit "logroll," he states that at least one of the justices he interviewed occasionally joined three because "he was interested in a more collegial process" (1991:168–69). Whereas the behavioralist model suggests that the behavior of justices is predetermined by their prevailing preferences, numerous studies of the *certiorari* process suggest that the evolving political dynamics thereto influence the choices of the justices.

Another important institution that constrains the ability of justices to see their individual preferences converted into legal policy is the process by which opinions are assigned on the Supreme Court. Since the tenure of Chief Justice Roger Taney (Schwartz 1993:152), the custom has been for the Chief Justice to assign opinions when in the conference majority; otherwise, the most senior associate justice in the conference majority assigns the opinion. This institution provides an opportunity for opinion assigners to attempt to affect the Court's decisions (Epstein and Knight 1998; Baum 1997). Since opinion authors have a disproportionate influence on the content of an opinion, the decision of who will write the opinion affects the policy content of the opinion as well as the breadth of the legal doctrine. Or, in the words of Justice Fortas, "If the Chief Justice assigns the writing of the Court to Mr. Justice A, a statement of profound consequence may emerge. If he assigns it to Mr. Justice B, the opinion of the Court may be of limited consequence" (Fortas 1975:405).

Studies of the opinion assignment process demonstrate that the Chief Justice frequently bases opinion assignments on strategic considerations. For example, Slotnick (1978, 1979), Davis (1990), Brenner (1982), and Maltzman and Wahlbeck (1995; 1996a) hypothesize that the Chief Justice is more likely to assign important cases to himself, since by doing so the chief increases the probability that the final opinion will be consistent with his policy preferences. Other scholars suggest that the Chief Justice strategically assigns opinions, especially in minimum winning cases, to ideological crossovers who may not write an opinion that perfectly reflects their policy views (Maltzman and Wahlbeck 1995, 1996a; Danelski 1960; McLauchlan 1972; Murphy 1964; Rohde 1972c; Rohde and Spaeth 1976; Ulmer 1970b; but see Brenner 1982; Brenner and Spaeth 1988; Rathjen 1974). Although some scholars speculate that such an assignment may stem from an attempt to preserve a fragile majority and the chief's preferred outcome (Murphy 1964; Rohde 1972c; Rohde and Spaeth 1976; Davis 1990; Maltzman and Wahlbeck 1995, 1996a), others contend the chief assigns for different, yet still strategic, reasons. For example, McLauchlan (1972) argues that the pivotal justice is assigned the case because of the chief's long-term goal of promoting Court harmony; Brenner, Hagle, and Spaeth (1990) argue that the Chief Justice is more likely to assign highly contested opinions to the pivotal justice to avoid the breakup of the original coalition majority and thus the need to reassign the majority opinion.

The opinion-writing process includes the key aspects of the formation of legal doctrine. It is during this stage that justices bargain, negotiate, and compromise about the content of the legal rules announced in majority opinions. In spite of the substantial influence of the opinion author, that justice is not a "free agent" (Rohde and Spaeth 1976:172). Instead, he or she is constrained by the actions and choices of other justices. This stems in part from the Court's rule that before an opinion can carry the imprimatur of the Court, it must gain the support of a majority of justices. Opinions that fail to gain the necessary support will not be seen as speaking for the Court, although they may announce the judgment of the Court, and their precedential impact will be lessened (Johnson and Canon 1984; Segal and Spaeth 1993).

Although Murphy may be the scholar most closely affiliated with a strategic approach to opinion-writing, he is not the only one to adopt such a theoretical framework. Even earlier, Westin (1958) wrote that justices may respond to a majority opinion draft with "returns [that] suggest detailed changes in argument, or even style. . . . Polishing the opinions is therefore a process of group adjustment, in which the Justice assigned the opinion to write must shape his statement to the wishes of his colleagues or risk separate concurrences or even defections to the minority" (127). Consistent with Murphy's and Westin's observations is the view that opinions are "the result of a cooperative process in which nine supreme individuals collaborate to bring about the desired result—a result that is the joint work of the Justices rather than the product of the named author alone" (B. Schwartz 1996:8). In short, opinion-writing is an interdependent process in which opinion writers are dependent on the support of their colleagues.

Given the importance of Court opinions, it is not surprising that each justice attempts to shape the majority opinion consistent with his or her policy objectives. Opinions contain legal rules that establish referents for future behavior and thus have an impact beyond the parties in the litigation (Hurst 1956; Knight 1993; McIntosh 1990; Spriggs 1996, 1997; Wahlbeck 1997). Justices therefore attempt to shape legal rules so that they can impact future social, economic, and political relationships. They thus do not necessarily join the first draft of the majority opinion. Instead, justices will often use a "mixture of appeals, threats, and offers to compromise" (Murphy 1964:42) to encourage opinion authors to write legal rules that reflect their policy preferences.

Murphy (1964), Spriggs, Maltzman, and Wahlbeck (forthcoming), Epstein and Knight (1998), and others argue that justices regularly make suggestions and threats and even circulate separate opinions as a mechanism for extracting concessions from the majority opinion author. And, they show that majority opinion authors frequently respond to these bargaining strategies by altering the opinion. During the Burger Court, justices requested that the author make a change to the majority opinion in about 23 percent of the cases.[15] Wahlbeck, Spriggs, and Maltzman (1998) also hypothesize and empirically demonstrate that these bargaining strategies are more likely to result in the author's willingness to accommodate, as seen in the number of majority opinion drafts circulated. For example, the greater the number of suggestions or threats by members of the majority conference coalition, the greater the level of accommodation by the author. Likewise, if the majority conference coalition is small in number, thus endowing its members

with leverage over the author, the author is more likely to accommodate. This finding is consistent with the claims made by the justices
themselves. Indeed, Chief Justice Rehnquist has explained: "The willingness to accommodate on the part of the author of the opinion is
directly proportional to the number of votes supporting the majority
result at conference. . . . [I]f the result at conference was reached by a
unanimous or a lopsided vote, a critic who wishes substantial changes
in the opinion has less leverage" (1987:302).

Another important component of the opinion-writing process is the
formation of majority opinion coalitions.[16] According to Murphy (1964)
and Epstein and Knight (1998), coalition formation reflects a series of
strategic calculations by justices fully cognizant of the dynamic and
interactive nature of the opinion-crafting process. The strategic portrait
of Court politics has been reinforced by a series of case studies looking
at opinion writing and coalition formation on the Court (Murphy 1964;
Woodward and Armstrong 1979; B. Schwartz 1985, 1988, 1996; Epstein
and Knight 1998), as well as a variety of papers focusing on the size
and composition of opinion coalitions (see Schubert 1959, 1964; Ulmer
1965; Rohde 1972a, 1972b; Rohde and Spaeth 1976; Brenner and Spaeth
1988; Brenner, Hagle, and Spaeth 1990).

Recently, we (Wahlbeck, Maltzman, and Spriggs 1996) have attempted to systematically test a strategic model of the coalition formation process. We hypothesize and demonstrate empirically that the
time it takes for a justice to join the majority opinion depends upon
more than just his policy preferences. Such choices also depend upon
strategic factors such as whether the majority opinion author already
has enough votes to win—a finding consistent with the argument that
an individual's bargaining leverage declines once a winning coalition
forms (Rohde 1972a:214; see Riker 1962; Riker and Niemi 1962)—and
the concurrent bargaining tactics of other justices, such as the circulation of suggestions or concurring opinions.

Justices also have an incentive to adopt tit-for-tat tactics, since their
lifetime tenure guarantees that they will continue to interact with the
same colleagues over the course of the near, and often distant, future.
Justices, that is, are engaged in repeated play, so it is reasonable to
expect them to embrace a long-term strategy designed to enhance their
future bargaining leverage and power. Murphy (1964:52), for example,
argues that a justice can "build up a reservoir of good will for later
use" by joining the majority opinion despite having reservations about
it. This tactic is useful because such a justice "may have put himself
in an excellent position to win reluctant votes from colleagues on other

issues" (Murphy 1964:53). Thus, in Wahlbeck, Maltzman, and Spriggs (1996), we hypothesize and show that justices are also likely to engage in tit-for-tat behavior. In particular, we show that even after controlling for preferences and other factors that might influence a justice's willingness to join a majority opinion, justices join majority opinions more quickly if the opinion's author has cooperated with them in the past. As they are political actors involved in a repeated game with their brethren, this finding is not surprising. (see Axelrod 1984; E. Schwartz 1996). In a separate paper (Wahlbeck, Spriggs, and Maltzman 1997), we further demonstrate that the more cooperative an opinion author has been with a justice in the past, the less likely that the justice will now concur or dissent.

The collegial nature of Supreme Court decision-making provides an institutional context in which justices' decisions are interdependent. As is obvious, however, scholars have just begun to offer theoretically and empirically rigorous models of this process and its effect on judicial outcomes.[17] We are confident that in the future, as more scholars examine this process, our understanding of the dynamic, political nature of the Supreme Court decision-making will be improved. The key to advancing our understanding rests in scholars' use of theoretically and empirically rigorous tests of their models.

Assessing the Strategic Approach

Critics of the strategic approach tend to take two different tacks. First, they accuse the strategic approach of being overinclusive. Indeed, in his contribution to this volume, Gillman writes: "In general, if one is being strategic whenever one considers the consequences of one's behavior in light of the behavior of others. . . .virtually all decisions handed down in the history of the Court, are properly labeled strategic." Our response to this criticism is twofold. First, Gillman is correct. We suspect that most decisions handed down by the Court are subject to strategic considerations by the justices. Nevertheless, despite the presence of institutional constraints on justices, which leads to strategic calculations, justices may be able to express their ideal policy preferences without concern for the choices of other justices or reactions by Congress and the President. Undoubtedly, there are cases that lack sufficient saliency to merit a congressional attack even though the decision is at odds with the views dominant in Congress. Likewise, justices may be free to author opinions that express their true policy views when there is general consensus on the Court or the case is relatively unimportant. This suggests, we think, not a limitation of the strategic model, but a potential research agenda as scholars attempt to discern the conditions under which justices modify their behavior in response to the threats and suggestions of their colleagues or the anticipated reaction by Congress. In short, scholars need to provide theories about the extent to which, and under what conditions, justices' choices are altered by interdependent decision-making.

Although we believe that most judicial behavior is influenced by strategic considerations, we are also confident that other factors play an important role in shaping judicial behavior. For this reason, we believe that it is imperative that when scholars employ either qualitative or quantitative evidence to explain outcomes, they are pluralistic enough to search for variables that are related to other approaches to the study of the Court. Inevitably, organizational factors, strategic considerations, attitudinal factors, and even legal factors influence the positions a justice is likely to embrace. Again, the principal task of judicial scholars is to provide theories for and empirical evidence of the circumstances under which these various factors affect justices' decisions. Furthermore, we also believe it is imperative that all empirical claims include information about what is not being explained. For quantitative studies, it is standard practice to inform the reader how much of the variance is being explained. Frequently, we see that statistically significant variables still only explain a modest amount of the variance.

Of course, Gillman's point raises a more serious consideration. If strategic behavior is defined so broadly, does it have any predictive power? We believe that a strategic approach does have uses if one recognizes that there is no single strategic model. Instead, the strategic approach represents a class of models that each individually helps us to understand judicial behavior and outcomes. In other words, the strategic model rests on one premise: that justices' choices are interdependent, a premise that must be given life through the use of specific conditional hypotheses about when and to what extent justices reflect on other actors' preferences and likely behavior. Thus, in the intra-court game, one of the hypotheses that the strategic approach leads to is that justices engage in tit-for-tat behavior. Even after controlling for preferences, we expect justices to join opinions of those colleagues who historically support them. Likewise, we expect justices to take into consideration the size of the winning coalition when deciding how to respond to a draft opinion. We further argue that most choices a justice makes during the opinion-writing process—from making a suggestion, to circulating a concurrence, to joining the majority opinion—depend in part on the concurrent actions of his or her colleagues. Each of these hypotheses represent specific and testable claims that fall under the strategic rubric.

The other criticism that has been lodged against the strategic approach is that it is underinclusive in that it cannot explain every aspect of Supreme Court decision-making. In particular, the strategic approach, like the attitudinal approach, continues to treat preferences as exogenous. As Clayton points out in his contribution to this volume (see also Smith 1988; March and Olsen 1984, 1989; Gates 1991), institutions do more than structure outcomes by affecting actors' beliefs; they shape preferences and values. We have no doubt that this is true: institutions affect individuals in a variety of ways, including the formation of values and preferences. Nevertheless, to account theoretically and empirically for all phenomena is a herculean task to which no one approach has yet risen. Thus, most scholars who embrace a strategic approach content themselves with clearly delimiting what they take to be exogenous (normally, institutional structures and preferences) and then determining what behavior is likely to flow from such assumptions. Even if preferences are endogenous to the Court's institutions, we can arguably still gain much insight into the dynamics of judicial choice by evaluating how a range of such preferences affects justices' subsequent choices. Finally, the strategic perspective—far more so than the attitudinal perspective—is appropriately attentive to the possibility of changing preferences in the course of Court decision-making. Recognizing the dynamic element of judicial decision-making and the interdependent character of justices' choices, the strategic approach recognizes that preferences indeed may shift. What is more, it is unclear why the historical-interpretive approach is considered to be better suited to untangling the linkages between institutional configurations and the formation of preferences. If one is interested in explaining the formation of and change in institutions (Knight 1992; North 1990), as well as in how such arrangements might affect actors' preferences, we suspect that a rational-choice perspective can offer valuable insight by focusing on the microanalytic linkages between them.[18] We, however, also suspect that an interpretive approach can also be of benefit, and thus urge scholars from both schools to tackle this issue.

An Emerging Source of Commonality: Focusing on Legal Rules

Both the attitudinal and strategic approaches emerge from distinct intellectual traditions. Their understanding of the motivations and factors that shape human behavior fundamentally differ. The lack of a common theoretical link between these approaches is matched by their divergent empirical interests. The attitudinal approach has been most fruitfully employed in understanding a justice's decision regarding how to vote on a case's merits. Attitudinalists claim that preferences alone account for a justice's decision to affirm or reverse a lower court decision.[19] In contrast, those scholars who embrace a strategic approach primarily, but not exclusively, cast their analytical scope on the opinion-writing process. This is one area in which the attitudinal approach has not been fruitfully employed. Even Harold Spaeth, the scholar most closely associated with the attitudinal model, notes that "opinion coalitions and opinion writing may be a matter where nonattitudinal variables operate" (Spaeth 1995:314).

We find the emphasis on the formation of legal rules to be an encouraging development that may eventually bridge the gap between scholars who embrace an interpretivist orientation to the study of the law and those who study the law from a more positivist perspective. While the strategic approach, we think, will result in a much richer understanding of how justices pursue their policy preferences, the interpretivists are beginning to demonstrate that noninstrumental goals may matter as well. We believe that a more comprehensive model may ultimately emerge which recognizes that, while a justice's principal goal is public policy, other goals also matter. Such a model, of course, would necessarily have to provide a theory for under what conditions various goals take primacy and the ways in which goals interact to result in judicial choice and ultimately legal policy. For the time being, however, we think that viewing justices as constrained seekers of legal policy provides a parsimonious, powerful way to conceptualize Court decision-making. We are thus hopeful that the strategic approach's success in helping to account for the development of legal rules will help reunite a subfield that has historically been so divided that some scholars have questioned whether it should be divided into two distinct subfields (Scheppele 1996).

Understanding the *certiorari* process, opinion assignments, opinion-drafting, accommodation amongst the justices, and competition between the three branches is central to explaining the development of the law. However, it would be a mistake to claim that strategic factors alone can fully account for the precise wording of Court opinions. Inevitably, opinions take the form they do because of a variety of factors that will never be fully accounted for by any single model of Supreme Court decision-making. Legal factors, a variety of endogenous and exogenous strategic calculations, role orientations, and numerous idiosyncratic factors that can never be completely captured in a reasonably parsimonious model are all likely to shape the Court's final opinion. Whether one's evidence is in the form of a statistical model or detailed, rich case studies, life is too complex, varied, and even random to be perfectly captured by any single model. Yet, we argue that viewing justices as pursuing their policy preferences within the constraints imposed by collaborative decision-making and other institutional constraints takes us a long way toward understanding the dynamics of the law's development.

For a good portion of the twentieth century, legal theorists and legal realists have vented their frustration with each other. We suspect that the lack of communication stems from unique theoretical perspectives, divergent empirical approaches, and the historical reluctance of judicial process scholars to study the opinion-writing process. Fortunately, theoretical and empirical advancements are enabling judicial process scholars to move beyond explaining justices' votes and instead to contribute to the issue that is central to public law scholars—the explanation for the development of Supreme Court opinions and thus the formation of legal precedent. In so doing, judicial scholars are developing a much richer and more dynamic understanding of the political, strategic nature of Supreme Court decision-making.

Notes

1. While Murphy's book represents the most comprehensive work on judicial strategy of his generation, he was not the only scholar making such an argument. In fact, Glendon Schubert, the principal innovator of the attitudinal model, argued that Supreme Court decision-making involves strategic behavior (1959:173–210, 1964; cf. Ulmer 1960, 1965).

2. For additional perspectives on strategic approaches and the U.S. Supreme Court, see Epstein and Knight (1997, 1998) and Baum (1998:chap. 4).

3. For a discussion of the early work on institutions, see Clayton's essay in this volume.

4. While we argue that a justice's principal goal is policy, we recognize that, at times, justices may pursue other goals, such as legitimacy of the Court (Epstein and Knight 1998; cf. Baum 1995).

5. Our preference for the term "strategic," rather than merely institutional, reflects the fact that rational-choice theoretic treatments are not the only tradition to claim the neo-institutionalist banner. Historical institutionalism, sociological institutionalism, and other institutionally focused approaches to the study of politics fall under the general rubric of neo-institutionalism. Neo-institutionalism incorporates a variety of theoretical and empirical perspectives. For an overview of the political economy of institutions, see the edited volumes by Alt and Shepsle (1990) and Knight and Sened (1995). For alternative theoretical approaches, see, for example, March and Olsen (1984, 1989) and Smith (1988, 1996). Distinctions between rational-choice and nonrational-

choice institutionalism are discussed in detail by Orren and Skowronek (1994) and Smith (1996).

6. In other words, sophisticated behavior (i.e., acting contrary to one's most preferred course of action) is a sufficient, but not necessary, condition for a justice to have been subject to strategic constraints. Again, the essence of a strategic explanation is the interdependency of choice among actors (see Elster 1986).

7. While a rational-choice approach emphasizes that actors are goal-directed, making choices based on the consequences of a particular course of action, such an explanation can also incorporate such factors as social norms (Elster 1986), normative notions about the duties of judges (Ferejohn 1995), and persuasion based on normative principles (Elster 1995).

8. Indeed, Marks maintains that "The Court is unconcerned with the impact of its decision on the legislature" (Marks 1988:2, as cited in Segal 1997:30).

9. Murphy (1964) explicitly rejects this line of reasoning when he writes:

> Accurate prediction of a political reaction is hardly an easy task. It involves weighing of intangibles on a scale calibrated to the unknown quantities of the future. Yet this is the sort of problem which decision-makers in other government positions must regularly handle. Thus it is also the kind of problem which most Justices, considering their wide range of political experience before coming to the bench, have also frequently handled. A Justice can get the facts on which he bases his estimate of the situation from newspaper reports, leaks, and analyses, from professional or scholarly journals, from the *Congressional Record*, from committee hearings and reports, from presidential press conferences, from statements by cabinet members or bureau chiefs, and of course, from the celebrated Washington grapevine (171–72).

10. The capacity to exploit a multidimensional space is enhanced by the fact that contrary to most treatments of Congress in separation of powers games, Congress is not a unitary actor (Baum 1997:96–97; Bawn and Shipan 1997).

11. The legal approach, like the attitudinal approach, suggests relative stability during the process of deciding a case. According to the legal approach, statutory and constitutional changes or alterations in precedent are the main factors that would lead a justice to alter his behavior in a case, but these factors normally do not change during the course of a single case.

12. Rohde and Spaeth define an attitude as "relatively enduring" (1976:75). Jones (1994) suggests as well that individual policy preferences tend to be stable over time.

13. If a single justice wants the Court to accept a particular appeal, the justice can place the case on the Court's discuss list (see Caldeira and Wright 1990). The discuss list is the list of appealed cases that at least one justice finds sufficiently compelling to merit discussion at the Court's conference. The Chief Justice first creates the discuss list from the appealed cases, and other justices may add cases to it. Chief Justice Burger initiated the present institutional arrangement. Prior to Burger, the Court used the "Dead List," which was a list of cases that did not merit discussion. The Chief created the list and any justice had the opportunity to remove a case from this "special" list.

14. Provine (1980) and Krol and Brenner (1990) believe that a justice's vote on *certiorari* is usually not influenced by their perception of a case's outcome. Perry (1991) concludes that a justice's perception about a case's outcome only plays a role in the cases that the justice finds central to their policy goals.

15. According to Justice Brennan's circulation records, justices circulated suggestions or threats in 527 of the 2,295 signed opinions or assigned cases decided during the Burger Court (1969–85 terms). For more information on these measures, see Wahlbeck, Spriggs, and Maltzman (1998).

16. On the importance of coalition formation, see Schubert 1959; Rohde 1972a, 1972b; Rohde and Spaeth 1976; Brenner and Spaeth 1988; Brenner, Hagle, and Spaeth 1990.

17. The capacity to systematically test hypotheses derived from the strategic approach has been facilitated by Justice Brennan's willingness to share his circulation records with judicial scholars. These records detail when every draft opinion was circulated, and when bargaining statements such as suggestions and threats were circulated by the justices (Epstein and Knight 1995a; Wahlbeck, Spriggs, and Maltzman 1998). These records are available in the Library of Congress's manuscript room.

18. If institutions shape preferences, one cannot determine preferences without understanding where institutions themselves emerge (Knight 1992; Knight and Sened 1995). Congressional scholars have fruitfully employed a rational approach to explain the development of institutional arrangements (Aldrich 1995; Binder 1997; Dion 1997). With a few notable exceptions (e.g., Walker, Epstein, and Dixon 1988), judicial scholars have not focused on the formation of institutional arrangements.

19. Howard (1968), B. Schwartz (1985, 1988, 1996), and Maltzman and Wahlbeck (1996b) argue that a justice's willingness to change their vote between the initial conference vote and the publication of the final opinion regularly result from strategic reasons such as an opinion author's willingness to alter their draft.

3

The Court as an Idea, Not a Building (or a Game): Interpretive Institutionalism and the Analysis of Supreme Court Decision-Making

Howard Gillman

> The concept of an institution has evolved to the point that we have lost track of what it means for an institution to give form or order to our politics. . . . Portrayal of an institution requires a leap from the common sense concreteness, evident in buildings and artifacts like robes and purpose curtains, to the shared perceptions that tell us what these things mean (Brigham 1987a:16).

Putting Attitudes in Context

For decades many behavioralists insisted that the best scientific procedures known to the social sciences repeatedly demonstrated that, when deciding cases on the merits, Supreme Court justices were properly viewed as policy makers who were remarkably free to make decisions on the basis of their political preferences or "attitudes" (Segal and Spaeth 1993; Rohde and Spaeth 1976). Scholars operating in this tradition would typically point out that this decisional freedom was made possible by features of the justices' institutional context, such as life tenure and the difficulties associated with overturning a Supreme Court interpretation of the Constitution. Still, once these institutional features were mentioned it followed that scholars interested in the determinants of Supreme Court decision-making should focus their attention on individual variables (associated with the characteristics of judges) rather than on institutional ones. After all, since institutional characteristics were considered significant to the extent that they made possible decision-making based on the personal preferences of the justices it made no sense to study how their institutional context might influence the justices' preferences, goals, or calculations.

Of course, throughout the reign of the attitudinal model there were scholars who questioned the assumption that institutional arrangements and historical contexts played little role in shaping or constraining the presumptive desire of judges to promote policy preferences. Some emphasized the effects of legal discourse on judicial attitudes and behavior (Brigham 1978, 1987a, 1987b; Harris 1982; Mendelson 1963, 1964), while others attempted to situate Supreme Court decision-making in a larger structure of political or social power (Dahl 1957; McCloskey 1960; Miller 1968; Shapiro 1964a). Now, thanks to a number of developments—including March and Olsen's (1984 and 1989) brief on behalf of "the new institutionalism," Smith's (1988) argument for why the new institutionalism should become "the future of public law," and the rising popularity of institutional analysis among students of American political development, comparative politics, and historical sociology (Orren and Skowronek 1994; Steinmo, Thelen, and Longstreth 1992; Ostrom 1995)—we are finding that many law-and-courts scholars have begun to shift their focus away from the long-standing question of how institutions are affected by the personal characteristics of judges and toward the question of how judges are affected by the institutional characteristics within which they are embedded. It is too early to declare that we have arrived at a "post-attitudinal" moment in public-law scholarship, but the accumulated evidence does suggest that there is an increasing consensus about the advantages of exploring how judicial decision-making is shaped by institutional contexts rather than viewing the Court primarily as a safe platform for the display of exogenous attitudes.

Within this consensus, however, are some disagreements over the nature of institutional analysis. One commentator has identified at least three camps within the new institutionalism (Koelble 1995)—rational-choice, sociological, and historical institutionalist—while others have configured the literature so that it is distributed among four categories constructed on the basis of whether researchers are using formal or informal methods and whether they are examining formal or informal institutions (Ethington and McDonagh 1995). Other permutations are also imaginable (see Heclo 1994).

In this essay I will contrast the conception of institutional politics that is embodied in the two major approaches represented in this volume—rational-choice institutionalism, a.k.a. the "strategic approach," and historical-interpretive institutionalism. Elsewhere in this volume Maltzman, Spriggs, and Wahlbeck discuss some of the advantages of studying Supreme Court decision-making through the use of rational-choice or positive political theory (PPT) approaches (also referred to as the positive theory of institutions or PTI [Orren and Skowronek 1994]), and Cornell Clayton explains why we might want to take some inspiration from the more traditional, pre-behavioralist, approaches to institutional politics, such as those associated with the "old institutionalism" of scholars such as Edward Corwin, Charles Haines, and Thomas Reed Powell as well as the more modern "political systems" analysis of Robert Dahl, Martin Shapiro, and others. As a methodological pragmatist I believe that all approaches have the potential of illuminating some questions in which we might be interested. Still, I will suggest that, given the way that "institutions" are conceptualized in each of these approaches, there is reason to think that researchers will be in a position to explore a broader range of institutional effects if they adopt historical-interpretive approaches than if they adopt rational-choice approaches.

To put the point simply: the strategic approach can only claim to shed light on those features of institutional politics that are properly considered strategic. Thus, while it may help us gain a perspective on how situations might lead people to act in ways that seem inconsistent with their most preferred positions (such as avoiding arms races, not confessing to crimes, or deciding cases on the basis of their sincere beliefs on the merits), it leaves unexplored a full range of other institutional effects on judicial decision-making, such as the possibility that institutions encourage affiliated members to pursue particular substantive political missions or functions (including institutional maintenance) that are not best characterized in the language of self-interest, or that institutions generate some decision-making routines that are less than fully deliberative. Perhaps more importantly, I will also suggest that we might not be able to understand even the narrow category of "strategic behavior" without the contributions of historical and interpretive methods, since these methods are indispensable to a reliable understanding of purpose and context.

For Supreme Court scholars who are interested in examining other aspects of institutional politics I will suggest that they consider adopting approaches that attempt to identify whether certain institutional contexts generate distinctive purposes, perspectives, or routines. In other words, rather than adopt approaches that exclude issues of preference formation, one might find it worthwhile to see whether affiliations with institutions influence the way people think of their interests and responsibilities. This alternative approach is part of a larger literature in interpretive social science which examines the "constitutive" effects of law and institutional arrangements on the behavior of social actors (see Brigham 1987b; Brigham and Gordon 1996; McCann 1994, 1996). While there is room within this approach for the possibility that people use their institutional positions to promote extra-institutional or personal agendas, it is also assumed that actors like Supreme Court justices may sometimes view themselves as stewards of institutional missions, and that this sense of identity generates motivations of duty and professional responsibility not easily incorporated into the world view of rational choice.

Institutional Politics and the "Strategic Justice"

If one is promising an examination of institutional effects on decision-making one must first identify those features of institutional life that are being isolated and examined. Advocates of the strategic approach define institutions in a way that makes their effects essentially equivalent to those experienced in any game-theoretical situation. Institutions are viewed as a structure of formal or informal rules that shape the strategic calculations of actors who are self-consciously pursuing a set of presumably fixed short-term preferences (Knight 1992). What makes the calculation strategic is the understanding that an actor's goals are a product of the interaction between his or her behavior and the behavior (or anticipated behavior) of others. Thus, institutional settings establish bargaining situations or "parameters of choice" (Ethington and McDonagh 1995:89) and thus require rational actors to settle for "the highest ranked element in the feasible set" (*ibid.*, citing Elster 1986:4; see also Aldrich 1994; Riker 1986; Shepsle 1989). And so while it may be assumed that Supreme Court justices want to promote their policy preferences, advocates of the strategic approach would want to add that this means that justices must also be mindful of an institutional terrain that includes (for example) the responsibility to make decisions about which cases to hear and which to ignore, the need to secure a majority in order to have one's preferred position become the law, an expectation that the justices pay homage to precedent, and the possibility that competing policy makers may try to overturn their decisions or remove them from office (Boucher and Segal 1995; Brenner 1979; Epstein and Knight 1998; Epstein and Walker 1995; Eskridge 1991a and 1991b; Knight and Epstein 1996b; Maltzman and Wahlbeck 1996b; Murphy 1964).

Advocates of the strategic approach are certainly correct to point out that justices are sometimes motivated to think beyond the merits of the case to the question of whether they need to take steps to mitigate the ability of others (both on the Court and off) to influence an outcome or to retaliate against the Court. In fact, even before the advent of the strategic approach interpretivists have drawn attention to both intra-court and inter-institutional elements of this dynamic (see, e.g., Kutler 1968; Mason 1956). The most frequent examples of intra-court dynamics involve considerations that are associated with granting *certiorari* and securing a majority by manipulating opinion assignments and bargaining over the language of opinions. Inter-institutional examples involve various opportunities that other powerholders might have to exercise "checks and balances" against a Court that is acting in ways that are inconsistent with the preferences of other institutions. These so-called "separation of powers games" are reflected in concerns about (for example) whether Congress may try to reverse the Court's interpretation of a statute, or whether the amendment process may be initiated in order to overturn a constitutional interpretation, or whether those charged with enforcing a decision might attempt instead to undermine it, or whether a coalition of forces might be prompted to assault the Court's personnel or jurisdiction.

What these examples of strategic behavior have in common is an image of justices as a) focused exclusively on short-term goals, that is, on shaping the outcome of a particular case in a way that gets as close as possible to their preferred position, b) willing to decide a case on the basis of their sincerely held positions on the merits only when there are no discernible intra-court or inter-institutional challenges to that position, c) inclined to decide a case on the basis of something less than their most preferred positions if concessions seem necessary to secure a majority or to evade an unwanted response from powerholders in other institutions, and d) prepared to make a decision on the basis of positions with which they fundamentally disagree in order to avoid the threat of a consequence they consider even worse than losing a particular case. In short, the strategic approach assumes that justices will bargain or retreat in the face of a challenge or will adopt insincere positions on the merits in order to avoid a conflict with powerholders who are in a position to thwart the will of the Court.

I will momentarily suggest that strategic behavior need not be limited to decisions to bargain or retreat. But assuming for the moment that advocates of the strategic approach are mostly interested in pointing out (as an addendum to the attitudinal model) that there are times when a calculation of political risks leads justices to abandon their "sincere" or "raw preferences" (Epstein and Walker 1995b:323–25), it should be noted that there is little reason to think that Supreme Court justices are frequently forced by circumstance to back away from their position on the substantive merits of a case. We have known for some time that justices sometimes bargain among themselves, but with the decline of "consensus norms" and the rise of individual opinions, there are fewer professional constraints on the ability of justices to stake out their own distinctive position, and this means that justices are rarely in a position where they feel pressured to vote in a way that does not reflect their sincere preferences (see O'Brien's essay in this volume). Moreover, while there are some notorious examples of the Court retreating in the face of external pressure from other powerholders, there is still reason to believe that the justices are not particularly concerned with the possibility that their decisions might be overturned or that their jobs might be in jeopardy (see Segal's essay in this volume).

If there is a disagreement about how frequently the justices engage in strategic decision-making rather than sincere decision-making (if these are to be considered two different things), then interpretivists think that the best way to resolve this question is through the use of interpretive methods. This is because the issue raised by this question refers to the subjective state of mind of the actor rather than to a particular course of conduct. After all, the mere fact that a justice may have changed her mind during the opinion-writing stage, or that the Court appears to have avoided a conflict with a coordinate branch of government, is not evidence of a strategic bargain or retreat. One of the first points made by Walter Murphy in his classic *Elements of Judicial Strategy* about intra-court dynamics is that justices often attempt to influence each other by making arguments on the merits, and "collections of judicial papers show that time and again positions first taken at conference are changed as other Justices bring up new arguments" (1964:44). The influence of professional training and legal argument can even lead a justice who was originally assigned a majority opinion to conclude that "additional study had convinced him that he and the rest of the majority had been in error" (*ibid.*), which I assume is not considered a strategic shift under any definition of "strategic." The way that Murphy determined whether a shift in position was a strategic retreat or a principled change of heart was to use "traditional legal-historical" methods (e.g., reviewing conference notes, draft opinions, memos, and memoirs) in order to better understand the substance of the justices' jurisprudence and deliberations (1964:3).

The same kind of interpretive analysis is necessary in order to determine whether justices are motivated primarily by a desire to evade conflicts with powerholders in other institutions. I think the evidence suggests that Marshall acted strategically when he refused to order the Virginia Supreme Court to release the Cohen brothers in *Cohens v. Virginia* (1821), but this conclusion is based on Graber's (1995) careful legal analysis of Marshall's interpretation of the District of Columbia lottery statute and his thoughtful political analysis of the institutional rivalries between the United States Supreme Court and the high court in Virginia. Without such interpretive evidence scholars would be more likely to consider it possible that Marshall allowed the Cohen brothers to stay in jail because he sincerely believed that the D.C. statute did not apply to them. At the same time, I also think that the evidence suggests that when the Court refused to issue an injunction against President Andrew Johnson in *Mississippi v. Johnson* (1867) it was not, as some have suggested (Epstein and Walker 1995:335; Hughes 1965:588), merely acting prudently to avoid a risky political battle, but rather was applying well-established constitutional principles (Neiman 1992). Even in a case such as *Ex parte McCardle* (1869)— which for quite some time has been viewed by historians as a prime example of strategic evasion—the question of whether the justices were being sincere or evasive in allowing the Congress to strip the Court of its appellate jurisdiction requires us to know, not just the treacherous terrain of Reconstruction politics, but the justices' attitudes about whether Congress had the constitutional authority to make adjustments in the Court's appellate jurisdiction, and in most discussions of the case there is no evidence provided on this central point of interest (Epstein and Walker 1995). In each of these cases, interpretive methods would seem to add quite a bit to our understanding of whether the justices thought of themselves as playing a "separation of powers game" or as applying separation of powers principles—or, perhaps, as doing both, which is an option that seems disallowed by the definition of strategic as "insincere."

While the strategic approach is often sold as a more sophisticated version of the attitudinal model (in that it sheds light on those circumstances when judges are forced to back off their preferred positions), it is important to note that there is nothing about the definition of strategic behavior that requires strategic decision makers to adjust their preferences when faced with pressure or uncertainty. In fact, for an institution that is expected to remain independent of political pressure, it would seem that the least strategic course of action would be to develop a reputation for bargaining, retreating, and evading. Indeed, the course of action that might best maximize the interests of the justices in the long run would be to act in a way that appeared principled rather than strategic (see Murphy 1964:174–75). Thus, just as the game of Chicken generates the paradox that acting irrationally may be a rational way of forcing one's opponent to swerve, so too might it be that, for the Supreme Court, nonstrategic decision-making might be viewed as a paradoxical form of strategic decision-making. However, if this is so, then the idea of a "strategic decision maker" suddenly expands beyond the idea of being forced to abandon one's "sincere preferences" to encompass almost any imaginable course of conduct.

Advocates of the strategic approach may view this as evidence of how their approach is capable of capturing a fuller range of judicial behavior. But those who are inclined toward historical-interpretive institutionalism think that this paradox exposes a possible weakness in the concept of "strategic decision-making," or at least exposes the dependency of the concept on interpretive analysis. A justice such as Scalia who fancies himself an ideological spokesperson—or perhaps Brennan and Marshall with respect to death penalty cases, or any justice with clear and consistent views on an issue—may often find himself in a position where he would need to make a concession in order to secure a majority, but after considering the alternatives he may conclude that his preferred position is best promoted by its more pure articulation in a plurality or concurring opinion than by elaborating a watered-down version in an opinion of the Court. It would be difficult to understand the sense in which this calculation should be characterized as nonstrategic rather than just strategic in a different sense than a decision to bargain. Moreover, some justices, when faced with intransigent competitors, may think that both their short-term and long-term interests are best served by standing firmly behind an unpopular but principled judgment rather than by retreating or evading a conflict, as with (perhaps) the four conservatives who held firm during the New Deal battles; the majority in the second flag-burning case (*U.S. v. Eichman* 1990, decided after Congress attempted to overturn *Texas v. Johnson* 1989 with the passage of the Flag Protection Act of 1989); and the Court as a whole in the famous joint opinion in *Cooper v. Aaron* (1958). What, if anything, makes these decisions any less strategic than those cases in which the justices may have attempted to steer clear of a collision with another branch?

In general, if one is being strategic whenever one considers the consequences of one's behavior in light of the potential behavior of others, then all of these examples, plus virtually all decisions handed down in the history of the Court, are properly labeled strategic. (The only example of nonstrategic voting that currently comes to mind is the aging Justice Grier's wandering votes during the conference on the *Legal Tender Cases*. His behavior earned him an invitation to retire.) In *Dred Scott* (1857), for example, would the strategic decision have been to avoid the slavery issue entirely by invoking the precedent of *Strader v. Graham* (1851) in order to establish the point that the Missouri high court had the final say on matters of state law (as Justice Nelson was initially prepared to write), or would it have been to address the constitutional issues that were previously sidestepped (as Justice Wayne proposed)? If the latter, was it more strategic to uphold the power of Congress to address the issue of slavery in the territories through the political process (as Justices Curtis and McLean suggested) or to write an opinion that might have had the effect of keeping the issue of slavery from dividing the Union by ruling that neither Congress nor the federal judiciary have any authority to determine the status of slaves (as Chief Justice Taney indicated in his majority opinion)? Raising these questions makes clear that what distinguishes these alternative courses of action is not the degree to which the justices exhibited a concern about the interactive effects triggered by the behavior of others, but rather the influence of different sets of preferences and concerns on the justices' calculations. (See also Murphy's [1964:202–7] discussion of the different approaches taken by Black and Stone toward economic substantive due process.)

If we think there are benefits to be gained by putting judicial attitudes and motivations in context, then what needs to be illuminated is not the abstract question of whether the justices are engaged in strategic decision-making but the more specific question of what sorts of considerations lead a particular judge to conclude that a particular course of action—whether bargaining or not bargaining, retreating or standing firm, evading or confronting, acting sincerely or insincerely—is the best course to adopt under the circumstances. Once these motives and contexts have been illuminated, the question then becomes how much do we gain by way of explanation when we add the extra concept of "strategic decision-making."

From an interpretivist perspective, the reason that the question, "Do the justices engage in strategic decision-making?" quickly transforms into the question, "What were those justices caring about or worrying about in that case?" is that all deliberate behavior, strategic (if one can make sense of the term) or otherwise, becomes understandable only in the context of particular purposes and preferences (see Kloppenberg 1995:126). In other words, before one can view institutional politics as a strategic terrain it is first necessary to understand it as a normative terrain. As Skowronek (1995:94) puts it, "[A]ny a priori notion of individual interest will very quickly succumb to historically derived and institutionally embedded rationalities of action."

Because the strategic approach claims to be a kind of institutional analysis, Skowronek's point about how "rationalities of action" are "institutionally embedded" deserves more elaboration. While Supreme Court scholars who use PTI want to distinguish their approach from the traditional "attitudinal model," the two approaches do share one assumption, which is that justices view their institutional position as a platform from which they pursue essentially extra-institutional preferences. Of course, there is nothing about institutional politics that prevents actors from importing into institutional arenas attitudes or interests that have extra-institutional origins; Justice McLean, for example, has been accused of using his position on the Court to run for the presidency. But if we are interested in understanding the factors that influence Supreme Court decision-making, it would seem appropriate to adopt an understanding of institutional politics that is able to take into account the possibility that some judicial preferences are shaped or constituted within the normative terrain of their institutional context. In Smith's (1988:95) words, institutions may "influence the self-conception of those who occupy roles defined by them in ways that give those persons distinctively 'institutional' perspectives." Moreover, beyond providing rules for decision-making procedures, they influence "the relative resources and the senses of purpose and principle that political actors possess," and this may mean that these purposes and principles are "better described as conceptions of duty or inherently meaningful action than as egoistic preferences." As Skowronek (1995:94) put it:

> Different institutions may give more or less play to individual interests, but the distinctive criteria of institutional action are official duty and legitimate authority. Called upon to account for their actions or to explain their decisions, incumbents have no recourse but to repair to their job descriptions. Thus, institutions do not simply constrain or channel the actions of self-interested individuals, they prescribe actions, construct motives, and assert legitimacy. That indeed is how institutions perpetuate the objectives or purposes instilled in them at their founding; that is what lies at the heart of their staying power.

Rather than address the question of whether Supreme Court justices place value on a set of institutionally derived purposes and responsibilities, PTI scholars typically adopt the attitudinalist assumption that the driving force beyond judicial decision-making is an interest in promoting personal policy preferences. This means that one of the most important effects that the Supreme Court as an institution may have on the decision-making of the justices is left unexplored in this version of institutional analysis.

Also unexplored is the extent to which the inclination to bargain or retreat from one's preferences (to the extent that this happens on the Court) is also a by-product of institutional forces (see more generally Bohman 1991:105–6). With respect to intra-court dynamics it should be kept in mind that our image of justices as insistent on having their idiosyncratic points of view represented in almost every case, either by extracting concessions from majority opinion writers or by writing separate concurring or dissenting opinions, is relatively recent. Bargaining among the justices was mostly unnecessary before John Marshall's time, when the practice was to hand down seriatim opinions rather than opinions of the Court. During the age of Marshall the practice might have been possible but, by most accounts, it was not very much in evidence, perhaps because of Marshall's leadership abilities, or because there was a high degree of jurisprudential consensus among early-nineteenth-century justices, or because the justices felt that it was important for their infant institution to speak in a strong, solitary voice about the great constitutional disputes of the day. In fact, up through the tenure of Chief Justice Stone it appears as though there was a consensus among the justices that writing concurrences and dissents should be a rare event, even if it meant signing on to an opinion of the Court with which a justice disagreed—which means that, during this period, efforts to secure a majority may have had more to do with marshaling a selfless commitment to institutional norms than with engaging in the strategic pursuit of self-interest. In many cases where a justice felt inclined to dissent from an opinion it was considered appropriate merely to indicate the dissent without writing an explanatory opinion. It was not until the breakdown of these consensus norms that the dynamics of intra-court negotiation could even become a serious object of inquiry. To put it another way, bargaining among the justices is not merely a function of preferences plus an awareness of interactive effects; it is also an activity that is constituted by an evolving set of normative institutional perspectives. Because of these sorts of institutional effects the justices internalize an understanding of whether such behavior is to be considered professional, as well as an understanding of what forms of bargaining are acceptable (e.g., circulating comments on a draft opinion or threatening to write a separate concurring opinion) or are not acceptable (e.g., leaking embarrassing information to the press or threatening to write a separate concurring opinion).

Since strategic behavior follows countless logics rather than predictable patterns, and since these logics are made comprehensible only after careful attention to evolving institutional norms and distinctive judicial preferences and concerns, it would be best if advocates of the strategic approach would formulate their research questions more narrowly. Rather than claim to be exploring the question, "Does the Court's institutional environment lead the justices to act strategically?," it would be more straightforward to ask, "Are there times when justices who are pursuing short-term policy victories display a willingness to abandon their beliefs about the merits of a case when they believe they are in a position of weakness or vulnerability vis-à-vis competing powerholders on and off the Court?" Interpretivists believe that there is nothing much new about the question and that the question can be (and has been) adequately explored without the use of the stylized conventions of rational choice. Then again, there is really no harm in using new methods of presentation to clarify our understanding of this dynamic, as long as we keep in mind Murphy's (1964:xi) warning that "the formal theory of games" often leads to "distortions of reality" when applied to judicial decision-making. Maybe this means that our division of labor will consist of interpretive scholars identifying a range of judicial motivations and concerns—the pursuit of personal policy preferences, the maintenance of jurisprudential traditions, the commitment to consolidate national power, the desire to protect the independence of the Court, the interest in avoiding impeachment, the promotion of the political agenda of a dominant coalition or class, perhaps even the ambition to run for president—while advocates of the strategic approach will see which of these is productively translated into rational-choice models and which can be presented without the use of those stylized conventions. (For example, compare Epstein and Walker 1995, which is an exemplary interpretive discussion of the "Reconstruction Game," with Epstein and Knight 1996, which supplements the history of Marbury with formal modeling.) Once we are aware of the extent to which historical-interpretive analysis makes rational-choice models possible we will be in a better position to discuss which side "is doing the most work" (Smith 1995:135) and how much the translation into models adds to what we already know from the interpretive evidence.

The second point is that, once we appreciate the limited scope of the strategic approach, it becomes clear that for scholars interested in examining a more full range of institutional effects on Supreme Court decision-making an alternative approach is necessary. The strategic approach is not well designed to help us understand (for example): whether justices acquire distinctive preferences, goals, or conceptions of duty by virtue of their understanding of the role of the Supreme Court in the political system; how internal norms relating to proper judicial conduct may regulate, or even severely constrict, the opportunities for bargaining or the tactics employed by the justices to influence each other; the circumstances under which the justices' concern about the maintenance of the institution's power and legitimacy mitigates their temptation to indulge their personal points of view; whether the establishment of decision-making routines results in decisions that are better viewed as habitual rather than deliberate or strategic; and the influences that historically contingent configurations of social and political power may have on the range of decision-making considered acceptable or appropriate. If one of the virtues of institutional analysis is to address these other sorts of questions alongside those questions typically addressed by PTI scholars, then we need to be mindful to develop a conception of "institution" that is capable of capturing the various motivations that institutional actors might possess and the various influences on their behavior exerted by institutional forces.

In elaborating an alternative conception of the nature of institutional politics it would also be useful if the conceptual apparatus made it easier to link our research to important normative debates. Obviously PTI is capable of informing certain kinds of normative questions, particularly when a case can be made that a change in institutional rules might channel behavior in a way that produces more desirable social consequences. Still, more often than not, rational-choice institutionalism is preoccupied with questions relating to how judges jockey for position in a potentially risky terrain, and while these questions can be very interesting to law-and-courts scholars they are, relatively speaking, fairly inconsequential for the rest of society. Even if PTI scholars devise research agendas that break out of this "inside the beltway" mentality, it would still be the case that the central image of institutional behavior within the strategic approach is essentially Hobbesian, and unless one thinks that all institutions exist in order to facilitate or mitigate Hobbesian impulses (and what's the evidence for that?) this

assumption precludes us from using institutional analysis to examine:
a) the actual normative foundations of our institutional practices, and
b) the constitutive effects of these foundations on social and political
relations. Institutional arrangements may be important in the way that
they channel self-interest, but they are also important because they give
corporal form to our concerns about what we should value and how
we should pursue those values. In embracing institutional analysis we
should be careful not to limit ourselves to a conception of institutional
politics that marginalizes these central questions.

Interpretive Institutionalism and the Concept of "Mission"

What is different about the way that interpretivists conceptualize institutional politics? While there are some intramural disagreements (see
Clayton in this volume, as well as the symposium introduced by Ethington and McDonagh 1995), in general what ties together those who
have embraced "the interpretive turn" in the social sciences (see Hiley,
Bohman, and Shusterman 1991; Bohman 1991) is an interest in understanding and explaining behavior in terms of the meanings that people
associate with their behavior. It bothers some interpretivists when behavioralists assume that justices act on the basis of hypothesized motives without carefully examining the justices' actual beliefs and concerns. We think the behavioralist practice of assuming motive and then
trying to find behavioral patterns that reflect particular motives, while
useful for illuminating certain questions, also leads to some obvious
mistakes, such as the claim that the Social Darwinistic Justice Holmes
may have been voting his policy preferences when he voted to uphold
progressive regulation of the economy. Rather than focus on ostensibly
universal motivations such as rationality or selfishness (which we think
do not get us very far), interpretivists try to reconstruct intentional
states of mind and cultural or political contexts in the hope that we can
induce with some confidence the reasons that led a particular person to
adopt a particular course of conduct. In other words, "Taking an internal view of the practice means viewing the activity in consideration of
the understandings of the participants involved (interpretivism); taking an external view means ignoring these understandings and instead
focusing on the patterns reflected in the activity (positivism)" (Tama-
naha 1996:183).

Given this perspective it should not be a surprise that most interpretivists are interested in reconstructing those bundles of ideas and
motivations that are associated with particular institutions. To be more

specific, from an interpretivist perspective what makes something a recognizable institution is a *mission*—an identifiable purpose or a shared normative goal that, at a particular historical moment in a particular context, becomes routinized within an identifiable corporate form as the result of the efforts of certain groups of people. All social activities (including a game of Chicken) are purposeful, but some have a more transient purpose and they might be better characterized as games or events. However, when an effort is made to organize a purposeful activity as an ongoing enterprise we tend to think of that activity as having been institutionalized. Part of this effort at routinizing a mission typically involves the establishment of certain *organizational attributes*, such as foundational documents (which typically specify missions), leadership positions, divisions of responsibility, decision-making mechanisms, and standard operating procedures; and the combination of an identifiable mission and a set of organizational attributes makes it possible for some actors to have a formal *affiliation* with the institution.

While it may be possible to elaborate other features of generic institutions, at bottom what makes it possible to identify an institution like a "court," and what makes a court different than the Federal Reserve or a university, is not its unique location in a strategic terrain but rather the fact that affiliated actors think of themselves as working together to promote specific goals or perform specific functions. From this point of view, to examine institutional effects on decision-making is, in part (the part that parallels the "intra-court bargaining" side of the strategic approach), to determine whether institutional actors are influenced in their attitudes and behavior by their relationship to their institution's mission and to the organizational attributes that have been constructed in service of that mission.

For interpretivists, focusing on the internal institutional characteristics of the Supreme Court means, first of all, drawing attention to the structures of meaning that are embedded in that particular corporate form. In other words, is there evidence that the justices view the Supreme Court as promoting specific goals or performing specific functions in the political system, and do they feel a sense of personal or professional responsibility to act in ways that facilitate the accomplishment of its distinctive mission? If so, then (reiterating Smith's point) we can say that the idea of the Court influenced "the self-conception of those who occupy roles defined by them in ways that give those persons distinctively 'institutional' perspectives," including a sense of duty that is designed to filter out the influence of those nonjudicial interests and preferences that are inconsistent with sustaining institutional functions (i.e., the overt use of judicial power to advance partisan goals). Once we identify the "institutional perspective" of the Court we will be in a position to explore the extent to which this perspective transforms, tames, or mitigates the influence of extra-institutional factors such as conventional political ideologies or partisan preferences.

The first step toward the identification of the Court's distinctive mission in this political system would be to review those foundational documents (such as Article III) that essentially articulate the justices' "job description"; this follows from Skowronek's (1995:94) suggestion that "the analysis of institutional action will itself be driven to a consideration of origins, toward an understanding of official behavior in terms of original purposes." This leads to the question of whether the justices' decision-making reflects a sense of responsibility to resolve legal disputes in accordance with their best understanding of the law. Evidence of this influence would emerge from a consideration of (for example): a) whether the Court's standing and justiciability requirements, while obviously susceptible to manipulation, nevertheless shape decisions regarding what counts as a legitimate case for purposes of invoking judicial power; b) whether decisions about which cases to hear reflect professional judgments about the substantive importance of the legal issues being raised or the role of the Court in managing a judicial hierarchy (see Perry 1991); and c) whether the substantive decision on the merits reflects the justices' concern with maintaining coherent and defensible jurisprudential traditions and not merely the promotion of conventional partisan or ideological preferences (Gillman 1993, 1994b, 1996; and the essays by Bussiere and Kahn in this volume).

There is evidence that most justices act in accordance with the Court's formal responsibility to decide actual legal disputes based on their best understanding of the law. If this is not always apparent in political science accounts of Supreme Court politics, which emphasize variation on the Court rather than the remarkable similarities in the justices' understanding of their responsibilities, then one need only contrast the routines and motivations of Supreme Court justices with actors who are affiliated with other sorts of institutions, such as university professors, bank presidents, senators, and preschool directors. Still, while adjudication and legal interpretation are central to the justices' understandings of their responsibilities, it would be wrong to assume that Article III purposes are the only ones that make up the Court's mission. Foundational documents do not always provide a reliable or comprehensive indication of the actual goals and purposes; in some cases (as perhaps with courts in more authoritarian regimes) they may be downright deceptive. And so as a check on, or supplement to, these formal statements it is essential to examine the substantive political goals that proponents of a federal Supreme Court sought to accomplish, as well as the actual agendas and concerns of the justices. For example, it may be the case that judges, like most state officials, feel an obligation to promote and protect the interests and stability of the political system as a whole, and this may make them exhibit a sense of loyalty not just to Article III purposes but also to those regime interests they consider compelling—whether the consolidation of national power during the early years of the republic (Casto 1995), the defense of Union efforts during the Civil War (e.g., *The Prize Cases* [1863], but compare Nelson's dissent), or the accommodation of Cold War repression (Belknap 1977).

Moreover, as with any institution, those who are affiliated with the Court should be expected to deliberate about protecting their institution's legitimacy and (relatedly) adapting their institution's mission to changing contexts and the actions of other institutions; in other words, in addition to performing a mission, institutional actors must consider issues of institutional maintenance in the context of a dynamic social setting. Maintaining legitimacy or authority may at times lead the justices to avoid perceived "self-inflicted wounds" which may undermine the distinction between an independent judiciary and a partisan policy-making institution (as with *Dred Scott* and the *Legal Tender Cases*); it may also lead the justices to work harder to establish a united front in high-stakes cases, as with *Brown v. Board of Education* (1954), *Cooper v. Aaron* (1958), and *U.S. v. Nixon* (1974). (Note that PTI scholars might be tempted to characterize these examples as "strategic" adjustments to what would otherwise be the preferences of particular justices; however, if the justices are motivated by a sense of institutional stewardship they are not properly viewed as strategic in the sense of personal preference maximizing—the behavior more closely resembles altruism than selfishness [but see Rand 1965]). Institutional maintenance might also require the justices to rethink their mission in light of larger changes in the political system; for example, when the Court's early twentieth-century efforts to enforce traditional constitutional limits on federal power collapsed with the rise of the modern regulatory welfare state, the justices in *U.S. v. Carolene Products* (1938) retooled the Court's mission so that the institution would be principally concerned with adjusting constitutional rights to a new age rather than with maintaining older conceptions of delegated constitutional powers (see Gillman 1994b). And then there are those institutional norms that elaborate boundaries of professional conduct, which on the Court include everything from standards of recusal to the dynamics of opinion-writing.

In general, then, the key question in determining if actors are influenced by institutional perspectives is whether relevant decision makers are committed to acting as stewards of discernible institutional purposes. Still, the process by which particular political functions or agendas become routinized typically includes the creation of organizational attributes which are designed to establish roles, relationships, procedures, and norms by which a group of actors can work together to pursue institutional missions. With respect to Supreme Court decision-making there are too many organizational attributes to mention, but among those that (at one time or another) have had an impact on the justices' behavior would be: the Court's relationship to a central government in a federal system, the fact that decisions are made by a majority of a small group of people, the elaborate (and changing) norms governing justiciability and the authority of *stare decisis*, the creation of intermediate courts of appeals, the expansion of the Court's constitutional and statutory jurisdiction, the elimination of mandatory appeals, the Rule of Four, the hiring of law clerks, the secrecy of the conference, the ability to print and circulate drafts of opinions, even the move to the so-called Marble Temple in 1935.

Some of the best institutional analyses of Supreme Court politics focus on selected organizational attributes without attention to the substantive mission of the judiciary (see the contribution of Hall and Brace in this volume). In these analyses researchers attempt to find patterns between the particular institutional characteristics (such as the method of appointment or election, the availability of discretionary jurisdiction, or the partisanship of coordinate branches) and decision-making tendencies (such as the likelihood of casting liberal votes or writing dissenting opinions). On the basis of this research we can discover whether, at a certain moment in time, different organizational attributes of judicial politics make it more or less likely that judges will vote in particular ways; for example, we can find out whether judges who are elected are more likely to hand down decisions that reflect the prevailing political attitudes of voters.

There is no questioning the value of this sort of information. But

interpretivists would suggest that there are explanatory benefits to focusing on how organizational attributes relate to the performance of
the Court's mission. In fact, without reference to the larger corporate
purposes that tie together these constituent elements it would be difficult to understand why courts are associated with certain powers and
responsibilities, methods of appointment, terms of office, internal
norms, rituals, even "languages of authority" (Brigham 1987a:211). For
example, the Rule of Four, which describes the practice of reviewing
a case if four justices favor granting the petition for *certiorari*, emerged
around the time of the creation of federal Courts of Appeals when the
Supreme Court was being transformed from an institution that was
expected to review the soundness of almost all lower federal court decisions to one that was expected to focus more specifically on those legal
and policy issues that were of greater import to the judicial system and
the country as a whole (Ely 1992); it is only with an understanding of
this background that it becomes possible to comprehend the sorts of
legal or institutional concerns that influence the process of granting
certiorari (Perry 1991), as well as the reason that so many of the Court's
institutional practices began to shift "from legal to bureaucratic forms"
(Brigham 1987a:177). The process by which Supreme Court justices are
nominated and confirmed also reflects changing understandings of the
Court's mission in the political system (Silverstein 1994). Similar constitutive effects on the justices' conceptions of their roles and responsibilities can be imagined with respect to virtually all of the Court's organizational attributes, from Marshall's reasons for creating "the Opinion
of the Court" to the norms that govern the interactions that take place
during the opinion-writing process (for an overview see Brigham
1987a).

   In general, it seems highly unlikely that organizational attributes affect judicial behavior only to the extent that they channel or constrain
the pursuit of self-interest. While it is true that life tenure might make
it easier to promote policy preferences, it may also be central to a
judge's sense of duty to resist political pressure and decide a case in
accordance with the law. If we see organizational attributes as derived
from a concern about the accomplishment of substantive concerns and
functions, and if we see the maintenance of these functions as central
to the identity of a particular institution, then we have a conception of
institutional politics that helps us gain a perspective on "the Supreme
Court's ability to transcend the changing personalities that have taken
a seat behind the bench" (Brigham 1987a:6). Moreover, when we move

beyond viewing institutions as facilitating or impeding self-interested behavior we are able to incorporate into our understanding of institutional effects certain experiences that are frequently missed by more positivist approaches, including: experiences of duty and professional obligation, understandings of shared purpose, concerns about the maintenance of corporate authority or legitimacy, and participation in a routine—each of which suggests the presence of a kind of motivation that is something other than rational, self-interested, strategic, and calculating (Granovetter and Swedberg 1992; see also Powell and DiMaggio [1991] on "embeddedness").

So far, the discussion of institutional effects has focused on the internal influences of Supreme Court norms on the attitudes and behavior of the justices. However, there is another advantage to using the idea of mission as the anchor for institutional analysis, and that is that it helps us understand how the Supreme Court interacts with, and becomes vulnerable to the influence of, other institutions and actors in the political system. When PTI scholars want to place the Court in a larger political structure they typically construct "separation of powers games" in which justices are envisioned as individual preference maximizers competing against other individual preference maximizers in coordinate branches of government. This game-theoretic metaphor, while useful in certain circumstances, may also obscure or neglect those cases where state actors in different institutions view themselves as having distinct and perhaps noncompetitive relationships to a particular issue area; in other words, it cannot adequately address how institutional relationships reflect ongoing and changing judgments about how to divide governing responsibilities. It may be the case that in 1936 Roosevelt viewed himself and the Court as having equal but diametrically opposed interests in the outcome of New Deal policymaking, and we might be tempted to suggest that he and the Court were engaged in a game of Chicken (although we would need to keep in mind that, at best, only one or two justices were playing); but Congress's unwillingness in 1937 to cooperate with FDR's court-packing plan was almost certainly a function of a consensus among those institutional actors that it was illegitimate for the Congress to assault the Court's role as an independent arbiter of constitutional disputes.

When we think of institutions as having particular responsibilities or promoting particular agendas we can also understand how they attract supporters, opponents, and even clients. On this latter point we know that changes in the numbers, needs, experiences, and perspectives of litigants establish the context within which the justices perform their responsibilities, and may even cause dramatic shifts in the justices' behavior (as Epp discusses in his contribution to this volume). Moreover, if every mission is a political project, then institutions can be expected to survive only to the extent that they attract enough supporters to sustain and defend them. In fact, by focusing on the idea of mission rather than potential battles over discrete cases we can understand why groups or classes in a society orient themselves to an institution like the Supreme Court (or the ACLU, NRA, or PTA) on the basis of whether they support or oppose the performance of the ongoing mission rather than on the basis of whether they support or oppose discrete decisions. One of the reasons why the game theorists' separation of powers games often ring hollow is that it is almost unheard of that people will seek to punish the Court simply on the basis of a short-term disagreement about the outcome of a particular case. In general, then, the ability of the justices to maintain the Court's general reputation in the political system, and to carry out a substantive political mission that is favored (or at least not opposed) by dominant classes or coalitions, has more to do with the institution's longevity and efficacy than discrete acts of effective bargaining with strategic adversaries. This is why, in the end, it is essential to situate the Court as an institution in larger structures of social relations and regime configurations—the sort of work that was the hallmark of the "old institutionalists" and that Clayton (in his chapter for this volume) characterizes as a "political systems approach" to Supreme Court politics.

In fact, rather than view intra-court dynamics and inter-institutional relationships as separate sorts of games, interpretivists are well positioned to explore the interactive effects between larger conflicts in the political system and the internal norms and decision-making patterns generated by the justices as they try to maintain a distinctive and valued presence in the political system. It would seem as though the successful accomplishment of this effort would have to be about more than wrestling with similarly motivated policy makers over short-term goals; among other things it would be about promoting or imposing a normative vision of political and social life, which of course would include a vision of the special functions that the Court should perform in a system of divided powers and responsibilities. As we gain an enriched understanding of the justices' beliefs about their role, and about how to keep that role current and legitimate, and about the interests served in the performance of that role, we will be in a position to link

our empirical research to the essentially normative questions that motivate us in the first place to be interested in this extraordinary institution.

Conclusion

Attitudinalists feel that the justices' institutional context is such that
we could learn a lot about judicial politics by simply focusing on their
policy preferences. PTI scholars believe that if you spend more time
thinking about the Court's context you find that the justices may also
exhibit different motivations beyond those identified by attitudinalists.
Advocates of historical-interpretive institutionalism agree that more
careful attention to context exposes more complicated motivations than
have been typically attributed to justices, but we think that there is
more to learn about the effects of institutional contexts on judicial preferences and interests than can be incorporated into a rational-choice
perspective. If there is value in putting attitudes in context, then interpretivists think that we should go all the way.

From the point of view of many interpretivists, the major weakness
in conventional political science accounts of judicial politics has been
the assumption that judges engage in "instrumental politics"—the self-
conscious manipulation of legal rules and rhetoric in order to promote
preferred political outcomes (see Brigham 1987a; Brigham and Gordon
1996; Burgess 1993; Kahn 1993; McCann 1996). This neo-realist theoretical orientation has been prevalent in the literature associated with "political jurisprudence" and judicial behavioralism, and it is now a central
feature of the rational-choice version of institutional analysis. Interpretivists understand that this sort of motivation may be a feature of
judicial politics, but we also think it is prudent that scholars of judicial
politics embrace theoretical frameworks that are capable of investigating alternative hypotheses, such as the possibility that the world view
of judges is constituted by institutional norms, jurisprudential traditions, and related social structures of power. This would mean that
judges view the law, not as a tool for the promotion of exogenous
preferences, but as reflective of their most deep-seated professional
convictions. At the same time, to say that judges may have sincere
attachments to legal values is not to deny the political nature of
decision-making; we just need to remember that politics is embedded
in jurisprudence, and does not merely come into play when legal values are set aside in favor of personal ones. If law-and-courts scholars

think that noninstrumentalist motivations are worth investigating, then interpretive-institutional analysis may be the most productive way to proceed. If not, then it may be worth discussing why "instrumentalism" has such a hypnotic hold on the imagination of our field.

Maybe the reason has to do with the possibility that abandoning instrumentalism puts pressure on parsimony. When Rogers Smith first suggested that historical-interpretive institutionalism may be the future of public law he also wondered whether interpretivists could do anything to prevent their "thick descriptions" from becoming "so hopelessly complex and foggy as to be impossible to bring into focus" (Smith 1988). Since then, he has explored the question of whether theoretically elegant explanatory models can be reconciled with careful interpretive accounts of the actual experiences and motivations of institutional actors (Smith 1992:26–27, discussing Ferejohn 1991). McCann (1994) has also urged interpretivists to be as clear and systematic as possible when explaining relationships among key variables. At the same time, careful attention to judicial attitudes in context may force us to acknowledge ways of knowing about the Court that cannot be reduced to formal models or parsimonious hypotheses. The more we take seriously human agency and substantive politics the more likely we are to see that Supreme Court decision-making is a much more complicated, and interesting, activity then is suggested by some hypothesis tests. This should not stop us from clearly specifying the relationships we are trying to explore and from inducing whatever modest generalizations we can persuasively defend—for example, about the principles or agendas driving decision-making in particular periods or the relationship between Court power and particular social interests. But we should also be prepared to acknowledge that the more we see decision-making as arising out of "historically derived and institutionally embedded rationalities of action" the more we may insist upon the contingent nature of our explanations. If some are tempted to worry that this puts interpretivists at a disadvantage in relation to positivists I would quickly add that a deeper appreciation of the embedded nature of Supreme Court politics may give us some perspective on whether the "general theories" offered by positivists amount to anything more than contestable interpretations of historically contingent patterns of behavior. Whether or not this is true, we may still find that after decades of work on Supreme Court decision-making that gave only perfunctory attention to the justices' institutional context there may be much to learn by immersing ourselves in it.

PART TWO

Legal Norms and the Internal Structure
of Supreme Court Decision-Making

4

Institutional Norms and Supreme Court Opinions: On Reconsidering the Rise of Individual Opinions

David M. O'Brien

Like other political institutions, the Supreme Court of the United States has its own unique set of internal practices, norms, and traditions. Along with jurisdictional doctrines and formal rules, institutional norms govern the Court's operation (see O'Brien 1996). Among the traditional norms are those of secrecy about deliberations prior to the announcement of decisions; majority rule in deciding cases and other matters; and respect for seniority during discussions at conference and in assigning opinions for the Court, which the Chief Justice does if he votes with the majority or, alternatively, the senior associate justice in the majority.

Another traditional norm governing the Court's work is that of consensus on an institutional opinion—the opinion announcing the Court's decision. Opinions for the Court represent a collective judgment and as such are negotiated documents forged through compromise. They became devalued in the twentieth century, however, with the rise of individual opinions. Individual opinions may concur in the result but disagree with the reasoning offered in the Court's opinion, dissent from both the outcome of and reasoning for the Court's decision, or both—that is, separate opinions in part concurring and in part dissenting. In contrast to opinions for the Court, justices writing separately do not labor under the burden of joining with other justices. Dissenting opinions, in the often quoted words of Chief Justice Charles Evans Hughes (1930–40), constitute "an appeal to the brooding spirit of the law, to the intelligence of a future day, when a later decision may possibly correct the error into which the dissenting judge believes the court to have been betrayed" (Hughes 1928:68). The rise of individ-

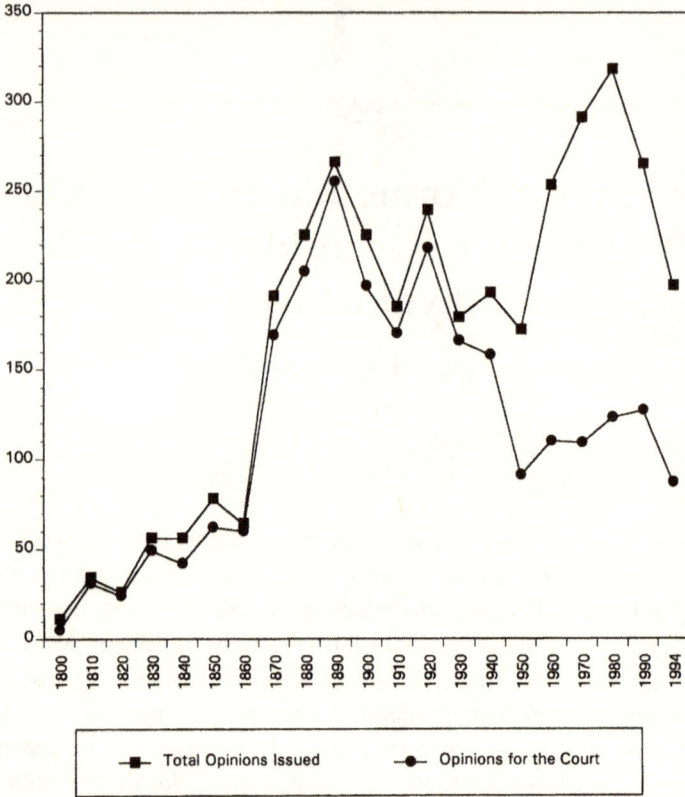

Figure 4.1 Opinion-Writing, 1800–1994.

ual opinions is shown in figure 4.1 (O'Brien 1996:319). Notably, by the mid-twentieth century the total opinions (including concurring, dissenting, and separate opinions) annually outnumbered those announcing the Court's decisions, though since the mid-1980s the number of individual opinions has declined slightly.

Chief Justice John Marshall (1801–35) is credited with forging the tradition of consensus in arriving at opinions for the Court. Prior to his arrival on the bench, during the Court's first decade (1790–1800) the English practice of rendering seriatim opinions was followed, whereby every justice delivered an opinion in each case. Marshall changed that in order to achieve his overriding institutional goal—unanimity. Marshall believed that unanimous decisions would build the Court's prestige and legitimacy. He therefore discouraged dissenting opinions and wrote the overwhelming number of the Court's opinions, even when he disagreed with a ruling. Not all of the justices shared his view, but he made it difficult for them not to follow.[1]

The Taney Court (1835–64) and subsequent ones generally emulated the Marshall Court's collegial decision-making practices, and consensus on the Court's opinions became an institutional norm. "The business of the Court," as Justice Potter Stewart once observed, "is to give institutional opinions for its decisions"(O'Brien 1996:265–66). Still, this is not to suggest that there was not also a tradition of dissent. Rather, institutional opinions were simply much more highly prized. Justices in the nineteenth and early twentieth century tended not to publish many dissenting or concurring opinions. Chief Justice Salmon P. Chase (1864–73), for one, seldom filed dissents because he thought "that except in very important causes [filing a] dissent [was] inexpedient" (Niven 1993:517). Chief Justice William Howard Taft (1921–30) suppressed more than two hundred dissents, explaining: "I don't approve of dissentings generally, for I think in many cases where I differ from the majority, it is more important to stand by the Court and give its judgment weight than merely to record my individual dissent where it is better to have the law certain than to have it settled either way" (Mason 1956:66, 223).

Published dissents are a manifestation of "institutional disobedience" (Campbell III 1983). In the nineteenth and early twentieth century, though, the justices tended to conform to the will of the majority and to refrain from publishing their differences. Justices Oliver Wendell Holmes and Louis D. Brandeis, for example, were among "the great dissenters" (Zobell 1959). Yet, according to Brandeis, Holmes was "reluctant to [dissent in subsequent and similar cases] again after he had once had his say on a subject."[2] In contrast, Justices Hugo L. Black and William O. Douglas, among others, noted every dissent. The change in judicial norms is evident from a comparison of the dissent rates of "the great dissenters" and of those serving on the Burger Court (1969–86) and the Rehnquist Court (1986–). Table 4.1 shows that recent justices publish dissents at higher rates than the "great dissenters."

With the publication of increasing numbers of individual opinions, the norm governing institutional opinions became devalued. As figure 4.2 underscores, throughout the nineteenth century opinions for the Court accounted for 80 to 90 percent of all opinions issued.[3] That changed rather dramatically in the twentieth century, however. The percentage of opinions for the Court of the total opinions annually produced declined throughout the 1940s and 1950s, and from 1960 to 1986

Table 4.1
Comparison of Dissent Rates

Justice	Number of Dissenting Opinions	Average per Term
"The Great Dissenters":		
W. Johnson (1804–1834)	30	1.0
J. Catron (1837–1865)	26	0.9
N. Clifford (1858–1881)	60	2.6
J. Harlan (1877–1911)	119	3.5
O. Holmes (1902–1932)	72	2.4
L. Brandeis (1916–1939)	65	2.9
H. Stone (1925–1946)	93	4.6
F. Frankfurter (1939–1962)	251	10.9
Justices Serving on the Burger and Rehnquist Courts:		
W. Douglas (1969–1974)	231	38.5
J. Stevens (1975–1994)	400	21.0
W. Brennan, Jr. (1969–1990)	402	19.1
T. Marshall (1969–1991)	335	15.4
W. Rehnquist (1972–1994)	269	12.2
H. Blackmun (1970–1994)	245	10.2
L. Powell, Jr. (1971–1987)	159	9.9
B. White (1969–1993)	233	9.3
A. Scalia (1986–1994)	61	7.6
R. Ginsburg (1993–1994)	7	7
S. O'Connor (1981–1994)	89	6.8
W. Burger (1969–1986)	111	6.5
C. Thomas (1991–1994)	19	6.3
A. Kennedy (1988–1994)	37	5.2
D. Souter (1990–1994)	17	4.2

Source: David M. O'Brien (1996), p. 331.

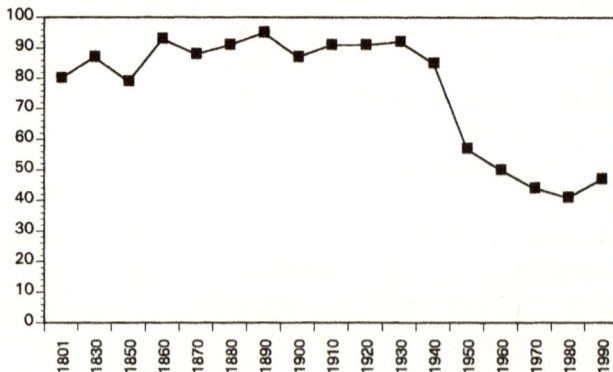

Figure 4.2 Percent of Opinions for Court of Total Opinions Issued, 1801–1990.

never again rose above 50 percent, with the exception of two terms. In other words, whereas in the nineteenth century individual opinions amounted to no more than 20 percent of the Court's total opinion production, in the latter half of the twentieth century institutional opinions constituted less than half of the annual output of opinions.

What explains the rise of individual opinions? That question is addressed in the next section, along with various hypotheses for explaining "the mysterious demise of consensual norms in the United States Supreme Court" (Walker, Epstein, and Dixon 1988). The following section, then, takes up the issue of why individual opinions grew increasingly numerous throughout the 1960s, 1970s, and into the mid-1980s, and then, after more than three decades, declined during the chief justiceship of William H. Rehnquist.

Revisiting "The Roosevelt Court"

In his pioneering work, *The Roosevelt Court: A Study in Judicial Politics and Values, 1937–1947*, C. Herman Pritchett inaugurated the so-called "behavioral revolution" in judicial studies (1948).[4] Focusing on the rise in the number of concurring and dissenting opinions that accompanied the appointments made to the Court by President Franklin D. Roosevelt between 1937 and 1943, Pritchett sought to explain the justices' increasing rates of disagreement.

The ironic story of FDR's Court-packing plan and success in remolding the Court is well known. During FDR's first term, the Court invalidated most of the early New Deal program and other progressive legislation. Yet FDR had no opportunity to fill a seat on the bench. After his landslide reelection in 1936, he proposed reforms that would have expanded the size of the Court to fifteen by allowing him to appoint a new member for every justice over seventy years of age. FDR aimed to thereby secure a majority on the Court supportive of the New Deal. In the spring of 1937, however, while the Senate Judiciary Committee was debating his "Court-packing plan," the Court abruptly upheld major pieces of New Deal legislation. The Court had been badly divided five to four when striking down earlier progressive legislation. Justices George Sutherland, James McReynolds, Pierce Butler, and Willis Van Devanter—the "Four Horsemen"—voted together against such legislation, while Justices Harlan F. Stone and Benjamin Cardozo followed Brandeis in supporting progressive economic legislation. Chief Justice Hughes and Justice Owen Roberts were the "swing votes," with the latter, more conservative justice casting the crucial fifth vote to strike down FDR's programs. Justice Roberts then changed his mind, and a bare majority of the Court now upheld major pieces of progressive legislation. That "switch in time that saved nine" was widely speculated to have been due to FDR's Court-packing plan. Yet even though the rulings did not come down until the spring of 1937, Roberts switched his vote at conference in December 1936, two months before FDR announced his plan. The reversal of the Court's position nonetheless contributed to the Senate's rejection of FDR's proposal the following May. Then, Van Devanter told the President that he would resign at the end of the term. And FDR had the first of nine nominations to the Court during the next six years.

When FDR made his first appointment, he was angry at the Senate for defeating his Court-packing plan and angry at the Court for striking down much of the early New Deal program. For the appointment, FDR chose Alabama's Democratic Senator Hugo Black, who had led the unsuccessful fight for the Court-packing plan. FDR thus took from the Senate one of the Court's sharpest critics and put him on the high bench. All of FDR's subsequent appointments turned on support for the New Deal. When Sutherland retired in 1938, the President named his Solicitor General, Stanley Reed, who had unsuccessfully defended New Deal programs before the Court. In 1938, Cardozo also died, and FDR turned to Harvard Law School professor Felix Frankfurter, who was widely known as a liberal adviser to the President. The following year, FDR filled Brandeis's seat with his Securities and Exchange Commission chairman and former Yale Law School professor, William O. Douglas. When Butler died in 1939, FDR nominated his attorney general, Frank Murphy. In spring of 1941, then, the last of the "Four Horsemen"—McReynolds—retired, and Chief Justice Hughes informed FDR that he would step down at the end of the term. Hughes suggested that the chief justiceship go to Associate Justice Stone, who had been a Columbia University Law School professor before joining the Court and who had been disappointed when his friend, Republican President Herbert Hoover, appointed Hughes Chief Justice in 1930, because Chief Justice Taft deemed Stone too divisive to be Chief Justice. FDR agreed, and the 1941 term opened with Stone in the Court's center chair. Democratic Senator James Byrnes filled McReynolds's seat, and Attorney General Robert H. Jackson took Stone's old seat as associate justice. A little over a year later, FDR made his last appointment, when Byrnes was persuaded to take another position in the administration, and yet another law school professor, Wiley Rutledge, was named to the Court.

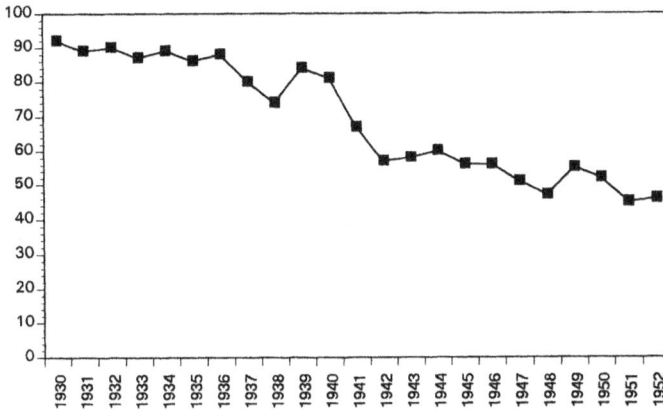

Figure 4.3 Percent of Opinions for Court of Total Opinions Issued, 1930–1952.

"Looking backward," Pritchett pointed out, "the 1941–42 term was definitely a turning point for the Roosevelt Court" (Pritchett 1948:40). Disagreement rates increased, and the percentage of opinions for the Court of the total opinions issued plunged from 81 percent in Hughes's last term to 67 percent in Stone's first term as Chief Justice. Moreover, the percentage continued to fall sharply, as indicated in figure 4.3, throughout Stone's chief justiceship (1941–45) and that of his successor, Chief Justice Fred Vinson (1946–53).

Pritchett offered a number of explanations for what happened. First, the New Deal appointees "may have felt a certain sense of relief from the previous constraint of being only a bare majority, or less than a majority, of the Court. The battle being won, they broke ranks. Second, the practical disappearance of the old conservative bloc . . . may have operated to remove the polarizing force which had kept the Court divided into two definite blocs." In other words, the New Deal justices began working out their individual differences and competing judicial philosophies. Finally, the 1941 term "saw the debut of Stone as Chief Justice" and, as Pritchett noted, "it seems to be agreed that as presiding officer he lacked some of the talents of his very able predecessor" (Pritchett 1948:40).

Chief Justice Stone's conduct of conference deliberations became widely accepted as the principal explanation for the erosion of the Court's consensual norm. That is due largely to the fact that Pritchett's students and others focused on the leadership abilities of the Chief Justice, along with the strategies justices might employ to marshal the Court (Murphy 1964). In particular, David Danelski argued, in presiding over conferences and when exercising the power of opinion assignment, Chief Justices may assert two kinds of leadership—"task" and "social" leadership—or fail at one or the other, or both (Danelski 1960). In exercising task leadership, the Chief Justice leads conference discussions with force and clarity, drawing the esteem of his colleagues; writes or assigns more opinions; and generally conducts the Court's business with efficiency. By contrast, social leadership eases tensions arising from disagreements in deciding cases and facilitates the justices' interpersonal relations. On the basis of examining the papers of justices who sat on the Court between 1921 and 1946, Danelski concluded that Chief Justice Taft (1921–30) was a social leader who relied for task leadership on Van Devanter, who Taft as President in 1911 had appointed to the Court. Whereas Hughes combined both kinds of leadership, Stone failed at each.

By all accounts, Hughes's photographic memory, authoritative demeanor, and personal charisma made him a respected task and social leader. At conference, he strove to limit discussion by giving crisp three-and-a-half-minute summaries of each filing. His "machine gun style" was largely successful, for, as Justice Roberts recalled, "so complete were his summaries that in many cases nothing needed to be added by any of his associates" (Roberts 1946). Although vigorously defending dissenting opinions, Hughes nevertheless maintained that unanimity was critical to public confidence in the Court's decisions (Hughes 1928, 67-68). Hughes would not "knock heads together" (McElwain 1949, 18), in the words of one of his law clerks, to achieve unanimity but he nevertheless deemed dissents best reserved for exceptional cases in which agreement proved impossible. As he put to Stone on a draft opinion: "I choke a little in swallowing your analysis; still I do not think it would serve any useful purpose to expose my views" (Danelski and Tulchin 1973, xxvi).

By comparison, Stone viewed conference deliberations and the value of consensus very differently. As an associate justice, he was annoyed that Hughes ran conferences "much like a drill sergeant" (O'Brien 1996: 228; see, generally, Mason 1956). When elevated to Chief Justice, he encouraged lengthy discussions, at the cost of prolonging conferences and carrying unfinished business over to special conferences held in the following weeks. Personally inclined to debate every point, he was not disposed to cut short the debates that erupted between Black and Frankfurter or Jackson and Black. As a result, Douglas observed, the justices were "almost in a continuous Conference" (Douglas 1980:223). Moreover, Stone wrote more separate opinions as Chief Justice than he had as an associate justice. In terms of his contribution of individual opinions as a proportion of the total opinions written during his chief justiceship, Stone's proportion was far above that of his predecessor and that of his two successors, though about the same as those of Burger and Rehnquist. (See table 4.2 below.)

There is little doubt that Chief Justice Stone's style and view of the Court's decision-making played a part in the erosion of the institutional norm of consensus. Thomas Walker, Lee Epstein, and William Dixon offered further confirmation by examining the possibility that other factors contributed to proliferation of individual opinion-writing (1988). Specifically, they examined whether the decline in consensus was attributable to: 1) the enactment of the Judiciary Act of 1925, which expanded the Court's discretionary jurisdiction, giving the justices (see table 2) greater power to decide what to decide and to set their own substantive agenda; 2) the increasing caseload; 3) the promotion of an associate justice to the chief justiceship; 4) changes in the Court's composition; and 5) the leadership of Chief Justice Stone. They found no correlation between either of the first two and the demise of the Court's consensual norm. They ruled out the third—namely, that internal promotions to the center chair lead to greater intra-Court conflict—by pointing to the chief justiceship of Edward White (1910–20). Chief Justice White, who like Stone had served as an associate justice for sixteen years, maintained the norm of consensus in the face of personality conflicts on the Court at the time.

The impact of changes in the Court's composition was more com-

Table 4.2
Individual Opinion-Writing of Six Chief Justices

	Number of Opinions	Number of Dissents	Number of Concurrences	Dissent* Proportion	Concurrence* Proportion
Hughes (1937–1940)	575	4	1	0.006	0.001
Stone (1941–1945)	710	33	8	0.046	0.011
Vinson (1946–1952)	731	13	3	0.017	0.004
Warren (1953–1968)	1,538	45	7	0.029	0.004
Burger (1969–1985)	2,366	115	104	0.048	0.043
Rehnquist (1986–1994)	1,099	56	11	0.050	0.010

* Number of dissenting and concurring opinions handed down by chief justice divided by number of cases decided by written opinion.

plex. On the one hand, according to Walker, Epstein, and Dixon, the high turnover rate during Stone's years as Chief Justice carried "with it the potential of creating a disruptive situation." They also noted that the 1941 term opened with five of the eight associate justices having little experience on the Court and that FDR's appointees came as well "from occupational traditions that encouraged individual expression"—that is to say, from law schools, the U.S. Senate, and high positions in the Department of Justice. On the other hand, they dismissed ideological division as explanation on the ground that during the Hughes Court there were well-defined left- and right-wing voting blocs but on the Stone Court intra-bloc agreement declined and the number of concurring and dissenting opinions proliferated. "Almost overnight," in their words, "the justices began expressing their personal views at extraordinarily high levels, demonstrating little compulsion to defer to the opinion of either the Court majority or of their own attitudinal sub-groups. This indicates that ideology alone cannot account for the sharp rise in individual judicial expression" (Douglas 1980:373–74). Nor, they contended, were FDR's appointees "dissent prone," because, prior to Stone's elevation to the chief justiceship, only Black and Roberts had disproportionately high dissent rates, while "Reed, Frankfurter, Douglas, and Murphy expressed minority viewpoints at relatively low levels" (Douglas 1980:378).

Turning, then, to Stone's dissent behavior in relation to prior Chief Justices, Walker, Epstein, and Dixon found that he cast more dissenting votes and wrote more dissenting opinions than his predecessors. On the basis of that quantitative analysis, they concluded "that much of the responsibility for changing the operational norms of the Court from institutional unity to permitting free expression of individual views can be attributed to the leadership of Harlan Fiske Stone" (Douglas 1980:384).

Although Stone's chief justiceship contributed to the devaluation of institutional opinions, the conclusion drawn by Walker, Epstein, and Dixon remains problematic. For one thing, as Stacia L. Haynie underscores, concurring opinions were on the rise prior to Stone's chief justiceship (Haynie 1992:1167). Furthermore, the proportion of unanimous decisions began dropping before Stone's chief justiceship and continued to decline during the next three decades, before more or less stablizing (Douglas 1980:384). In addition, the drop in the percentage of opinions for the Court of the total number issued began during the last four years of the Hughes Court, coinciding with the arrival of FDR's first five appointees (Black, Reed, Frankfurter, Douglas, and

Table 4.3
Percentage of Court Opinions of Total Opinions, 1933–1994

	Average Percentage of Opinions for the Court of Total Opinions	Average Percentage of Individual Opinions of Total
Hughes Court (1933–1936)	87.5	12.5
Hughes Court (1937–1940)	79.7	22.3
Stone Court (1941–1945)	59.6	40.4
Vinson Court (1946–1952)	50.2	49.8
Warren Court (1953–1968)	47.2	52.8
Burger Court (1969–1985)	39.2	60.8
Rehnquist Court (1986–1994)	44.8	55.2

Murphy). During the 1933 to 1936 terms, when the Court's composition remained stable, the traditional norm of consensus prevailed. That norm, however, began to fail to hold in the last four years of Hughes's chief justiceship, as indicated in table 4.3. In short, the transformation of the norm supporting consensus preceded Stone's chief justiceship and the leadership of the Chief Justice remains only one factor in explaining the devaluation of opinions for the Court.

It is worth recalling that Pritchett's explanation for the increasing rates of disagreement was more profound and philosophical. Simply put, the arrival of the New Deal justices brought the full force of American Legal Realism and liberal legalism to bear on the Court. Holmes and Brandeis had been on the Court, to be sure, yet they failed to command a majority. By contrast, FDR's appointees not only constituted a majority but embodied the intellectual forces of a generation of progressive liberals who had revolted against the legal formalism of the old conservative order (White 1957). American Legal Realism was not a school of thought but rather an intellectual movement embracing a range of diverse, though generally progressive and pragmatic, positions on judging and legal reform (Rumble 1968; Fisher, Horwitz, and Reed 1993). American Legal Realism, nonetheless, highlighted the indeterminacy of law, taught that judges make law, and advocated judicial pragmatism or the balancing of competing values. Legal realism about matters of degree and judicial balancing, instead of reliance on fixed formulas and tests, however, also made consensus more difficult. At the same time, precisely because Legal Realism debunked legal formalism, along with attacking the pre-1937 conservative Court's invalidation of progressive legislation, and taught that judges make law, the premium was raised on justifying the justices' decisions, individual and collective.

Moreover, liberal legalism developed out of the progressive and Legal Realist movements and embraced diverse viewpoints but lacked coherence (Kalman 1996). At bottom, as Pritchett observed, were "the short-comings of American liberalism as a social and economic philosophy. . . . Its failure was in producing any consistent social and economic philosophy" (Pritchett 1948:265). On the bench, the tradition of liberal legalism inherited from Holmes and Brandeis, and perpetuated by FDR's appointees, was also a divided, incoherent one. Holmes stood for judicial self-restraint and deference to legislatures, whereas Brandeis also championed progressive legal reforms. Although dominating the Court, FDR's New Deal justices split into two camps: Frankfurter-Reed-and-Jackson stood for judicial self-restraint and became more conservative during their time on the bench, while Black-Douglas-Murphy-and-Rutledge pushed toward greater liberal judicial activism. These two camps in turn further fragmented over where and how to draw the line between judicial self-restraint and activism in constitutional interpretation and legal policy. In short, as a result of their disagreements over the course of liberal legalism and constitutional interpretation, the New Deal justices were inclined to articulate their distinctive views in individual opinions.

In addition to the reconstruction of constitutional doctrines and to the new intellectual directions pursued by FDR's justices were other changes in the Court's operation that facilitated an increase in individual opinions. First, throughout the nineteenth century, the author of the Court's opinion did not circulate drafts of the opinion. Instead, drafts were read at conference, where other justices could offer suggestions for changes. In the 1920s and 1930s, with the technological advantage of typewriters, the Court began the practice of circulating drafts prior to conference. Justices thus had more time to study the wording of opinions and to make suggestions for changes or to decide to write separately. Threats of a dissent undoubtedly carried greater weight when the consensus norm prevailed: the author of the Court's opinion would accommodate as much as possible and as a kind of compromise the justices tended to refrain from publishing dissents, even when still disagreeing with the opinion for the Court. As the norm supporting institutional opinions began to erode, threats of dissent carried less force and their publication became easier.

Second, and rather ironically, coinciding with the higher disagreement rates was the Court's move into its own building. Prior to the completion of the building in 1935, the justices worked alone at their homes and held their sessions and conferences in the Capitol. Though

Chief Justice Taft managed to persuade four others—a bare majority—to support his lobbying for the construction of the building, he would have found it difficult to get them to move into the Marble Temple. Indeed, although the Hughes Court held its sessions and conferences there, none of the justices moved their offices into the building. In 1937, Black became the first to move in, leading the way for FDR's subsequent appointees. Still, even after his elevation to Chief Justice, Stone continued to work at home. Not until the Vinson Court (1946–53) did all nine justices regularly work in the building.

With the justices' move into the Marble Temple, the institutional life of the Court changed. While the building insulated the justices from the political life of the Capitol, it brought about greater interaction and, perhaps, intensified their psychological interdependence and independence. Some, like Frankfurter, constantly tried to lobby the others in their chambers, which often proved counter-productive by heightening personal tensions and undoubtedly contributed to the increasing rates of disagreement. In turn, as further discussed below, these tensions undoubtedly contributed to the ongoing breakdown of the consensual norm.

Finally, along with settling into the Marble Temple, the number of law clerks also began to increase. By Chief Justice Stone's time, it was well established for each justice to have one law clerk but he decided to hire a second as well. During Fred Vinson's chief justiceship, then, each justice had two law clerks, the number that remained throughout the years of the Warren Court. Although their duties varied from justice to justice, law clerks certainly facilitated the production of more opinions.

In sum, the demise of the norm of consensus preceded Stone's chief justiceship. While Stone's conduct of the Court's deliberative process undoubtedly contributed to the rise in the number of individual opinions, too much weight has been given to his influence and too little to the impact of changes brought by FDR's other eight appointees. The New Deal justices infused American Legal Realism and liberal legalism into the Court, but they were not of one mind. They quickly began disagreeing and pursuing their differences over conflicting tenets of liberal legalism in individual opinions. Although Stone encouraged individual expression more than his predecessors, he would have had little alternative. Other changes in the Court, such as circulating draft opinions, may also have contributed to the expression of individual differences. In any event, the ascendance and incoherence of liberal legalism brought by the New Deal justices better explains both the increase in individual opinions before Stone's chief justiceship and the continued increase long after his chief justiceship, as further discussed in the next section.

From the Warren to Burger to Rehnquist Court

The continued increase in individual opinions long after Stone's departure further undercuts the theory that Stone bears "much of the responsibility for changing the operational norms of the Court" (Walker, Epstein, and Dixon 1988:386). President Harry Truman had hoped that Stone's replacement would end the quarreling among the justices. But Chief Justice Vinson failed to do so. Although more of an administrator than Stone, Vinson was neither as intellectually equipped nor as interested in the law. Besides, Vinson faced an already contentious Court, given to individual expression. Chief Justice Warren could not reverse the tide, in the view of Walker, Epstein, and Dixon, because he "came to the Court directly from the political world having no exposure to the traditional norms of the judiciary. He could hardly be expected to value pre-1941 behavioral expectations, or impose them on associate justices who were by then accustomed to readily engaging in dissenting and concurring opinions" (Walker, Epstein, and Dixon 1988: 386). The proliferation of individual opinions continued throughout Warren's chief justiceship. Consequently, the percentage of opinions for the Court of the total opinions declined almost yearly, as indicated in figure 4.4, until it fell to just 31 percent in the 1969 term, the first term of Chief Justice Burger.

Post-FDR justices were clearly socialized into individual expression. Still, what remains to be explained is the rather steady decline in the

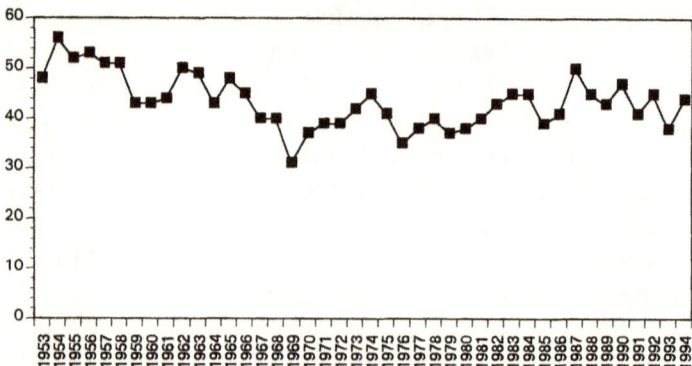

Figure 4.4 Percent of Opinions for Court of Total Opinions Issued, 1953–1994.

percentage of the Court's opinions of the total number annually issued throughout the chief justiceships of Stone, Vinson, and Warren, and then a gradual reversal of direction during the chief justiceships of Burger and, especially, Rehnquist. That trend, highlighted in figure 4.4, appears especially problematic for those who focus on Stone's chief justiceship, rather than on the impact of changes in the Court's composition brought by the New Deal justices. For, while the percentage of opinions for the Court declined during his chief justiceship, Warren was highly respected by his colleagues, some called him the "Super Chief" (Schwartz 1983). By contrast, the percentage began to increase during Chief Justice Burger's tenure, even though by most accounts he failed both as a task and a social leader. The percentage continued to grow until reaching the mid-to-upper 40 percent range—a range higher than that of most of the Burger Court years and yet only half of that of the pre-Roosevelt Court—under Chief Justice Rehnquist, who according to some accounts excels as both a task and social leader (Steamer 1986; Schwartz 1996; O'Brien 1996).

On closer examination, the influence and impact of the New Deal justices on the rise of individual opinions is evident in tables 4.4 and 4.5, showing the dissenting and concurring behavior of justices from the Hughes Court to the Rehnquist Court. Notably, on the post-1937 Hughes Court, conservative Justice Butler led in dissents but was followed by Stone and Black; Black and Reed also led in concurrences. Compared to the Hughes Court, all of the justices on the Stone Court had higher rates of dissent and issued more concurring opinions. They in turn increased their dissent and concurring behavior under Chief Justice Vinson, with Reed, Frankfurter, and Jackson doubling their rates of dissent. The behavior of the two New Deal justices with the longest tenures on the bench—namely, Black and Douglas—is also especially noteworthy: they steadily increased their dissent and concurring behavior throughout their very long careers. In particular, the most liberal justice, Douglas, more than doubled his dissent behavior on the Vinson and Warren Courts from that on the Stone Court, and then doubled it again during the more conservative Burger Court.

Post–New Deal justices were clearly socialized into higher rates of individual expression, as Tables 4.4 and 4.5 also indicate. The justices, to be sure, differed in their rates of individual expression. But, virtually all tended to increase their dissent and concurring behavior during their time on the bench. On the Burger Court, for instance, Rehnquist and Stevens exhibited higher rates of dissent than other justices. With the exception of Justice Byron White, they were also the only two of

Table 4.4
Dissent Behavior of Selected Post-1937 Justices*

Justice	Hughes Court	Stone Court	Vinson Court	Warren Court	Burger Court	Rehnquist Court
Hughes	0.006					
Sutherland	0.020					
Brandeis	0.003					
Butler	0.043					
McReynolds	0.009					
Roberts	0.029	0.050				
Stone	0.031	0.046				
Black	0.038	0.057	0.087	0.093	0.137	
Reed	0.005	0.036	0.079	0.061		
Frankfurter	0.002	0.074	0.150	0.100		
Douglas	0.009	0.053	0.128	0.122	0.279	
Murphy	0.000	0.050	0.071			
Jackson		0.047	0.103	0.092		
Rutledge		0.041	0.084			
Vinson			0.017			
Clark			0.016	0.064		
Warren				0.029		
Harlan				0.135	0.055	
Brennan				0.051	0.140	0.350
Stewart				0.058	0.087	
White				0.066	0.071	0.068
Marshall				0.023	0.124	0.116
Burger					0.048	
Blackmun					0.074	0.100
Powell					0.069	0.071
Rehnquist					0.109	0.033
Stevens					0.180	0.177
O'Connor					0.058	0.068
Scalia						0.080
Kennedy						0.039
Souter						0.050
Thomas						0.067

* Number of dissenting opinions divided by number of cases decided by written opinion.

their contemporaries to have served as law clerks to New Deal justices, respectively, Jackson and Rutledge. Rehnquist, the most conservative justice on the Burger Court, filed so many "solo dissents" that he earned the nickname "Lone Ranger." The record for solo dissents, nevertheless, belongs to Douglas (Epstein et al. 1994). Justice Brennan's dissent behavior also stands out because of his highly acclaimed skills at forging majorities on the Court for advancing his liberal positions. His dissent behavior more than doubled as the Court moved in more

Table 4.5
Concurring Behavior of Selected Post-1937 Justices*

Justice	Hughes Court	Stone Court	Vinson Court	Warren Court	Burger Court	Rehnquist Court
Hughes	0.001					
Sutherland	0.000					
Brandeis	0.000					
Butler	0.002					
McReynolds	0.009					
Roberts	0.000	0.006				
Stone	0.006	0.011				
Black	0.010	0.015	0.016	0.028	0.060	
Reed	0.017	0.005	0.014	0.006		
Frankfurter	0.006	0.045	0.073	0.054		
Douglas	0.000	0.020	0.027	0.053	0.052	
Murphy	0.000	0.021	0.010			
Jackson		0.029	0.046	0.092		
Rutledge		0.019	0.065			
Vinson			0.004			
Clark			0.013	0.015		
Warren				0.004		
Harlan				0.078	0.162	
Brennan				0.033	0.068	0.064
Stewart				0.038	0.052	
White				0.044	0.054	0.047
Marshall				0.004	0.030	0.011
Burger					0.043	
Blackmun					0.076	0.063
Powell					0.075	0.045
Rehnquist					0.033	0.010
Stevens					0.089	0.081
O'Connor					0.066	0.072
Scalia						0.132
Kennedy						0.065
Souter						0.051

* Number of concurring opinions divided by number of cases decided by written opinion.

conservative directions under Chief Justice Burger and, then, Chief Justice Rehnquist. Still, all of the more conservative justices, appointed by Republican Presidents from Richard Nixon to George Bush, had comparable or higher rates of dissent and concurrence to those on the Roosevelt Court and those appointed afterward.

By the end of the Warren Court, the New Deal justices had effectively transformed the Court's norm of consensus into one of individual expression. "Unanimity is an appealing abstraction," as Frankfurter once put it, but "a single Court statement on important constitutional issues and other aspects of public law is bound to smother differences that in the interests of candor and of the best interest of the Court ought to be express" (1959 Memorandum for Conference quoted in O'Brien 1996:334). The one area where Chief Justice Warren insisted on unanimity, and the other justices agreed, was in dealing with school desegregation cases, beginning with the landmark *Brown v. Board of Education of Topeka, Kansas* (1954). When Frankfurter angered the others by insisting on filing a concurring opinion in the Little Rock school desegregation case (*Cooper v. Aaron* 1958), all of the justices signed the Court's opinion in order to highlight their unanimity and to show that his concurrence was not a "dilution of the views expressed in the Court's joint opinion."

The devaluation of unanimity on institutional opinions continued during the Burger Court years. The unanimous decision on President Richard Nixon's claim of executive privilege during the "Watergate affair"[5] proved the exception to rule. On the major controversies over capital punishment in *Furman v. Georgia* (1972) and the "Pentagon Papers" case, (1971), for example, in each case the justices produced ten opinions—a *per curiam* opinion, announcing the Court's decision, six concurrences, and three dissents. In the no less vexing yet important ruling on affirmative action in higher education, in *Regents of the University of California v. Bakke* (1978) the only part of Justice Lewis F. Powell's opinion, announcing the Court's decision, joined by other justices was a one-paragraph statement of the facts.

Although the percentage of opinions for the Court of the total annually issued began to increase after the last New Deal justice, Douglas, left the bench in 1975, during the Burger Court years there was a sharp increase separate opinions—opinions in part concurring and dissenting. Figure 4.5 shows the increase in separate opinions after Burger became Chief Justice and the no less steep decline after Rehnquist succeeded him. In addition, during Burger's chief justiceship more opinions for the Court commanded the support of only a plurality of the justices than had been rendered in the Court's entire previous history (Davis and Reynolds 1974; O'Brien 1996:321). The sharp increase in separate opinions and plurality decisions underscores the continued decline in the weight given to reaching consensus on an opinion for the Court.

In the 1980s, Chief Justice Burger, among others on and off the bench, complained about the increase in plurality opinions and individual expression. In his view, the "proliferation of concurring opinions and even some dissenting opinions [was] the result of 'an increasing case-

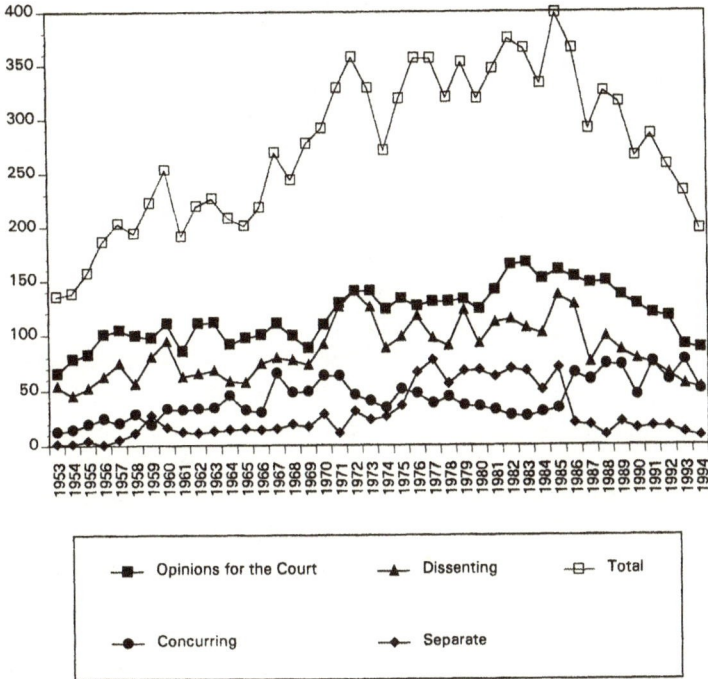

Figure 4.5 Opinion-Writing, 1953–1994.

load' and the consequent lack of time to hammer out differences" (O'Brien 1996:334). But, the increasing caseload was not the determining factor, for the percentage of opinions for the Court increased and the total number of opinions declined during the Rehnquist Court, which granted fewer cases review even in the face of a still growing docket. Instead, a combination of factors contributed to greater dissensus during the Burger Court and to the slight reversal of that trend under Chief Justice Rehnquist.

First, Chief Justice Burger tended to be more like Vinson, basically managerial in his approach and more interested in judicial administration than in jurisprudence. At conference, his discussion of cases left some of the others feeling that he was "the least prepared member of the Court." Moreover, Justice Powell recalled that under Burger, "the justices at conference [had] a great deal of latitude. You could speak as long as you wanted, and you could interrupt another justice if you wanted to." Confusion occasionally resulted over who voted how and which justices later switched their votes. Besides Burger's lack of precision contributing to the confusion at conference, he would later join a perceived majority and assign the Court's opinion, in turn angering the senior associate justices, notably, Douglas and later Brennan. As a result of Burger's conduct of conferences and opinion assignments, the justices became even more interested in a mere tally of votes than in arriving at an institutional decision and opinion.

Second, on the administrative side, Chief Justice Burger brought managerial changes and modern office technology into the Marble Temple, which certainly facilitated the production of more individual opinions. As noted earlier, each justice had two law clerks during the chief justiceships of Vinson and Warren. Beginning in 1970 the number assigned to each justice gradually grew to three and then four, with Burger having a fifth senior clerk. The number of secretaries likewise increased, at first in the place of additional clerks and later to help the growing number of clerks. The introduction of modern office technology also undoubtedly affected the operation of the chambers. In the late 1970s, each chamber acquired a photocopying machine and five or more terminals for word processing and legal research. As a result, the justices' chambers began to resemble, in Rehnquist's words, "opinion writing bureaus" (Rehnquist 1982). The managing of their chambers and supervising of paperwork consumed more time than in the past and contributed to keeping the justices apart. They talked less to each other, delegated more responsibility for opinion-writing to their clerks, and read and wrote more memoranda and opinions. The justices in turn became less willing to withdraw concurring and dissenting opinions because of the time their clerks devoted to them. As one justice put it, even though his concerns had been accommodated in the majority's opinion, "it would break my law clerk's heart" to suppress his concurring opinion (O'Brien 1996:335).

In comparison to Burger, Chief Justice Rehnquist discouraged lengthy exchanges at conference and proved to have the intellectual and temperamental wherewithal to be a leader, in Justice Thurgood Marshall's words, "a great Chief Justice." Notably, as indicated in Tables 4.4 and 4.5, unlike Stone, Rehnquist wrote fewer dissents and concurrences after becoming Chief Justice. A shrewdly articulate advocate of his own views, Rehnquist has the sense of humor of a practical joker and he moves conferences along by concisely and firmly discussing cases. In addition, Rehnquist also has prevailed in reducing the number of cases annually granted plenary consideration by over fifty. Whereas the Burger Court heard between 150 and 180 cases a year, under Rehnquist that number has dropped to less than 100, even while the caseload has continued to grow to over eight thousand cases on the annual docket. By virtually all accounts, Rehnquist's success as Chief Justice is attributable to his strong social and task leadership.

The decline in the percentage of individual opinions of the total opinions issued during Rehnquist's chief justiceship (as shown in figure 4.4), however, is not solely due to his leadership abilities. There is ample evidence that by the late 1980s, Brennan, as senior associate justice and increasingly finding himself in the minority as the Rehnquist Court drifted further to the right, insisted on assigning or writing a joint opinion for the dissenters. Because of workload pressures, and except for cases deemed especially important, the others agreed. And thus the number of individual dissents declined (Cook 1995). The practice of the senior associate justice in the minority to assign an author to write a dissent to the majority's ruling, as Justice Sandra Day O'Connor confirms, continued into the 1990s after Brennan's retirement (O'Brien 1996:332).

The increase in the percentage of opinions for the Court of the total annually issued during the Rehnquist Court, nevertheless, does not indicate a restoration of the norm of consensus. There is little evidence that Rehnquist strives to build consensus or that the others give great weight to achieving institutional opinions for the Court's decisions. To the contrary, for the first time in the Court's history, during the 1990 term, the Court handed down what Chief Justice Rehnquist dubbed "doubleheaders or twins": two cases in which there were two opinions announcing different (and somewhat contradictory) parts of the Court's ruling for two different majorities in each case (see *Arizona v. Fulminante* 1991; *Gentile v. State Bar of Nevada* 1991). Nor were those "doubleheader" opinions the last of such rendered by the Rehnquist Court, which further underscores how individual opinions and a mere tally of votes have replaced the norm of consensus.[6]

In sum, agreement on an institutional opinion for the Court's decisions was once deemed central to the Court's prestige and legitimacy, and to preserving the myth that law is not merely a reflection of politics. The forces of American Legal Realism and liberal legalism brought to the Court by the New Deal justices transformed that norm into one of individual expression. Still, when individual opinions are more highly prized than opinions for the Court, consensus not only declines but the Court's rulings appear more fragmented, uncertain, less stable, and less predictable.

In any event, liberal justices, such as Douglas and Brennan (Brennan 1986), are no longer alone in defending individual expression. One of the most conservative justices on the Rehnquist Court, Antonin Scalia, vigorously defends the filing of dissenting and concurring opinions. Scalia praises individual opinions for their internal and external consequences. "The most important internal effect of a system permitting dissents and concurrences is to improve the majority opinion." The prospect of a dissent, he emphasizes, may make the Court's opinion writer receptive to suggested changes, and a draft dissent "often causes the majority to refine its opinion, eliminating the more vulnerable assertions." In addition, Scalia claims that "dissents augment rather than diminish the prestige of the Court. When history demonstrates that one of Court's decisions has been a truly horrendous mistake, it is comforting—and conducive of respect for the Court—to look back and realize that at least some of the Justices saw the danger clearly, and gave voice, often eloquent voice, to their concern." A second external consequence of a concurring or dissenting opinion is that it can help change the law, as well as "inform the public in general, and the bar in particular, about the state of the Court's collective mind." "By enabling, indeed compelling, the Justices of our Court, through their personally signed majority, dissenting and concurring opinions, to set forth clear and consistent positions on both sides of the major legal issues of the day," Scalia adds, "it has kept the Court in the forefront of the intellectual development of the law." Still, that also reflects a very different view of the role of the Court, though a view ushered in by the Roosevelt Court. For, as Scalia puts it, "The Court itself is not just the central organ of legal *judgment;* it is center stage for significant legal *debate*" (Scalia 1994).

Whatever the merits of Justice Scalia's defense of individual expression and view of the Court, a return to the consensual norm appears highly unlikely. The demise of that norm remains a legacy of liberal legalism brought to the Court by the New Deal justices, whose disagreements made possible, as Pritchett foresaw, behavioral studies of law, courts, and judicial politics.

Notes

This chapter is dedicated to the memory of Professor C. Herman Pritchett.

1. See, e.g., Justice William Johnson's letter to President Thomas Jefferson, December 10, 1822, quoted by D. Morgan (1944).

2. L. Brandeis, quoted by Alexander Bickel (1967:18).

3. This figure is based on data collected and explained in O'Brien (1993:430–31n.146), and after 1937 on the annual "Statistical Sheet" of the Office of the Clerk, Supreme Court of the United States.

4. Besides the studies cited elsewhere in this chapter, see Stuart Nagel (1961); Glendon Schubert (1962a, 1964); Sheldon Goldman and Charles Lamb, eds. (1986); and Jeffrey A. Segal and Harold J. Spaeth (1993).

5. *United States v. Nixon* (1974). For further discussion, see Ball (1990).

6. See, *Morse v. Republican Party of Virginia*, 116 S.Ct. 1186 (1996). See also *Bush v. Vera*, 116 S.Ct. 1941 (1996), where Justice O'Connor's opinion for the Court was joined only by the Chief Justice and Justice Kennedy, and she undertook to file a concurring opinion to her opinion for the Court.

5

The Incidence and Structure of Dissensus on a State Supreme Court

Charles H. Sheldon

Introduction

Ideally, appellate courts should reach three equally elusive goals. Appellate courts should be effective, cohesive, and authoritative. When all three goals are reached and balanced in a delicate web of interdependence a court actually moves beyond viability toward eminence (Sheldon 1988:241–54). But what role does dissent play in this balance?

Although disagreement among judges affects in some manner all three goals, it is, of course, the crucial variable in cohesion. An appellate court has both individual and collective decisional components. Each justice votes separately and prepares and justifies his or her version of the case. The individual versions are fused into a collective court decision.[1] However, the two decisional components often collide. The individual component may take the form of dissenting or separate concurring opinions, which have a long and accepted tradition at both the federal and state levels.[2] Nevertheless, too much dissension weakens precedent, confuses the law, encourages further appeals, and leads to dissatisfaction among the justices.[3] A reconciliation of the two components is achieved through a deliberately prolonged process which considers alternatives but encourages agreement. Protracted discussions, involving explanation, debate, persuasion or compromise constitute the means of reconciliation.[4]

Dissent and Dissonance

The range of disagreement among judges on an appellate court varies from mild and general difference involving but one judge and possibly expressed informally in conference to sharp and specific disagreement recorded in angry dissenting opinion signed by a near majority of a court's membership. One or more judges have a wide range of deci-

sional alternatives that permit them to record a disagreement with the
majority's perspective. A dissenting opinion, a draft of a dissenting
opinion threatened or circulated but not filed, and a vote with a dissenting opinion constitute various forms dissent can take. Whatever
the form, dissents urge change. They argue for either innovation, moving forward with new solutions or renovation, moving backward to
earlier resolutions.[5]

A separate concurring opinion, draft, or vote adds to the range of
disagreement. Judges who write separate concurring opinions accept
the outcome reached by the majority, but reject all or part of the reasons
supporting the outcome. Concurring opinions expand or contract on
the majority's view (Coffin 1994:226–27). In either case they subtract
from the court's consensus.

Dissensus refers to dissents and separate concurrences, along with
the votes they may attract which constitute less than a majority of a
multi-member bench. Dissensus competes with consensus in a zero-
sum game, the result of which is not final until the decisional process
has run its course.

Inevitability of Dissent

Dissensus is dictated if not encouraged by forces common to a democracy as well as to the Anglo-American judicial system. Dissent is part
of the American ethic, and is natural to a democratic political system.
Percival Jackson expressed it well: "Dissent is endemic in a country
won by blood spilled for conscience and expression. It is natural, essential, and inevitable. Its absence marks a graveyard of conformity, to
paraphrase Justice Jackson. And its value and inevitablity is no less
within the precincts of the law" (Jackson 1969:4). Majoritarian democracy means nothing unless a minority is to be heard and given the
opportunity to replace or to change the view of the majority. The requirement applies equally to the judiciary.

The Anglo-American judicial system guided by *stare decisis* encourages dissent. The outcome of cases reviewed by courts of last resort
is an either/or proposition. Appellate courts either affirm or reverse
appeals in whole or in part. However, the confusing and perplexing
policy and legal issues confronting these courts rarely lend themselves
to simple either/or answers. To achieve a clear decision, a majority
of judges must all agree, however reluctantly, to one set of relevant
rationales. Extended explanations or *obiter dicta* are discouraged. Only
through an unencumbered dissent or a well-crafted concurrence can

the "maybe" or "perhaps" be expressed and the several nuances that bring the majority's certainty into question be discussed.[6] Judge Frank M. Coffin understood: "There is a feeling of unjudicial glee as one shucks off the normal retraints of writing for a panel and proceeds to thrust and parry with gay abandon" (Coffin 1994:227).

Recent trends at both the state and federal levels toward more diverse benches bring varied perspectives to bear on legal questions. Also, more contentious policy and political issues are finding their way into courts for resolution, prompting disagreement and dissents. The nature of the law coupled with courts composed of judges with varied experiences and perspectives assure disagreement and compel compromise. According to Judge Richard A. Posner: "The more diverse the judiciary, the more robust are the decisions that command strong support within it. . . . A diverse judiciary exposes—yet at the same time reduces—the intellectual poverty of the law, viewed as a method not just of settling disputes authoritatively but also of generating cogent answers to social questions" (Posner 1990:458).

Judicial decision-making is based on the results of the adversary process, with two sides arguing for opposite results before judges who must choose between the contending parties. Reasons for reaching opposite results are thus always made available to potential dissenters. It is no accident that the membership on courts of last resort is nearly always in uneven numbers—three, five, seven, or nine. Dissents are anticipated and inconclusive tie votes avoided.

The Dissensus Dilemma

Pulling at those nonconforming judges who would dissent to construct or to reconstruct or those who would concur separately to add or to subtract from the majority is the collective need for consensus. An appellate court, especially a court of last resort, must reach and maintain a high level of consensus.[7] As the judges edge toward unanimity, the authority surrounding their decisions, the court, and the law deepens. Charles Evans Hughes put it nicely when he wrote: "When unanimity can be obtained without sacrifice of conviction, it strongly commends the decision to public confidence" (Hughes 1928:67). The dissensus dilemma confronting judges, then, is to encourage dissent but also to strive for unanimity (Sheldon 1988:317). Early in his tenure on the Washington bench, one justice felt the tension the dilemma created: "As a person is on the Court longer, maybe you don't see the need for dissent quite as much as you see a greater need to try to get everybody on the same side and are willing to give and take, perhaps compromise more and I'll learn more about the law. Maybe some of my dissents are rather foolish but as I learn more about what is going on I may change."[8]

Because of their contribution, those who express their dissension must not be silenced, but they must not be so persistent and strong so as to threaten the authority of the court.[9] Over time, does disagreement on an appellate court increase or decrease and does it take a particular shape as it confronts the challenge presented by the dissensus dilemma?

Researching the Structure of Dissensus

The focus here is directed toward the interaction between consensus and dissensus which provides a framework for understanding the structure of dissensus. Further, within this structure, what have been the trends in the level and content of disagreement over the years? Are there institutional explanations for these trends?

The subject of the inquiry is the Washington State Supreme Court, a typical state court of last resort. Lessons learned from its experience with dissent may be generalized to other benches.[10] The Washington high bench has nine members, elected to six-year terms on nonpartisan ballots (Sheldon 1986). The average tenure on the bench is twelve years, and, as expected, incumbency largely assures retention in nonpartisan elections. Since 1969, the justices largely control their docket, taking for the most part only those appeals they feel are in need of review. The decisional process involves conferences to grant appeals as recommended by five-member departments of the court, assignments of initial research for bench memos, oral arguments to a full bench, conferencing on the merits, writing assignments by rotation with exceptions, depending upon conference vote, and circulation of drafts until all signatures are accounted for. Throughout the deliberative process, dissension and consensus interact, and either one or the other builds. Does the rate of dissensus vary and what might explain this variance should it appear to be excessive?

The Incidence of Dissensus

All other things being equal, the results of the interplay between consensus and dissensus should remain fairly stable and not experience abrupt changes over the years. However, should the rate of disagreement vary erratically, explanations might be forthcoming by isolating

Table 5.1
Rate of Dissensus on Washington Supreme Court, 1955–1995

Year	1955	1965	1975	1985	1995
Number of Opinions	335	322	161	134	127
Total Dissents	27	44	34	42	33
Percent Dissents	8.0%	13.7%	21.1%	31.3%	26.0%
Total Concurrences	21	7	30	23	18
Percent Concurrences	6.3%	2.2%	18.6%	17.2%	14.2%
Total Dissensus	48	51	64	65	51
Percent Dissensus	14.3%	15.8%	39.8%	48.5%	40.2%

institutional changes that had been implemented from time to time. Table 5.1 records the percentage of dissents and separate concurrences from selected years beginning in 1955 and continuing through 1995. Table 5.1 confirms that the incidence of dissensus does, indeed, vary, increasing over the years especially after 1965. Perhaps the increase can be explained by institutional changes that taxed the traditional dissensus norms, although some practices that successfully resolved the dissensus dilemma may remain viable. What institutional changes occurred during the years which may help explain variation in dissensus?

INSTITUTIONAL CHANGES (1969)

In 1968 a constitutional amendment was approved by the voters establishing an intermediate court of appeals to provide relief from the state supreme court's overwhelming caseload. Beginning in 1969, the new intermediate appeals bench heard the bulk of appeals and the state supreme court gained near complete control over its docket. Previously the court had to review nearly all appeals that met fairly flexible reviewing standards. Now, Washington's high bench is confronted only with those cases the justices feel compelled to hear. Except for a review of all death penalty appeals, a unanimous vote of a five-member department brings under original appellate review from the trial benches only those appeals that involve a state officer, a declaration of unconstitutionality of a statute or ordinance, conflicting statutes or rules of law, or an issue "of broad public importance and requires prompt and ultimate determination." Simply stated, the new jurisdiction signifies that "[T]he type of cases considered by the Supreme Court means that they are the more difficult cases and will result in more important announcements of the law."

The jurisdictional change also prompted a new decisional process.

Previously, the justices decided appeals in five judge departments with the chief justice presiding over both departments. Only in about one out of five cases did the full nine-member court sit *en banc* to decide these more troublesome cases when members of a department couldn't agree. In the pre-1969 era two dissents in a department would automatically shift the case to a full *en banc* hearing, adding to an already formidable workload.

As a result of the establishment of the intermediate court of appeals, the state supreme court 1) heard all cases *en banc*; 2) had fewer cases to review; and 3) was confronted with more problematic and controversial issues to resolve. All together or separately, the 1969 institutional changes seem to account for the decrease in caseload and the increase in the incidence of dissent and separate concurring opinions reported in table 5.1. First, all nine justices decide cases, making dissent less troublesome than when five were responsible for decisions in the old departments. Second, almost all of the cases now involve important issues which likely generate more disagreement among the justices. Third, with a smaller docket more time is available for researching and writing dissents and separate concurring opinions. Finally, justices gain further decisional assistance from an added law clerk.

Dissensus does become more common. In 1968, just prior to the change, a 14.9 percent dissensus rate was recorded, in line with previous years. In 1970, after one year under the new process, the court recorded a 38.6 percent dissensus rate, an abrupt increase which is maintained in the following years.

The Norms of Dissent: What Are the Acceptable Functions?

Are there changes in how justices express their disagreement that can be attributed to the beginnings of the court of appeals? The data on dissensus and consensus come from mail surveys of law clerks who had served with justices of the state supreme court over the years.[11] Most of the law clerks worked closely with their judges and constitute a prime source on the inner workings of the decisional process.

The degree of involvement of clerks with opinion-drafting varied but most were familiar with their justice's efforts. For example, one clerk wrote that he and the judge:

> followed the practice of alternating the preparation of the
> initial draft of an opinion in cases assigned my Justice. On
> one case he would write an original draft and I would pre-

pare a detailed line by line critique—sometimes suggesting
. . . language of my own. We would then meet and go over
all my suggestions. He would adopt a good many and
would explain why he rejected others. On the next case I
would do the first draft and we would meet to discuss it.[12]

However, another wrote that "[s]ometimes a post-argument memorandum was sought from the law clerk, to help the Justice sort out his
thinking on a case. Sometimes this helped him, sometimes not." All
were involved in discussions about cases, and some clerks were responsible for an occasional draft of majority, concurring, and dissenting opinions. Their views of what shaped dissension provide us
with the data the research requires.

The law clerks were asked a series of questions pertaining to their
justice's dissenting and concurring behavior. What are the acceptable
functions of dissent? What are the norms surrounding dissent and did
the 1969 changes affect the norms? Dissents are drafted for compelling
reasons, and those reasons may vary with individual justices and the
particular case context. However, over the years some reasons for dissent are more acceptable than others and become institutionalized into
norms shaping dissenting behavior.

Dissenting opinions have internal and external thrusts. Internally directed dissents are aimed at the other members of the bench, urging
them to heed the dissenter's warnings, to be persuaded to join the dissenter, or to correct aspects of the majority opinion. In contrast, some
dissents are directed beyond the immediate bench to the environment,
explaining, warning, and advocating to other audiences. With the out-
wardly directed dissents, persuading colleagues is less important than
alerting attorneys, other courts, the legislature or the public about the
error into which the majority has fallen. The externally directed dissents might tempt a justice to be drawn into a policy issue. Norms of
collegiality likely assist the justices in settling the appeal and reconcil-
ing differing views of legal issues. Table 5.2 compares the pre– and
post–court of appeals years and records what law clerks recalled about
their justice's idea of what ought to be the purposes of dissenting votes
or opinions. It is fairly clear from these data that dissents are largely
meant for internal consumption. Disagreement is to remain in-house
and is designed to persuade. Even if directed externally, dissents are
kept in the family by providing guidance to attorneys and other courts.

Although the level of dissensus increased after 1969, with only a few
exceptions the clerks felt that the justices changed very little. Testing

Table 5.2
Norms of Dissent

Question: A dissenting opinion may be written with a variety of purposes in mind and may vary with its context. One dissent may be directed beyond the immediate court context, while another may be aimed more at the other justices. Below are listed a number of both externally and internally directed purposes for writing dissenting opinions. Please rate on a scale of one (strongly agree) to five (strongly disagree) to what degree your justice would have agreed with each of the purposes.

Purposes for Writing Dissenting Opinions	Percent Agreeing with Statement	
	Before 1969 (n = 55–50)	After 1969 (n = 46–41)
Internal Norms:		
To refute a specific contention found in majority opinion	86.1	93.5
To make the majority consider all it should	81.2	93.5
To pick-up enough votes to become majority	80.5	91.3
To lay groundwork for consideration by future court	73.8	89.1
Little hope of becoming majority but strengthen dissent vote	50.0	56.1
To defend the dissenter's previous decision now under attack	40.4	47.6
To reprimand or embarrass the majority	7.6	20.4
External Norms:		
To give guidance to lower courts	81.1	71.8
To give guidance to attorneys	76.0	66.7
To represent ignored or rejected ideas, persons or groups	36.0	52.2
Written because dissent is needed in democracy and court	41.3	46.7
To test a creative or innovative idea	**27.4**	**50.0**
To alert other jurisdictions of decision's implications	39.2	36.3

Bold = statistically significant ($P < .05$)

a "creative or innovative idea" by means of a dissent became more acceptable as did using a dissent to represent "ignored or rejected ideas, persons or groups."

Of course, a single dissent may be written for several purposes. In fact, according to the clerks, those few opinions that are written to test a "creative or innovative idea" often are used to "represent ignored or rejected ideas, persons or groups" and "to alert other jurisdictions" of the decision's implications. Providing "guidance to" both attorneys as well as to lower courts motivates a large number of dissenters. Giving guidance to attorneys also is coupled with refuting a "specific contention found in the majority opinion." Within the internally directed norms of dissent, only making "sure the majority considered all it should" is significantly associated with refuting a "specific contention of the majority."[13] What is perhaps of more interest is the absence of any significant correlations among the other norms of dissent. They apparently have evolved separately as guides for the justices.

Proper Decisional Options

What are the decisional alternatives available to justices as they express their disagreement and what are the degrees of disagreements represented by these alternatives? Each law clerk respondent was asked to "indicate how *your Justice* would . . . rate" the level of disagreement for each of the following decisional options. Table 5.3 records the ratings from the mildest level of disagreement to the sharpest.

Obviously, dissonance can vary considerably from a threatened concurrence to a strong dissent joined by other justices. A concurring opinion which may question the majority's reasoning but still reach the same outcome does not subtract from consensus as other forms of dissensus. With the exception of a slight increase in the use of solo dissents, the association between the degree of disagreement and the means of expressing this disagreement has remained fairly steady despite the intervention of the intermediate court.

However, is there a connection between these decisional alternatives

Table 5.3
Preferred Decisional Options and Levels of Disagreement

Question: Below are listed several decisional options indicating varying degrees of disagreement. On a scale of one (greatest disagreement) to five (least disagreement), indicate how your justice would have regarded the rate of disagreement for each.

	Percent Felt Opinion Indicated Disagreement	
Decisional Options	Before 1969 (n = 46–36)	After 1969 (n = 33–26)
Circulating a concurring draft but not filing it	22.2	19.2
Voting with a separate concurring opinion	36.4	25.0
Circulating a draft dissent but not filing it	37.8	33.3
Writing a concurring opinion agreed to by others	42.2	31.0
Writing a solo concurring opinion	41.9	34.5
Dissenting in part and concurring in part	43.2	43.8
Voting with a dissenting opinion	57.8	63.6
Writing a solo dissent	70.2	84.9
Writing a dissenting opinion agreed to by others	73.9	84.4

available to the justices for recording their disagreement and the norms of dissent? For example, does a justice tend to write a "solo dissent" in order to "represent ignored or rejected ideas." Several significant connections are detected. Writing a solo dissent is, indeed, the preferred means of testing a "creative or innovative idea" both before and after 1969; writing a concurring opinion also continues to be motivated by the hope of gathering "enough votes to become the majority." Justices before 1969 would write a concurring opinion to strengthen the minority even if there was no hope of becoming the majority, and, again, strengthening the minority was accomplished by voting with a dissenter.

Contextual Influences on Dissent

Of course, a disagreement, however expressed, varies with its context. Each clerk respondent was asked the following question: "Listed below are a number of contextual factors which may more often than not have shaped *your Justice's* dissents. On a scale of one to five rate how the following contextual factors influenced your Justice's dissents."

According to their clerks, for nine out of ten of both pre- and post-1969 justices whether to dissent depends "upon the legal issue involved." The "number of Justices agreeing with the dissent," and "the state's econ-socio-political environment" are not important contextual variables with only one out of four clerks noting them as influences on dissents. Not until after 1969 does "with whom the Justice was agreeing" or "disagreeing" become somewhat important in writing a dissent, with over one-third of the clerks regarding this as influential on their justice's dissenting behavior.

What has been suggested is that dissents ought to be designed to influence the other members of the bench rather than those outside the judicial process and that certain decisional alternatives are available depending upon the intensity of the disagreement. Some of the decisional alternatives lend themselves better to particular purposes of dissents, and clearly, the nature of legal issues dictates the context for dissent, although who agrees or disagrees with whom influences some recent dissenting justices.

The Decisional Process and the Building of Consensus

Confronting the norms and practices of dissensus are the various constraints and opportunities available for reaching a consensus among the justices and either lessening the impact of disagreements or eliminating their influence altogether. What are the more acceptable meth-

Table 5.4
Methods for Reaching Consensus

Question: Please rate from one (very often) to five (never) each of the consensus methods listed below according to how often your justice used them to reach agreement, if not unanimity, on the bench?

Consensus Methods	Percent Used "Very Often" or "Often"	
	Before 1969 (n = 50–39)	After 1969 (n = 43–33)
Persuading on the merits	92.0	95.3
Compromise (agreeing on some issues but not others)	56.8	36.8
Mediation (urging both sides to agree)	46.2	44.4
Threatening a critical dissent or separate opinion	27.5	39.5
Bargaining (trading preferences)	10.3	16.2
Appealing to image of the court	9.1	21.2
Capitulation (giving in on most or all issues)	2.4	2.9

ods by which a majority can be forged and consensus built, approaching if not reaching unanimity? For example, is it acceptable to bargain over votes? Table 5.4 records the responses of the law clerks to the question: "Please rate . . . each of the consensus methods . . . according to how often your Justice used them to reach agreement, if not unanimity, on the bench."

Despite evidence to the contrary which attributes political motives and strategic behavior to high court judges, at least from the perspectives of those clerks who were involved to a significant degree in the decisional process, consensus is reached by persuasively arguing the merits of any particular case. Only on occasion can compromise, mediation, and the threat of a critical dissent bring about agreement. Except for a slight decrease in the use of compromise since 1969, the means of reaching agreement changed very little over the years.

Judicial decision-making is structured to reach a reasoned and considered judgment, and, in addition, it is designed to reach a consensus, if not unanimity. Where does the drive for consensus show itself along the decisional process and did the intermediate court bring about changes? Table 5.5 places stages of the decisional process in their proper sequence from the initial discussions with law clerks on petitions for review to the final deliberations as draft opinions are circulated for signatures.

As anticipated, consensus builds as the decisional process progresses for the courts both before and after 1969. The preparatory stages, from

Table 5.5
Decisional Sequence and Consensus Factors

Question: Disagreement or consensus can change as the decisional process progresses. Below is a list of the various phases of the decisional process. On a scale of one (very conducive to resolving disagreement) to five (not conducive to resolving disagreement), please rate each phase according to when your justice's disagreement tended to be resolved or at least softened.

Decisional Phases	Percent Regarding Stage as Contributing to Consensus	
	Before 1969 (n = 56–53)	After 1969 (n = 43–39)
Discussions with law clerks	30.2	48.9
Conferences on petitions for review	35.1	41.9
Pre-hearing memos from Reporting Judge	48.8	53.8
Questions during oral arguments	38.5	26.8
Post-argument conferences on merits	86.8	79.5
Opinion drafting	88.1	72.1
Informal discussions among justices during drafting	69.1	82.5
Opinion circulation and comments on passing sheets	73.2	66.7
Opinion circulation and informal talks among justices	72.7	83.7

initial discussions on petitions for review through the oral arguments, contribute little to bringing about agreement. These steps are the individual components of the decisional process. The opportunities for consensus-building surge with the post-argument conferences until finally all signatures on opinions are accounted for. These later stages of the deliberations bring to the justices more information on their respective positions, which is vital for consensus building. One clerk's impression confirms the importance of the secret conference following oral arguments: "Post argument conference often brought all or most of Justices into agreement. If not, drafts of majority and dissenting opinions would be produced and considered by the other Justices. . . . Opinions were modified, to most specific concerns of individual Justices, and this often permitted more consensus than would otherwise occurred."

Also, it is clear that informal communication through memoranda, on passing sheets, or in person contributes significantly to reaching agreement. The consensus-building of the decisional sequence remains strong throughout the two time periods under consideration.

FACTORS CONTRIBUTING TO CONSENSUS

As an opinion moves through the decisional process, several persons and practices make their contribution to the ever increasing consensus.

Table 5.6

Factors Contributing to Consensus

Question: Many factors contribute to consensus. To what extent do you think the following factors contributed to consensus on the court? Please rate each factor on a scale of one (large contribution) to five (no effect on consensus).

	Percent Rating Factors a Positive Influence	
Factors	Before 1969 (n = 56–46)	After 1969 (n = 45–38)
Extensive communication during draft circulation	89.1	81.8
Similar legal/political perspectives between justices	**65.4**	**84.1**
Personal contacts	65.4	78.3
Leadership from other justice	60.4	75.0
Reporting judge's pre-hearing memo	**43.8**	**81.0**
Law clerk discussions	27.8	25.6
Leadership from Chief Justice	**46.3**	**30.3**
Leadership from Acting Chief Justice	17.4	10.5
Commissioner's office recommendations	**9.4**	**28.2**

Bold = $P < .05$

Table 5.6 reports the rating law clerks gave to "factors contribut[ing] to consensus on the Court."

The persons and practices that assist in building consensus parallel the stages of the decisional process for both sets of data. Personal contacts during the circulation of draft opinions between justices with similar political and legal perspectives, often under the leadership of one justice, provide the dynamics for agreement. However, "similar legal/political perspectives," the court commissioner's recommendations, and the "reporting judge" play increasing roles after the court of appeals changes the process. The tightening of the state supreme court's jurisdiction to include only important cases often involving public policy questions necessitates forging a majority of justices with similar legal and political perspectives to resolve case issues. The supreme court commissioner's office was set up only in 1975 to recommend which petitions for review the justices should consider. Also the reporting judge, responsible for pre-argument review of cases for other justices, now recommended disposition to a full nine-member court rather than to a three-judge panel, which was the practice prior to 1969.

Although not a significant factor before 1969, the role of the chief justice in encouraging agreement has decreased even more in recent times. This can be attributed to the short tenure automatically rotated among senior members every two years.[14] The chief justice presides over oral arguments and conferences, as well as coordinates support agencies, but when compared to those accorded to U.S. Chief Justices, the prerogatives are few.

The Structure of Dissensus

Dissensus as an institution both shapes and is shaped by the behavior of judges. Washington State supreme court justices, not unlike judges on other courts of last resort, have evolved a fairly narrow range of acceptable choices as they confront disagreements with one another. Over time, these choices tend to be reinforced, becoming norms that guide, if not control, dissensus behavior even as the jurisdiction and decisional processes are altered by the establishment of the court of appeals.

It is clear that following the beginnings of the intermediate appeals bench the incidence of dissensus increases substantially. Nonetheless, the changes in the nature of dissents and concurrences are minimal. These few changes are directly related to this increase in dissensus among the justices. Post-1969 justices become more contentious and experimental as they confront fewer but more important and troublesome cases that often involve policy issues. Similar legal and political perspectives between justices becomes an important factor in bringing about the consensus needed to resolve troublesome appeals. In order to secure at least four more signatures, dissenters should directly refute the majority's contentions in the debate during post-argument conferences or during circulation of draft opinions. In contemplating dissent, it is important for them to consider who agrees and disagrees with whom and whether a separate concurring draft would win over a majority. Hesitant justices may wish to take the opportunity dissents provide to test a creative and innovative legal theory which may be adopted by a future court.

The experience of the Washington State Supreme Court shows that dissents—and to a lesser extent, separate concurrences—perform dual purposes, and that these purposes or norms have withstood the jurisdictional changes required by the establishment of the court of appeals. Dissensus retains its institutional identity as it confronts changes from the beginnings of the intermediate court. The dominant norm compels justices to direct their disagreements over the merits of the case to each other in an effort to reach a consensus through persuasion. The intermediate appeals bench did not change the rewards for a compelling and persuasive argument. Throughout the court's history, the satisfactions of winning a case from other competitive colleagues and of writing a majority opinion that is recorded in the reports and may establish a new and notable precedent are the rewards.[15] The challenge to write a compelling dissent or concurrence to win over other justices is often accepted. According to a senior member of the Washington bench: "You have to ask yourself what the purpose of it is if eight of the people on the Court have agreed that the majority is correct. . . . So then what are you trying to accomplish, parading your own ideas out? . . . I think I write them to try to persuade four other people and that sometimes happens even after the vote in conference."[16]

Support from another colleague may tempt a dissenter to circulate a draft that he or she hopes will attract four or more votes. A frequent dissenter on the court confirmed that the temptation cannot often be ignored: "If it looks like an 8-1 dissent I'm going to look very carefully but if I've got one or two on the passing sheet that looks like they're going with me and maybe a chance to pull some others in, why, I'll [try]."[17]

If it appears that gathering enough votes to become the majority is unlikely, dissenters attempt to "critique" the majority opinion and to correct any mistakes or oversights in the majority's version. For example, one reluctant dissenter on the state's high bench would, on occasion, take the majority to task and with some success, even though he remained alone.

> Sometimes I write a dissent because I'm outraged at the far-reaching effect, and I want to open their eyes, and "what are you doing here?" And I might use rather stark language, but try not to. I want to get their attention, and I don't want to be overbearing, and if I were to do that I would take it out. In other words, if I didn't get their attention, and they insisted in their view, then I would maybe take out some strong language and still get my dissent.[18]

Of course, some caution must be exercised when acting as a critic. As one justice pointed out, today's enemy may be tomorrow's friend.

To a lesser extent but still an acceptable purpose, dissents are directed outside the membership of the bench, but only to draw the attention of attorneys and other courts to the implications of the majority's ruling. Although such a dissent may be "crippling [to] the force of the majority opinion" and involve extra effort, "it's a hallmark of laziness not to write a dissent. You're not playing fair with the public. You owe the Court and the profession a delineation of your reasons."[19]

Each justice must weigh the temptations of dissensus against the need to achieve a consensus on important issues. The result should be a balance, leaving the dissensus dilemma unresolved.

The establishment of the intermediate court of appeals had an impact on the incidence of dissensus but for the most part the norms of dissent survived. However, did the 1969 changes alter the content of those dissents and separate concurrences? Were the jurisprudential perspectives of the justices affected by the court of appeals?

Conflicting Jurisprudential Perspectives

The nonpartisan election of justices, supplemented by interim gubernatorial appointments to vacancies, has brought to the Washington bench predominately middle-of-the-road judges (Sheldon and Maule 1997). However, within this moderation, conflicting jurisprudential perspectives still remain. The jurisprudential view which sometimes intervenes in the deliberations of state judges involves an age-old issue: What is the role of courts in the separation of powers scheme of state government? Although the issue was not new at the time, the U.S. Supreme Court, under the leadership of Chief Justice Earl Warren, popularized it. Should judges be activists, substituting their view of what is needed by the community for that of the elected officials, or should judges exercise restraint and defer to the political branches? The activists would be lured into policy debates, while the restraintist would reject such opportunities.

Responses to previous surveys of former supreme court law clerks and experienced appellate attorneys provide measures concerning the impact of the 1969 changes on the activism versus restraint ideological debate.[20] Assuming that ideological conflict divided the justices before 1969, did the institutional change accompanying the establishment of the court of appeals exacerbate that division or did the new opportunity for dissensus actually soften the conflict? Was the increase in dissensus largely due to moderates on the bench?

Table 5.7 reports the 1965 through 1975 ideological line-up on the Washington State supreme court as well as the dissensus rate for each justice.

Indeed, prior to 1969 justices located toward the ideological extremes of the activist/restraint scale tended to dissent or write separately more often than did their more moderate colleagues. For example, restraintist Justice Hill and activist Justice Finley consistently rated higher on the dissensus scale than their more moderate colleagues. However, the changes associated with the establishment of the court

Table 5.7
Ideological Perspectives and Dissensus Rates

Res/Act Score*		# of Dissensus Votes and Opinions	Res/Act Score		# of Dissensus Votes and Opinions	Res/Act Score		# of Dissensus Votes and Opinions
	1955			1965			1968	
1.36	Ott	7)	1.36	Ott	10	1.55	Hill	16
1.55	Hill	13	1.55	Hill	15	1.75	Weaver	10
(1.66	Grady	3)	1.71	Donworth	14	1.84	Neill	10
1.71	Donworth	13	1.75	Weaver	7	1.86	McGovern	6
1.75	Weaver	7	1.90	Hamilton	6	1.90	Hamilton	7
1.82	**Hamley**	9	1.96	Hale	13	1.96	Hale	11
1.89	Mallery	6	2.00	Hunter	6	2.00	Hunter	6
1.96	Schwellenbach	10	2.30	**Rosellini**	23	2.30	Rosellini	10
2.80	Finley	14	2.80	Finley	15	2.80	**Finley**	12

Res/Act Score		# of Dissensus Votes and Opinions	Res/Act Score		# of Dissensus Votes and Opinions	Res/Act Score		# of Dissensus Votes and Opinions
	1970			1971			1975	
(1.75	**Weaver**	4	(1.58	Wright	6)	1.58	Wright	15
1.84	Neill	19	1.84	Neill	22	1.86	**Stafford**	21
1.86	McGovern	9	1.86	Stafford	13	1.90	Hamilton	12
(1.86	Stafford	3)	(1.86	McGovern	8)	(1.96	Hale	16)
(1.90	Sharp	3)	1.90	**Hamilton**	10	2.00	Hunter	13
1.90	Hamilton	6	1.96	Hale	18	(2.00	Horowitz	9)
1.96	Hale	10	2.00	Hunter	12	2.10	Brachtenbach	11
2.00	Hunter	6	2.30	Rosellini	18	2.30	Rosellini	22
2.30	Rosellini	11	2.80	Finley	20	2.68	Utter	27
2.80	Finley	16				2.80	Finley	15

* Restraint = 1 to Activism = 3.
(***) Justice did not serve full year.
Bold = Chief Justice

of appeals, rather than exacerbating the jurisprudential division, have appeared to create a tendency toward an equalization of the dissensus ratings. The adjustments to the new system in 1970 and 1971 find the "extremists" Justices Finley, Rosellini, and Neill continuing to dissent but not at the rate expected when compared to the increase in dissensus for all the justices.

Also, a shift in the view of the court majority is evident. Initially, only Justice Finley took an activist stance, joined later by Justices Rosellini and Hunter. However, by 1975 the activists have a majority on the bench and yet they continue to record disagreements with the colleagues. Additionally, the chief justice's location among the dissenters confirms the minor role the office plays in consensus.

The increased rate of disagreement after 1969 is associated with the shift in emphasis in the content of that dissensus. The complex and controversial cases now challenging the justices prompt them to look beyond a simple activist versus restraintist issue. It is no longer of great concern for the modern court. By the 1980s, politicans, the public, and judges had accepted, although perhaps reluctantly, the proposition that state courts of last resort do make public policy. The concomitant tendency is for litigants to take more policy questions to the courts and for politicians to pass on to courts political issues they themselves feel unable or unwilling to resolve.

Also, the activists are now in the majority. If dissents and separate concurrences are primarily used for convincing other members of the bench to sign on, when the occasion arises, dissenters might well focus on persuading their colleagues to accept their arguments on questions of policy. Justices would best focus on the immediate legal or doctrinal issues, quite apart from whether it is their role to do so.

Summary

Jurisdictional and decisional changes in what the supreme court reviews which can be attributed to the establishment of the intermediate court of appeals have stimulated greater dissensus among the justices. Additionally, the decisional changes have tended to soften the divisions among the justices concerning the role of courts in the separation of powers constitutional scheme.

Dissensus has its own structure, constraining the justices. Certain acceptable alternatives to uses of dissent, to decisional options, and to methods for resolving disagreement have shaped dissensus. Within the limits of these institutionalized alternatives the "dissensus dilemma" remains. A balance between the creativity of dissensus with the stability of consensus is needed. The search to resolve the dissensus dilemma continues to provide the dynamism to the supreme court's deliberations.

Notes

1. "There is some tension between these two, but the reconciliation lies in the distinction between deliberating about a case and deciding it. . . . Traditional appellate process in America has assured both imperatives by providing for group deliberation based on independent preparation." Meader, Carrington, and Rosenberg (1976:9–10).

2. The first recorded dissent on the U.S. Supreme Court was Justice William Paterson in *Simms & Wise v. Slacum* (1805). Justice Theodore Stiles filed the first dissent in the Washington Supreme Court's first year in *Brotton v. Langert* (1890).

3. Judge Learned Hand saw dangers in dissent. He wrote that with the habit of dissents "[p]eople become aware that the answer to the controversy is uncertain, even to those best qualified, and they feel free, unless especially docile, to ignore it if they are reasonable sure they will not be caught" (1962:72).

4. "If each judge is effectively to apply a personal imprimatur to the decision, he must have at least the opportunity, and must present the appearance, of doing individual thinking and evaluating. Yet the functions of appeal are adequately served only if the decision is a joint decision based upon shared thinking" (Meader, Carrington, and Rosenberg 1976:9).

5. Although now rare, a judge may simply state "I dissent" or "I concur in the results" without a written explanation.

6. Chief Justice Harlan Stone (1942:78) saw value in dissents that warn of too much innovation: "A considered and well stated dissent sounds a warning note that legal doctrine must not be pressed too far. It sometimes. for better or for worse, arrests a trend and sometimes reverses it."

7. "Dissenting opinions enable a judge to express his individuality. He is not under the compulsion of speaking for the court and thus securing the concurrence of a majority. In dissenting, he is a free lance" (Hughes 1936:68).

8. Interview, April 15, 1977 (Author's files). Years later, the same justice apparently had learned more about what was going on. He explained his developing reluctance to dissent: "It may be that after you are here for awhile you a. don't give a damn, b. are tired, c. recognize that it is valuable to have an opinion without a dissent." Letter dated September 16, 1996 (Author's files).

9. Article 19 of the American Bar Association's 1960 Canons of Judicial Ethics cautioned, "It is of higher importance that judges constituting a court of last resort should use effort and self-restraint to promote solidarity of conclusion and the consequent influence of judicial decision. A judge should not yield to pride of opinion or value more highly his individual reputation than that of the court to which he should be loyal. Except in cases of conscientious difference of opinion on fundamental principle, dissenting opinions should be discouraged in courts of last resort" (Sanders 1963). By contrast, Justice Robert Jackson cautioned that "[a] court opinion which puts out a misleading impres-

sion of unanimity by avoiding, or confusing, an underlying difference is a false beacon" (Jackson 1951).

10. For rare accounts of dissent at the state level see Goldman and Lamb, eds. (1986).

11. An earlier study of Washington Supreme Court law clerks is reported in Sheldon (1988/89, 1981).

12. Not unlike law clerks with the U.S. Supreme Court, those who served the Washington justices assumed opinion-drafting responsibilities and, after consultation with and in anticipation of their justice's desires, crafted at least the initial version of opinions. For U.S. Supreme Court clerks who became "parajustices," see B. Schwartz (1996:48–55). For an account of Washington clerks acting as "Puisne Judges," see Sheldon (1988/89:45).

13. The overlap of dissenting purposes is based upon a simple bivariate correlation test with $p<000$ as the significance level.

14. According to the Washington Constitution, the senior justice serving the last two years of his or her elected term automatically becomes Chief Justice. The Acting Chief Justice is simply the justice next in line to become the Chief. This finding is in contrast to the literature on the U.S. Supreme Court that attributes some of the discord to the Chief Justice's style of leadership. In 1995 the Washington State Constitution was amended to allow the justices to elect the Chief without regard for seniority; once elected he or she could now serve beyond the two-year limit.

15. Washington justices have another reward for winning a case. They earn credits if their initial dissents become the majority. They are assigned correspondingly fewer opinions in the next term of the court.

16. Interview dated April 13, 1983 (Author's files).

17. Interview dated April 14, 1983 (Author's files).

18. Interview dated April 14, 1983 (Author's files).

19. Interview dated April 14, 1983 (Author's files).

20. Two hundred appellate attorneys and 163 former clerks responded to surveys which solicited their views on the ideological leanings of the justices. The activism/restraint ratings are the average of both law clerk and attorney responses. The surveys were supported by NEH and NSF research grants. See, for example, Sheldon 1988:283, 299.

The attorneys and law clerks rated justices according to the following definitions: A restraintist was exemplified by Justice Felix Frankfurter. He tended to believe that cases should be decided on narrow grounds; precedent should be closely followed; deference must be granted to the political branches; important economic, social, and political issues should be avoided; and moral judgments eschewed. An activist, exemplified by Justice William O. Douglas, generally took the "opposite" approach.

6

The Chief Justice and Judicial Decision-Making: The Institutional Basis for Leadership on the Supreme Court

Sue Davis

The New Institutionalisms

Institutions have always been important in the study of judicial deci-sion-making. Nevertheless, what has come to be viewed as a renewed focus on institutions in the study of politics (March and Olsen 1984) and specifically in public law (Smith 1988) has given rise not only to the increasing popularity of a "new institutionalism" but also to a rein-vigorated debate over methodologies (see, for example, Ethington and McDonagh 1995).

March and Olsen (1984) emphasized the importance of moving away from the assumption that humans are self-interested, calculating power maximizers to assigning a more autonomous role to social and political institutions, and exploring the interplay between those institutions and the behavior of political actors. The new focus on institutions, in their view, held possibilities for building a new theoretical understanding of political life—one that goes beyond politics as the allocation of re-sources to recognize the importance of participation in the life of the community. Like March and Olsen, Smith (1988) argued that the new institutionalism can be used to challenge the instrumental view of poli-tics. It will be essential, he emphasizes, for political analysis to recog-nize the centrality of institutions as

> themselves created by past human political decisions that were in some measure discretionary, and to some degree they are alterable by future ones. They also have a kind of life of their own. They influence the self-conception of those who occupy roles defined by them in ways that can give those persons distinctively "institutional" perspectives. Hence such institutions can play a part in affecting the polit-

ical behavior that reshapes them in turn—making them appropriate as units of analysis in their own right (1988:95).

The approach that Smith prescribed for the future of public law has
come to be called the historical-interpretive institutionalism; the other
major institutionalist approach—rational-choice institutionalism—embraces very different assumptions about human behavior and methodologies for studying that behavior. Rational-choice institutionalism
takes as its starting point assumptions that the historical-interpretive
scholars have rejected, namely that the behavior of political actors can
be explained on the basis of self-interest and strategies for maximizing
power. For rational-choice institutionalists, institutions provide incentives and are important in structuring the strategic behavior of political
actors.

Since the late 1980s, as a growing number of law-and-courts scholars
have adopted the new institutionalism, they have arranged themselves neatly into two groups, with one adopting Smith's historical-
interpretive approach and the other following the lead of rational-
choice theory.[1] Although the differences between the two versions of
the new institutionalism are vast, both challenge the view that judicial
decision-making can be explained merely with reference to the preferences of the judges.

This chapter begins with an examination of the uses to which scholars
have put the new institutionalism in both of its forms to study leadership on the United States Supreme Court. I then offer some observations concerning Chief Justice Rehnquist's leadership from a historical-
interpretive perspective and conclude with some suggestions for future
research.

Studies of Leadership on the Court

The existing work on leadership in the Supreme Court demonstrates
how true it is that—as both advocates and critics of the new institutionalism admit—institutions never entirely disappeared from the discipline of political science. Indeed, it is difficult to imagine how one
might approach leadership without taking institutional factors into account. By tradition, for example, the Chief Justice has the prerogative
to assign the Court's opinion when he is in the majority; institutional
norms also govern the practices of conference discussion and voting;
a norm of equality and a dynamic of group interaction among the nine
justices constrains the Chief Justice's ability to dictate his policy preferences to the others. While earlier studies did not ignore such institu-

tional factors, more recent research tends to include a wider range of institutional variables, to treat them in a more systematic fashion, and to focus more explicitly on what Smith has referred to as the "interplay of meaningful actions and structural contexts" (1988:91).

The analysis of styles of individual Chief Justices is one approach to studying leadership. In his well-known paper, David J. Danelski (1960) developed a theory of conference leadership according to which a Chief Justice might perform the role of task leader or social leader, both, or neither. He posited important consequences for the various possibilities: when a Chief Justice performs both leadership functions conflict tends to be minimal, and social cohesion and satisfaction with the conference tend to increase, as does productivity. If the Chief Justice does not perform either role, and none of the associate justices provide leadership, just the opposite occurs. By examining the justices' private papers, Danelski found that Chief Justice Taft was a social leader who depended on Associate Justice Van Devanter to act as task leader. Chief Justice Hughes performed the roles of both task and social leader, thereby reducing conflict, increasing cohesion, satisfaction, and production. In contrast, Chief Justice Stone performed neither role, which resulted in conflict, tension, antagonism, and low levels of productivity. Danelski's typology of leadership incorporated institutional concerns insofar as it considered how styles of leadership promote the goals of the Court, including productivity and maintaining congeniality. Still, the analysis did not treat institutional factors explicitly as independent variables that might have an effect on the behavior of the Chief Justice nor did it explore the interaction between structural elements and the justices' behavior. Instead, Danelski treated leadership primarily as a matter of an individual's interpersonal skills and personality and the impact that those qualities had on the output of the Court. Murphy (1964) devoted only seven pages to what he called "The Special Case of the Chief Justice," but his entire examination of judicial strategies is relevant to leadership and the powers of the Chief Justice; it also explicitly takes institutional constraints into account. His analysis treated institutional factors as components that the self-interested, strategic, power-maximizing judge is forced to take into account.

Most studies of leadership have focused on an aspect of leadership that is clearly an institutional factor: the rule that gives the Chief Justice the authority to assign the majority opinion. Danelski (1960) explained that the selection of the author of the majority opinion is important because the opinion determines not only the value of a decision as a precedent, but also how acceptable it will be to the public. The author of the opinion, moreover, may be responsible for holding the majority together in a close case, and may persuade would-be dissenters to join the majority. David W. Rohde (1972c) underlined the importance of assigning the majority opinion by identifying two sets of concerns: intra-Court and extra-Court factors. The first set of concerns includes holding together a tenuous majority, increasing the size of a solid majority, and promoting harmony among the justices. Extra-Court factors include those that involve the relationship between the Court and the rest of the political system. The Chief Justice should be sensitive to "public relations" in assigning opinions, for example, particularly those that will be unpopular to a large segment of the public. Rohde also pointed to a third factor that "has to do with the personal policy preference of the assigner" (1972c:658). The Chief Justice can make assignments to members of the Court whose views are most similar to his own in order to maximize the likelihood that majority opinion will further his policy objectives.

Efforts to substantiate the assertion that Chief Justices use the tool of opinion assignment to advance their policy goals have yielded results that are less than conclusive. Danelski (1960) formulated two assignment rules that a Chief Justice might use to influence others to join the majority. First, he might assign the opinion to the justice whose views are the closest to the dissenters in the belief that he or she would take an approach upon which both majority and minority could agree. Second, where there are blocs on the Court and a bloc splits, the Chief Justice might assign the case to a majority member of the dissenters' bloc. Danelski found that of the three Chief Justices he studied, only Hughes appeared to follow such rules. A number of studies, seeking to determine whether assigners follow Danelski's first rule, have found a pattern of overassignment to the justice closest to the dissenters in cases in which a change in one vote would have altered the outcome (for example, Ulmer 1970b).[2] Brenner and Spaeth (1988), however, found that assigning the majority opinion to the marginal justice did not actually help maintain an original minimum winning coalition.

Rohde (1972c) hypothesized that the justice who assigns the majority opinion will either write the opinion or assign it to the justice whose position is closest to his own on the issue in question. Analyzing civil liberties cases decided during the Warren era, he found that the pattern of opinion assignments supported his hypothesis.[3] Moreover, the assigner's tendency to give opinions to the justice closest to him increased in important cases and as the size of the majority increased. When Gregory Rathjen (1974) replicated Rohde's study using economic rather than civil liberties cases, he found that the pattern of assigning opinions to the closest justice disappeared. While Rathjen endorsed the theory that justices assign opinions on the basis of policy preferences, he suggested that Rohde's hypothesis was most viable in cases that involved issues of primary concern to the Chief Justice. He conjectured that the issues presented in economics cases were less salient to Warren than those of individual rights, so that he may have placed policy concerns aside in those cases in order to assign opinions in a manner that would help to equalize the workload.

Departing from the primary focus on opinion assignment as a means to further policy preferences, and looking to institutional concerns, Slotnick (1979) explored the possibility that the Chief Justice may be more concerned with achieving equality of workload than getting his preferences into the law. Examining two models of opinion assignment—the opinion assignment ratio (OAR), which is conditioned on the frequency with which each justice is a member of the majority, and the model of absolute equality of caseloads, whereby all justices would have substantially the same number of majority opinions regardless of how often they agreed with the majority—he found that the six Chief Justices from Taft through Burger followed a norm of absolute equality. Moreover, it was Chief Justice Burger's behavior that most closely approximated the model of absolute equality. Likewise, Spaeth (1984) found that Burger practiced equal distribution to an extent that was unmatched by any of his five predecessors. Two of Slotnick's (1979) findings, however, suggested that in spite of a concern for equal workload, policy outcomes did in fact play an important role in opinion assignments. First, Chief Justices departed from the norm of equality in important cases, assigning opinions to themselves at a substantially higher rate than they did for the universe of cases. Second, those who most often voted with the Chief Justice were favored in the assignment of opinions in important cases. Spaeth's (1984) analysis of Burger's assignments revealed the same pattern. My study of the first three terms of the Rehnquist Court (Davis 1990) suggested that Rehnquist has been more concerned with distributing the workload equally than with using his opinion-assigning prerogative as an instrument to shape the outcome of the Court's decisions. Other studies have revealed that additional motivations may be relevant to opinion assignments, including encouraging issue specialization (Brenner 1984; Brenner and Spaeth 1986) and promoting efficiency (Brenner and Palmer 1988).

In the most important recent contribution to the literature on opinion assignment, Forrest Maltzman and Paul J. Wahlbeck (1995 and 1996a) developed a multivariate model and applied it to analyze the assignments of Chief Justices Earl Warren, Warren Burger, and William Rehnquist. The results of their study of Rehnquist's assignments revealed that his choices are primarily driven by institutional constraints rather than by an ideological agenda (1996a).[4] When they expanded their analysis to include Warren's and Burger's assignments (1995), they discovered that in certain circumstances ideology does influence the Chief Justice's choices. They concluded that the importance of ideology in opinion assignment is conditioned on the political and institutional contexts and the nature of the cases.

The sophistication of the methodology that Maltzman and Wahlbeck employ is an important aspect of their contribution to an understanding of opinion assignments. More important for present purposes, however, is the way they have worked within the framework of the new institutionalism. They not only seek to challenge the assumptions of the attitudinal model by demonstrating that institutional considerations, namely a desire to be evenhanded in distributing opinions, play an important role in opinion assignments but they also seem to be willing to depart from the assumptions of the rational-choice model by allowing that factors other than power-maximizing strategy considerations may motivate opinion assignments.

It is unfortunate that so much of the scholarship has focused on just one dimension of leadership on the Supreme Court.[5] Joseph F. Kobylka (1989) pointed out that studies of leadership that are limited to analyzing opinion assignments are incomplete and claimed that Chief Justice Burger's leadership cannot be understood without considering contextual influences including the intra- and extra-judicial environments. In order to examine Burger's leadership, Kobylka analyzed the twenty-eight Establishment Clause cases decided during the Burger Court years with regard to voting behavior, opinion content, and doctrinal development as well as opinion assignments. He argued that the explanations for Burger's failure to reformulate Establishment Clause doctrine are found in the positions of the other justices, the factual circumstances of the cases, and political forces from outside the Court—in the face of pressure from the Reagan Administration to reverse precedents, justices whose votes were crucial declined to vote with Burger out of a concern that the Court might be seen as caving in to political pressure. Kobylka incorporated institutional considerations into his analysis, structuring it around the premise that Burger's desire to accommodate state support of religious activities was the primary concern driving his behavior.

Studies of leadership on the Supreme Court reflect the renewed emphasis in political science on the importance of institutions in political life. What stands out about the research is that the heightened focus on institutional factors has expanded the scope of analysis. Thus, although the extent to which Chief Justices use their power to get their preferences into the Court's decisions will always be a major concern in studies of leadership, other dimensions have begun to receive more attention as scholars have made it a priority to understand the ways in which institutional factors shape the powers of the Chief Justice. In the following section, I offer some comments on Chief Justice Rehnquist's leadership, paying particular attention to the importance of institutional norms.

Rehnquist's Leadership: Ideology, Strategy, and Institutional Constraints

> *Accentuate the positive*
> *Eliminate the negative*
> *Latch on to the affirmative*
> *Don't mess with Mr. In Between.*[6]

> [My colleagues] defer not in the slightest on matters of law. [But] if there's a problem in the parking garage or the temperature is set uncomfortably in the conference room, they are quick to invoke my authority.[7]

> He has no problems, wishy-washy, back and forth. He knows exactly what he wants to do, and that's very important as a chief justice.[8]

October 1996 marked the tenth anniversary of the Rehnquist Court. William H. Rehnquist's position during the previous fourteen and a half years as the Court's most conservative member had made him the Reagan Administration's logical choice to replace Warren E. Burger. When Rehnquist took his seat at the center of the Court a number of commentators anticipated that he would be an effective, perhaps even a great Chief Justice. Qualities such as his "extraordinary intellectual power" (Schmidt 1986), his strong convictions that his positions are correct and his desire to win ("Reagan's Mr. Right" 1986), plus his good nature, his sense of humor, and his ability to get along well with his colleague—even those who disagree with him—seemed to enhance his prospects for success.

How effective has Rehnquist been in leading the Supreme Court? The new Chief Justice brought a well-developed agenda to his office. In fact, when Rehnquist joined the Court he already had a general outline of that agenda. In 1985, he reflected, "I came to the court sensing,

without really having followed it terribly closely, that there were some
excesses in terms of constitutional adjudication during the era of the
so-called Warren Court." He continued, "So I felt that at the time I
came on the court, the boat was kind of heeling over in one direction.
Interpreting my oath as I saw it, I felt that my job was, where those
sort of situations arose, to kind of lean the other way" (Jenkins 1985:
33). It is now well known that the overarching theme of Rehnquist's
decision-making is state-centered federalism. Thus, he has used various devices to shift power from the federal government to the states,
including interpreting Congress's power narrowly (see, e.g., *United
States v. Lopez* 1995). Perhaps most important in understanding Rehnquist's agenda, however, is his campaign to reduce the role of the federal courts. A major component of that agenda is ideological. Indeed,
an examination of his votes in cases coming from state courts demonstrated that he has been considerably more likely to respect the decisions of such courts when they reached conservative results (Davis
1992). Much of his behavior as Chief Justice may be understood as
strategic behavior designed to maneuver the four other justices to vote
with him so that he may shape the law according to his own preferences. In short, his agenda and his ideology are central to an understanding of his leadership. Nevertheless, there are important institutional factors that also need to be considered, including norms and
rules structuring the powers of the Chief Justice that Rehnquist inherited from his predecessors and that are likely to have an important
influence on his understanding of the powers of the office and well as
his ability to lead the Court.

Most of the journalistic commentary on the Rehnquist Court reflects
the assumption that the most important—perhaps the only—measure
of the effectiveness of the Chief Justice is his success in commanding
a majority of the Court. In that view, Rehnquist has been a successful
leader to the extent that the Court's decisions are conservative. By such
a measure, Rehnquist's leadership varies from term to term but invari-
ably comes up short, particularly in light of his failure in 1992 to convince a majority to overrule *Roe v. Wade* (*Planned Parenthood v. Casey*
1992),[9] and the majority's decision to invalidate Colorado's constitutional amendment that banned policies prohibiting discrimination on
the basis of sexual orientation (*Romer v. Evans* 1996). Indeed, David
J. Garrow argued that "[t]he Rehnquist Court is only sometimes the
Rehnquist Court. When Kennedy chooses to side with the four moderates it is turned into the Kennedy Court" (1996:65).

One of the problems with such an approach is that it fails to take sufficient account of the extent to which Rehnquist has been successful in shaping the law in selected areas that are central to his agenda. His campaign to limit federal habeas corpus is a prime example. As an associate justice, he played a leading role in the Burger Court's attack on the Warren Court's expansive use of habeas corpus as a vehicle for reform.[10] His view is captured by his complaint in 1981 that in spite of the Court's determination that capital punishment statutes did not violate the Constitution, there had been only one execution of a defendant who had persisted in challenging his sentence. He placed responsibility on the Court for allowing the death penalty to become "virtually an illusion," which made a mockery of the criminal justice system (*Coleman v. Balkcom* 1981). Although Rehnquist stood alone in 1981, his position came to prevail.

In 1989, as head of the Judicial Conference of the United States, Rehnquist appointed a committee chaired by former Justice Lewis Powell to recommend changes in the availability of habeas corpus for death-row appeals. The result was the Powell Report, which recommended that condemned prisoners be allowed only one appeal to the state courts and, if that failed, one appeal to the federal courts, allowed only if filed within six months. When the Judicial Conference decided to postpone consideration of those recommendations Rehnquist sent the proposals directly to the House and Senate judiciary committees. Fourteen of the conference's twenty-six other members sent a letter to the committees objecting and asking the committees to delay any action until they had heard from the senior federal judges. Undeterred, Rehnquist asked Congress to act on the proposals as soon as possible. Although Congress did not act, the Court did. In 1991, in *McCleskey v. Zant* the Court limited successive habeas petitions by requiring petitioners to show cause in second or subsequent petitions for failing to raise a claim in an initial habeas petition.[11] In 1996, when Congress did take some action to restrict habeas corpus in the Antiterrorism and Effective Death Penalty Act by providing that second or subsequent habeas petitions cannot be filed unless a federal appeals court grants a motion giving the prisoner permission to file a petition, the Court unanimously and quickly upheld the legislation in *Felker v. Turpin* (1996).

While reducing the availability of habeas corpus clearly promotes Rehnquist's goal of reducing the role of the federal judiciary and elevating the importance of state courts, it is also consistent with the his longstanding desire to allow states that choose to use the death penalty to carry out sentences without long delays. Rehnquist's victory in reducing habeas corpus, thus, points to his success in leading the Court where he wants it to go. In the same vein, not only has he managed to get the Court to reconsider long-settled principles of federalism, but in 1995 he emerged triumphant when, for the first time in sixty years, a majority invalidated a federal law on the ground that Congress had exceeded its constitutional authority to regulate interstate commerce (*U.S. v. Lopez*). Finally, in 1996 he substantially advanced his goal of extending the reach of the Eleventh Amendment to enhance state power by limiting the ability of citizens to bring suit against a state. The decision in that case brought longstanding legal principles into question by limiting Congress's power to waive state immunity through legislation (*Seminole Tribe v. Florida* 1996). The substance of the Court's decisions in areas that are central to federalism and, thus, likely to hold a high priority for Rehnquist suggests that he has been an effective leader insofar as he has managed to amass at least four other votes for the results that he desires.

A second problem with measuring Rehnquist's effectiveness in terms of the extent to which the Court's decisions have been consistent with his conservative preferences is that such an approach fails to take account of institutional factors and the ways in which they structure the powers of the chief justice. While ideological preferences, strategy, and personality are important, systematic treatment of institutional norms should be central to an analysis of Rehnquist's leadership. In the remainder of this section I consider several norms that are likely to have an important impact on the dimensions of the Chief Justice's power to lead the Court.

Several scholars have examined the norm of the individual opinion, which replaced the norm of consensus and the institutional opinion. The demise of the norm of consensus has been attributed variously to Chief Justice Stone's style of leadership (Walker, Epstein, and Dixon 1988) and to a shift in behavioral expectations among the justices that Chief Justice Hughes precipitated (Haynie 1992). Minimizing the importance of the Chief Justice's style in running the conference to the demise of the norm of the institutional opinion, David M. O'Brien (see his essay in this volume) emphasized the impact of the uncertainties that came with Legal Realism and the effect of changes in the operation of the Court, including the circulation of drafts prior to conference, the justices' move to the new Supreme Court building beginning in 1937, and the increase in the number of law clerks. While it was firmly established by the end of the Warren Court, the norm of individual opinions may have grown even stronger under Chief Justice Rehnquist. Just as Roosevelt's appointees began to disagree once they had a majority, so

too did the conservative Reagan and Bush appointees over such matters as constitutional interpretation and the importance of *stare decisis*.
Additionally, while it became easier to revise opinions with the type-
writer in the 1920s and 1930s, as O'Brien points out, rapid developments
in computer technology in the late 1980s further enhanced the ease with
which opinions could be shared and revised. Further, if Legal Realism
and liberal legalism contributed to the rise of the individual opinion by
introducing new possibilities and uncertainties to the justices, the proliferation of legal theories in the academic literature in the 1980s and 1990s
must have had a similar and perhaps even stronger effect.

Efficiency, both in running the conference and in completing the
work of the Court, is another institutional norm that is likely to have
played an important role in Rehnquist's leadership. As the workload
of the Court increased during the Warren and Burger years it became
imperative for the Chief Justice to run the Court efficiently, even bureaucratically. Efficiency was particularly important to Rehnquist's immediate predecessor, Chief Justice Burger, who stated during his confirmation hearings that the Chief Justice has "a very large responsibility
to try to see that the [federal] judicial system functions more efficiently
[and] should certainly be alert to trying to find these improvements"
(Fish 1984). As an associate justice, Rehnquist saw Burger introduce a
number of reforms geared to improving the efficiency of the judiciary.
For example, it was Burger who appointed the Freund Committee to
study the problem of the growing caseload. That committee recommended the creation of a national court of appeals to screen *certiorari*
petitions for the Supreme Court. Rehnquist inherited the norm of efficiency from Burger, adopted it, and developed it further. Rosen (1993)
blamed Rehnquist's "mania for efficiency" for lack of intellectual debate among the justices and contended that the Chief Justice's most
conspicuous legacy has been to make the Court more coldly bureaucratic. Justice Scalia has commented that the conference has become
less of an interchange than a statement of the views of the justices (B.
Schwartz 1996:42). Rehnquist has been labeled a stickler for operating
on time and on schedule (Savage 1996b).[12] He has allegedly adopted a
policy of reducing the share of majority opinions assigned to justices
who fail to complete their dissents within four weeks after the majority
opinion circulates. Moreover, some of the justices have professed that
they feel pressure to join a majority opinion as soon as it circulates
(Rosen 1993). While rushing through the cases with a minimum of intellectual exchange among the justices is consistent with the norm of efficiency, it also is likely to enhance Rehnquist's ability to control the deci-

sions of the Court. Moreover, the decline in collegiality with the disturbing increase in incivility among the justices and its reputed failure to resolve national controversies (Schwartz 1989) are developments that serve to promote Rehnquist's goal of reducing the role of the Court.

Rehnquist is commonly credited with the shrinking docket—during the 1995 term the Court decided only seventy-five cases, less than half of the 175 decided in the 1984 term and the lowest number since the 1953 term. The sharp decline in the number of cases the Court accepts for review is most often explained as part of Rehnquist's strategy to reduce the role of the Court and to let conservative decisions of Reagan-Bush–packed lower federal courts stand. Nevertheless, reducing the number of cases serves to promote efficiency and thus the institutional interests of the Court. The reduction in the Court's caseload may also be examined as an element of the Court's process of agenda-setting and the Chief Justice's role in that process. Pacelle (1991) reported that the Rehnquist Court had begun to show signs of reopening parts of the federalism and economic agendas. My own examination of the plenary agenda revealed that for all the terms of the Rehnquist Court through 1992, criminal appeals comprised a higher percentage of all cases than any other single issue. That pattern is consistent with the argument that Rehnquist has been successful in his campaign to overrule or at least limit liberal precedent in the area of the rights of the accused.

Traditionally, much of the research on case selection has presented justices' decisions on *certiorari* as preliminary strategic votes on the merits (see, for example, Ulmer 1972, 1978; Brenner 1979). More recent work, however, points to a subtler and more complex interplay between internal norms and external factors in addition to strategic concerns that shape the Court's agenda. H. W. Perry (1991) captured the complexity of the Court's internal norms when he described the process of deciding whether to grant *certiorari* as composed of two different sets of decisional steps in which a case travels one channel, or decision mode, or the other. The choice of decision mode depends on both the justice and the case. If a justice cares strongly about the outcome of a case on the merits, he or she will enter the outcome mode to decide whether or not to take the case. Alternatively, if a justice does not have strong feelings about the outcome of the case on the merits, he or she will enter the jurisprudential mode to consider whether there is a legitimate inter-circuit conflict, whether the conflict involves an important issue, needs more percolation, and is a good vehicle. Perry concluded that most of the justices most of the time operate in the jurisprudential mode; even in the outcome mode, however, the decision is far more complex than a strategic, "If I can win, grant" (281). As Perry describes it, the outcome mode is composed of a series of steps or questions, including whether the case is a good vehicle or whether there is likely to be a better case for pulling a swing justice and for achieving one's long-range goals. Perry's model suggests that there are substantial constraints on the power of the Chief Justice to control the Court's agenda. It seems quite likely that Rehnquist may operate in the outcome mode when deciding whether to vote to grant *certiorari* in the cases that are most important to him and he tries to bring his powers of persuasion to bear on the other justices. Regardless of his personal qualities as a leader, however, the complex interaction between the outcome and jurisprudential modes among his eight colleagues is likely to diminish his ability to secure the three necessary votes to grant *certiorari*.

The Solicitor General's role in case selection is an institutional factor that has major implications for the ability of the Chief Justice to shape the Court's agenda. The Solicitor General acts as gatekeeper to the Supreme Court by deciding which cases in which the government is a party merit a petition for *certiorari* and in cases in which the government is not a party, by filing an *amicus curiae* brief in support of or in opposition to review. The Solicitor General's success in getting the Court's attention has been thoroughly documented. Salokar (1992:25, 27), for example, found that for the terms 1959 through 1989 the Solicitor General was successful in gaining review in 69.78 percent of the 1,294 cases that the government filed, compared to 4.9 percent of private litigants' petitions. When the Solicitor General filed an *amicus* brief on behalf of the appellant, the Court granted review in 87.6 of the cases.[13] Thus, the Court's norm of relying on the advice of the Solicitor General in the selection of cases is one that is firmly established. The existence of that norm suggests that during periods when the policies favored by the White House are consistent with those of the Chief Justice, the latter will enjoy increased success in shaping the agenda of the Court primarily because the Solicitor General's arguments would lend support to his own. Thus, during the Reagan and Bush years, Chief Justice Rehnquist's own priorities may have prevailed more than they did during President Clinton's first term in office.[14]

Alternatively, it is possible that the "politicization of Justice Department policy" (Clayton 1992:147) during the Reagan era had a damaging effect on Rehnquist's ability to shape the Court's agenda. The Justice Department's adoption of a more aggressive litigation program and a more explicitly political strategy may have violated the norms of the Solicitor General's relationship with the Supreme Court. If so, the

Court's norm of paying particular attention to the Solicitor General's arguments would have declined, disagreements among the justices would have increased, and Rehnquist would most likely have experienced less success in convincing the others to go along with his preferences in the selection of cases. A comment from a former Solicitor General underlines such a possibility. The key to maintaining influence on the Court, he noted, is to draw on the credibility of the office. "But if [the Solicitor General] draws too deeply, too greedily, or too indiscriminately, then he jeopardizes not only the advantage in that particular case, but also an important institution of government" (Salokar 1992: 99).

Caplan (1987) contended that the Reagan Administration transformed the role of the Solicitor General and in so doing, damaged its relationship with the Supreme Court. The administration's attitude was that the courts had misbehaved and that it was the Justice Department's responsibility to straighten them out. Emphasizing the political goals of the Reagan Administration, Caplan argued, the Solicitor General, "sometimes made the law an afterthought" (1987:168). Caplan pointed to the resulting deterioration of the relationship between the Court and the Solicitor General with comments from several justices. "Generally, until recent years, I've always welcomed any filing by the Solicitor General. Now the clerks tell me consistently that you can't trust the SG about the facts or the law the way you'd like, and I rely on their judgment. So we pause a bit longer in granting cert. just because the government says to, and we may grant a few less." Another justice remarked, "I scrutinize the cert. petitions more so than I used to. . . . I don't give them the same benefit of the doubt I used to and I have to spend more time combing through their work" (Caplan 1987: 265, 266).[15]

Recent studies of the Solicitor General have challenged Caplan's claim that the Reagan Administration diminished the Solicitor General's credibility as a reliable adviser to the Court (Clayton 1992; Salokar 1992; Fisher 1990). Although Salokar concedes that "[b]y focusing on the politically-oriented task, these solicitors general risked devaluing the reputation of the office by violating gatekeeper norms, offering less-than-rigorous arguments to the justices, and showing a general lack of respect for legal precedent," she maintains that, at the stage of the decisions on the merits:

> the arguments of these solicitors general were not dismissed by the Supreme Court out-of-hand; the government's positions may not have mustered the support of a majority of the nine justices, but they did manage to secure some votes

on each of the issues. I suggest that the arguments advanced by these solicitors general merely reflected the controversies that were being debated both within the Court and in the broader political environment—specifically the lack of agreement that these issues were "settled" areas of law (1995:79).

Clayton (1992) traced the development of the role of the Solicitor General to profound changes in the American political system, which began with Franklin D. Roosevelt's administration and introduced the regularization of institutional conflict, the legalization of policy disputes, and a more independent judicial politics, all of which led to the politicization of the Justice Department. The assertion that the Reagan Justice Department's litigation strategy was consistent with its historic role and did not violate the Solicitor General's independence or change the traditional role of the office is supported by the Solicitor General's continued success before the Court. Clayton (1992:58) reported that Solicitors General Rex Lee (1981–85) and Charles Fried (1985–89) had the highest overall rates of success in Supreme Court litigation since the administration of Calvin Coolidge.

Finally, the transformation of the role of the Supreme Court in the American political system that began with the New Deal and was completed by the end of the Warren Court provides the institutional context for assessing Rehnquist's leadership.[16] The Court over which Rehnquist has presided since 1986 is one that continues to carry on the legacy of the Warren Court. That legacy includes a willingness to use judicial power to shape social policy in key areas of individual rights; a commitment to basic fairness and to reaching the right outcome sometimes without much concern for consistent legal principles; and an increase in the Court's independence, in part as a result of alliances with interest groups. Because the Court's new role has become so firmly entrenched—so clearly a part of the institution—Rehnquist, as did Burger before him, faces tremendous obstacles in his quest to reverse the trend that culminated with the Warren Court in order to reduce the role of the Court. In short, Rehnquist's leadership should be examined both in terms of the ways in which his Court has continued, even expanded, the role established by the Warren Court and the ways in which he has succeeded in challenging that role.

Suggestions for Future Research

While the extant scholarship on leadership in the Supreme Court is enormously valuable, it is clear that a great deal of work remains in the task of developing a full understanding of the multitude of ways in which Chief Justices have used the prerogatives of the office to shape the decisions of the Court, how their leadership has affected the institution itself, and how institutional factors have structured the powers of the Chief Justice. As I emphasized in the previous section, it is important to recognize that ideological preferences and strategies, personality, and style of a Chief Justice need to be considered in conjunction with the institutional attributes that have a profound effect on a Chief Justice's goals and expectations and ability to lead the Court. In short, systematic attention to "the dialectical interplay of meaningful decisions and structural constraints" (Smith 1988:103) will be a useful tool in studying leadership on the Court.

The questions with which scholars of law and courts have been preoccupied—how and to what ends have Chief Justices used one of the prerogatives of the office—the authority to assign opinions—is but one question out of the many that need to be addressed. Although patterns of opinion assignment are readily quantifiable and amenable to increasingly refined and sophisticated techniques of analysis, they provide only a partial view of the wide panorama of leadership. Even that partial view, however, is valuable. Maltzman and Wahlbeck's (1995, 1996a) recent work, for example, confirms the importance of looking beyond policy preferences to institutional considerations to explain patterns of opinion assignment.

For those who choose to delve further into the way Chief Justices utilize the tool of opinion assignment it will be beneficial to follow the example set by Maltzman and Wahlbeck by not treating the power to assign opinions as merely a tool to influence who wins and who loses; that is, analyses should not simply assume that Chief Justices use their prerogative to assign opinions in a strategic way in order to get their policy preferences into the law. More information about the development of the norms of opinion assignment over time may also shed light on current practices. The patterns of opinion assignment that scholars have analyzed going back as far as Chief Justice Taft (Slotnick 1979) are likely to have had an important influence on the development of the current norms of assigning opinions. Thus, it should be useful to delve into the past to study opinion assignments in order to explore the importance of changing norms on the activities of the Chief Justice.

Moving beyond work on opinion assignment, historical analysis will be helpful not only in increasing our understanding of the ways in which past practices have affected the development of institutional norms but also of how changing norms shape the dimensions of the

power of the Chief Justice. While I suggested in the previous section
that it may be useful to view Rehnquist's leadership in light of the changing role of the Court since the New Deal, an understanding of leadership
is also likely to be enhanced by going back even earlier in the history of
the Supreme Court to explore the impact of the changes in the norms
regarding opinion-writing[17] on the development of the institution. An
examination of the process by which the Court moved from the custom
of delivering seriatim opinions to the practice of issuing an "opinion of
the court," which Chief Justice John Marshall instituted (and most of
which were attributed to him), could shed more light on the viability of
the argument that by reforming the way that opinions were delivered,
Marshall enhanced the power of the Supreme Court.

Studies of leadership on the Court will benefit by the conscious
adoption of the posture that "[h]istory provides the dimension necessary for understanding institutions as they operate under varying conditions. Beyond that it is also a natural proving ground for the claim
that institutions have an independent and formative influence on politics" (Orren and Skowronek 1986:vii). Thus, scholarship can be informed by a concern with how the office of the Chief Justice has
evolved over the years in terms both of the way in which individuals
have shaped the office and of how the office has influenced the behavior of its occupants. How has the development of the office of Chief
Justice helped to define the possibilities for leadership? And how have
individual Chief Justices used their powers in the past to shape both
the law and the Supreme Court? While scholars who choose to pursue
such questions can look to Gillman's (1993 and 1994b) work as a model
of the new institutionalism in the area of doctrinal development, they
will also benefit from ground-breaking work of law-and-courts scholars who have examined some of the historical and developmental dimensions of leadership (see, Walker, Epstein, and Dixon 1988; Epstein
and Walker 1995; Knight and Epstein 1996a).[18]

While still focusing on historical development but moving to the
more recent past, one might structure a study of leadership around the
norms that Burger inherited from Warren and that Rehnquist inherited
from Burger. I barely began to suggest the importance of a few of those
norms in the previous section. Systematic analysis of the origins of institutional norms, the impact they have had on the powers of the Chief
Justice, and the consequences for the decision-making of the Court
would be a tremendously important undertaking. It would also be useful to examine various aspects of Rehnquist's leadership in light of
practices of earlier Chief Justices. For example, an examination of Chief

Justice Hughes's responses to President Roosevelt's court-packing plan may provide a useful parallel to Rehnquist's defense of judicial independence in the midst of the controversy over the Clinton Administration's attack on federal district judge Harold Baer Jr. in April 1996 and his condemnation in 1993 of the Library of Congress's decision to open the Marshall papers. Such a possibility points to another institutional norm that influences the Chief Justice's behavior—one of his jobs is to act as defender of the Court—which would profit from careful historical analysis.

Conclusion

While the suggestions offered above might generate ideas for research, they are intended primarily to demonstrate how a historical-interpretive institutionalist approach can increase the understanding of leadership on the Supreme Court. Some caution is warranted, however. Paying constant attention to the "interplay of meaningful actions and structural contexts," emphasizing the relative autonomy of political actions from structural determinants, and assuming that political actions can have an effect on those structures, as Smith urges (1988: 91,101), could lure unwary scholars into a morass in which "everything is somehow connected to everything else" (Smith 1988:101). If researchers take particular care to design their research projects with well-defined limits they should be able to avoid such a problem. Additionally, to refute the charge that the new institutionalism "is a return in certain respects to a more or less traditional political science" (Shapiro 1989, 89), researchers should take particular care to explain how the new approach encompasses alternative conceptions of politics and human behavior, new and broader definitions of institutions, and how their methodologies take those new perspectives into account (see Clayton's essay in this volume).

The contrasting ways that law-and-courts scholars have conceived and applied the new institutionalism belie Smith's (1988) expressed hope that adopting the approach would facilitate the development of connections between empirical and normative concerns and bridge the gulf between qualitative and quantitative methods to transcend the persistent tensions within the field. Although the two versions of the new institutionalism overlap to the extent that they share the conviction that institutional arrangements matter, from there they take very different paths. To some extent it may be possible to develop a viable argument that there is room in law-and-courts scholarship for both approaches. For example, qualitative work that focuses on the ways in which the office of the Chief Justice have developed over the years in order to describe the interaction between structures and decisions may make quantitative studies of opinion assignment more complete. Moreover, Lee Epstein and her co-authors have demonstrated that quantitative methods often provide for illuminating analyses of historical developments. Be that as it may, the viability of the reconciliation-under-the-rubric-of-the-new-institutionalism argument is severely limited by the fact that the assumptions of the rational-choice model are clearly incompatible with the visions of politics and human agency to which those who embrace the historical-interpretive approach subscribe (see Gillman's essay in this volume).

Although its value to law-and-courts scholarship is clear, the new institutionalism is not going to end the clashes between scholars who simply see things differently, use contrasting methods to answer their questions, and often even ask different questions. Given the limited prospects for agreement, I conclude with a plea for tolerance on both sides—no more disparaging remarks assessing the work of the other side as marginal to the discipline, for example. We would do well, as always, to take C. Herman Pritchett's counsel and "let a hundred flowers bloom."

Notes

The author would like to thank Howard Gillman and Cornell Clayton for their helpful comments on an earlier draft of this chapter and Seth Birdoff for diligent research assistance.

1. For examples of the historical-interpretive approach see Gillman (1993 and 1994b) and Orren (1995b). Examples of the rational-choice approach include Epstein and Knight (1995a), Knight and Epstein (1996a), see Hall and Brace (1989 and 1992) and Brace and Hall (1990).

2. See also, McLauchlan (1972). McLauchlan found a pattern of overassignment to justices occupying the position closest to the minority in close cases (the pattern was more pronounced in civil liberties than in economic cases), which he construed as evidence of a strategy to reduce conflict among the members of the Court. Although Rohde found that there was some advantage to being closest to the dissenters and concluded that the "marginality hypothesis does, at one point, add to our understanding of the process" he actually found only limited support for that hypothesis. The marginal justice had an advantage only where he was both marginal and a member of the group closes to the assigner (Rohde 1972c). Brenner (1982) also questioned the claim that the opinion favors the marginal justice in order to prevent defection.

3. Ulmer (1970b) also found that closeness in terms of policy preferences of the assigner and the assignee had an influence on the assignments of Chief Justice Warren.

4. But see Cook (1992), whose multivariate analysis suggested that political ideology was the most useful variable in explaining opinion assignment.

5. A notable exception is Robert J. Steamer's (1986) study of the fifteen Chief Justices from John Jay through Warren Burger, which provides a wealth of descriptive information that may help to provide an impetus for further research.

6. In a 1991 memorandum transmitting a draft opinion in *Barnes v. Glen Theatre, Inc.*, Rehnquist argued that Indiana could outlaw nude dancing. The verse was an attempt to downplay precedent that did not support his case. As quoted in Biskupic (1994a:C4).

7. Rehnquist's comment about his authority as Chief Justice (Savage 1996b: A5).

8. Justice Thurgood Marshall, commenting on Rehnquist in 1987. As quoted in B. Schwartz (1996:34).

9. For a discussion of Rehnquist's attempts to overrule *Roe* in *Webster v. Reproductive Health Services* (1989), see B. Schwartz (1996:55–64).

10. See, for example, Rehnquist's opinions in *Davis v. United States* (1973); *Wainwright v. Sykes* (1977); *Sumner v. Mata* (1981). Garrow notes the existence of a memo in Justice Jackson's papers that Rehnquist prepared as his law clerk in 1953 for the case of *Brown v. Allen*. In that memo, Rehnquist argued that federal courts should not grant habeas petitions involving any issue that had been considered by a state court unless the defendant had been denied the right to counsel (1996:66).

11. See also, *Herrera v. Collins* (1993); *Keeney v. Tamayo-Reyes* (1992); *Coleman v. Thompson* (1991); *Arizona v. Fulminante* (1991).

12. See also Biskupic (1994a:C4): "[H]is no-nonsense timetable leaves little room for serious discussion of cases."

13. Scigliano (1971:174–75) found that for the 1958 through the 1967 terms the Court accepted 70 percent of the government's *certiorari* petitions. Clayton (1992:67) notes that the Supreme Court granted more than half of the petitions the Justice Department filed or supported for every term from 1925 through 1988 except for 1933, 1934, 1949, and 1951. The average success rate for the entire period was just over 70 percent. In contrast, the Supreme Court granted over 20 percent of petitions filed by other litigants in only two terms (1929 and 1930). Caplan (1987:4) notes that for the 1983 term the Court granted 79 percent of the petitions for *certiorari* submitted by the Solicitor General where the government was a party and 78 percent of the cases in which the government supported a petition as *amicus curiae*.

14. Such a trend might be mitigated by something that Salokar found. Even in Democratic administrations arguments tend to be conservative (at least in individual rights cases) because the conservative position often coincides with support for government (1992:155).

15. But Fisher (1990) questions the reliability of Caplan's interviews.

16. That transformation has been described at length. See, for example, Shapiro (1983, 1990); Hall (1996); Tushnet (1993); Silverstein and Ginsberg (1987).

17. It was not until 1834 that all opinions were required to be filed with the clerk (Garner 1992:609)

18. See also Murphy (1964:88) on how Stone's five years as Chief Justice shaped the expectations for Vinson's Court.

7

The Supreme Court and the Development of the Welfare State: Judicial Liberalism and the Problem of Welfare Rights

Elizabeth Bussiere

On August 22, 1996, President Clinton signed a Republican-authored bill abolishing the sixty-one-year-old federal welfare entitlement program known as Aid to Families with Dependent Children (AFDC), which provided government assistance to impoverished single mothers and their dependent children. Presidential scholars will likely underscore the ironic juxtaposition of a Democratic President dismantling an important part of the welfare state and of Republican President Richard Nixon attempting to create a guaranteed income for all Americans a quarter century earlier. But a less appreciated irony of welfare politics—and the centerpiece of this chapter—is that the *liberal*-oriented Warren Court, not the *conservative*-oriented Rehnquist Court, was the first U.S. Supreme Court in the post–New Deal period to refuse to identify subsistence as a constitutionally protected right.

In fact, when the Rehnquist Court confronted the claim of a "constitutional right to life" in 1989, the majority cited two Warren Court precedents in ruling that the Fourteenth Amendment contains no "affirmative duties" mandating states to give individuals the necessary aid to sustain life or liberty.[1] Even Justices William Brennan and Thurgood Marshall, two Warren Court liberals who still sat on the Supreme Court then, agreed with Chief Justice Rehnquist that the Fourteenth Amendment embodies no "positive liberties."[2]

In that closely watched case, *DeShaney v. Winnebago County Dept. of Social Services* (1989), the Rehnquist Court addressed the "right to life" argument in the context of child abuse and state liability. The case involved the near death of a young boy, Joshua DeShaney, at the hands of an abusive father who had been the subject of a Wisconsin Social Services Department investigation into allegations of child abuse. Reaffirming the Warren Court's position that the Fourteenth Amendment contains no substantive "right to life," Chief Justice Rehnquist's majority opinion denied the claim of state liability made on Joshua's behalf. Interestingly, in insisting that the decision hinge on reason, not "sympathy," the conservative Chief Justice echoed his liberal predecessor, Chief Justice Earl Warren. Expressing grave doubts about a constitutional right to welfare, Chief Justice Warren had written: "To the extent that [lawyers expose] the handicaps upon the poor of the Nation, they appeal to the right instincts of all men. However, instinct cannot be our guide . . . ."[3]

Justices Brennan and Marshall, joined by Nixon-appointee Justice Harry Blackmun, dissented in *DeShaney;* nevertheless, they accepted the majority's proposition that the Fourteenth Amendment protects individuals from mistreatment by the state rather than eliciting affirmative government duties to safeguard human life (*DeShaney v. Winnebago County Dept. of Social Services* 1989:204). But unlike those who joined the majority opinion, the dissenting justices characterized the state's decision to keep Joshua in his father's custody as potentially negligent state action (not mere "inaction") in violation of the Fourteenth Amendment's Due Process Clause (*ibid.*).

DeShaney serves as a reminder that the Warren Court, although it formulated legal doctrines that appreciably expanded welfare "entitlements," never conferred constitutional status on welfare assistance. In declining to identify welfare as a constitutional right, the Warren Court rendered the poor politically vulnerable to just the sort of attack embodied in the 1996 welfare law. Although very different in other areas of constitutional law, the Warren and Rehnquist Courts agreed that the substance of government's obligations to meet the poor's needs is defined by statute, not by the Constitution. Indeed, the Court's approach to questions of human needs in *DeShaney* illustrates a way of thinking that has transcended the partisan ideologies of the individual justices and helped shaped the Supreme Court's role in the U.S. welfare state.

This article attempts to explain why the Warren Court decided against identifying welfare assistance as a constitutional right, and then considers subsequent judicial interpretations and political consequences. The explanation lies not in some inherent characteristic of the American liberal tradition, for, as I have argued elsewhere, a powerful strain of Anglo-American natural-law thought made the property rights of the rich conditional on the fulfillment of the poor's subsistence needs (Bussiere 1997:chap. 2). Nor does the explanation lie primarily in the underlying shifts in the balance of political power and public opinion after 1968 (although those shifts almost certainly played a role). Rather, the Warren Court's decision to exclude welfare from the category of nonenumerated "fundamental rights" was the product of the intellectual bases of legal doctrines and the institutional dynamics of judicial decision-making (Bussiere 1994, 1997).

Far from acting upon their liberal "instincts" unrestrained by precedents, the Warren Court justices were so inhibited by their fidelity to existing doctrinal constructs that, during an admittedly brief "window of opportunity" at the close of the 1960s, a majority of the justices turned decisively against those very "instincts"—and doomed to oblivion the notion of a constitutionally based right to welfare. Thus, even while introducing new constitutional and statutory interpretations, the Warren Court operated within a framework of ideas created by the Roosevelt Court that constrained its ability to "constitutionalize" a right to welfare. Ironically, President Franklin Roosevelt, the political figure who best personifies the U.S. welfare state, acted in such a way as ultimately to impair the Warren Court's ability to define welfare as a constitutional right.

Like the other chapters in this volume, the analysis offered here utilizes the insights of the "new institutionalism" perspective. My own use of this body of literature most resembles "interpretive" approaches to judicial decision-making, which emphasize both the constraints of inherited legal doctrines and the fluidity, multiplicity, and "indeterminacy" of legal meanings among state and nonstate actors (see Gillman 1994b, 1996; Ignatieff 1983; Leyh 1992; McCann 1994; Sarat and Kearns 1993).[4] Interpretivists highlight the open-ended, culturally embedded nature of legal doctrines and their internal normative tensions, which judges strive to make coherent and which interest groups and social movements can exploit in pursuit of their own political goals (see especially McCann 1994). Yet, even among interpretivists, there are diverse interests and methods of analysis. My own preference is for close textual analyses of court opinions, including earlier draft opinions that change over time, in order to illuminate judges' patterns of reasoning and rhetoric and in some cases the reciprocal effect of a court's collective deliberation on the final decisions.

While litigation is a form of political "mobilization," legal doctrines, in my view, hold more than purely instrumental value for the judges charged with the duty to interpret them. To some degree, judges who interpret the law through the filter of legal doctrines are acted upon by such doctrines because the existing categories of analysis shape judges' very perception of, and reasoning in, the cases before them. (That, according to the new institutionalism, is what gives judges their uniquely institutional outlooks.) Furthermore, usually what is of value to social movements, interest groups, or other audiences is not just the outcome of a case but the mode of reasoning that justifies a court's decision. For, the line(s) of reasoning embedded in a court opinion helps condition the kinds of cases to be subsequently litigated, or avoided, and influences the direction of political struggles inside and outside the judiciary. As such, careful textual analysis of judges' opinions can be just as important to political actors bent on maintaining or changing the status quo as it is to scholars themselves. Tracking the changes or revisions made in draft opinions in cases also provides a glimpse of the conflict on a court and the processes of resolution used in judicial decision-making.

Analyzing the Warren Court's Equal Protection doctrines regarding the poor, this chapter describes the intellectual structures and the ideological dimensions of the justices' opinions. In addition to elucidating the intellectual and ideological content of those doctrines, it looks at another key institutional attribute of judicial decision-making: the process of deliberation and negotiation through which the justices sometimes build, maintain, or try to rebuild coalitions in order to arrive at a collective decision. In short, both the doctrinal categories and the process of deliberation and negotiation among the justices mediate between any one individual justice's attitudes and the Court's opinions. Attention to institutional dynamics of Supreme Court decision-making thus enriches both behaviorist and structural analyses of the justices' opinions.

Part 1 of this chapter describes the Warren Court's understanding of the Fourteenth Amendment's Equal Protection Clause, with particular attention paid to one welfare case. Part 2 examines a key statutory doctrine in the Warren Court's interpretation of AFDC, which affected the decisions of the Supreme Court well into a more politically conservative political era. The third part briefly considers the overall pattern of the Burger and the Rehnquist Courts' rulings, laying bare the institutionalist pressures reflected therein.

The Warren Court and Constitutional "Welfare Rights"

THE POST–NEW DEAL "DOUBLE STANDARD"

The "double standard" arose out of the conflict between the Roosevelt Administration and the Supreme Court during the 1930s. Where Roosevelt perceived "economic royalists" flouting the general welfare in pursuit of their own profits, a majority of the Court perceived federal and state regulations as interferences with individuals' (and corporations') liberty and property rights. Emblematic of the Court's conservativism was its interpretation of the Fourteenth Amendment's Due Process Clause as safeguarding "liberty of contract."

Critics, including Roosevelt, derided the "liberty of contract" decisions as textually unsupported by the Constitution and anachronistic in an age of concentrated economic power (but see Gillman 1993; Keynes 1996; and McCann 1989). Laborers responded that, since "an empty stomach can make no contracts," the notion of liberty of contract was a "sham" (quoted in Montgomery 1967:252). Roosevelt's support for the National Labor Relations Act demonstrated his own belief in the need to level the playing field between employers and employees. Nevertheless, from 1890 until 1937, the Supreme Court insisted that, although not listed in the document, liberty of contract was of the essence of individual liberty protected by the Fourteenth Amendment. This time period became known as the "Lochner era," named after the Court's ruling in *Lochner v. New York* (1905), striking down New York's regulation of bakers' work hours. A consensus during and after the New Deal period was that the Court was abusing its authority by reading its own conservative political philosophy, under the guise of natural law, into the Constitution.

With the Court's plummeting popularity and his own at a peak after his landslide reelection in 1936, Roosevelt entered his second term of office determined to rein in the "nine old men." To dilute the power of the conservatives on the Court, Roosevelt proposed a "court-packing" plan, which would authorize the President to nominate an individual justice for each sitting justice age 70.5 years or older. Criticizing the plan as an executive assault on an independent judiciary, the Senate voted it down in 1937. The court-packing plan was defeated, but what it represented—the willingness of a President to exert political control over an independent judiciary—was enough of a jolt to the two "swing" voters on the Court, who henceforth voted with the liberal bloc to uphold Roosevelt's economic initiatives. The saying thus developed that, although Roosevelt had "lost the battle," he "won the war."

Just one year after the court-packing plan failed, the Supreme Court signaled its new approach to constitutional issues. In an otherwise innocuous case, *U.S. v. Carolene Products Company* (1938)—and in a footnote, no less—the Court suggested that it would employ a "double standard" in constitutional interpretation (*U.S. v. Carolene Products Co.*

1938:footnote 4). In economic cases it would employ judicial restraint for the very reason offered by Justice Oliver Wendell Holmes in his *Lochner* dissenting opinion: the Constitution enshrines no particular economic theory because in a democracy citizens are free to decide for themselves what form their economy ought to take. A stricter constitutional standard would be applied, however, to cases involving: 1) rights in the Bill of Rights; 2) the integrity of the democratic process; and 3) "discrete and insular minorities" (see, for example, Greenhouse 1992a; Simon 1995; and Savage 1995). The Court's "double standard," as John Hart Ely and Michael J. Sandel have each elucidated from different vantage points, ushered in a new era of "proceduralist" constitutional interpretation in which the Court sought to define due process, personal liberty, and equality under the Fourteenth Amendment, while the Executive Branch was given relatively free rein to "create" programmatic rights to economic security (Ely 1980; Sandel 1984, 1995; see also Milkis 1993).

The Warren Court's "New Equal Protection"

The Warren Court introduced innovations in Equal Protection review that made it an attractive forum for federally funded Legal Services Program (LSP) lawyers and their indigent clients. The Equal Protection Clause states: ". . . nor [shall any state] deny to any person within its jurisdiction the equal protection of the laws." The original purpose of the Fourteenth Amendment was to protect the newly freed slaves following the Civil War; thus, it is not surprising that the Supreme Court came to identify race as a "suspect classification" under the Equal Protection Clause. Any law containing a racial classification aroused the Court's suspicion that discrimination lay behind it, and the Warren Court placed the burden on the states to prove otherwise.

Significantly, however, during the 1950s and 1960s the Court extended the scope of "suspect classification" to include economic class. In a series of decisions, the Warren Court ruled that classifications amounting to "wealth discrimination" violate the Fourteenth Amendment's Equal Protection Clause. For example, in 1956 the Court invalidated a trial transcript fee that Illinois required of all criminal defendants seeking appeals. Noting the corrosive effects of wealth disparities on criminal justice, Justice Hugo Black's plurality opinion in *Griffin v. Illinois* (1956:18–19) asserted: "There can be no equal justice where the kind of trial a man gets depends on the amount of money he has."[5] A decade later, the Court extended the wealth-discrimination doctrine to the electoral arena. In *Harper v. Virginia Board of Election Commissioners* (1966), Justice Douglas's majority opinion voided a Virginia poll tax as an "invidious discrimination" between rich and poor. LSP attorneys regarded the wealth-discrimination doctrine as a powerful tool to challenge laws and institutional practices that were biased against the poor.

The *Harper* ruling embodied two doctrinal innovations that delighted LSP lawyers. In addition to the wealth-discrimination doctrine, Justice Douglas's *Harper* opinion contained the "fundamental rights" doctrine. Citing an earlier Warren Court decision, Justice Douglas identified voting in a state election as a "fundamental right," even though there is no mention of it in the Constitution.[6] Since voting enables individuals to effectively exercise their constitutional rights, it is "fundamental" for Equal Protection purposes (*Reynolds v. Sims* 1964). The year preceding *Harper*, in *Griswold v. Connecticut* (1965), the Court had proclaimed the "right to privacy" as a "fundamental right."[7] Although not enumerated in the document, privacy was said to be an inextricable part of several rights listed in the Bill of Rights.

Legal Services lawyers regarded both the wealth-discrimination and the fundamental-rights doctrines—what came to be called the "new Equal Protection"—as powerful litigation weapons in the War on Poverty. If voting in a state election were a "fundamental right" under the Equal Protection Clause, LSP attorneys reasoned, surely subsistence must also be considered "fundamental." After all, how could the poor exercise their constitutional rights in any meaningful sense when they lacked the very means to survive? Wasn't welfare assistance even more elemental—more "fundamental"—than the right to vote in a state election? Weren't all rights secondary to a "right to life"? By 1966, LSP lawyers and leaders of a growing national welfare rights movement plotted a litigation strategy aimed at persuading the Warren Court to "constitutionalize" a right to welfare.[8]

The Failure of a Constitutional Right to Welfare

The Supreme Court's handling of *Shapiro v. Thompson* (1969) vividly illustrates both the promise and the limits of the Warren Court's understanding of the Equal Protection Clause. *Shapiro* consolidated three cases challenging durational residence requirements attached to AFDC programs in Connecticut, Pennsylvania, and Washington, D.C. In the 1967–68 term, the Court upheld the laws conditioning receipt of AFDC on one year of residence. Chief Justice Warren's majority opinion found that, however searing to the "conscience" the prospect of needy new-

comers being temporarily denied assistance, the justices' "best instincts" could not "be [their] guide" in determining whether the regulations violated either the Social Security Act or the Constitution. Since
the laws were an economic (budgetary) and not a rights matter, the
Chief Justice explained, the loose reasonable basis test was the appropriate one in this case. Finding no inconsistency between the one-year
residence rules and either federal statutory or constitutional law, the
Chief Justice's six-member majority upheld the state laws. The decision
was a blow to LSP attorneys, who had hoped the Court would accept
a constitutional right to welfare and thus invalidate the residence rules.

Lingering doubts about the case, however, led the Court to schedule
a re-argument of *Shapiro* in the 1968–69 term. Between terms, the LSP-
funded Center on Social Welfare Policy and Law, which was the litigation nerve center of the welfare rights movement located in New York
City, decided to exploit the justices' discomfort with the durational
residence requirements (Bussiere 1997:chap. 6). Executive Director Edward Sparer recruited Archibald Cox, the former Solicitor General with
extensive experience arguing cases in the Supreme Court, to re-argue
Shapiro on behalf of the AFDC recipients. Cox and Sparer agreed that
the Washington, D.C., and Connecticut LSP lawyers had pushed too
abruptly for a constitutional welfare right, leaving the Court little
choice but to uphold the residence requirements. A more modest approach was necessary.

Cox made two significant changes in the original LSP lawyers' arguments and set in motion a process of deliberation and negotiation
among the justices that resulted in Justice Brennan's successfully re-
drafting the opinion to build a coalition striking down the durational
residence requirements. First, instead of characterizing the durational
residence regulations as constituting a wealth discrimination on the
part of "the rich" against "the poor"—as the LSP attorneys and dissenting Justices Fortas and Douglas had done—Cox couched the discrimination as that of in-staters toward out-of-staters, of "neighbors"
toward "strangers."[9] In so doing, he neutralized the incendiary language of class peppered throughout the original dissenting opinions
circulated by Justices Fortas and Douglas. Explaining that the AFDC
mothers' precarious situation lay in their lack of political representation in a new state and not simply in their poverty, Cox likened the
unequal treatment of newcomers to racial discrimination. In short,
whereas Justices Douglas and Fortas had underscored the unequal effects of the residence laws on rich and poor, Cox stressed the Privileges
and Immunities component of the Fourteenth Amendment: the idea

that states are constitutionally prohibited from discriminating against citizen-strangers from other states.

Cox's second doctrinal revision of the LSP lawyers' original brief was to transform the claim of a constitutional right to *welfare* into a right to *interstate travel*. Although Cox himself believed state discrimination in relation to the "bare essentials of life" made the durational laws constitutionally vulnerable, he also grasped that a "much narrower ruling" was possible. The nagging legacy of the *Lochner*-era liberty of contract decisions—the lingering consensus that the Court has no authority to define the substantive content of economic justice—made Cox averse to hinging *Shapiro* on a "fundamental right" to welfare assistance. Therefore, he amplified the right to interstate travel, which the Court had acknowledged in precedents dating back to the 1940s, while conceding a constitutional basis for a right to welfare.

Cox's revision here was ingenious, for by making the right to interstate travel—a right established in precedents—the centerpiece of the case, he persuaded Justice Brennan to abandon Chief Justice Warren's majority coalition upholding the durational residence requirements.[10] In fact, Cox had wound up zeroing in on the very part of Justice Fortas's original draft dissent that Justice Brennan himself had found alluring. As the archival materials on *Shapiro* reveal, Justice Brennan had penciled in the word "compelling," for the "compelling interest" strand of the strict scrutiny test, in the margin where Justice Fortas had written that the durational residence laws erected a "material interference" with the poor's right to interstate travel."[11] The abridgment of the right to interstate travel enabled Justice Brennan to subject the durational residence laws to the rigorous strict scrutiny test. Perceiving *Shapiro* initially as raising the "novel" idea of a constitutional right to welfare during the first term the case was heard, Justice Brennan agreed with the Chief Justice that welfare programs appropriately triggered the deferential reasonable basis test. With Archibald Cox's dazzling presentation of *Shapiro* as essentially bearing on the right to interstate migration, however, Justice Brennan found middle ground between the dissenting opinions of Justices Douglas and Fortas, on one side, and the majority opinion of Chief Justice Warren and the rest of the Court, on the other. With this new casting of the case in hand, Justice Brennan then persuaded Justices Potter Stewart and Byron White to nullify the durational residence requirements used in welfare policy.

Particularly revealing of the Court's internal deliberations is Justice Stewart's final concurring opinion in *Shapiro*. He had criticized the majority in *Harper*, the poll tax case, for using the Equal Protection Clause to commit the same sins as the *Lochner* Court had, albeit in pursuit of liberal rather than conservative ends. Believing that reasonable people could disagree over the substance of electoral rules, Justice Stewart had lambasted the majority for remaking the Equal Protection Clause in the justices' own egalitarian image. Yet, in response to Chief Justice Warren's argument in *Shapiro*, Justice Stewart could now claim that when government "penalizes" the "virtually unconditional personal right" to interstate travel, it must do more than prove that a welfare regulation is not an irrational way to distribute scarce resources.

After *Shapiro* was reargued, then, a dramatic shift occurred. Chief Justice Warren's original majority coalition upholding the durational residence laws collapsed, and in its place Justice Brennan cobbled together a winning coalition by drawing on the essential points in Cox's brief. In what thus became the *Shapiro* majority opinion in 1969, Justice Brennan appropriated Cox's analogy between the durational residence laws and the Elizabethan Poor Law tradition. The modern welfare regulations, no less than the ancient ones, Cox had stated, were predicated on the hostility of "neighbors" toward impecunious "strangers."[12] In striking down the durational residence rules, Justice Brennan insisted, the Court was merely preventing states from denying formal equality under the law to outsiders who settled in their jurisdictions. And rather than reading "equality of results," or a substantive, need-based theory of economic justice, into the Fourteenth Amendment, Justice Brennan gave voice to the twin ideals of negative liberty and equal opportunity.

Archibald Cox, and then Justice Brennan, in fact, successfully revised *Shapiro* by anchoring the case not only in "well established case law" but also in familiar ideological language. They skillfully tethered the constitutional basis of the right to interstate travel to the powerful ideology of negative liberty and equal opportunity. For example, in his final opinion Justice Brennan stated that the claim asserted in *Shapiro* was not a right to welfare but the right to be free of burdensome government intervention: the "liberty . . . requir[ing] that all citizens be free to travel . . . uninhibited by statutes, rules, or regulations which unreasonably burden or restrict this movement" and the right "to leave an old and personally unsatisfying environment for new opportunities . . ." (629, 631–32). Justice Brennan showed how the right to interstate travel was embedded in the Privileges and Immunities Clause of the Fourteenth Amendment and its vision of the United States as a "national community" with open borders that bars state discrimination. The transcript of the oral argument in *Shapiro* also exhibits Cox deftly turning the right to interstate migration into a basic right of national citizenship, thus disarming those who had trivialized the right by asking whether citizens had a constitutional right to travel *internationally*.

In addition, Justice Brennan highlighted the Commerce Clause basis of the right to interstate migration, the longstanding interpretation being that labor must be unencumbered by state barriers in its search for a market. He agreed with the *amicus curiae* briefs submitted by the American Civil Liberties Union and the Center on Social Welfare Policy and Law (CSWPL), which characterized the durational residence requirements as an "invisible tariff" because "[t]he integrity of the free trade area intended by the framers of the Constitution in creating the commerce clause is seriously compromised by the 'barriers caused by restrictive residence or settlement requirements'. . ." (Kurland and Casper 1975:171). Intriguingly, the ACLU and CSWPL briefs read like an Adam Smith tract against England's Act of Settlement in 1662, which barred parish assistance to any indigent person except official parish residents who had established a legal settlement. (The Act of Settlement was a punitive measure aimed at curbing vagrancy.) By privileging the right to interstate travel over a collective obligation to meet the poor's needs, Justice Brennan made the "fundamental right" to interstate travel attractive not only to the swing voters, Justices Stewart and White, in the *Shapiro* case but also to a more conservative Burger Court. At the same time, by linking the states' durational residence requirements with the archaic Poor Laws of England, Justice Brennan was able to ascend the high moral ground without venturing into the much shakier ground of a constitutional right to welfare assistance. In sum, Justice Brennan's revisions of *Shapiro,* in transforming the controversial wealth-discrimination and right-to-welfare assertions into well-established constitutional principles, made good sense not only at the level of judicial doctrine but also at the level of political ideology (Bussiere 1994, 1997:chap. 7).

In voiding the durational residence laws, *Shapiro* was a victory for Cox, the Center on Social Welfare Policy and Law, and the welfare rights movement. Clearly buoyed by the ruling, the CSWPL, however, also felt ambivalently about the Court's ruling because it seemed so apparent that the justices would strictly scrutinize welfare laws only if they impinged on some "well-established" right.[13] CSWPL attorneys realized that Justice Brennan mustered a majority vote only by recasting *Shapiro* as implicating the right to interstate travel and the classical liberal values of equal opportunity (not equal results) and negative (not positive) freedom. To put the point another way, only by neutralizing the language of class and of economic entitlement did Justice Brennan secure a majority vote.[14] The consequence, however, was to strip *Shapiro* of any need-based theory of economic justice and of its downwardly redistributive policy implications.

The CSWPL lawyers had good reason to doubt whether the Warren Court would "constitutionalize" a right to welfare. The very next year after *Shapiro* the Court handed down *Dandridge v. Williams* (1970), upholding Maryland's regulation limiting AFDC monthly benefits to $250 per family regardless of family size.[15] In *Dandridge* the Court dispelled any doubt about whether the justices were somehow trying to smuggle a constitutional right to welfare into its *Shapiro* opinion. In response to the LSP attorneys' assertion of a "fundamental right" to procreation and to life, Justice Stewart's majority opinion revealed just how strongly the "double standard," arising out of the *Lochner* era, shaped the Court's perception of the case: "For here we deal with state regulation in the social and economic field, not affecting freedoms guaranteed by the Bill of Rights . . ." (*Dandridge* 1970:484).

Applying the lax reasonable basis test, Justice Stewart characterized the law as a rational way to allocate scarce resources. His opinion seemed haunted by *Lochner*. While acknowledging that "The Constitution may impose certain procedural safeguards" in the administration of AFDC, Justice Stewart stressed that the "intractable economic, social, and even philosophical problems presented by public welfare assistance programs are not the business of this Court" (*Dandridge* 1970: 484, 487). To admit welfare into the precious category of "fundamental rights," Justice Stewart believed, "would be far too reminiscent of an era when the Court [believed it had the] power to strike down laws because they may be unwise, improvident or out of harmony with a particular school of thought" (*Dandridge*, 484).

Justice Stewart was genuinely sensitive to the argument that *Dandridge*, unlike most economic cases, involved subsistence needs and not commercial interests; nevertheless, he could see no way around the "double standard." Echoing Chief Justice Warren and foreshadowing Chief Justice Rehnquist, Justice Stewart's opinion in *Dandridge* equated the idea of a constitutional right to welfare with "right instincts," "natural sympathy," and ultimately pure sentiment unattached to sound judicial reason.

Drawing on the "new institutionalism" perspective, one sees that the intellectual or ideological structure of the Warren Court's "new Equal Protection" doctrines contained the following mutually reinforcing attributes: the distinctions between procedural and substantive economic justice,[16] human needs and individual rights, and negative and positive rights / freedom, as well as the dichotomy between the sphere of economics and the sphere of rights. By fortifying a cognitive wall separating rights from economics, the decision in *Dandridge* had the effect of divorcing the *content* of rights from the *capacity* to exercise them. *Dandridge* thus exposed the frailty of the Warren Court's "new Equal Protection" doctrines in wrestling with the "paradox of poverty amidst plenty."

Statutory Welfare Rights in the Warren and Early Burger Courts

The Warren Court disappointed AFDC mothers looking for a safe haven from hostile political forces through the establishment of constitutional welfare rights. Nevertheless, it would be a mistake to assume that *Dandridge* represented the Court's definitive position on all claims made by welfare recipients. For, in treating welfare as a *statutory entitlement* rather than a mere form of charity, the Court was able to use the Fourteenth Amendment to require the states to adhere to certain procedural standards in the administration of AFDC. Furthermore, as R. Shep Melnick persuasively argues, through statutory interpretations the Warren and Burger Courts invalidated a whole host of state eligibility restrictions on AFDC (Melnick 1994). In fact, at about the same time Chief Justice Warren stated that moral conscience alone was insufficient to justify *constitutional* welfare rights, he established a *statutory* principle which privileged children's needs over the other goals of state welfare programs.

In *King v. Smith* (1968), Chief Justice Warren's unanimous opinion for the Court declared Alabama's notorious substitute-father rule a violation of the federal Social Security Act of 1935.[17] Used in nineteen states at the time the litigation was initiated in 1966, the substitute-father and man-in-the-house rules allowed state authorities to deny AFDC to women who were even suspected of living with a man out of wedlock. Alabama defended its regulation on both monetary and moral grounds, contending that a woman who is presumed to be living with a man is likely to be receiving some sort of financial support from him and, in any event, is violating moral standards by having sexual relations outside of wedlock. In practice the regulation was often a way for states to deny benefits to black women, who were perceived as promiscuous and as irresponsible mothers (L. Gordon 1994:292). For example, at a dinner the night before the oral argument before the Supreme Court, the Alabama attorney remarked to the attorney representing the welfare recipients: "Good Alabama citizens don't think there should be sex outside of its 'proper' domicile—the wedded couple. You know that they [Negroes] aren't like us" (quoted in Garbus 1971:189).

Despite evidence of racial discrimination in Alabama's administration of AFDC, Chief Justice Warren found it unnecessary to reach the constitutional issue since the substitute-father rule violated statutory law. Although back in 1935 Congress accepted that welfare regulations properly promoted "moral" purposes (e.g., anti-fornication), the Congress of the late 1960s, the Chief Justice asserted, had a more "enlightened" view of government assistance. The overriding intent of AFDC, according to Chief Justice Warren, was to meet the needs of single mothers and their impoverished dependent children and not to promote morality among the mothers themselves. He also maintained that any man who is not legally obligated to support a woman's child(ren) cannot be presumed to be supporting her or her offspring and hence cannot have his income taken into account in the calculation of the AFDC mother's welfare grant. To do otherwise, the Chief Justice asserted, would be to adopt a definition of "parent" that Congress had not meant in the Social Security Act. And yet, as Melnick points out, the legislative history was not at all clear on Congress' meaning of "parent"; nor was the Court's characterization of Congress' attitude toward welfare recipients as being "enlightened" (nonpunitive) convincing (1994:86–88). Congress, after all, had just passed amendments to AFDC penalizing states that failed to decrease illegitimate births and adding a work requirement. Nevertheless, in identifying the key purpose of AFDC as serving children's needs and questioning state regulations aimed at controlling AFDC mothers' behavior, the Warren Court opened the door for statutory challenges to state welfare regulations.

Chief Justice Burger had already replaced Earl Warren by the time the Court issued another unanimous opinion expanding on the liberal statutory interpretation of AFDC offered in *King*. In *Townsend v. Swank*, in 1971, Justice Brennan offered an interpretation of *King* that led the lower federal courts to issue broad rulings declaring state welfare regulations inconsistent with the Social Security Act. In the context of a fairly narrow case involving AFDC coverage for dependents between the ages of 18 and 21 who were enrolled in school, the Court held that unless Congress explicitly authorized in the Social Security Act particular restrictions on AFDC, the states were prohibited from enacting them to limit coverage. The significance of that interpretation of the Social Security Act in *Townsend* was to deprive the states of sub-

stantial discretion in the administration of AFDC. At the time the Social
Security Act was enacted, the states were perceived as the main locus
of power over welfare programs for the poor; therefore, few national
standards were written into the law. Franklin Roosevelt himself supported a large state role in AFDC, and the impressive power of Southern Democrats in Congress prevented efforts by liberal legislators to
"federalize" the program by creating more uniform national standards.
But, as in *King*, the Court put a more liberal gloss on the AFDC program
than the legislation itself (its text and history) had actually warranted.

The doctrinal principle underlying *King* and *Townsend* was to make
children's *needs* the main test of whether welfare regulations were (in)-
consistent with the Social Security Act. The institutional consequence,
at least with respect to some kinds of welfare regulations, was to shift
power from the states to the national government.

The Supreme Court's Retreat from Statutory Welfare Rights

The Burger Court, although more solicitous of state government power
than the Warren Court ever was (the Warren Court tended to equate
"states' rights" with local prejudice), built on the Warren Court's *King*
ruling and on its own decision in *Townsend* to strike down state eligibility restrictions on AFDC (Melnick 1994:93–94). Many lower courts followed suit and were even more activist than the Supreme Court in
striking down state regulations on statutory grounds (*ibid.*, 97). Yet,
the Burger Court was inconsistent; in some cases, especially those involving standards of need and work programs, the Court was much
more deferential to the states than to AFDC recipients' claims. And
by the mid-1970s the Burger Court began to scale back on the broad
interpretation of the Social Security Act underlying *King*. The overall
unpredictability and confusion of the Burger Court decisions, however,
had the effect until the mid- to late 1980s of giving more leverage to the
lower federal courts, which were predominantly liberal until President
Ronald Reagan was able to appoint approximately 60 percent of the
federal court bench. As such, deference to principles of federalism was
not uniform throughout the federal court system; there were still jurisdictions where AFDC mothers could count on prevailing.

Just as the Burger Court by the late 1970s deferred ever more to state
authority, the justices also increasingly began to rule in favor of Executive Branch agencies, based on their policy expertise. Interestingly, in
ceding authority over the content of welfare policy to administrative
agencies, the Burger and Rehnquist Courts behaved more like the New

Deal Court than the Warren Court had. For, after President Franklin
Roosevelt had threatened to pack the Court, the justices became quite
acquiescent to the Roosevelt Administration. Many of the Legal Realists, who put a premium on the policy knowledge and experience of
administrative experts, actually staffed the executive agencies under
Roosevelt.

By the 1960s, however, the Warren Court was much less willing to
bow to administrative authority. Believing that bureaucrats too often
placed efficiency or utilitarian ends ahead of individual rights or fair
treatment, the Supreme Court began to scrutinize bureaucratic rules
and regulations. Following the ideas of Charles Reich, the influential
legal scholar, the Warren Court demanded that government benefits,
including welfare assistance, be treated as akin to old "property" and
be administered in accordance with the standards of due process of
law (Reich 1965). Thus, when the Burger and Rehnquist Courts gave
pride of place to administrative agencies during the 1980s, the consequence was to serve the conservative policy goals of the Reagan presidency (Melnick 1994:247).

The Rehnquist Court's concern about protecting state authority from
encroachments from the federal government is well known. William
Rehnquist, as an associate justice, was the author of *National League of
Cities v. Usery* (1976), an opinion that gave voice to the idea of the states'
Tenth Amendment police powers serving as a substantive limit on
Congress's commerce power.[18] One of the key swing voters in such
explosive areas as abortion rights has been Sandra Day O'Connor, a
champion of state government power.[19] Perhaps most vividly, in the
1995 term the Court surprised legal commentators by striking down a
gun-free buffer zone in the environs of a school, contending that the
law was not really of a commercial nature and thus exceeded the
bounds of the Commerce Clause and encroached upon the states' police powers.

It is beyond the scope of this chapter to determine whether the
Burger and Rehnquist Courts' approaches to welfare are best explained
by doctrinal factors, i.e., as an institutionalist commitment to federalism and separation of powers principles, or by a politically conservative understanding of poverty. Whatever the case, just as the Warren
Court's fidelity to the double standard did not guarantee liberal outcomes on welfare policy, a judicial commitment to "states' rights" or
separation of powers hardly guarantees conservative outcomes. The
actual outcomes, after all, depend on the political occupants of the presidency, Congress, state houses, and governors' mansions.

What is clear, however, is that the tenacity of the Rehnquist Court's loyalty to federalism and separation of powers doctrines will be seriously tested in the remaining years of the twentieth century, as the new welfare law is implemented throughout the nation. As indicated at the outset of this chapter, the new welfare law gives considerable flexibility to the states to structure their programs in ways they see fit. In some states, such autonomy may mean drastic cutbacks and severe penalties imposed on welfare recipients, but in other states it could mean more liberal policies. In fact, New York City's *Republican* mayor, Rudolph Giuliani, who is not known as an advocate of welfare recipients, has challenged on constitutional grounds the new welfare law's restrictions on aid to legal immigrants. Furthermore, if states' welfare-to-work programs falter because businesses prove resistant to hiring former welfare recipients, state governments could conceivably crack the whip and impose expectations that might arouse business opposition. In an ironic twist on the *Lochner* era, businesses might seek haven in the (currently) predominantly conservative federal courts by challenging state programs on constitutional and (federal) statutory grounds. Such challenges, at least in the current Supreme Court, would pit institutionalist principles or doctrines, such as judicial deference to state governments and to federal administrative agencies, against *laissez-faire*–minded businesses seeking relief from government intervention. And in cases involving the expertise of administrative agencies, it is possible that the Rehnquist Court's usual deference would signify more liberal than conservative policy goals since, at least as of this writing, the Clinton Administration speaks of softening the new welfare law (Pear 1996). If the administration cannot do so legislatively, it may try to do so through the use of bureaucratic power (*ibid.*).

Conclusion

Focusing on the Warren Court, this chapter has used the insights of the "new institutionalism" literature to show the importance of legal doctrines and the process of deliberation/negotiation in judicial decision-making. From the ideological composition of the Warren Court, one would have predicted it to have "constitutionalized" a right to welfare. Instead, under the leadership of the Chief Justice himself and then of the crucial swing voters, Justices Potter Stewart and Byron White, the Court ultimately treated a "right to live" in the same way that the Rehnquist Court had treated that claim in the *DeShaney* case— as an expression of pure sentiment and not sound judicial doctrine.

Only when the "well-established" constitutional right to interstate migration became a viable doctrinal route did Justice Brennan attract enough justices to invalidate the durational residence requirements.

The importance of the Warren Court's generous reading of the Social Security Act, which served as the basis for more liberal statutory interpretations into a more conservative Burger Court era, cannot be overlooked. Once again, based on political ideology alone, one would not have predicted the Burger Court to have rendered unanimous decisions that so clearly favored welfare recipients. But the force of precedent and the nature of analogical reasoning (extending one principle to a new fact situation) are institutional attributes of judicial decisionmaking that are too powerful to be ignored. It remains to be seen whether, and to what extent, doctrinal principles will exert their force over political ideology on the Rehnquist Court in the coming litigation over the new welfare law.

Notes

1. *DeShaney v. Winnebago County Dept. of Social Services* (1989). The two Warren Court precedents were *Goldberg v. Kelly* (1970) and *Dandridge v. Williams* (1970), both explained in the chapter (for *Goldberg*, see note 16).

2. By "positive liberties" the Court meant the individual's right to government assistance so as to guarantee life or liberty. By "negative liberties" the Court meant the individual's right to be free of arbitrary government intervention in his or her life.

3. Draft Opinion of the Court, *Shapiro v. Thompson*, June 3, 1968. Filed in the Earl Warren Papers, container number 566, Library of Congress. *Shapiro*, which will be dealt with later in the chapter, was reargued the following year, and, unable to maintain a majority coalition in urging the statute to be upheld, Chief Justice Warren ultimately dissented. In his official opinion rendered in 1969, he omitted the passage quoted in the text.

4. At least on the academic left, the interest in legal ideology has gradually shifted from a Marxist to a critical-legal, and most recently to a postmodern understanding. In the 1970s and 1980s, critical-legal scholars began to critique traditional Marxist notions of legal ideology, posited as a mere "superstructure" reflecting (and rationalizing) the interests of a ruling class (Gordon 1984). Postmodern theory has pushed the critical-legal critique further. Legal ideology, although an important dimension of understanding power relations, is said to be "indeterminate" because of the contradictory aims and purposes underlying basic norms of legal justice.

5. In *Douglas v. California* (1963), the Court invoked the wealth-discrimination doctrine once again, overturning a California law that required defendants to pay a fee for appellate review. See also the famous decision in *Gideon v. Wainwright* (1963), in which the Court ruled that states must pay for legal counsel for indigent criminal defendants in noncapital felony cases (and not just death-penalty cases).

6. See *Reynolds v. Sims* (1964), and precedents cited therein.

7. Specifically, the Court ruled that the Connecticut birth control law infringed on marital privacy.

8. For a meticulously researched and elegantly written account of the relationship between LSP attorneys and the welfare-rights movement, see Davis 1993. Within the legal academy, meanwhile, Frank I. Michelman of Harvard Law School began to formulate a theory of constitutional welfare rights that defined the Equal Protection Clause as guaranteeing the poor "minimum protection" to secure their basic needs. Although not influential on the Supreme Court, Michelman's work has been influential among law professors.

9. Transcript of the Oral Argument, reprinted in Kurland and Casper, eds. (1975:387).

10. Here Justice Brennan cited *U.S. v. Guest* (1966), and *Edwards v. California* (1941).

11. See Justice Fortas's draft dissent and accompanying memoranda filed in the Earl Warren Papers, the Library of Congress. The William Brennan Papers, housed in the Library of Congress and New York University, also contain memoranda, draft opinions, and other materials relied upon here.

12. Since Chief Justice Warren had defended the California law overturned in *Edwards v. California* in 1941 as a legitimate exercise of the states' police power and not a violation of the right to interstate travel implicit in the Commerce Clause, it is not altogether surprising that he continued to believe in the constitutionality of the durational residence requirements. Chief Justice Warren was not, however, insensitive to the problem of pervasive negative stereotypes of the poor. In fact, he was the author of the Court's opinion in *King v. Smith* (1968), which revealed an awareness of disparaging attitudes toward welfare recipients. But perhaps having once been a governor, he might have been more nervous than the other liberals on the Court about judges rendering decisions that had a direct and overt impact on the budgetary process.

13. Interview with Henry Freedman, Executive Director, Center on Social Welfare Policy and Law and then a staff attorney at the Center.

14. I do not suggest that Justice Brennan's doctrinal revisions and ideological recasting of *Shapiro* were purely instrumental moves on his part in order to secure a majority vote. That he himself was initially uncomfortable with the LSP lawyers' claim of a constitutional "right to live" as a kind of liberal reincarnation of *Lochner's* "liberty of contract," despite his own personal and political sympathy for the AFDC mothers, suggests, if anything, the force of doctrinal categories in shaping the justices' perception of cases. The same can be said for Chief Justice Warren and Justice Harlan. Clearly, the Chief Justice was "troubled" by the poor's impoverished circumstances, but he saw no doctrinal vehicle for asserting a constitutional right to welfare. Conversely, although perceiving the right to interstate travel as being of the essence of the liberty protected by the Fourteenth Amendment, Justice Harlan did not see the durational residence requirements as creating the kind of barrier to the exercise of that right that Justices Brennan, Stewart, and White ultimately did in the 1968–69 term.

15. The fact that Chief Justice Burger had already replaced Chief Justice Warren by the time *Dandridge* reached the Court was inconsequential, since the latter, like the former, had rejected the idea of a constitutional right to welfare. The outcome in *Dandridge* was unaffected by President Nixon's appointment

of Warren Burger and Justice Fortas's resignation from the Court because of cries of financial impropriety.

16. See, for example, the Court's ruling in *Goldberg v. Kelly* (1970), two weeks prior to the announcement of *Dandridge*. In *Goldberg* the Court ruled that the Fourteenth Amendment requires states to provide AFDC recipients with a "fair hearing" prior to any termination of benefits. The Court emphasized in *Goldberg* that AFDC is a *statutory* right. The different outcomes in the two cases hinged on three of the nine justices distinguishing between the two on grounds that *Goldberg* was a proceduralist decision while *Dandridge* raised substantive issues of distributive justice.

17. That is, he claimed the rule was a violation of Title IV of the Act, involving AFDC.

18. *Usery* was overturned by *Garcia v. San Antonio Metropolitan Transit Authority* (1985). *Usery* struck down while *Garcia* upheld the extension of provisions of the Fair Labor Standards Act to municipal employees.

19. For an eloquent statement of Justice O'Connor's philosophy of federalism, see her dissenting opinion in *Garcia*.

8

Institutional Norms and Supreme Court Decision-Making: The Rehnquist Court on Privacy and Religion

Ronald Kahn

Introduction

Supreme Court decision-making can be viewed as instrumental or constitutive. While drawing on quite disparate explanations, all instrumental approaches reject constitutional principles, institutional norms, and legal concepts, such as the rule of law, as significant to Supreme Court decision-making. They are united in a central premise, really a heuristic device, that justices draw upon institutional norms, precedent, constitutional principles, and theories of interpretation only to justify preconceived policy preferences. Two prominent instrumental approaches center on the individual justice. One, the attitudinal approach,[1] argues that justices decide cases on the basis of their personal policy preferences; the other, the strategic approach, argues that justices are rational actors whose decisions reflect a desire to promote policy preferences in a way that is attentive to the competitive preferences of their colleagues and other policy makers.[2] A second major set of instrumental approaches centers on external influences on the Court—proceeding on such assumptions as that the Court follows election returns,[3] responds to interest group pressures,[4] or responds to other political events (but see Clayton's essay in this volume).[5]

By contrast, the constitutive approach to Supreme Court decision-making is based on the premise that justices' decisions are "constituted" of a distinctive set of institutional norms and customs, including legal principles and theories.[6] It assumes that members of the Supreme Court believe that they are required to act in accordance with particular institutional and legal expectations and responsibilities. Thus, the constitutive approach is consistent with the assumptions about institutional behavior held by the new wave of "historical institutional" schol-

ars who seek to meld the study of politics and history. They argue that
institutions both structure one's ability to act on a set of beliefs that
are external to the institution and are a source of distinctive political
purposes, goals, and preferences.[7] Therefore, the constitutive approach
assumes that justices make their decisions in an institutional context
which informs the choices that they make. It assumes that the Court's
institutional norms and commitments are important for the maintenance of constitutional principles and Court decision-making. Moreover, justices must be principled in their decision-making process if
they are to have the continued respect of their colleagues, the wider
interpretive community, citizens, and leaders. Justices must not only
convince us that a specific case decision is wise, but also that the principles upon which they based their decision, and upon which future
cases should be based, are appropriate.

There are distinctive institutional purposes, preferences, or discrete
and discernible habits of thought that are considered appropriate for
members of the Supreme Court.[8] One of the basic foundations of our
constitutional thought is a vision of political power concerned with
protecting individual rights and with ensuring all citizens the right to
participate in our political process. Thus, Supreme Court decisions are
constituted through a respect for and application of what I shall call
rights and polity (or institutional) principles.[9] Rights principles are defined as beliefs about legally enforceable claims for individual powers,
privileges, or immunities guaranteed under the Constitution, statutes,
and laws. Rights can also be described as "cocoons" that shield citizens
from government intrusion and respect individual choice.

Polity principles are deeply held ideas about the role, nature, and
structure of political institutions and courts and where to locate
decision-making, especially on questions of constitutional significance.
They involve beliefs about whether courts or electorally accountable
political institutions are the more appropriate forum for decisions on
constitutional issues. The constitutive approach to Supreme Court
decision-making helps us understand how institutional and rights
principles interact to form the basis of a justice's decision in a particular
case and doctrinal area, as well as his general approach to constitutional questions across doctrinal areas. In contrast to instrumental approaches, the constitutive approach assumes that a particular justice's
conceptions of institutional and rights principles are not merely a justification of policy preferences. Rather, they inform a justice's decisions
and become quite important as they evolve over the course of her years
on the Court as she develops a coherent approach to constitutional

questions. A justice does not think only in terms of specific case outcomes, but must consider the implications of how issues are formulated in each decision in terms of prior and future definitions of institutional and rights principles.

I will analyze landmark privacy and religion cases from the 1990s to ask whether the Rehnquist Court (1986–present) continues to be constitutive in its decision-making. As with the Warren Court (1953–69) and Burger Court (1969–86) before it, Rehnquist Court justices do not follow election returns, the policies of the presidents who appointed them, or even personal policy wants, as my evidence will show. I find that institutional norms, including the following of precedent, or *stare decisis;* respect for the difference between law and politics; and concerns for institutional legitimacy inform Court decision-making in important ways.[10] The doctrinal areas of privacy (abortion choice and sexual intimacy) and religion were chosen for study here because they have generated very strong views by the Presidents who nominated Rehnquist Court justices; thus they present a good test of whether justices act instrumentally or constitutively. The Rehnquist Court, like the Warren and Burger Courts, is often misunderstood by commentators who focus exclusively on the policy views of the justices or on the influence of Presidents and politics on Court decision-making. Also like its predecessors, this Court would disappoint instrumental scholars.[11]

Rights of Privacy and Abortion Choice

The key Rehnquist Court right of abortion choice case, *Planned Parenthood of S.E. Pennsylvania v. Casey,* was not decided until 1992. By 1991, there were six Reagan-Bush appointees on the Supreme Court: Sandra Day O'Connor (1981); William H. Rehnquist as Chief Justice (1986); Antonin Scalia (1986); Anthony Kennedy (1988); David Souter (1990); and Clarence Thomas (1991). Before the 1991–92 term, it was not clear what direction the Rehnquist Court would take in crucial areas such as the right of privacy and abortion choice and freedom of religion. Would the Rehnquist Court, like the Warren and Burger Court eras before it, be constitutive in its decision-making; or would it change the pattern, by following election returns; disregarding important legal norms, such as *stare decisis;* and failing to protect the institutional needs of the Court?

At the core of a constitutive approach to Supreme Court decision-making are the following six major premises: First, the Court does not follow elections or politics, but views itself as autonomous from direct and indirect political pressure. Second, justices do not follow personal policy wants. Third, respect for precedent and principled decision-making are central to Supreme Court decision-making. Fourth, to follow precedent and other institutional norms rather than politics and personal policy wants is an important means with which to achieve Court legitimacy. Fifth, to sustain its legitimacy and support for its principles, the Supreme Court must interpret principles and precedents in light of what they mean as applied in a changing society. And sixth, a constitutive decision-making process requires that justices weigh institutional and rights principles, with the final decision being a reflection of the application of both principles. We shall take up each of these premises in order.

THE SUPREME COURT, PRESIDENTS, AND ELECTION RETURNS

If justices on the Rehnquist Court are simply instrumental in their decision-making, what might we expect from this Court? Pushed by the religious right, the Reagan-Bush Administrations sought to end the right of abortion choice, except where the life of the mother is threatened. They also opposed the expansion of various rights of sexual intimacy. Nevertheless, in the face of such pressure, the Rehnquist Court refused to reject the basic holdings of *Roe*, that a woman has a right to abortion choice prior to viability. Rehnquist Court justices refused to vote their personal policy preferences on abortion, or those of the Presidents who appointed them, even in the face of the Reagan-Bush Administrations' long-term, spirited attack on the right of abortion choice, as evidenced by their five attempts over a decade to overturn *Roe*.

Justices O'Connor, Souter, and Kennedy—three Reagan-Bush appointees—refused to overturn *Roe*. Their joint opinion in *Casey* begins with a rebuke of the Reagan-Bush administrations' efforts to overturn the right of abortion choice: "Liberty finds no refuge in a jurisprudence of doubt. Yet, 19 years after our holding that the Constitution protects a woman's right to terminate her pregnancy in its early stages, that definition of liberty is still questioned. Joining the respondents as *amicus curiae*, the United States, as it has done in five other cases in the last decade, again asks us to overrule *Roe*" (*Planned Parenthood of S.E. Pennsylvania v. Casey* 1992:844).

In the *Casey* decision, Justices O'Connor, Kennedy, and Souter explain the importance of institutional rules such as the need to follow precedent and to view the Supreme Court as an institution that follows the rule of law and not simply politics. They write:

The Court must take care to speak and act in ways that allow people to accept its decisions on the terms the Court claims for them, as grounded truly in principle, not as compromises with social and political pressures having, as such, no bearing on the principled choices that the Court is obliged to make. . . . A later decision overruling the first [would be viewed as] a surrender to political pressure, and an unjustified repudiation of the principle on which the Court staked its authority in the first instance (865–66).

Casey shows three Reagan-Bush appointees committed to the polity principle of maintaining the Court's autonomy from politics, even though to do so they must reject the Reagan-Bush Administrations' and their own, views on abortion. O'Connor, Souter, and Kennedy argue that the Court, unlike political branches, cannot go back to the people on election day for a renewal of the people's faith in its principles. They write, "If the Court's legitimacy should be undermined, so would the country be in its very ability to see itself through its constitutional ideals" (868). Justice Blackmun, in a opinion that concurs and dissents in part, agrees: "While there is much to be praised about our democracy, our country, since its founding, has recognized that there are certain fundamental liberties that are not to be left to the whims of an election. A woman's right to reproductive choice is one of those fundamental liberties. Accordingly, that liberty need not seek refuge at the ballot box" (943).

The Rehnquist Court must remain a counter-majoritarian institution: It must uphold precedent, the rule of law, and its own legitimacy. It could have chosen not to confront the constitutionality of abortion choice head-on; it could have overturned *Roe v. Wade* (1973), following the wishes of Presidents Reagan and Bush, who appointed most of the justices. If the Court had done so, it would have confirmed the views of instrumentalists who emphasize that the Court is willing to listen to invitations from elected officials. The point is not that this position (the plurality's and Blackmun's) is the only one consistent with a commitment to institutional values; the dissenters may also have acted on the basis of similar commitments. Rather, the more limited point is that these justices did not act as if they were succumbing to conventional partisan pressures.

Principles, Not Personal Policy Preferences, Followed

As justices do not follow elections returns, they do not simply follow personal policy preferences. In the joint opinion in *Casey*, O'Connor,

Kennedy, and Souter wrote, "Some of us as individuals find abortion offensive to our most basic principles of morality, but that cannot control our decision. Our obligation is to define the liberty of all, not to mandate our own moral code" (*Planned Parenthood of S.E. Pennsylvania v. Casey* 1992:850).

This upholding of principles was not new to the Supreme Court: evidence that institutional norms, conceptions of rights, and theories of constitutional interpretation, not personal policy preferences or those of appointing Presidents, influence decision-making can be seen earlier in *Griswold v. Connecticut* (1965). In this case the Warren Court found there is a right of privacy in the Constitution that permits married persons to use contraceptives. Dissenting Justices Stewart and Black called the Connecticut anti-contraception law "uncommonly silly" but found it constitutional because they viewed the role of a justice as not to determine whether a law is "unwise or even asinine," but rather whether "it violates the United States Constitution" (*Griswold v. Connecticut* 1965:527). Moreover, in support of the institutional norm of following precedent, Justice Stewart did not dissent in *Eisenstadt v. Baird* (1972), a Burger Court case which declared unconstitutional a state law prohibiting the distribution of contraceptives to unmarried persons. Nor did he dissent in *Roe v. Wade* (1973), the Burger Court case which established the right of abortion choice, even though he had dissented in *Griswold*. One cannot say that personal preferences never enter the calculations; the evidence of attitudinalists makes clear that judicial votes can be quite consistent with what we would expect if we assumed that judges voted on the basis of their political ideologies. However, a new institutional gloss helps us understand some of the circumstances under which judges might subordinate their preferences in order to serve institutional goals and purposes.

The Importance of Precedents

The joint opinion in *Casey* emphasizes that a continuing commitment to *stare decisis* requires a reaffirmation of *Roe*. It states, "The obligation to follow precedent begins with necessity, and a contrary necessity marks its outer limit" (*Planned Parenthood of S.E. Pennsylvania v. Casey* 1992:854). Justices O'Connor, Souter, and Kennedy crafted an important new test in *Casey* to determine when the Court should overturn past decisions. The joint opinion states that decisions will be overruled only if they 1) prove unworkable in practice, 2) cause inequities in effect, 3) damage social stability, 4) are abandoned by society, or 5) rely on key fact assumptions that have changed. Applying this test to *Roe v. Wade*, the plurality finds that it meets none of the conditions (855–61).

In a constitutive decision-making process, the Supreme Court applies polity and rights principles and precedent in light of the nation's reliance that a rule of law will prevail. For example, the *Casey* Court, in deciding whether to overturn *Roe*, considers the reliance people have placed in the rule of law in *Roe* and whether overturning the rule of law in *Roe* would create special hardships. They also consider the citizens' reliance on the rule of law in light of whether related principles of law have developed, making the law under question "a remnant of abandoned doctrine" (855). They ask whether facts have so changed or come to be seen so differently, as to have robbed the old rule of significant application or justification . . . whether *Roe's* central rule has been found unworkable, whether the rule's limitation on state power could be removed without serious inequity to those who have relied upon it or significant damage to the stability of the society . . . whether the law's "growth in the intervening years has left *Roe's* central rule a doctrinal anachronism discounted by society . . . [and] whether *Roe's* premises of fact have so far changed in the ensuing two decades as to render the central holding somehow irrelevant or unjustifiable in dealing with the issue addressed (855–56). They find none of the above conditions that might warrant overturning precedent.

The Court also considers new doctrine. They find that the continuation of *Roe's* essential holdings is supported "not only as an exemplar of *Griswold* liberty but as a rule (whether or not mistaken) of personal autonomy and bodily integrity, with doctrinal affinity to cases recognizing limits on governmental power to mandate medical treatment or to bar its rejection" (*Planned Parenthood of S.E. Pennsylvania v. Casey* 1992:857). In stating this the Court refers to *Cruzan v. Director, Missouri Dept. Of Health*, a 1990 right-to-die case. Moreover, the Court views prior abortion rights cases, including *Akron v. Akron Center for Reproductive Health* (1983), *Thornburgh v. American College of Obstetricians and Gynecologists* (1986), and *Webster v. Reproductive Health Services* (1989), as either reaffirming *Roe* or as declining "to address the constitutional validity of the central holding of *Roe*" (*Planned Parenthood of S.E. Pennsylvania v. Casey* 1992:858). Because the relationship of the right of abortion choice to society's reliance on the basic values of liberty and privacy has grown stronger and has been reinforced by events in the lives of women since the establishment of the right of abortion with *Roe* in 1973, the Court finds that the essential holdings of *Roe* must be retained.

To do otherwise in 1992 would seriously undermine the legitimacy of the Supreme Court and the rule of law itself, they asserted.

Institutional Legitimacy

The joint opinion makes frequent mention of the danger to the Court's legitimacy that would come from overturning *Roe:* "To overrule under fire in the absence of the most compelling reason to reexamine a watershed decision would subvert the Court's legitimacy beyond any serious question" (*Planned Parenthood of S.E. Pennsylvania v. Casey* 1992:867). Finally, Blackmun's concurring opinion seems to offer a clear rebuke to the Reagan-Bush Administrations and to the instrumental election-returns theories of Dahl and Rosenberg. Blackmun writes, "The Court's reaffirmation of *Roe's* central holding is also based on the force of *stare decisis.* . . . What has happened today should serve as a model for future Justices and a warning to all who have tried to turn this Court into yet another political branch" (924).

One cannot claim that precedent always controls in a straightforward way; there is extensive evidence that judges do not always mindlessly follow a clear precedent even in those rare circumstances when cases are covered by precedent (Segal and Spaeth 1996). However, *Casey* demonstrates that there are times, for reasons having to do with the Court's institutional position in the political system and the justices' conceptions of their professional obligations, when a commitment to precedent takes priority over a more instrumental approach to the law, and the new institutionalist perspective helps draw attention to these circumstances.

Personhood, Not Privacy

As might be expected, given what we know of the Warren and Burger Courts, in a constitutive decision-making process, in which precedents, new constitutional theories, and social realities are considered, even moderate and conservative Courts can be forums for social change and new rights. A commitment to institutional principles and constitutive decision-making guided all but the most originalist of justices. It led the Court not only to reaffirm *Roe's* central holding, but also to strengthen the doctrinal basis of the right of abortion choice by viewing the right of abortion choice as a right of personhood, not simply a right of privacy. In the explication of liberty interests in the *Casey* decision, the Court goes beyond *Griswold's* and *Roe's* flat and untextured statement of the concept of privacy. There is a more affirmative right of "personhood" in *Casey*. The definition of liberty interests behind the right of abortion choice is far more detailed and filigreed than in *Roe*. The Rehnquist Court notes:

> These matters [personal decisions relating to marriage, procreation, contraception, family relationships, child rearing, and education], involving the most intimate and personal choices a person may make in a lifetime, choices central to personal dignity and autonomy, are central to the liberty protected by the Fourteenth Amendment. At the heart of liberty is the right to define one's own concept of existence, of meaning, of the universe, and of the mystery of human life. Beliefs about these matters could not define the attributes of personhood were they formed under compulsion of the State (*Planned Parenthood of S.E. Pennsylvania v. Casey* 1992:851).

In placing greater emphasis on physical autonomy as a rights value, the Court emphasizes that at stake here are "the most intimate and personal choices a person may make in a lifetime, choices central to personal dignity and autonomy" (*ibid.*).

Most important, the joint opinion acknowledges for the first time that women's equality in self-definition of their personhood is a component of the right of abortion choice. In so doing, it emphasizes that the right of self-definition by a woman is more important than the majoritarian expectations of a particular state or the nation as a whole. The joint opinion reads: "The liberty of the woman is at stake in a sense unique to the human condition, and so, unique to the law. . . . Her suffering is too intimate and personal for the State to insist, without more, upon its own vision of the woman's role, however dominant that vision has been in the course of our history and culture" (852).

The plurality attempts to answer scholarly criticisms of the concept of privacy by grounding it in a more tangible framework of physical autonomy, personal choice, and equality. Therefore, *Casey* is more than a confirmation of the central premise of *Roe v. Wade*. When read in light of subsequent landmark cases, it is a clear statement that Justices Souter, O'Connor, and most surprisingly Kennedy, have decided to make constitutional choices based on precedent, considered in light of developments in constitutional scholarship and the changing complexities of life in the United States.

Casey demonstrates that rights principles are not static; rather, they continue to evolve as our nation changes. The plurality gives greater

voice to a new right of personhood that complements, and even en-
larges, the right of privacy developed in *Griswold v. Connecticut* (1965),
Eisenstadt v. Baird (1972), and *Roe* (1973). In important ways, this shift
in emphasis to a right of personhood reflects the Supreme Court's continuing commitment to the rule of law and to institutional values that
are critical of majoritarian politics. It demonstrates that the Court is
innovative and responsive to new ideas from the interpretive community of constitutional scholars, jurists, journalists, and the informed
public.

CONSTITUTIVE DECISION-MAKING: WEIGHING INSTITUTIONAL AND RIGHTS PRINCIPLES

Polity or institutional concerns, not only rights principles, have been
important to Supreme Court decision-making well before *Casey*. Wo-
ven throughout the *Griswold* case are arguments about the responsibilities of the Supreme Court in protecting fundamental rights such as
liberty and the relationship of the role of the Court's deference to political or elected bodies (*Griswold v. Connecticut* 1965:485, 493, 500–501).[12]

The intersection of rights and polity principles is crucial to *Roe* itself.
In *Roe*, the Burger Court chooses to support the polity principle of deference to state legislatures over the "rights" of the mother or fetus by
allowing state legislatures to decide whether abortions are to be permitted after viability, except when the mother's life is in danger. All
states have chosen to protect potential life after viability rather than
permit post-viability abortions when the mother's health in not in danger. But this is less significant with regard to the legitimacy and acceptance of *Roe* than the Burger Court's decision to move from a rights
basis (before viability) to a majoritarian political question to be decided
in state legislatures (after viability). In my view, this decision under-
mines the clarity of the liberty principles in *Roe*, and the personhood
principles in *Casey*, and continues to cloud the place of mothers and
potential life before the law. It is an important factor, rarely discussed,
that adds to our society's conflict over the right of abortion choice.[13]
(See *Maher v. Roe* 1977 on Medicaid payment for nontherapeutic abortions and *Harris v. McRae* 1980 on government payment for certain therapeutic abortions.)

Moreover, the doctrinal innovations in *Casey* do not stand alone as
simply a redefinition of a right. They result from the Court's consideration of polity and rights principles as related to liberty interests and
from a concern by the justices as to whether or not they distrust the

capacity of majoritarian institutions and politics to define women's right to abortion choice. *Casey* demonstrates that institutional and rights principles work together and that innovative protections of individual rights can be derived from strong institutional principles. In *Casey*, the newly recognized equality component of personhood as a basis for abortion choice stems from the Court's recognition of changing dynamics of political representation and empowerment of women in society: "The ability of women to participate equally in the economic and social life of the Nation has been facilitated by their ability to control their reproductive lives" (*Planned Parenthood of S.E. Pennsylvania v. Casey* 1992:856).

The Supreme Court's landmark abortion decision in *Casey* invalidates key assumptions in the instrumental theories of Robert Dahl, Martin Shapiro, and the more recent contribution of Mark Graber.[14] Moreover, the rare joint plurality opinion in *Casey* by Reagan-Bush appointees O'Connor, Souter, and Kennedy confirms that individual justices, and the Court as a decision-making institution, make choices based on both individual rights values, such as a woman's constitutional liberty right to abortion choice, and key polity principles, such as a commitment to *stare decisis* and Supreme Court autonomy from the majoritarian political system. *Casey* is a landmark decision because it sets out polity principles for the Court to follow in the future and also suggests Court commitment to a new right of personhood.

The Rehnquist Court and Religion

STATE ESTABLISHMENT OF RELIGION

In addition to the rights of abortion choice and privacy, one also sees the constitutive nature of Supreme Court decision-making when analyzing Rehnquist Court cases regarding questions of state establishment and free exercise of religion in the 1990s. If the Rehnquist Court was instrumental in its decision-making, we would expect it to reject precedents and institutional norms and follow election returns and personal policy wants, or those of Presidents Reagan and Bush, who had wide political support among the religious right and appointed a majority of sitting Rehnquist Court justices in the 1990s. If the Rehnquist Court in the 1990s was constitutive in its decision-making, we would expect it to respect the polity principle of church-state separation and free exercise rights principles in the Establishment Clause and freedom of religion in the Free Exercise Clause, principles that are respectful of the nonreligious and minority religions as well as main-line religions.

Doctrinally, if the Rehnquist Court were moving to be far more accommodative to religion it would reject Burger Court Establishment Clause principles, codified in *Lemon v. Kurtzman* (1971), under what has become known as the *Lemon* test. The *Lemon* test requires that for a law or policy to be upheld under the Establishment Clause it must 1) have a secular purpose; 2) have a principle or primary effect that neither advances nor inhibits religion, and 3) not foster excessive entanglement with religion (*Lemon v. Kurtzman* 1971:612–13). Scholars and politicians that desire to increase state support of religion have argued for a test which almost completely emphasizes free exercise rather than the institutional separation principles in the Establishment Clause. They seek to replace the *Lemon* test with what is called the coercion test. All the state cannot do under this weaker test is coerce a child or citizen to engage in religion under public institutional auspices.[15]

The Rehnquist Court rejects the "coercion" test and keeps the central elements of the *Lemon* test. In the landmark school prayer decision *Lee v. Weisman* (1992), the Rehnquist Court found that a prayer at a junior high school graduation violates the religion clauses of the First Amendment, despite encouragement from the Bush Administration to decide in favor of school prayer. As in *Casey, Weisman* shows Reagan-Bush appointees Justices Kennedy, O'Connor, and Souter staking out important institutional principles in the area of state establishment of religion. As with *Casey,* the *Weisman* majority, written by Kennedy, emphasizes the Court's autonomy from politics and the need for the Court to follow established precedents (*Lee v. Weisman* 1992:587). Rather than centering on the freedom of conscience, the majority stays with a state endorsement of religion test. The Court refuses to conflate individual conscience and institutional norms under liberty of religious thought.

The *Weisman* majority emphasizes the Supreme Court's autonomy from the majoritarian political system. As in *Casey,* the Court rebuffs the Bush Administration's attempt to lead it: "Thus we do not accept the invitation of petitioners and *amicus* the United States to reconsider our decision in *Lemon v. Kurtzman*" (*ibid.*). In language nearly identical to that in *Casey,* the majority emphasizes the need to maintain Court legitimacy as an important polity principle: "Our timeless lesson is that, if citizens are subjected to state-sponsored religion exercises, the State disavows its own duty to guard and respect that sphere of inviolable conscience and belief which is the mark of a free people. To compromise that principle today would be to deny our own tradition and forfeit our standing to urge others to secure the protections of that tradition for themselves" (592). In a concurring opinion, Justice Souter emphasizes the value of Court autonomy: "We have not changed much since the days of Madison, and the judiciary should not willingly enter the political arena to battle the centripetal force leading from religious pluralism to official preference for the faith with the most votes" (618). This is a quite clear statement of Court autonomy and the importance of counter-majoritarian polity principles to protecting individual rights.

For the majority, Justice Kennedy renews the Court's support of the institutional separation principles in the Establishment Clause. Justice Kennedy takes a strong stand that the public and private spheres need to be viewed in different and separate terms. He writes, "It must not be forgotten, then, that while concern must be given to define the protection granted to an objector or a dissenting nonbeliever, these same Clauses exist to protect religion from government interference" (589–90). Kennedy refuses to meld individual conscience and polity/institutional norms under liberty of religious thought as the Reagan-Bush Administrations and religious supporters had favored. Moreover, Justice Kennedy also considers the question of whether the prayer leads to political divisiveness, an institutional principle that was important to Brennan, but one that never made it formally into the Burger Court's *Lemon* test. Kennedy is concerned that political divisiveness can occur in the choice of who delivers a prayer at the graduation (587–88). Thus, he seems to suggest that fear of political divisiveness, not an actual finding of divisiveness, should be a concern of the Court.

In contrast to those who favor a coercion test, Justices Blackmun, Stevens, and O'Connor, as well as Kennedy, view both the rights principles of free exercise of religion and church-state separation polity principles in the Establishment Clause as important, separate, and distinct. Justice Blackmun, joined by O'Connor and Stevens, states, "The mixing of government and religion can be a threat to free government, even though no one is forced to participate" (606). As in a dialogue with the interpretive community, Souter specifically mentions that he rejects Michael McConnell's coercion theory and suggests that such a view violates precedent and the central meaning of the Religion Clauses. He writes, "But we could not adopt that [McConnell's] reading without abandoning our settled law, a course that in my view, the text of the Clause would not readily permit" (618).

In *Agostini v. Felton* (1997), the Supreme Court overturned *Aguilar v. Felton* (1985) and parts of *School District of Grand Rapids v. Ball* (1985), two cases that prohibited public school teachers from teaching in parochial schools. Upon first look, it may appear that this reversal of precedent was simply a decision based on the justices' policy choices. However, *Agostini* demonstrates the Court is actually very much concerned that it follow precedent. For a majority of the Court, failure to overturn *Aguilar* and the part of *Grand Rapids* dealing with the Shared Time Program would undermine institutional norms, including *stare decisis*. Justice O'Connor delivered the opinion of the Court, joined by Justices Rehnquist, Scalia, Kennedy, and Thomas. Justices Souter, Stevens, Ginsburg, and Breyer dissented in the case.

The overriding question for both the majority and dissent in *Agostini* is the interpretation of precedent. The majority contends that *Zobrest v. Catalina Foothills School District* (1993) created "fresh law" when the Court allowed state-provided aids for a deaf student in parochial schools (*Agostini v. Felton* 1997:2007). Justice O'Connor does not view the interpreter as any different from an instructor in *Aguilar*: "The signer in *Zobrest* had the same opportunity to inculcate religion in the performance of her duties as do Title I employees, and there is no genuine basis upon which to confine *Zobrest's* underlying rationale—that public employees will not be presumed to inculcate religion—to sign-language interpreters" (2011).

In arguing that the majority is following *stare decisis*, Justice O'Connor emphasizes that in *Zobrest* the Supreme Court had "expressly rejected the notion—relied on in Ball and Aguilar—that, solely because of her presence on private school property, a public employee will be presumed to inculcate religion in the students" (*ibid.*). In *Agostini* the Court accepts the long-held O'Connor view that entanglement between church and state must be excessive before it is a violation of the Constitution.

The Court takes the position, which is in agreement with the O'Connor, Kennedy, and Souter joint opinion in *Casey*, that *stare decisis* does not preclude the Supreme Court from recognizing substantial change in Establishment Clause jurisprudence and overruling *Aguilar* and portions of *Grand Rapids*. In line with case law, considering that *Aguilar* would be decided differently under current Establishment law, adherence to *Aguilar* would be an injustice. In discussing *stare decisis*, O'Connor specifically cites the joint opinion in *Casey* as "(observing that a decision is properly overruled where 'development of constitutional law since the case was decided has implicitly or explicitly left [it] behind as a mere survivor of obsolete constitutional thinking')" (*Agostini v. Felton* 1997:2016–17). Thus, the primary basis on which to overturn is whether the Court's later Establishment Clause cases have so undermined *Aguilar* that it is no longer good law.

We see the Court complying with changing law in relation to changing facts and experience in society—that government employees in schools for secular subjects have not caused the political divisiveness and endorsement of religion and indoctrination that the *Aguilar* Court had feared would occur. The Court here is referring to prior cases, *Witters* and *Zobrest*, in suggesting that when aid is given to private schools on neutral, secular criteria that neither favor nor disfavor religion, and is made available to both religion and secular beneficiaries on a nondiscriminatory basis, such programs are not likely to have the effect of advancing religion. Because *Zobrest* abandoned the presumption that public employees will inculcate religion simply because they happen to be in a sectarian environment, there is no longer any need to assume that entanglement problems will occur from pervasive monitoring of Title I teachers. Thus, the change in the definition of what might influence students leads for a majority of justices to less concern that entanglement between church and state will be excessive.

The interesting aspect of *Agostini*, then, is how the Court views the Title I professionals, and specifically, how the Court views their professionality. No evidence or reason had been presented for the Court to believe that the instructors were in any way inculcating religion, nor was any evidence or reason advanced to support the claim that allowing public money to be used for secular purposes in sectarian settings necessarily advanced the notion that there was an excessive entanglement of church and state. As in *Weisman*, the Rehnquist Court continues to specifically refer to the *Lemon* test and says the New York City program does not run afoul of the three primary criteria currently used to evaluate whether government aid has the effect of advancing religion: it does not result in government indoctrination, define its recipients by reference to religion, or create an excessive entanglement. Nor can this carefully constrained program reasonably be viewed as an "endorsement of religion" (*Agostini v. Felton* 1997:2016).

Because of institutional concerns and Court-legitimacy concerns, the Court is very precise on restating the conditions under which a decision may be overturned. It admonishes lower courts to follow the controlling precedent until the Supreme Court overturns a case. The Court does not want lower courts to determine or conclude that recent cases have, by implication, overruled an earlier precedent. Rather, lower courts should follow the case which directly controls, leaving to the Supreme Court "the prerogative of overruling its own decision" (*ibid.*). The Court says that Rule 60(b)(5) should not be viewed as a vehicle for effecting change in law because "it will erode the Court's institutional integrity" (*ibid.*).

One view of this case is that the Court is in the process of forming a new principle, one that rests upon the need for actual evidence that there is misuse of the public funds in the sectarian environment. This potential principle is very much related to the anti-discrimination principle, in that specific evidence of mal-intent is needed for the Court to conclude that there is abuse of the system. In *Agostini*, Title I funds are available to all children who meet eligibility requirements, regardless of religious beliefs. Thus, by one reading, it is possibly unconstitutional to deny access to these funds, or to make the acquisition of these funds unnecessarily difficult, on the basis of religious beliefs.

The majority opinion gives lower courts "directions" in employing precedent in hopes of solidifying the rule of law in future cases. Writes O'Connor: "It is true that the trial court has discretion, but the exercise of discretion cannot be permitted to stand if we find it rests upon a legal principle that can no longer be sustained" (*Agostini v. Felton* 1997: 2017). Thus the use of precedent is directly related to the rule of law, and if the rule of law is to be maintained, a principled use of *stare decisis* is mandatory. The issue is not whether one agrees with the majority's view of the precedents and the Establishment Clause; rather, it is their principled use of such notions that is of importance. There is a deeper issue present in this case as to the relationships among Court decisions, new findings of facts, and the linkage of those facts to key constitutional norms, relationships that were alluded to in both *Casey* and *Weisman*, the parallel aspects of which are explored elsewhere.[16] What we see in *Aguilar* is a principled overturning of precedent with the necessary steps taken to insure that *stare decisis* is employed correctly by lower courts.

FREE EXERCISE OF RELIGION

Most cases under the Free Exercise Clause revolve around questions as to whether citizens should be permitted the free exercise of religion at times when laws would prohibit such acts were they not based on a religious motivation. In *Employment Division, Department of Human Resources of Oregon v. Smith* (1990), the Rehnquist Court decided that the Free Exercise Clause permits a state to prohibit the sacramental use of peyote, a controlled substance, using a legal test which was far more solicitous of state discretion over the free exercise of religion than in prior cases. In this case Oregon could deny unemployment benefits for a Native American dismissed from a job for using peyote for religious purposes. The Court found that the law banning the use of peyote is permissible if it is neutral in its content and enacted for reasons unrelated to religious expression. It allowed a state to permit the use of peyote for sacramental use if it so chooses, but the Court refused to make the use of peyote for religious purposes a right protected under the Free Exercise Clause.

Justice Scalia wrote for the 5–4 majority. For the majority, a religious motivation in the use of peyote did not place citizens beyond the reach of the law. Scalia emphasized that when a government law is passed with neutral (nonreligious) intent, a compelling government interest is present and may be applied against citizens whose motivation for breaking the law is religious (*Employment Division, Department of Human Resources of Oregon v. Smith* 1990:885–86). Justice Scalia preferred that judges not be given the power to weigh the social or policy objectives of laws which are passed by states, or to weigh the importance of government interests against the requirements of the First Amendment Free Exercise Clause. Thus, a majority of the Court supported the institutional principle of state determination of its criminal laws.

Justice O'Connor, joined by Brennan, Marshall, and Blackmun, rejected the majority view that the Free Exercise Clause contains "a single categorical rule" that "if prohibiting the exercise of religion . . . is . . . merely the incidental effect of a generally applicable and otherwise valid provision, the First Amendment has not been offended" (892). O'Connor argued that we always have to balance religious concerns with generally applicable regulations, as the Court did in prior cases. Thus, the dissent opposed Scalia's test of the constitutionality of laws regarding religious practices. They would apply the following test: to allow religious exemptions from a general criminal law if such exemptions do not unduly interfere with the fulfillment of a governmental interest—in this case the prohibition of the possession and use of a controlled substance.

O'Connor supported the decision in the case not to allow sacramental use of peyote, but opposed Scalia's test. She wrote, "Although the question is close, I would conclude that uniform application of Oregon's criminal prohibition is essential to accomplish its overriding interest in preventing the physical harm caused by the use of a Schedule I controlled substance" (905). Justice Blackmun, in dissent, joined by Brennan and Marshall, wanted the Court to look at this law under the standard that a statute which burdens the free exercise of religion can only stand if the law is general and the state's refusal to allow a religious exemption is justified by a compelling interest which cannot be served by less restrictive means. For Blackmun, if we do not require strict scrutiny when a law burdens religion, we allow "the repression of minority religions" as an "unavoidable consequence of democratic government," and thus distort and undermine long-held precedents and constitutional values (909). The dissenting justices agreed with O'Connor's view of the need for Court power on such questions, but not her answer to the question as to whether peyote use could be permitted in religious services. As in the abortion rights and Establishment Clause cases, this case demonstrates the importance of the institutional principle that the Court, not elected bodies, must decide questions of individual rights. It also shows differences among the justices as to their views of basic free exercise principles and how these principles are to be juxtaposed with institutional principles in Court decision-making.

That the constitutive process is at work is quite evident if we compare *Smith* (1990) with *Church of Lukumi Babalu Aye, Inc. v. City of Hialeah* (1993). In *Hialeah,* a majority of the Rehnquist Court rejected Scalia's test for free exercise cases. In moving away from the *Smith* rule that a law that is simply neutral in intent and general in application is enough to limit the free exercise of a religious practice, the Court, in *Hialeah,* emphasized that neutrality and general applicability of a law that limits religious practice are interrelated. The failure to satisfy one requirement is a likely indication that the other has not been satisfied. In *Hialeah,* the Court found that the city's anti-animal sacrifice law had been "gerrymandered," in the Court's words, to proscribe the religious killings of animals by Santeria church members, but to exclude the killing of all other animals (*Church of Lukumi Babalu Aye, Inc. v. City of Hialeah* 1993:542). Moreover, the regulations suppressed far more religious conduct than was needed in order to meet the valid public health concerns of the law. The Court found that the laws as applied to the sacrifice of animals for religious purposes are over and under inclusive with regard to animal killings for food, eradication of insects and pests, and the euthanasia of excess animals. Scalia and Rehnquist disagreed with the equal protection aspects of the Kennedy decision, which seeks to protect minority religions. Scalia's majority opinion in *Smith* left such protection up to state legislatures, not federal courts.

Justice Souter concurs with the principle of this case in that "the Free Exercise Clause bars government action aimed at suppressing religious belief or practice" (559). However, he refuses to join part II of the majority opinion because in *dicta* the *Smith* rule is mentioned, and he opposes the *Smith* rule. Unlike *Smith,* here the Court finds that laws are restricting religion, while the anti-peyote laws in *Smith* were on the books as general anti–drug use laws. Souter would not support the use of a law that is neutral with regard to religion on its face or in its purpose but may lack neutrality in its effect by forbidding something that religion requires. Souter wants to ensure not only formal neutrality of laws with regard to religion, but also what he calls "substantive neutrality" (562). He argues that the *Smith* rule is of limited use as precedent because it is too statute-specific in terms of the interest offered by the state for the law, and is not solicitous of the needs of our nation to balance state interests with support for the free exercise of religion (562–77). Blackmun, joined by O'Connor, agrees with Souter that "the First Amendment's protection of religion extends beyond those rare occasions in which the government explicitly targets religion" (577–78).

In *Smith* and *Hialeah*, we see the Court considering institutional principles of an elected body compared to Court power, rights principles as to free exercise of religion, and how institutional and rights principles are balanced. We see the constitutive process occur across cases, as more recent Reagan-Bush appointees Kennedy and Souter work out how they view the application of institutional and polity principles. We also see that rights principles do not always trump institutional principles; nor do institutional principles trump rights.

Perhaps there is no better example of the constitutive decision-making process at work than *City of Boerne v. Flores, Archbishop of San Antonio, et al.* (1997). *Boerne* is a free exercise case in which the Rehnquist Court, in a 6–3 decision, declared that the Religious Freedom Restoration Act of 1993 (RFRA) exceeds Congress's power under section 5 of the Fourteenth Amendment. This decision surprised many scholars of the Supreme Court and constitutional law because the Rehnquist Court, comprised of six Reagan-Bush appointees, was opposing congressional power directly, seeking to limit Congress's enforcement powers under the Fourteenth Amendment, and not following election returns, as the decision was against the protection of free exercise rights.

RFRA was Congress's direct response to *Smith*, a case discussed above. In *Smith*, the Court declined to use the compelling interest test established in *Sherbert v. Verner* (1963), which requires the Court to ask whether the law at issue substantially burdens a religious practice and whether the burden is justified by a compelling government interest. RFRA reestablished these requirements as a matter of federal statute. The law's mandate applied to all federal and state officials, and to other persons acting under cover of law, regardless of when the statutes they were operating under were adopted.

Polity principles dominate the issues of concern to the Rehnquist
Court. It viewed Congress's enactment of RFRA as a clear violation of
separation of powers, as an infringement upon both the Supreme
Court's power of judicial review and the states' power to regulate. The
Court emphasized that it had the power to define only which acts
of Congress are legitimate remedial legislation under the Enforcement
Clause of the Fourteenth Amendment and which acts of Congress constitute an invalid substantive interpretation of individual rights. Justice
Kennedy, writing for the majority, argued that history and case law
demonstrate that the design and text of the Fourteenth Amendment
are inconsistent with the suggestion that Congress has the power to
decree the substance of the Fourteenth Amendment's restrictions on
the states. Kennedy argues that legislation which alters the meaning
of the Free Exercise Clause cannot be said to be enforcing it.

In *Boerne* we see the Court balancing weighty institutional concerns
of protecting the Supreme Court's power to interpret the Constitution
against incursion by Congress and issues of what constitutes an infringement on the free exercise of religion. Regardless of judicial philosophy, all justices were concerned that institutional norms basic to
the Constitution and the Supreme Court's power of judicial review not
be violated by Congress's interpretation of the Fourteenth Amendment
and passage of RFRA. That Justices Kennedy, Stevens, Thomas, Ginsburg, and Chief Justice Rehnquist, all of whom hold quite different
views on issues of religious freedom and church-state separation,
joined the majority opinion, except in part III-A-1, suggests the importance of the institutional norm that Congress adhere to legislative tasks
while the Supreme Court remains the final arbiter of Constitutional
questions. Justice Kennedy writes: "Our national experience teaches us
that the Constitution is preserved best when each part of the government respects both the Constitution and the proper actions and deter-
minations of the other branches. . . . RFRA was designed to control
cases and controversies, such as the one before us; but as the provisions
of the federal statute here invoked are beyond congressional authority,
it is this Court's precedent, not RFRA, which must control" (*City of
Boerne v. Flores, Archbishop of San Antonio, et al.* 1997:2172).

Moreover, the majority found that RFRA, in forcing states to demonstrate a compelling interest as well as to show that the law is the least
restrictive means of furthering that interest, burdens states and curtails
their traditional regulatory power. The Court is exhibiting the polity
principle that the judicial branch is better equipped to draw lines on
institutional powers under the Constitution than are institutions sub-

ject to direct political pressure. Justice Kennedy writes: "If 'compelling interest' really means what it says . . . many laws will not meet the [RFRA] test. . . . [The test] would open the prospect of constitutionally required religious exemptions from civic obligations of almost every conceivable kind. . . . Laws valid under Smith would fall under RFRA without regard to whether they had the object of stifling or punishing free exercise" (2171).

Although polity principles are of the foremost consideration in this case, rights principles remain of critical importance to the justices. All of the justices agreed that RFRA violates polity principles. However, the dissent found that the polity principles, though important, were not of enough "weight" to supercede the rights principle of free exercise of religion. The dissent, comprised of Justices O'Connor, Breyer, and Souter, stated that the statute was an unconstitutional use of Congress's power. However, the dissent centered on their opposition to the majority's interpretation of *Employment Division, Department of Human Resources of Oregon v. Smith* (1990), and their reluctance to employ it as a yardstick for Establishment Clause jurisprudence led them to reject the Court's holding. The dissent opposed the majority's view that the *Smith* case should be the precedent on such free exercise cases. Justice O'Connor, joined by Souter and Breyer, in dissent, writes, "The Free Exercise Clause is best understood as an affirmative guarantee of the right to participate in religious activities without impermissible governmental interference even where a believer's conduct is in tension with a law of general applicability" (*City of Boerne v. Flores, Archbishop of San Antonio, et al.* 1997:2184). The dissenters do not like the fact that *Smith* violates this premise of impermissible governmental interference, although they agree that RFRA violates this premise as well by requiring government to have a compelling state interest before interfering with the free exercise of religion. By dissenting, Justices O'Connor, Breyer, and Souter are not on record as supporting *Smith*, which leaves room for them to maintain what they view as the proper conception and application of free exercise rights when confronted by state law. For the dissent, the case was a difficult balance of polity and rights concerns, and with their decision, they were able to support the polity principles of the majority while maintaining a dialogue on the *Smith* decision and its consequences on the free exercise of religion.

In *Boerne, Smith, Aguilar, Weisman, Casey,* and all the cases we have analyzed, it is evident that when justices differ on the nature of what precedents stand for they make their decisions in line with important polity and rights principles, rather than simply on their policy wants.

This is not to say that there are no conditions under which justices act strategically. In *Boerne*, the majority emphasizes polity principles defining Supreme Court and Congress's power, while assuming that *Smith* is good law. The dissent emphasizes that they do not want *Boerne* to be read as supporting the *Smith* test on questions of the free exercise of religion. Some might view the strategic voting in *Boerne*, especially by the dissenters, as justices making instrumental choices in policy terms. This view is misguided because such choices were made on strongly felt needs by the justices that principles they hold dear must be supported.

When we look at the Establishment and Free Exercise Clauses cases together, we see that a majority of the Reagan-Bush appointees refused to turn their backs on key institutional principles in the Establishment Clause, even though they were under pressure to view all cases as pertaining to free exercise rights, to drop the institutional principles of the *Lemon* test, and to trust elected bodies on issues of free exercise of religion. Rather, a Supreme Court dominated by Reagan-Bush appointees chose to follow precedent and build doctrine upon principles developed during the Warren and Burger Court years. It chose to reject a call for school prayer in *Weisman* and a test in RFRA that would have limited the free exercise of members of minority religions. In the area of substantive due process, it chose to support the right of abortion choice and deepen the theoretical bases for the right by conceiving of the liberty issues facing women as not simply issues of privacy but of personhood, a change which may form the doctrinal basis with which to extend the rights of homosexuals beyond the landmark case of *Romer v. Evans* (1996).

The Constitutive Approach and the New Historical Institutionalism

Contemporary historical institutionalists, such as Stephen Skowronek, argue that there are distinctive criteria of institutional action (Skowronek 1995). Institutional actions are official and have legitimate authority. Institutions must account for their actions. Institutions do not simply constrain or channel actions of self-interested people; they prescribe actions, convert motives, and assert legitimacy. In so doing they perpetuate the objectives or purposes instilled in them at their founding—that is what is at the heart of their staying power. Because of the above characteristics, Skowronek writes:

> Any a priori notion of individual interest will very quickly succumb to historically derived and institutionally embed-

ded rationalities of action. . . . [T]he analysis of institutional action will itself be driven to a consideration of origins, toward an understanding of official behavior in terms of original purposes. If . . . institutional analysis is inherently historical, it is because a great deal of the work is simply to figure out the rationalities in play. . . . [Scholars] must locate the historical/institutional construction of the behaviors observed and their particular claims to authority (Skowronek 1995).

These criteria are evident both in the constitutive approach to Supreme Court decision-making that I have discussed here and in the Supreme Court—which has changed its internal process very little in its history, and, by doing so, has sustained its legitimacy as an institution. To emphasize, "the historical/institutional construction of the behaviors observed" speaks to the traditions that each justice must follow—the rule of law, *stare decisis,* the difference between law and politics, disdain of direct political pressure on the Court, and the equal counting of votes, to name but a few. The distinctive criteria of institutional action in the Supreme Court means that justices are not like elected officials, bureaucrats, or other policy makers, and their decision-making should not be analyzed in such terms. Because the constitutive approach is far more respectful of historical criteria of institutional action than are instrumental approaches, it is a more credible and useful way to inquire into how Supreme Court decision-making informs and is informed by processes of institutional and societal change.

Notes

1. See Segal and Spaeth (1993) for the most forceful and respected presentation of the attitudinal approach.

2. See Epstein and Knight (1995a) for an important statement of this position as applied to the Supreme Court.

3. See Dahl (1957) for the first major statement of this approach; see Kahn (1994) for evidence and reasons why the Warren and Burger Courts did not follow election returns.

4. Epstein and Kobylka (1992) for a recent example of this approach.

5. See Rosenberg (1991) for the most sophisticated study using this approach. Also see McCann (1994:290–93) questioning Rosenberg's "neo-realist" approach.

6. See Kahn (1994); also see Gillman (1993) for a sophisticated study of Supreme Court decision-making that rejects instrumental premises about Court behavior and employs many of the assumptions of a constitutive approach. Also see Michael McCann (1996) and Brigham and Gordon (1996), for discus-

sions of how a constitutive approach to law differs from a positivistic one using quite different legal contexts than the Supreme Court.

7. See Skowronek (1995) for a superb statement of how institutional rules shape individual decision-making and how to study institutional change.

8. See Skowronek (1995:94) for the argument that "institutions perpetuate the objectives or purposes instilled in them at their founding" and "that any a priori notion of individual interest will very quickly succumb to historically derived and institutionally embedded rationalities of action."

9. In this chapter the term "polity" and "institutional" principle will be used interchangeably, as contrasted to "rights" principles.

10. See Kahn (1994) for an examination of these questions by looking at Court decision-making concentrating on Supreme Court eras under Chief Justices Earl Warren (1953–69) and Warren Burger (1969–86).

11. For example, see Simon (1995).

12. See Justice Harlan's eloquent discussion in *Griswold*, alluding to *Poe v. Ullman* (1961), about the Court's responsibility to respect and define both the liberty interests of citizens as found in the Due Process Clause and the moral decision-making of political institutions.

13. The importance of both polity and rights principles is also seen in the abortion funding cases. The Burger Court chose to balance the right of abortion choice with the power of the states and the federal governments to decide whether or not they wish to support potential life, since poor people are not a discrete and insular minority and there is no affirmative responsibility for the state to pay so that a person may take advantage of fundamental rights. States may choose to pay for the birthing costs of poor people under Medicaid, and not choose to pay for therapeutic and nontherapeutic abortions—even when such choices by states lead to additional expense, or (as many argue) a denial of the right to choose abortion itself.

14. See Kahn 1994: chapters 1, 2, 3, and 8 for a discussion of Dahl's elections returns approach; chapters 1 through 6 and 8 for a discussion of Martin Shapiro's policy-making approach; and chapter 8 for a discussion of Rosenberg's view of the Court's following politics. For the most recent call by Martin Shapiro for scholars to use instrumental approaches to Supreme Court decision-making, see Shapiro (1989). Also, see Graber (1993) for a neo-Dahlian approach.

15. See Kahn (1993) for a detailed analysis of *Lee v. Weisman* (1992) in the context of prior cases and for the argument that the Rehnquist Court did not accept the no-coercion test in *Weisman*.

16. See Kahn (1994, 1996a, 1996b) for a discussion of the role of social facts in constitutional theory and practice.

PART THREE
Extra-Judicial Influences on Supreme Court Decision-Making

9

Recruitment and the Motivations of Supreme Court Justices

Lawrence Baum

Human behavior can be understood as a product of interaction between the attributes of individuals and characteristics of the situations in which they act. In its various forms, the new institutionalism assists in analysis of this interaction by showing how institutional situations influence the impact of individual attributes: choices by decision makers are structured by the formal and informal rules under which they work (Shepsle 1986; Moe 1987; March and Olsen 1989; Steinmo, Thelen, and Longstreth 1992). This theme of the new institutionalism has influenced the ways that scholars think about Supreme Court decision-making (e.g., Smith 1988), reinforcing a longstanding concern with the Court as an institution.

One central issue in institutional analysis is the relative weight of individual attributes and situational characteristics in shaping patterns of behavior. Most students of the Supreme Court subscribe to theories of decision-making that limit the impact of justices as individuals to an important but narrow domain. In other words, they have treated the Court's institutional features as greatly restricting the play of individualism.

There is considerable basis for this view of the Court, but there is also reason to think that the constraints on individualism in the Court have been exaggerated. In this chapter I argue that the individual characteristics of justices merit greater attention than they have received, and I explore their impact through the lens of recruitment.

People, Situations, and Supreme Court Behavior

By no means do students of the Supreme Court ignore justices as individuals. Most political scientists who study the Court treat individual policy preferences as the primary determinant of the Court's collective policies (e.g., Schubert 1965; Tate 1981; Segal and Spaeth 1993).[1] At a deeper level, however, the most influential theories of Supreme Court behavior depict the justices as homogeneous. That deeper level concerns motivation. Supreme Court justices typically are portrayed as people who all act on the same narrow set of goals, usually on a single goal carried out in a particular way. In turn, that homogeneity has been ascribed to characteristics of the situation in which justices make their choices.

By and large, the major theories of Supreme Court behavior held by social scientists and legal scholars share the assumption that justices act only on an interest in the content of legal policy—the outputs of the Court and, perhaps, those of other government institutions. Justices do not decide cases in ways designed to enhance their incomes or their prospects for other positions, to gain popularity or respect among the Court's audiences, to reduce their workloads or secure a pleasant working environment. Rather, they focus their efforts singlemindedly on the quality of law or policy for its own sake. In a world of skeptical scholars, nowhere else are public officials depicted as acting with so little concern for their self-interest.

The belief that justices focus on the content of legal policy to the exclusion of other considerations does not rest on an assumption of judicial altruism (see Epstein 1990). Rather, characteristics of the Court situation are seen as limiting the range of relevant motives. While this premise is often implicit in scholarship on the Court, Rohde and Spaeth (1976:72–74) and Segal and Spaeth (1993:69–72) presented an explicit rationale for it: the justices' life terms and the Court's attractiveness virtually eliminate both concern about retention of their positions and ambition for other offices.

While most students of Supreme Court behavior agree on the primacy of legal policy as a goal for justices, they differ in more specific conceptions of justices' goals and of the ways they act on their goals. The disagreement about goals concerns the focus of the justices' concern with the content of legal policy—the relative importance of their interest in making good law (primarily accurate interpretation of applicable legal rules) and good policy.

Disagreement over the ways in which justices act on goals concerns the balance between expressive and instrumental behavior (see Simon 1985:298) or, to use the more common terms, sincere and strategic behavior.[2] Justices who engage in expressive or sincere behavior simply take the positions that they regard as embodying good law or good policy. Justices who engage in instrumental or strategic behavior take positions that they believe will be most effective in promoting good law or good policy in the Court's collective decisions or in the decisions of government as a whole; those positions may diverge from the ones that justices most prefer in themselves (Gely and Spiller 1990; Eskridge 1991b).

Like the consensus that Supreme Court justices focus on the content of legal policy, scholars' differing views about specific goals and ways to advance them reflect conceptions of the justices' situation. This linkage is especially strong in the debate over law and policy as judicial goals.[3] Adherents to the attitudinal model of decision ascribe the dominance of policy over law to the legal ambiguity of cases selected by the Court: because good legal rationales can be offered for alternative choices in each case, legal considerations become largely irrelevant to decision, thereby freeing (or forcing) justices to decide on the basis of their policy preferences (Segal and Spaeth 1993:70). The justices can limit their decisions to legally ambiguous cases because of the Court's discretionary jurisdiction, established by Congress primarily at the behest of the justices themselves (O'Brien 1993:135).

Those scholars who believe that one goal for the justices is that of making good law attribute this motivation, explicitly or implicitly, to informal institutional constraints (e.g., Perry 1991; Brenner and Stier 1995; see Searing 1991). The prescribed job of the Supreme Court justice is to interpret the law.[4] Thus justices are socialized to accept that prescription and encouraged to do so by the legal community that serves as a reference group for them. From this perspective, justices may be free to leave legal considerations out of their calculus of decision in one sense, but in another sense they are constrained to include them.

In the major scholarly theories of Supreme Court behavior, justices differ in their behavior only to the extent that they make differing judgments about what constitutes good law or good policy; other sources of divergent behavior are largely ruled out. This position is quite reasonable as a general stance, in that psychologists have demonstrated the great power of situations to structure patterns of behavior. Even students of personality recognize the capacity of situations to channel the impact of personality traits (Snyder and Ickes 1985). Indeed, one lesson of psychological research is that the characteristics of situations probably have greater impact on behavior, and those of individuals less, than most people believe (Patry 1989; Ross and Nisbett 1991). It is a virtue of Supreme Court scholarship that it avoids undue emphasis on the idiosyncrasies of individual justices and focuses on identifying regularities that derive from the Court's situation.

Even so, the major scholarly theories of Supreme Court behavior arguably leave too little room for individualism. Powerful as situations are in shaping behavior, attributes of individuals do affect people's choices (see Kenrick and Funder 1988). More specifically, in two related respects the situation in which the justices make decisions places only limited constraints on the play of individuality.

First, the Court's institutional characteristics may free justices to ignore everything but their interest in legal policy, but justices are not precluded from seeking to achieve other goals as well. While the high prestige of their positions limits justices' ambitions for other positions, such ambition is not entirely absent. Justices occasionally leave the Court for other positions, as James Byrnes did in 1942 and Arthur Goldberg did in 1964. Some justices, such as William O. Douglas and Hugo Black, have shown an interest in the presidency or vice-presidency.

Ambition aside, justices may act to advance goals such as personal popularity and limited workloads. Certainly justices have demonstrated an interest in their personal standing with important audiences, particularly in the legal community. Their speeches to bar associations and articles in law reviews reflect that interest. Clarence Thomas, for example, has devoted considerable effort to strengthening his standing with audiences that are important to him (Biskupic 1994b; Fisher 1995). Similarly, justices care about the volume of work they face. They sometimes indicate their feeling that they need to work harder than they would prefer (e.g., Stevens 1982). The dramatic reduction in the numbers of cases that the Court accepted between the mid-1980s and the early 1990s suggests the importance of this concern.[5]

It is not clear how much an interest in personal standing or in workload influences the positions that justices take on case outcomes and legal doctrine. But it is easy to identify ways that these motivations could affect individual and collective positions in cases. The desire to limit workload, for instance, may encourage justices to adopt positions that reduce the need to decide future cases; this was one rationale articulated by William Brennan for his famous shift of position in obscenity law (*Paris Adult Theatre I v. Slaton* 1973:93).

Second, even if the Court situation made irrelevant all goals other than justices' interest in the content of legal policy, that interest itself could take multiple forms. Justices could act to achieve either good policy or good law. They could carry out either goal instrumentally, acting strategically on its behalf, or they could do so expressively, simply taking the positions that accord most closely with their own views. Current scholarly debates about these different possibilities underline the multiplicity of ways that an interest in legal policy could be manifested in justices' behavior.

Thus there is a wide range of goal orientations that might guide Supreme Court justices. One implication is that justices with different personal characteristics might behave differently; there is good reason to leave open the question of homogeneity in ends and means (see Gillman 1993:199–200). Some justices may give greater weight to legal considerations than do others (Dorsen 1993:118; Segal and Spaeth 1996: 983–84). Perhaps some are more inclined to behave strategically than others. Justices may differ considerably in the strength of their interest in minimizing their workloads or pleasing external audiences.

Moreover, if such variation does not exist, if justices' goal orientations are essentially homogeneous, this convergence of motivations could not be explained solely by the Court's institutional characteristics; it must reflect shared personal traits as well. If no justices decide cases with an eye to their workload, they must be the kinds of people who give a low priority to minimizing their labor. If they act on their policy goals in instrumental rather than expressive ways, they must be people who are inclined toward instrumental behavior.[6]

This point should not be overstated. Unquestionably, elements of the Court's institutional situation such as the partial insulation of justices from external control and their discretionary jurisdiction help to narrow and channel their motivations. Widely shared expectations of the justices have a similar impact. But there would seem to be a considerably broader range of possible goal orientations for justices than the most influential theories allow.

If so, the personal characteristics of justices merit more consideration. One good vantage point from which to consider these characteristics is recruitment, because recruitment determines the mix of traits that justices bring to their work on the Court.

Recruitment and the Goal Orientations of Supreme Court Justices

"Recruitment is a process by which individuals are inducted into active political roles" such as membership on the Supreme Court (Marvick 1976, 29). It is a long-term, multi-stage process (see Prewitt 1970; Prinz 1993). The process is driven by the actions both of aspirants and potential aspirants to office and of those who participate in selecting officials.

Recruitment to office is not entirely distinct from the situations in which officeholders serve. People tend to seek out situations that are compatible with their goals (Graham, Argyle, and Furnham 1980; Waller, Benet, and Farney 1994), and this undoubtedly is true of those who choose whether to seek or accept government positions. For their part, those who help to select officials work from their images or schemas of the characteristics appropriate to a particular office (Fiske 1993:239–40).

Recruitment is significant for an obvious reason: it determines what kinds of people hold particular positions in government. More subtly, the paths that people take to a position produce socialization processes that shape their attitudes (Marvick 1976:37). In this respect the goals and preferences that people bring with them to public office reflect the recruitment process itself.

Students of judicial politics have done considerable research on recruitment to the Supreme Court and other courts. Most process studies examine the nomination and confirmation of federal judges or the election of state judges (see Goldman 1991; Sheldon and Lovrich 1991). Attribute studies typically examine the relationship between background characteristics of judges and their decisional behavior (e.g., Tate and Handberg 1991; Songer, Davis, and Haire 1994).

These bodies of research are valuable, but they are deliberately limited in their scope. With a few exceptions (Watson and Downing 1969), process studies focus on the last stage of recruitment, the selection of judges from aspirants for judicial positions. Attribute studies are concerned with variation in judges' policy preferences, giving little attention to variation in their general goal orientations. Such variation is considered only in a small body of research on judges' needs and motives (Lasswell 1948; Caldeira 1977; Sarat 1977; Aliotta 1988). Biographical studies of Supreme Court justices often examine recruitment processes and justices' attributes more broadly (see Howard 1971), but their implications for recruitment to the Court as a general process have been considered only in limited ways (see Schmidhauser 1959).

At this point, then, analysis of the relationship between recruitment to the Supreme Court and the goal orientations of justices must be largely speculative. In this section I offer some speculations, necessarily focusing on a limited range of issues.

Of the most important patterns in recruitment to the Supreme Court, at least one is typical of recruitment to high government positions: nearly all justices have been involved in politics, defined broadly to include activities that range from party activism to the holding of nonjudicial offices. That involvement helps potential justices to establish the high level of achievement needed to be credible candidates for the Court, to amass credits with the officials who help to select justices, and—perhaps most important—simply to become visible to those officials.

Other patterns in recruitment to the Court are more distinctive. The most obvious is the informal but inflexible requirement of certification as an attorney. Lawyers are well-represented in other high government positions, but they hold no monopoly on those positions. And in contrast with many attorneys in those other positions, nearly all justices have had some experience in the practice of law (see Miller 1995:122–38).

Control over the selection of justices is held by a relatively small group of people, and the electorate plays no direct role. The result is to limit variation in the traits of people chosen as justices. Perhaps most important, the officials who choose justices demand at least a fairly high level of visible achievement in law or government as a prerequisite for selection. Because the electorate does not enforce that prerequisite so strongly, people who lack comparable records of achievement can win election to offices as high as the U.S. Senate (Canon 1990) and state supreme courts.

The scholarship on political recruitment appropriately emphasizes the role of ambition and the risks involved in seeking to move upward in politics (e.g., Schlesinger 1966; Fowler 1993). Neither ambition nor risk is as important in recruitment to the Supreme Court as it is for most other offices.

Certainly ambition is relevant to selection as a justice. People take actions intended to enhance their chances for selection, such as accepting a position that increases their credibility as a candidate (e.g., Thurgood Marshall, Robert Bork) or calling themselves to the attention of people involved in the selection process (e.g., Warren Burger). But it is not mandatory for a prospective justice to seek a position on the Court actively, because Executive Branch officials are themselves proactive in looking for potential justices from the large number of credible candidates. The Supreme Court is one of the few high positions for which there is an element of truth to the old saw that the office seeks the person. Moreover, the Court is a frustrating object for ambitious people. A very small proportion of the credible candidates become justices, and aspirants to the Court typically can do less to advance their prospects than can aspirants to elective office.

Candidacy for the Supreme Court involves relatively little risk, in that someone does not have to give up another position to be considered for the Court. The same is true of the most common penultimate position, a judgeship on a federal Court of Appeals. In combination with the relative passivity of aspirants to the Court, the absence of risk means that the sorts of calculations associated with potential candidacy for nonjudicial office (Black 1972; Rohde 1979; Abramson, Aldrich, and Rohde 1987) are much less relevant to the Supreme Court.

These patterns in recruitment might have several effects on the orientations of people who reach the Supreme Court. One pattern may help to account for the apparent primacy of legal policy as a goal for justices. Because Supreme Court justices have reached a high level of achievement, they typically sacrifice a substantial amount of potential income when they join the Court or a federal Court of Appeals. Most also sacrifice some of the pleasures of interaction with other people who have also reached high levels in law and politics. Those who are willing to pay these costs must see corresponding advantages to judicial service. One major advantage is likely to be the satisfaction of ruling on issues of legal policy (Landes and Posner 1975:887; Posner 1995:131). Thus the dominance of legal and policy considerations that most students of the Court have posited might reflect recruitment to the Court as well as the justices' situations.

To the extent that justices focus on the content of legal policy, the requirement of legal training and the near universal experience of law practice may elevate the importance of legal considerations in the justices' choices. More subtly, lawyers who seek or accept judgeships may differ from their colleagues in ways that strengthen the relative importance of legal considerations. As adjudicators rather than advocates, judges differ from most other lawyers and public officials. This characteristic may tend to screen out lawyers who are oriented to advocacy and attract those who prefer to consider choices in a relatively dispassionate way (Watson and Downing 1969:55–56). The latter group might be inclined to give greater weight to the goal of making good law.

Another element of the recruitment process may increase the importance of policy considerations to justices. A significant proportion of lawyers involve themselves in politics, but a great many do not. Those who do seek out political involvement, as future Supreme Court justices typically do, are likely to care more about public policy than do other members of the legal profession. This trait, then, may help to explain the importance of making good policy as a goal for justices. More broadly, the combination of legal training and political activity in the backgrounds of most justices seems likely to foster an interest in both good law and good policy on their part.

As noted earlier, justices need not be as ambitious as most other people who enjoy political success, and those who seek active control over the course of their careers may be more attracted to other kinds of positions. One effect might be to favor sincere over strategic behavior. Lacking a strong interest in power and a strong inclination to seek it, perhaps most justices are inclined more to express their preferences than to seek to impose those preferences on the Court or government as a whole. On the other hand, people may be more willing to accept the costs of service on the Supreme Court if they value the opportunity to influence the course of law and policy, an influence that is enhanced by strategic behavior.

Of course, there is no single path to the Court. Justices differ in their involvement in legal practice, elective office, and lower-court judgeships. Some have played highly active roles in politics, while others have participated in more peripheral ways. A multiplicity of paths to a particular office is typical of political recruitment in the U.S. (Canon 1990; Williams 1993). That characteristic fosters diversity among officeholders, and it may enhance differences in their motives for government service (Barber 1965; Payne et al. 1984; Winter 1987).

Much of the variation in paths to the Supreme Court can be captured by a crude but meaningful dichotomy between law and politics. The extreme example of a legal path—approximated by John Paul Stevens—involves a career devoted solely to some combination of private legal practice, law-school teaching, and lower-court judgeships, with minimal involvement in partisan politics. The extreme political path to the Court—approximated by Earl Warren—involves a career spent entirely in public positions and primarily in elective office and its pursuit.

Over time, recruitment patterns to any office are likely to change (Bogue et al. 1976; Peabody, Ornstein, and Rohde 1976; Canon 1990). Schmidhauser (1959, 1979) characterized justices by their primary careers before reaching the Court and documented some patterns of change. Most important, after 1862 there were fewer justices with predominantly political careers and more with predominantly judicial careers (Schmidhauser 1959:32–34).

Table 9.1 presents data on trends in the backgrounds of justices beginning with the Civil War era. These trends are uneven, except for a steady and sharp decline in the proportion of justices who had experience as candidates for elective office. Standing out most clearly in the table is the distinctiveness of the era that began in 1969: the legal path to the Court has been dominant to an unprecedented degree. Of the

Table 9.1

Selected Background Characteristics of Supreme Court Justices Appointed
in Different Eras (in percentages)

| | | Lifetime | | Time of Appointment | |
| | | Electoral | Judicial | Political | |
Years	N	Candidacy	Experience	Office	Judgeship
1861–1895	22	86.4	68.2	13.6	45.5
1896–1932	19	57.9	57.9	26.3	42.1
1933–1968	21	38.1	47.6	61.9	28.6
1969–1996	12	8.3	83.3	8.3	83.3

Notes: Only a justice's first appointment to the Court is counted. "Electoral candidacy"
refers to candidacy for any nonjudicial office in government that was, or appears to have
been, elective. Seats in the U.S. Senate are treated as elective throughout this period. The
proportions in this column may be slightly inaccurate because of incomplete information.
"Political office" refers to any official, full-time position in the executive or legislative
branches. "Judicial experience" refers to any judgeship, including part-time positions.

Sources: Witt (1990); L. Epstein, Segal, Spaeth, and Walker (1994); Jost (1995); biographies
of justices.

twelve justices appointed in this era, ten (all but Sandra Day O'Connor
and Clarence Thomas) spent essentially all of their pre-Court careers
in legal positions in government or the private sector.

Many justices in this era have participated substantially in politics.
But only O'Connor ever ran for elective office, and she chose to leave
the state legislature for the judiciary at an early stage in her career.
Moreover, while about 60 percent of all the pre-1969 appointees to the
Court had known the President who appointed them (Scigliano 1971:
95), at most one of the twelve appointees since then could be classified
as a presidential acquaintance.[7] In the current era, Presidents frequently meet their nominees for the first time shortly before selecting
them.

The distinctive recruitment pattern of the past quarter century might
not continue. Moreover, had events proceeded differently in a few instances (for example, Senator George Mitchell's accepting a nomination
in 1994), this pattern would be less distinctive. Still, it suggests a change
in the schemas that Presidents and other participants in the recruitment
process bring to their selection of Supreme Court justices.

In turn, this change may have produced a shift in the collective goal
orientations of Supreme Court justices. This is not because background
characteristics such as prior judicial service necessarily have strong
linkages with judicial behavior (Schmidhauser 1959:43). After all, justices do not come randomly from the sets of people who share particu-

lar backgrounds; rather, certain types of people from those sets are selected and self-selected purposively (see Segal and Spaeth 1993:232–33). But evolution in the general distribution of justices' backgrounds is a sign of change in the sorts of people who are able and willing to secure positions on the Court. And that change may be reflected in what justices want and how they go about achieving it.

The most likely effect of the distinctive recruitment pattern in the current era is an enhanced focus of justices' attentions on the Court itself. Justices in the era since 1969 have been less likely to devote substantial time to outside activities than was true in earlier periods (see Scigliano 1971:61–84). It appears that only Warren Burger engaged in the presidential consulting that was moderately common in past eras; this decline reflects the lack of pre-nomination relationships between Presidents and their appointees.[8] And there is little evidence of interest in other offices—essentially none, other than what some observers perceived as Sandra Day O'Connor's interest in the vice-presidency (Davis 1994:128). That lack of interest is understandable in light of the decline in political experience among justices; those who serve on the Court today are inclined to view their current positions as more attractive than high positions in the other branches.

If justices now focus more on the Court than they did in the past, then the dominant models of their behavior apply better to the current Court than they do to its predecessors. There is nothing inherent about the Court as an institution that makes its members care solely about its outputs to the exclusion of other goals, but the sorts of people who reach the Court today may have attitudes and perspectives that cause them to give the Court's outputs a very heavy priority—and a higher priority than did the cohorts of justices who served in past eras.

A second possible result of the current recruitment pattern is a stronger concern with legal considerations in decisions. On average, today's justices were immersed longer and more fully in the work of lawyers and judges prior to reaching the Supreme Court than were the justices of past eras. Most directly, such immersion could reinforce a tendency to see choices in terms of law as well as policy. Further, a justice who has risen within the legal system rather than the political system may be oriented primarily to legal audiences, so that the most relevant feedback comes from people who give a high priority to skillful interpretation of the law (see Grossman 1965:206–7). If justices with this orientation predominate on the Court, they could structure the general atmosphere in which issues are considered and decisions made.

This effect should not be exaggerated even as a possibility. If justices are more law-minded today than in past eras, policy considerations still might predominate. The Court's discretionary jurisdiction has created a situation in which it now hears primarily cases with high levels of legal ambiguity—a situation in which a justice's policy preferences are guaranteed to exert considerable impact (see Kunda 1990). Moreover, even legal audiences may reinforce particular policy positions rather than the more abstract goal of good law. Still, the balance between legal and policy considerations may have shifted enough to influence subtly the Court's decisions and doctrines.

Conclusions

Little can be said with certainty about the impact of recruitment on the behavior of Supreme Court justices. Scholarship on the kinds of people who reach the Court and the ways they get there has not gone far in probing this impact. The limits to what we know about recruitment to the Court are suggested by the speculative tone of the preceding section.

What can be said is that there is room for recruitment to make a difference. The situation of Supreme Court justices has powerful effects in freeing justices to concentrate on the content of legal policy. But that freedom is not a constraint: justices could act to advance interests other than their legal and policy goals. Further, the relative weights that they give to legal and policy considerations and to expressive and instrumental behavior can vary. And if such variation is possible, one determinant of the mix of goals and means for the justices is the recruitment process.

If we are to gain a clearer understanding of recruitment as a process shaping Supreme Court behavior, that understanding will come through extensive research taking diverse approaches. At least some of that research should look broadly at the recruitment process, examining the whole series of stages that determine who gets to the Supreme Court rather than only the final set of selection decisions. Some research also should look deeply at the impact of the process, examining its impact on justices' general goal orientations as well as on their policy preferences. Approaches that such studies might take are suggested by some studies of recruitment to judgeships (Schmidhauser 1959, 1979; Watson and Downing 1969) and to other offices (Matthews 1960; Canon 1990).

Whatever the form in which recruitment is studied, it merits more consideration from students of Supreme Court behavior. Proponents of the new institutionalism are right to emphasize the impact of institutions in structuring behavior. But that emphasis can coexist comfortably with an interest in the characteristics of people that shape their choices in institutional contexts (Canon 1990:21–32, 145–54). If the behavior of Supreme Court justices reflects the interplay between their traits as individuals and the situation in which they make decisions, both individual and situation require attention.

Notes

1. Of course, there are also a great many biographies (Howard 1971) and studies of the thought and behavior of particular justices (e.g., Lamb and Halpern 1991).

2. There is considerable variation in the use of these terms. My usage is similar to that of Rodriguez (1994:58) and Calvert and Fenno (1994:349).

3. The linkage also exists in the debate over strategic behavior. Among those scholars who believe that Supreme Court justices think strategically, there is disagreement about the extent of the Court's autonomy from Congress; in turn, that disagreement leads to differing judgments about how much of a constraint is placed on the justices' choices by the congressional power to override decisions (see Segal 1997). More generally, some scholars have argued that the Court situation powerfully influences the justices' choices of strategies (Knight and Epstein 1996a).

4. As this language suggests, this view of the Court can be understood in terms of prescribed role conceptions for justices. As indicated in the preceding paragraph, however, one may believe that this role conception is strong and yet conclude that legal considerations have little impact on the justices' choices.

5. The mean number of cases accepted per term was 180 in the 1984–1987 terms and 99 in 1992–1995. These figures, which exclude original jurisdiction cases and summary decisions, are based on data collected by the Court and published annually by *United States Law Week*.

6. To anticipate a point that is discussed in the next section, recruitment links individual and institution and thus blurs the distinction between them. Decisions whether to seek a position and whom to select for a position are influenced by the perceived characteristics of an institution such as the Supreme Court. Thus, for instance, homogeneity in justices' attributes that produces similar patterns of behavior may reflect institutional characteristics to a considerable degree. But if those characteristics place only limited constraints on variation in justices' behavior, recruitment may have a largely independent impact on the mix of goal orientations on the Court.

7. That one was William Rehnquist, who served in the Nixon Justice Department. But three months before nominating Rehnquist, Nixon remembered his name as "Renchburg" (Abraham 1992:319).

8. It also may reflect the strong criticism of Abe Fortas for his continuing consultation with President Johnson after joining the Court.

10

Mapping Out the Strategic Terrain: The Informational Role of *Amici Curiae*

Lee Epstein and Jack Knight

Without a doubt, most members of Congress (MCs) seek to be reelected to their positions; indeed, some scholars suggest that this is their primary goal (Mayhew 1974). If that is so, then we would expect MCs to take into account the preferences of their constituents when deciding whether or not, say, to vote for a bill. But from where do legislators learn about the desires of their constituents? The answer, according to many legislative specialists, is from interest groups. On this account, lobbyists provide information to MCs about the consequences of alternative courses of action (such as voting for or against a bill). With this information in hand, MCs can then make rational choices, that is, choices designed to maximize their preference for reelection as opposed to electoral ouster.[1] This is one reason why reelection rates for MCs remain so high. Or so the argument goes.

In this chapter, we argue that organized interests—participating as *amici curiae*[2]—play a role for justices similar to that lobbyists play for legislators: they provide information about the preferences of other actors, who are relevant to the ability of justices to attain their primary goal—to generate *efficacious* policy that is as close as possible to their ideal points.[3] In other words, just as information permits legislators to make rational decisions, so too does it enable justices to make choices to maximize their preferences. Perhaps that is why Congress so rarely overturns Supreme Court decisions.

Since this argument follows from a more general account of Supreme Court decision-making—what we call a strategic account—we begin by providing a brief summary of it.[4] Within this discussion, we lay out our assumptions about the goals of justices. This is a necessary step because we can hardly talk about organized interests as helping justices to maximize their preferences if we do not specify the nature of those preferences. The discussion also helps to establish why it is that justices require information. Next, we describe the sources from which justices can gather information (with particular emphasis on briefs *amicus curiae*) and consider the evidence bearing on our argument. Finally, we provide some directions for future research adopting strategic approaches to study the role of organized interests in court.

A Strategic Account of Judicial Decisions

Throughout this chapter, we invoke a strategic account of judicial decisions. This account rests on a few simple propositions: justices may be primarily seekers of legal policy, but they are not unsophisticated actors who make decisions based merely on their own ideological attitudes; instead, justices are strategic actors who realize that their ability to achieve their goals depends on a consideration of the preferences of other actors, of the choices they expect others to make, and of the institutional context in which they act. We call this a strategic account because the key ideas it contains are drawn from the rational-choice paradigm,[5] an approach that has been advanced by economists and political scientists working in other fields.[6] We can, thus, state our primary argument as follows: we can best explain the choices of justices as strategic behavior, and not merely as responses to ideological values.

Shortly we detail how *amici curiae* fit into this account. For now, we simply want to be clear about its major components: justices' actions are directed toward the attainment of goals, justices are strategic, and, institutions structure justices' interactions.

JUSTICES AS GOAL-ORIENTED ACTORS

A key assumption of rational-choice explanations is that actors make decisions consistent with their goals and interests. Indeed, we say that a "rational" decision occurs when an actor takes a course of action (makes a decision) that satisfies her desires most efficiently. All this means is that when a political actor selects, say, between two alternative courses of action, she will choose the one that she thinks most likely to help her attain her goals; all we need to assume is that she acts "intentionally and optimally" toward some specific objective.

To give meaning to this assumption, namely, that people maximize their preferences, however, we must specify the content of actors' goals.[7] And that is where the notion of justices as "seekers of legal policy" comes in. On our account, a major goal of all justices is to see the law—over the long term—reflect their preferred policy positions, and that they will take actions to advance this objective.[8]

This is not a particularly controversial claim. Justices may have goals other than policy,[9] but no serious scholar of the Supreme Court would claim that policy is not prime among them. Indeed, this is perhaps one of the few things over which most students of the judicial process agree.

STRATEGIC JUSTICES

The second part of the rational-choice account ties back to the first: For justices to maximize their preferences, they must act strategically in making their choices. By "strategic," we mean that judicial decision-making is interdependent. That is, a justice acts strategically when she realizes that her fate depends on the preferences of other actors and the actions she expects them to take (not just on her own preferences and actions) (Cameron 1994).

For obvious reasons, justices who care about policy must take account of what other Court members will do.[10] But strategic considerations do not simply involve calculations over the preferences and likely actions of colleagues. Justices must also consider the preferences of other key political actors, including members of the elected branches of government and the American people. The logic here is as follows.[11] As all students of U.S. politics recognize, two key concepts undergird our constitutional system. The first is the separation of powers doctrine, under which each of the branches has a distinct function: the legislature makes the laws, the executive implements those laws, and the judiciary interprets them. The second is the notion of checks and balances: each branch of government imposes limits on the primary function of the others. For example, as figure 10.1 shows, the judiciary may interpret federal laws (and even strike them down as being in violation of the Constitution). But congressional committees can introduce legislation to override the Court's decision; if they do, Congress must act by adopting a committee's recommendation, adopting a different version of it, or rejecting it. If Congress takes action, then the President has the option of vetoing the law. In this depiction, the last "move" rests again with Congress, which must decide whether to override the President's veto.[12]

It is just these kinds of checks that lead policy-oriented justices to concern themselves with the positions of Congress, the President, and even the public.[13] For if their objective is to see their favored policies become the ultimate law of the land, then they must take into account the preferences of the key actors and the actions they expect them to

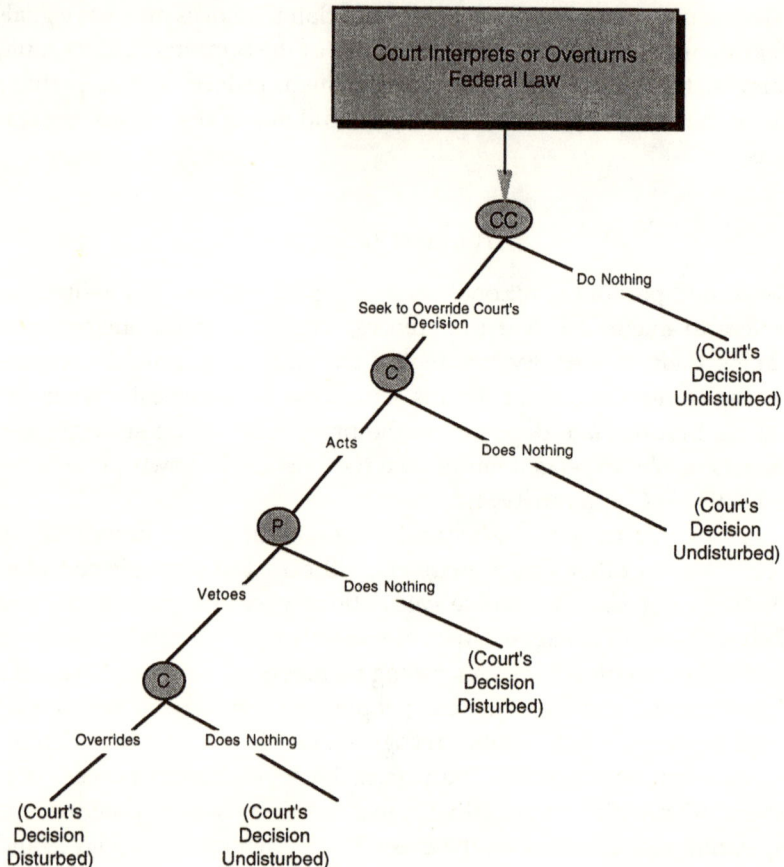

Figure 10.1 The Separation of Powers/Checks and Balances in Action: An Example.

take. Or else they run the risk of seeing Congress replace their most preferred position with their least. Or the risk of massive noncompliance with their rulings, in which case their policy fails to take on the force of law.[14]

INSTITUTIONS

Even from this brief discussion, we can see that policy-oriented justices face a complex strategic decision in their efforts to affect the nature of the law. In attempting to create policies that reflect their own preferences, they must take account of two sets of rules governing two different strategic relationships: 1) the *internal* relations among the justices, and 2) the relations between the Court and relevant *external* actors, such as members of the other branches of government and the American people. Their success in creating particular laws depends on their ability to anticipate the reactions of those other actors in these relationships to their own decisions. That is, the effectiveness of a particular justice is in part a function of how well she is able to develop reliable expectations of the actions of others. It is in this important task of expectation formation that social and political institutions—sets of rules that structure social interactions in particular ways—play a crucial role.

There are many *internal* Court rules that assist the justices in this way. The requirement of a majority for precedent is certainly one. Under this norm, justices know that they must attain the signatures of at least four justices for their decisions to become precedent. The "Rule of Four" is another institution that provides information to assist justices in making choices. Most obvious is that justices know that they *generally* must attract at least four votes to hear a case. If they do not, they will need to bargain with their colleagues to attain the requisite number.[15]

More relevant to our immediate concerns about the role of organized interests in litigation, however, are those rules that govern the relationship between the Court and *external* actors—with an especially important one being an institution underlying the U.S. Constitution, the separation of powers system.[16] As we have already noted, that system, along with informal rules that have evolved over time (such as the power of judicial review), endows each branch of government with significant powers and authority over its sphere. At the same time, it provides explicit checks on the exercise of those powers such that each branch can impose limits on the primary functions of the others (see, generally, figure 10.1).

Seen in this way, the rule of checks and balances inherent in the system of separation of powers provides justices (and all other governmental actors) with important information: *policy in the United States emanates not from the separate actions of the branches of government but from the interaction among them.* Thus, it follows that for any set of actors to make efficacious policy—be they justices, legislators, or executives—they must take account of this institutional constraint by formulating expectations about the preferences of the other relevant actors and what they expect them to do when making their own choices.

SOURCES OF INFORMATION

But from where do justices obtain the information necessary to formulate such beliefs? This is a critical question, for, if justices cannot obtain the necessary information, they cannot act in the manner we suggest or, at the very least, cannot do so effectively. That is, just as members of Congress require information to help them to make decisions that will enhance their chances of reelection, justices need information to guide them toward making choices that will maximize their preferences for establishing law that is as close as possible to their ideal points—and efficacious law at that. This is not to say that justices need know with certainty where other political actors stand on particular issues; it is just to say that they must be able to make some calculation about the nature of the political context in which they are operating.

Two sources, it seems to us, have the potential to supply the information necessary to enable justices to formulate such beliefs. The first is the media. Simply put, we have no reason to suspect that justices, just like other Americans, do not obtain information about current events from television, the radio, and newspapers. Indeed, all the available evidence suggests that justices do, as the saying goes, "follow the election returns." For example, because so many Court members held political positions prior to their ascension to the bench,[17] it would be virtually impossible to believe that they give up their interest in politics when they don their black robes any more than they shed their political preferences (see Baum's chapter in this volume). Moreover, as we know from our research into the private papers of Justices Marshall, Brennan, and Powell, Court members regularly clip articles and editorials about specific cases—those the Court has decided and those awaiting action. At the very least, this suggests that justices are paying attention to how the press reports on their activities; and we can hardly imagine that these are the only articles that they read.

From journalistic accounts justices—like all of us—are able to formulate *general* beliefs about the political environment. Based on the results of the 1996 election, for instance, current Court members know that Congress is led by the Republican Party and that the President is a Democrat, suggesting that Clinton is to the left of (more liberal than) the median members of the House and the Senate.

This sort of information, of course, was also available to justices of earlier eras. From press reports—coupled with their own political insights—they too could make guesses about the preferences and likely actions of other political actors. And these guesses, as accounts of cases of historical import suggest, often turned out to be good ones (See Murphy 1964; Epstein and Walker 1995; Knight and Epstein 1996a:87–120). The 1803 case of *Marbury v. Madison* provides a good example. At issue here were several judicial appointments that President John Adams

had made but that the incoming president, Thomas Jefferson, refused
to deliver. When some of the men denied their commissions (William
Marbury et al.) brought suit, the Supreme Court, led by Chief Justice
John Marshall, had to decide whether or not to force the new administration to deliver the commissions. To be sure, Marshall, himself an
Adams appointee, wanted to give Marbury his appointment. But his
political instincts and his reading of the newspapers of the day suggested that such a move would be risky: forcing the administration to
deliver Marbury's commission, Marshall believed, would lead Jefferson to initiate an effort to have him impeached—an effort Congress
would have supported. *Marbury*, thus, posed a dilemma for the Chief
Justice: vote his sincere political preferences and risk the institutional
integrity of the Court (not to mention his own job) or act in a sophisticated fashion with regard to his political preferences and elevate judicial supremacy in a way that Jefferson could accept. Perhaps not so
surprisingly, Marshall chose the latter course of action, which proved
to be a rational one in light of the politics of the day.

In some sense, Marshall was quite fortunate: he was able to formulate an accurate guess about the nature of the political environment.
But, because that guess was based on sketchy and imprecise information, it could have turned out, like all guesses, to have been wrong.[18]

Today's justices, we believe, are less handicapped. For, in addition
to journalistic accounts, they can draw on a second source of information—briefs *amicus curiae*. And, even more to the point, these submissions potentially enable them to make more *precise* calculations.

We base these assertions on three factors. First, and most obvious,
is that briefs *amicus curiae* are now an ever present part of the Court's
litigation environment, as figure 10.2 shows. Whereas in John Marshall's day—and even into the Warren Court era—friend-of-the-court
submissions were rare,[19] contemporary justices can expect to receive at
least one *amicus curiae* brief in virtually all of the cases they accept for
review; in fact, the typical *amicus* case (a case with one or more *amicus
curiae* briefs) contains not one but 4.4 such briefs (see Epstein 1993:639–
717).

Second, because *amicus curiae* briefs almost always take a position on
a case, they not only inform the justices that a particular constituency is
concerned with their decision but of the preferences of that constituency as well. This information can be especially valuable when it comes
from briefs submitted by members of Congress or the U.S. Solicitor
General (SG), who represents the United States in the Supreme Court.
Since such participation is voluntary (that is, these political actors usu-

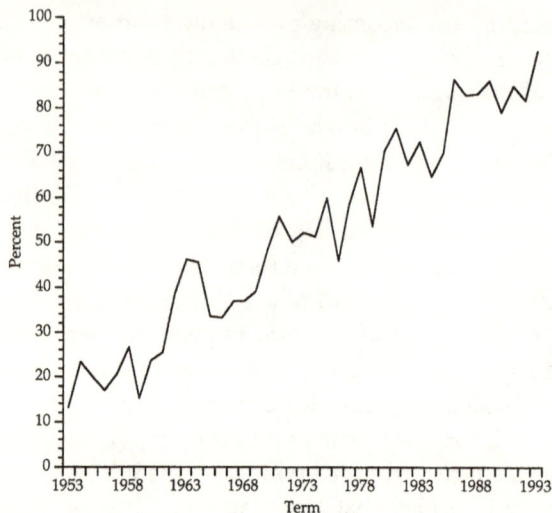

Figure 10.2 Percent of U.S. Supreme Court Cases Containing at Least One *Amicus Curiae* Brief, 1953–1993 Terms.

ally file briefs *amicus curiae* at their discretion),[20] it provides a seemingly reliable indication of where members of the other branches stand on matters of public policy. Indeed, scholars have used the position taken in *amicus curiae* briefs filed by the SG, in particular, to gauge the President's preferences.[21] We suspect that justices do the same.

The final factor centers on the content of *amicus curiae* briefs. It is eminently plausible to believe that organized interests, in filing such briefs, seek to provide information about the preferences of actors (such as Congress, the President, the states, and the public) who are relevant to the justices' ability to attain their policy goals—just as lobbyists provide information to members of the legislature about their constituents' preferences. In other words, we argue that in their friend-of-the-Court submissions, organized interests engage in preference delineation, pointing out to the justices where various political actors stand on the extant policy.[22] And that such information helps the justices to formulate more accurate beliefs about the context in which they are operating than, say, information they obtain from journalistic accounts.[23]

AN EMPIRICAL ASSESSMENT OF THE ACCOUNT

We are, of course, not the first to view organized interests in these terms. As we have already noted, scholars studying legislative politics have long viewed lobbyists as the bearers of information relevant to the ability of members of Congress to attain their goals. Caldeira and Wright have also applied similar logic to briefs *amicus curiae* (1988). They posit that *amicus* submissions filed by organized interests on *certiorari* reduce the U.S. Supreme Court's uncertainty about the importance of a case—in other words, such briefs provide information about the economic, political, and social significance of a petition, thereby increasing the likelihood that the Court will hear it. Their data, consisting of petitions the Court granted and denied during the 1982 term, support this prediction. When more than one *amicus* brief supports review, the probability of review jumps from .08 to .35; even briefs filed against *certiorari* increase the likelihood that the Court will review the case, because, however inadvertently, they too signal that a case is sufficiently important to generate participation. Finally, in a paper advancing a theoretical argument akin to ours, Spriggs and Wahlbeck present empirical evidence to show that *amici* often submit new information to the justices, that is, information not present in the briefs of the parties (forthcoming).

These works suggest the plausibility of our argument but they fall short of providing empirical support for it. Caldeira and Wright focus exclusively on the *certiorari* stage and Spriggs and Wahlbeck, while showing that *amici* provide new information, do not specify the nature of that information. Hence, in what follows, we turn to the task of providing some documentation for the informational role of friends of the Court.

INDIRECT EVIDENCE

There are several pieces of evidence, albeit of an indirect nature, that lend support to our argument. One comes from the rules that the justices have promulgated over time to govern *amicus curiae* participation.

Throughout most of its history, the Court maintained a simple, informal rule regarding *amici*: they need only demonstrate "an interest" in the extant case in order to participate (see *Northern Securities Company v. United States* 1903). But, largely because of ambiguity created by this policy (it was unclear to potential *amici* what the Court meant by "interest"), in 1938 the justices found it necessary to generate a formal rule:

> A brief amicus curiae may be filed when accompanied by written consent of all parties to the case, except that consent need not be had when the brief is presented by the United States or an officer or agency thereof and sponsored by the Solicitor General, or by a State or a political subdivision

thereof. Such brief must bear the name of the bar of this Court.[24]

Since 1938, the Court has revised the rule several times, with the current version as follows:

> An amicus curiae brief submitted before the Court's consideration of a petition for a writ of certiorari, motion for leave to file a bill of complaint, jurisdictional statement, or petition for an extraordinary writ, may be filed if accompanied by the written consent of all parties. . . . When a party to the case has withheld consent, a motion for leave to file an amicus curiae brief before the Court's consideration of a petition for a writ of certiorari, motion for leave to file a bill of complaint, jurisdictional statement, or petition for an extraordinary writ may be presented to the Court . . . .
>
> No motion for leave to file an amicus curiae brief is necessary if the brief is presented on behalf of the United States by the Solicitor General; on behalf of any agency of the United States allowed by law to appear before this Court when submitted by the agency's authorized legal representative; on behalf of a State, Commonwealth, Territory, or Possession when submitted by its Attorney General; or on behalf of a city, county, town, or similar entity when submitted by its authorized law officer.[25]

Two aspects of the evolution of this rule are relevant to our concerns. Note, first, the plain words of both the 1938 and the current policy: all interests wishing to participate as *amici curiae* must obtain the consent of the parties—with the exception of governments.[26] That the Court has always excluded governments from this requirement is quite consistent with our account. For, from these briefs, the justices learn (with some degree of precision) the preferences of sets of actors who are relevant to their ability to attain their goals. It is no wonder, then, that the Court has attempted to facilitate their discretionary participation. Worth noting too is that the justices occasionally invite governments— especially the United States—to participate as *amici* when they have not submitted briefs. Such requests further facilitate the Court's efforts to assess the desires of these important political actors. To see this, we only have to consider the 1993 term, during which the justices issued eighty-four signed opinions. Of those eighty-four, the U.S. government was a party to twenty-one, a voluntary *amicus curiae* in thirteen, and an invited "friend" in five;[27] in other words, in nearly half the opinions issued that term did the justices have some idea of the preferences of the United States.

The second aspect concerns a change in the rules. Note that the 1938 rule provided nongovernmental *amici* with only one way to participate: they had to obtain the permission of the parties to the case. The present rule includes an escape valve. If the parties withhold consent, *amici* can petition the Court. Of course, this valve would not be so important if the Court rejected most of the requests. But that is hardly the case. A study by O'Connor and Epstein shows that between 1969 and 1981, the Court granted 89 percent of the 832 total motions it received.[28] Updated data suggest that the Court has become even more willing to grant such requests; during its 1994 term it denied only one of the 111 motions.[29] Such figures—not to mention the change in rules itself—are again consistent with our account. If we are correct and justices obtain valuable information from these briefs, they would have every reason to create a liberal rule and, in turn, apply that rule leniently.

Another piece of evidence in support of our account comes from data on the participation of the Solicitor General as an *amicus curiae*. It follows from our argument that, if it wanted to create efficacious policy, the Court would pay a good deal of attention to information contained in *amicus curiae* briefs reflecting the interests of the United States Congress, and, at the very least, the preferences of the President. This seems to be the case, as figure 10.3 shows. Overall, between the 1954 and 1993 terms, the Court adopted the disposition advocated by the Solicitor General in 72 percent of the 691 cases in which his office participated as an *amicus*. These findings, as Segal shows, hold regardless of presidential administration (Segal 1991; see also Puro 1971). In other words, even when the United States presents liberal arguments to a conservative Court (and vice versa), it does quite well.

MORE DIRECT EVIDENCE

Certainly, we recognize that the evidence offered above, while consistent with our account, is indirect at best,[30] and that to provide more direct support for it we require data to gauge whether *amici curiae* are actually providing information to the justices about the larger political context.

To make this assessment, we drew a random sample of cases decided during the Court's 1983 term.[31] We then read the *amicus curiae* briefs filed in the cases and coded the kinds of information presented as falling into five possible preference-delineation categories: 1) preferences

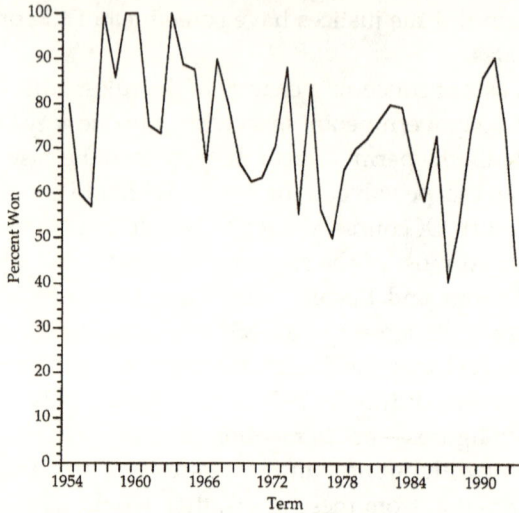

Figure 10.3 Success Rate of the Solicitor General as *Amicus Curiae*, 1954–1993 Terms.

of the enacting (state or national) legislature; and the current preferences of 2) members of the U.S. legislative branch, 3) members of the
U.S. Executive Branch, 4) the states, and 5) the public.[32] By preferences
of the enacting legislative body, we mean claims in *amicus curiae* briefs
about intent, such as "Congress [in Title VII of the Civil Rights Act of
1964] intended to eradicate barriers preventing women and minorities
from reaching all rungs of professional life and contemplated no exemption for lawyers."[33] Illustrations of the current preferences of the
U.S. Congress and Executive are mentions in briefs of recent action
(or inaction) on the matter at hand, including reports and proposed
legislation / rules; and citations to the positions taken by legislators and
the Solicitor General in *amicus curiae* briefs. More concretely, we coded
the following assertion, from a brief filed by several states in *United
States v. Leon* (1984),[34] as containing information on the current preferences of members of Congress and the Executive: "Several justices have
expressly stated that the exclusionary remedy is not of constitutional
dimension, and *this view is concurred in by the current President [Reagan]
and a number of members of Congress.*"[35]

We take information about the current preferences of states to include references to the number that engage (or do not engage) in a
particular practice, as when one *amicus* pointed out that "[t]wenty-four
states have some form of percentage limit on fund raising costs."[36] Finally, evidence of current public preferences could take the form of
statements about the interests of the American people or citations to

Table 10.1
Preference Delineation in Briefs Amicus Curiae

Preference Delineation	Cases (N = 12)		Briefs (N = 58)	
	% yes	n =	% yes	n =
Mention Preferences of Enacting Legislature	33.3	4	32.8	19
Mention Current Preferences of Congress	41.7	5	22.4	13
Mention Current Preferences Executive	66.6	8	50	29
Mention Current Preferences of States	66.6	8	29.3	17
Mention Current Preferences/Interest of Public	91.7	11	62.1	36

Note: Data collected by the authors from *U.S. Supreme Court Records and Briefs*, BNA's Law Reprints.

public opinion data, such as this argument (also made in *Leon*): "According to figures cited by Attorney General William French Smith, *the percentage of the public which felt that the courts do not deal harshly enough with criminals reached 90% by 1981.* Though the exclusionary rule is certainly not entirely responsible for this perception of undue judicial leniency, it cannot have failed to contribute to it."[37]

With these coding rules noted, let us turn to the results of our analysis, displayed in table 10.1. Looking first at the cases in our sample, we note that organized interests filed *amicus curiae* briefs in 75 percent (twelve of sixteen) of cases, a figure well in line with the population.[38] Note, too, the degree of preference delineation that occurred in these twelve cases: in nearly half did at least one of the briefs make an assertion about the current preferences of Congress; that figure was over 90 percent for the interests of the American people. To think about the data in another way, in all but 16.6 percent of the cases were justices able to learn about the preferences of at least two actors relevant to the attainment of their goals.

Consider now the fifty-eight *amicus curiae* briefs filed in the twelve cases. As table 10.1 shows, half or more paid heed to the preferences of the current Executive and the public. And while *amici* were somewhat less attentive to the preferences of the other actors, they did not ignore them completely: 20 percent or more made some assertion about the preferences of the enacting legislature, and of the current preferences of Congress and the states.

In fact, we came across only three briefs that did not delineate one or more of the preferences we considered. But, it is important to note, even those briefs provided valuable information to the justices, though not of the sort we coded. For example, in *Nix v. Williams,*[39] the Legal Foundation of America et al. made several arguments about the potential impact of a Court decision affirming the lower court (which excluded evidence gathered by police), including this one:

> In the present case, there has been exclusion of the most relevant evidence, the fact that defendant led officers to the body of the [victim]. Excluding evidence that the State would have found in any event . . . would go far beyond the appropriate confines of the deterrence function [of the exclusionary rule]. In fact, it would deter good police work . . . and such efforts should not be discouraged.

By the same token, the National School Boards Association's submission—another brief containing none of the attributes for which we coded—in *Board of Education v. Vail* (1984) contained a pointed discussion of precedent:

> The court below grants short shift to *Parratt*[40] on the ground that the precedent in the case was, in the court's opinion below, laid to rest by [the Supreme] Court in its decision in *Logan v. Zimmerman.*[41] That is incorrect. The Supreme Court carefully distinguished *Parratt* from *Zimmerman* by stating that, unlike *Parratt*, *Zimmerman* dealt with an established state procedure that destroyed the "liberty" interest of the complainant without according him proper procedural safeguards. . . . *Zimmerman* in no way limits the clear ruling in *Parratt*.

Surely both kinds of information assist the justices in making their strategic calculations. From the Legal Foundation of America's brief, the justices may have learned something about the potential effect of their decision, which itself speaks to broader issues of compliance and efficacy; from the School Board submission they could have taken away information about how their opinion should treat previously decided cases, which in turn has implications for the opinion's legitimacy and ultimate acceptance by the community (Knight and Epstein 1996b).[42]

On the whole, then, what do we learn from our analysis? The most important lesson is this: Despite the limitations of the data (particularly the fact that we coded only certain types of information), we believe that they provide a convincing case for the informational role of organized interests. At the very least, they show that *amici curiae* more than occasionally provide justices with information about the preferences of actors relevant to their ability to attain their goals.

Discussion

We began this chapter by noting that information from lobbyists helps members of Congress to make rational decisions—ones designed to facilitate their goal of reelection. This provides at least one explanation as to why MCs are so often able to attain their objectives. The argument we have made in this chapter is that *amici curiae* play a similar role in the Supreme Court. They too provide information to the justices. But, of course, since justices do not need to attain reelection to retain their jobs, the information *amici curiae* provide is of a different sort. Largely it is information about the preferences of other governmental actors, who are relevant to the ability of justices to achieve their primary goal—to generate efficacious policy which is as close as possible to their ideal points. Perhaps that is why Congress, while it often considers overturning Supreme Court decisions, rarely does so (Eskridge 1991a).

And yet, ours is just the beginning of an inquiry into the role played by *amici curiae* as information transmitters. Because we have only dealt with information provided by organized interests, important questions remain about the recipients of their information: the justices. For example, do justices attempt to formulate beliefs about the preferences and likely actions of other governmental actors based on the information they obtain from *amici*? Surely we have several reasons to suspect that the answer is yes. For one thing, the fact that *amici* so often include information about the other political units in their written submissions suggests that they believe that justices do engage in expectation formation. After all, given length constraints on briefs, why would *amici* include this information if they thought it would be trivial to justices?

It is also true, as table 10.2 shows, that justices of the current Court regularly cite briefs *amicus curiae* in their opinions, and that at least some of these citations pertain directly to information about preferences. Consider, for example, *Morse v. Republican Party of Virginia* (1996), in which the Court considered whether the Republican Party of Virginia could charge a registration fee to citizens who wanted to become delegates to a convention to nominate the party's candidate for U. S. Senator. Two individuals challenged this policy on the grounds that it violated sections 5 and 10 of the Voting Rights Act of 1965. A three-judge District Court dismissed the suit, concluding that the general rule—that section 5 covers political parties conducting primary elections—does not apply to the selection of nominating convention delegates under a regulation promulgated by the U.S. Attorney General. In his opinion/judgment for the Court, Justice Stevens cited (with approval) the current preferences of the United States on the matter at hand: "[B]oth in its brief amicus curiae supporting appellants in this case and in its prior implementation of the regulation, the Department of Justice has interpreted it as applying to changes affecting vot-

Table 10.2
Citations to *Amicus Curiae* Briefs by Justices
of the Supreme Court

Justice	Number of Citations to *Amici Curiae*	Number of Citations to *Amici Curiae* Divided by Total Opinions Written
Breyer	9	.26
Ginsburg	17	.27
Kennedy	107	.52
O'Connor	311	.65
Rehnquist	474	.66
Scalia	192	.53
Souter	31	.25
Stevens	636	.65
Thomas	33	.30
Total	1810	.59

Source: Lee Epstein, Jeffrey A. Segal, Harold J. Spaeth, and Thomas G. Walker (1996), by the authors using the same data collection strategy as the *Compendium*.

Note: Total Number of Opinions Written includes opinions of the Court, judgments, and dissenting and concurring opinions.

ing at a party convention. We are satisfied that the Department's interpretation of its own regulation is correct."

Finally, we know from our previous research that justices attempt to formulate beliefs about other governmental actors during their conferences.[43] An examination of Justice Brennan's conference memoranda[44] and the notes he took during the justices' private discussions of cases orally argued during the 1983 term reveals that in more than half the cases at least one justice explicitly stated beliefs about the preferences and likely actions of other governmental actors. Exemplary are Brennan's comments in *Norfolk Redevelopment and Housing Authority v. Chesapeake & Potomac Telephone Company* (1983), in which the Court was asked to determine whether a utility company is a "displaced person" within the meaning of the Uniform Relocation Act of 1970. After noting his view of Congress's intent in the legislation at hand, Brennan said, "Congress is in the process of enacting legislation which would prospectively overrule the Fourth Circuit's holding, while also allowing utilities to obtain relocation assistance in certain limited circumstances. It is interesting to note that even if applicable, none of these circumstances would cover the present case." In other words, Brennan attempted to formulate beliefs about congressional preferences and likely actions by looking at the legislature's intent *and* its current behavior. Interesting too is that Congress was not the only actor to whom Brennan was attentive. In *Immigration and Naturalization Service v. Phinpathya* (1984), involving the meaning of the term "continuous physical presence" within the Immigration and Nationality Act, Brennan stated his belief that Congress's purpose was not to punish aliens who left the country to avoid "undue hardship." And that he drew "support for this position from the Attorney General's acquiesce in *Wadman*[45] in 1964, combined with his [position] in this case."

These bits and pieces of data are suggestive; they tell us that attorneys believe that justices find useful information about the preferences and likely actions of other actors; and that justices, at the very least, attempt to engage in expectation formation in their opinions and at their private conference discussions. But, clearly, the data do not allow us to say definitely that justices formulate beliefs about other relevant actors based on information they obtain from *amici*. To make that claim, more systematic research is required to map out the relationship between, say, justices' conference comments and information provided by Court "friends."

Nor does this evidence enable us to answer yet another question we have left unaddressed—one that centers on effect: Do justices' beliefs about the preferences and likely actions of other governmental actors affect the choices that they make?[46] On our theoretical account, the answer, again, is yes. Because the institution of the American separation of powers system (along with other norms structuring the relationship between the Court and external actors[47]) serves as a constraint on justices acting on their personal preferences, we would expect to find evidence of the constraint operating on many of the choices justices make and, ultimately, affecting the law that they create. Since scholars are only beginning to study this important issue, it is one that is quite ripe for future research. And we hope the data presented here, at the very least, will help to advance this line of inquiry. For they provide support for an assumption embedded in most of the existing studies, namely, that justices can obtain information about the preferences and likely actions of other relevant political actors in a great many of their cases.

Notes

This research was supported by the National Science Foundation (SBR-9320284) and the Center for Business, Law and Economics at Washington University. We also thank the editors of this volume for their help as we were developing the chapter. Some of our data come from the Papers of Justice William J. Brennan. We are, thus, grateful to Justice Brennan for allowing us to use his collection and to Mary Wolfskill and David Wigdor of the Library of Congress for easing considerably the data compilation process.

1. For interesting examples, see Caldeira and Wright (1995) and Hansen (1991).

2. *Amicus curiae* means "friend of the court," even though most *amici* support one party over the other.

3. By "efficacious" policy, we mean policy that other political actors and society as a whole will follow and respect. By "ideal point," we mean the justice's preferred position on the policy.

4. We offer a full version of the strategic conception of Supreme Court decisions in our book *The Choices Justices Make* (1998).

5. See Ordeshook (1992). We refer to nonparametric or strategic-choice accounts. Under these, individuals make rational decisions but the rational course of action is contingent upon their expectations about what other players will do unless they have a dominant strategy (a particular strategic choice that will produce the best outcome regardless of what the others do).

6. It also has been applied to the Court. In fact, in a book written over thirty years ago, *Elements of Judicial Strategy*, Murphy (1964) paints a portrait of shrewd justices, who anticipate or know the responses of their colleagues and of other relevant actors, and take them into account in their decision-making; of a group that would rather hand down a ruling that comes close to, but may not exactly reflect, its preferences than, in the long run, see another political institution (e.g., Congress) completely reverse its decisions or move policy well away from its ideal points. *Elements*, in other words, elucidates the strategic nature of judicial decision-making, just as does our account. As such, our intellectual debt to Murphy is huge.

We also owe a good deal to a group of (mainly) law and business school professors who have, in recent years, adopted rational-choice theory to study the role of the Court in the governmental system. See, for example, Eskridge (1991a), Farber and Frickey (1991), Ferejohn and Weingast (1992), Rodriguez (1994), Spiller and Gely (1992).

7. If we do not, then our resulting explanations take on a tautological quality, "since we can always assert that a person's goal is to do precisely what we observe him or her to be doing" (Ordeshook 1992:10–11).

8. By emphasizing "over the long term," we mean that justices wish to create efficacious policy. See note 3.

9. For other goals, see Baum (1994b; and his contribution to this volume).

10. For example, justices know that for an opinion to become the law of the land, at least five members of the Court must join it. (Opinions that fail to obtain the signatures of a majority become "judgments of the Court," which lack precedential value. This majority requirement for precedent is one of the Court's many norms, a subject we take up shortly.) This means that justices who care about maximizing their policy preferences (that is, most justices) are not necessarily free to craft majority opinions that reflect their most preferred positions; rather, they must take account of the preferences and likely actions of their colleagues.

11. We adopt this discussion from Epstein and Walker (1995).

12. In this figure, we depict a sequence in which the Court makes the first "move" and Congress the last. Of course, it is possible to lay out other sequences and to include other (or different) actors (see Zorn 1995). For example, we could construct a scenario in which the Court moves first; congressional committees and Congress again go next but, this time, they propose a constitutional amendment (rather than a law); and the states (not the President) have the last turn by deciding whether or not to ratify the amendment.

13. Virtually every study examining the separation of powers/checks and balances system lends support to this claim. See, e.g., Pritchett (1961), Murphy (1964), Eskridge (1991a), Spiller and Gely (1992), and Cohen and Spitzer (1994). An important exception is Segal (1997:42–43), which provides a good deal of empirical evidence to show that "the institutional protections granted the Court mean that with respect to Congress and the presidency" the justices almost never need to vote other than sincerely.

Whether Segal's conclusion will hold as scholars continue to produce research on this important topic (see, for example, Martin 1996) we cannot say at this point. But, as noted above, the great bulk of the research to date surely supports our assertion in the text.

14. They also open themselves up for other forms of retaliation on the part of Congress and the President: legislation removing their ability to hear certain kinds of cases and impeachment, to name just two (see Murphy 1964).

15. Such bargaining typically takes the form of a threat to publish a dissent from a *certiorari* denial. For more, see Epstein and Knight (1998) and Perry (1991).

16. There are other institutions structuring the relations between justices and external communities, such as legitimacy norms (e.g., the norm favoring respect for precedent and the norm disfavoring the creation of new issues). For more details, see Knight and Epstein (1996b), and Epstein, Segal, and Johnson (1996).

17. Eighty-nine of the 107 justices (including eight of the nine justices serving in 1998) engaged in some sort of political activity before ascending to the high Court. See Epstein, Segal, Spaeth, and Walker (1996:table 4.8).

18. Marshall did not know with certainty whether President Jefferson favored judicial review and whether Congress would have supported the President had Jefferson decided to seek Marshall's impeachment. For more on these points, see Knight and Epstein (1996a).

19. The *amicus curiae* practice traces back to Roman law but the first brief was not filed in the U.S. Supreme Court until 1823. In that year, in *Green v. Biddle* (1823), the justices permitted Henry Clay to participate as an *amicus* because they suspected collusion between the parties. See Wiggins (1976) and Krislov (1963). Although we lack data on the period between 1823 and 1927, Hackman reports that from 1928 through 1952, only seventy of the Court's 549 noncommercial cases contained briefs *amicus curiae* (see Hackman 1969).

20. Occasionally, as we discuss later, the justices will request the U.S. Solicitor General to file an *amicus curiae* brief. But, even in those instances, the Solictor General will typically take a position on the case.

21. See, e.g., Stimson, MacKuen, and Erikson (1995). Further support for this claim comes from studies showing that the position of Solicitor Generals varies

by administration, with those serving under Democratic Presidents filing more liberal briefs than those working for Republicans. See Epstein, Segal, Spaeth, and Walker (1996[1994]:table 7.14).

22. This is not to say that parties to cases could not also provide such information. But, as Spriggs and Wahlbeck (forthcoming) note, "Since litigants are more likely to be narrowly focused on the case outcomes, the broader policy ramifications of the decision may not be discussed in their briefs." The Court's own rules (37.1) make the same point: "An amicus curiae brief that brings to the attention of the Court relevant matter not already brought to its attention by the parties may be of considerable help to the Court. An amicus curiae brief that does not serve this purpose burdens the Court, and its filing is not favored." Moreover, participation as an *amicus curiae* is typically discretionary. This fact, as we note in text, is important for our account.

23. In this chapter, we beg the important question of whether information from *amicus curiae* briefs is credible and, thus, potentially able to influence the choices justices make. Suffice it to note here that, while organized interests have goals (and, certainly, present information that helps them to attain their objectives), this does not mean that the information they present to the justices is not credible. Indeed, the very fact that *amici curiae* incur costs in acquiring the information they put in their briefs, and that justices realize this, provides "a natural indication of credibility." For only if information is costly will there be asymmetry between the *amicus curiae* and the justice; otherwise the justice would be fully informed in which case the information provided by groups would not be influential (see Austen-Smith and Wright 1992:231).

24. Rule 27(9) at: 306 U.S. 708–709 (1938).

25. Rules of the Supreme Court of the United States, Rule 37, available at: http://www.law.cornell.edu/rules/supct/overview.html#24

26. The current rule enables *amici* to motion the Court for consent to file, if the parties refuse. We discuss this change momentarily.

27. The figure of five is not atypical. During the 1995 term, the Court issued seven invitations to the Solicitor General to "submit his views" as an *amicus curiae*; that number was five for the 1994 term. We collected these data via a LEXIS search.

28. The exceptions, as O'Connor and Epstein show, are readily explicable. Seven of the ninety-one leaves denied during this period were untimely, while sixteen were sought by groups represented by pro-life attorney Alan Ernest on behalf of Children Unborn or the Legal Defense Fund for Unborn Children. When these denials are excluded, the Court rejected only sixty-eight of the 832 motions. See O'Connor and Epstein (1983:40–41).

29. Data collected by the authors using the same procedure as did O'Connor and Epstein in "Court Rules and Workload."

30. For example, there are explanations other than the one we offer for the success of the Solicitor General as an *amicus curiae*. See Puro 1971, Segal 1991, Scigliano 1971.

31. Since there is nothing particularly unusual about *amicus curiae* participation during the 1983 term, we have no reason to believe that our sample is not representative of briefs filed in that term, or in earlier or later ones.

32. We obtained the *amicus curiae* briefs from *U.S. Supreme Court Records and*

Briefs, BNA's Law Reprints. We examined only briefs filed on the merits of cases. Data are available from the authors upon request. E-mail Epstein at: epstein@artsci.wustl.edu.

33. Brief Amici Curiae for California Women Lawyers, et al., filed in *Hishon v. King & Spaulding* (1984), no. 82-940. We do not include in this category the preferences of the framers of constitutions. These drafters are hardly able to override the decisions of justices or to pose threats to the institutional integrity of the Court.

34. *Leon* created a good faith exception to the exclusionary rule.

35. Our emphasis. Brief Amici Curiae filed by Kansas et al., in *Leon,* no. 82-1771.

36. Brief Amicus Curiae on Behalf of Independent Sector, et al., filed in *Secretary of State of Maryland v. J. H. Munson Co.* (1984).

37. Our emphasis. Brief of Amici Curiae filed by Kansas et al., in *Leon,* 82-1771.

38. Of the cases decided during the 1983 term, 72.3 percent contained at least one *amicus curiae* brief. Epstein, Segal, Spaeth, and Walker (1996[1994]:table 7.27).

39. *Nix v. Williams* (1984), establishing the inevitable discovery exception to the exclusionary rule. Under this exception, evidence discovered as a result of an illegal search can still be introduced in court if it can be shown that the evidence would have been found anyway.

40. *Parratt v. Taylor* (1981), asking whether negligent actions by state officials can be a basis for an action under 42 U.S.C. 1983.

41. (1982), asking the Court to determine whether a State may terminate a "complainant's cause of action because a state official, for reasons beyond the complainant's control, failed to comply with a statutorily mandated procedure."

42. One potential criticism of our study is that we operate under the assumption that justices (or their clerks) read briefs *amicus curiae,* when that may not be the case. To this, we offer two responses. First, as table 2 (and our discussion of it later in the text) indicates, justices regularly cite these briefs in their opinions. This provides evidence that the justices (or their clerks) read at least some of the submissions. Second, as we have learned from our examination of various *certiorari* and merits memoranda, clerks occasionally delineate the positions taken and rationales invoked by *amici.* Once again, this lends support to the notion that the briefs are getting perused.

43. We report these data, along with the coding procedures, in Epstein and Knight (1998:chap. 5). We obtained them from the Papers of Justice William J. Brennan, Jr., Library of Congress.

44. These are typed versions of the statements Brennan made at conference.

45. *Wadman v. Immigration and Naturalization Service* (1964), in which a lower federal appellate court wrote that a strict construction of the relevant section of the Immigration Act is "inappropriate."

46. Highly pertinent to the question of influence is the credibility issue. See note 23.

47. See note 16.

11

Supreme Court Deference to Congress: An Examination of the Marksist Model

Jeffrey A. Segal

There is a specter haunting political science. . . .

Introduction

No serious scholar of the judiciary denies that the decisions of judges, especially at the Supreme Court level, are at least partially influenced by the judges' ideology. Justices, like most politically sophisticated adults, have preferences of policy and presumably derive greater utility when those preferences are written into law than when they are not. Moreover, the ability of justices to vote their ideological preferences is not problematic. According to attitudinal theorists (e.g., Segal and Spaeth 1993), the legal discretion that exists in the type of cases that reaches the Court combines with institutional incentives that favor independence to produce a Court that is capable of acting like "single minded seekers of legal policy" (George and Epstein 1992:325).

The extent to which justices can realize their goals by acting in such a manner is the subject of much debate. Recent articles advocating rational-choice or positive theories of judicial decision-making claim that even if judges are single-minded seekers of legal policy, they must temper their decisions by what they can do (Eskridge 1991a; Epstein and Walker 1995; Ferejohn and Shipan 1990; Spiller and Gely 1992). The Court does not exist in a political or institutional vacuum, and in order to maximize its policy-based utility it must carefully consider the rules of the game that it is playing. In statutory cases, the relevant rules of the game include the possibility of overrides by Congress. For example, a liberal Court facing a conservative Congress might moderate its views so as to avoid overrides that would leave the policy outcomes even further to the right. Thus, according to these separation of powers models, justices can only maximize their policy goals by reacting to

the constraints imposed by other significant players in the Court's political and institutional environment.

The purpose of this chapter is to provide a series of tests of these
distinct models of Supreme Court decision-making in order to give us
a better empirical view about how the Court reaches the decisions it
does.

Policy-Based Models of Judicial Decision-Making

According to economic models of behavior, humans are utility maximizers. Though it is not necessarily the case that the goals that justices
will seek to maximize are policy goals, factors such as a lack of electoral
accountability and a lack of ambition for higher office make it likely
that policy goals will be at the forefront. Within these models, the major
dispute is over whether the justices can almost always vote their unconstrained preferences, as suggested by attitudinalists, or whether they
must frequently engage in sophisticated behavior, as suggested by
mainline positive political theorists.

THE ATTITUDINAL MODEL

The attitudinal model is well known among judicial scholars and is
discussed in the first chapter of this book, so I will only highlight its
main features. First, there is not one attitudinal programme, but two.
Narrowly speaking, the attitudinal model holds that justices decide
cases on the merits in light of the facts of the case vis-à-vis their sincere
ideological attitudes and values (Schubert 1965; Segal and Spaeth 1993;
Segal 1997). This version of the attitudinal model is a model of unconstrained choice. Because few areas in political life can be well represented by unconstrained choice, judicial attitudinalists have carefully
limited the model in its pure form to the one area where it might plausibly apply: the Supreme Court's decisions on the merits. Some of the
factors that lead to this unique institutional freedom include the following:

- no court can overrule the Supreme Court
- the justices have life tenure with no diminution of pay, and
- docket control weeds out legally unambiguous cases

Though it is true that Congress can overrule the Court by passing
ordinary legislation, the difficulty of passing override legislation combined with the even greater difficulty of the Court's knowing whether
that would happen creates an environment in which members of the

Court can rationally vote their sincere policy preferences. Thus, far from ignoring the institutional environment (see chapter 1), the application of the attitudinal model to the Supreme Court crucially depends on the institutional environment facing the Court in the decision on the merits.

More broadly speaking, attitudinal works have gone beyond the unconstrained-choice model when examining factors such as the vote on *certiorari*, bargaining over the majority opinion, opinion assignments, etc. In these areas, attitudinalists expect that attitudes will be a crucial factor shaping decisions, but not the only factor. For example, justices voting on *certiorari* must carefully consider the likely outcome on the merits before choosing whether to hear a lower court case (Schubert 1959:chap. 4; Segal and Spaeth 1993:chap. 5; Boucher and Segal 1995). So, too, Court rules requiring the support of a majority of the Court in order for a majority opinion to form leads to acceptance of suboptimal policies there (Rohde and Spaeth 1976:chap. 9; Segal and Spaeth 1993:chap. 7). In sum, outside of the decision on the merits, attitudinal works, broadly defined, very much resemble many of the strategic-choice hypotheses of more recent vintage (e.g., Epstein and Knight 1995b; Maltzman and Wahlbeck 1996b; but see Murphy 1964 for some early applications of rational-choice theory to judicial questions).

Whatever the similarities between the two models, they clearly diverge on the question of the vote on the merits. Positive political theorists argue that justices must frequently defer to Congress in order to avoid being overturned, while attitudinalists claim that justices are in fact capable of voting their sincere policy preferences.

Empirically, the attitudinal model is well supported in the literature. Various scholars have found high correlations between the justices' attitudes and their votes (Segal and Cover 1989; Segal et al. 1995; Segal 1997). Nevertheless, I must note that tests of the model prior to the Vinson Court and in areas other than civil liberties are in short supply.

Theoretically, the most plausible criticism of the model is that in order to be an effective policy maker, the Court would frequently have to defer to Congress and the President, especially in statutory cases. This, though, is an empirical question that I hope to answer, at least partially, in this paper.

Less convincing are criticisms that suggest that the attitudinal model is a model of naïve decision-making (Epstein and Knight 1995b:2; Epstein and Walker 1995; Maltzman and Wahlbeck 1996b:582). Despite these assertions, the model does not hold that justices are myopic decision makers who are unconcerned about what Congress might do;

rather, the model holds that justices act in a structural and institutional environment that allows them to be rationally sincere decision makers. If their preferences can rarely be overturned by Congress and if they only have vague notions as to when overrides might occur, sincere voting may readily dominate purportedly sophisticated voting.

Finally, critics have contended that under the attitudinal model, behavior beyond the decision on the merits is determined solely by raw preferences. For example, a few scholars have at times claimed that under the attitudinal model, justices would apply their unconstrained preferences and nothing else to, say, the joining of majority opinions (Epstein and Knight 1995b; Wahlbeck, Maltzman and Spriggs 1996). If the attitudinal model made such claims, it would certainly be in error. Clearly, though, it does not. First, the attitudinal model's notion of unconstrained choice has been applied only to the decisions on the merits because that is the one plausible area where Supreme Court decisions could be unconstrained. The unconstrained-choice model has never been applied by any attitudinalist to any other stage of Supreme Court decision-making. Second, where attitudinalists have considered other stages of Supreme Court decision-making, the arguments, though viewing policy preferences as primary, have explicitly taken into account contextual and strategic factors (Rohde and Spaeth 1976:chap. 9; Segal and Spaeth 1993:chap. 7).[1] In sum, careful attention to what attitudinalists have actually done provides models of rationally sincere behavior on the decision on the merits, where institutional rules and structures protect the Court; and the likelihood of sophisticated policy-driven behavior at other stages, where rules and structures are more constricting.

THE POSITIVE POLITICAL THEORY MODEL

The question over the extent to which the justices can successfully impose their policy preferences on society by acting sincerely on the merits derives from the separation of powers model of Marks (1988), who carefully examined the placement of preferences in Congress that prevented *Grove City College v. Bell* (1984) from being overturned prior to 1986.[2] While what I label "the Marksist model" spawned many of the positive models demonstrating judicial deference to Congress, Marks himself modeled Court preferences as exogenous. To Marks, the justices simply voted their ideal points, that is, their most preferred positions. The task of modeling Court decisions as dependent upon congressional preferences fell to subsequent neo-Marksist theorists, such

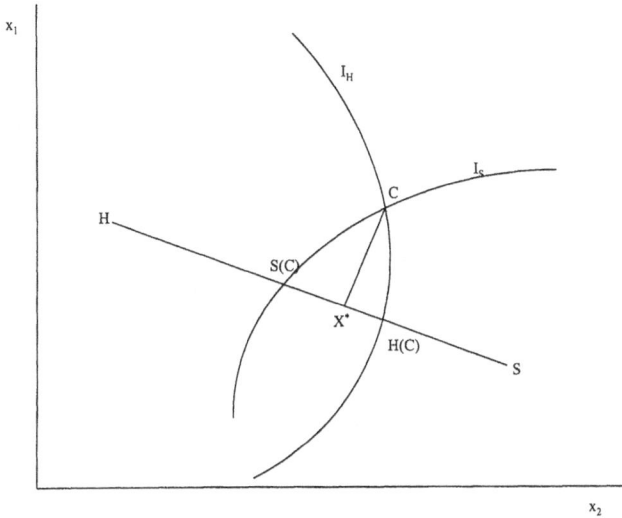

Figure 11.1 The Neo-Marksist Model.

as Ferejohn and Shipan (1990), Gely and Spiller (1990), and Spiller and Gely (1992). I present a standard representation of these models.

Consider the example in figure 11.1, where the Court must decide a case in two-dimensional policy space. The game is played as follows. First, the Court makes a decision in (x_1, x_2) policy space. Second, the House and Senate can override the Court decision if they can agree on an alternative. H, S, and C represent the ideal points of the House, Senate, and Court, respectively. The line segment HS represents the set of Pareto Optimals. That is, no decision on that line can be overturned by Congress, because improving the position of one Chamber by moving policy closer to its ideal point necessarily worsens the position of the other. Alternatively, any decision off of HC, call it x, can be overturned, because there will necessarily be at least one point on HC that both H and C prefer to x. Imagine, for example, a decision at the Court's ideal point, C. The arc I_s represents those points where the Senate is indifferent to the Court's decision. And obviously, the Senate prefers any point inside the arc to any point on the arc (or, obviously, outside the arc). Similarly, I_h represents those points where the House is indifferent to the Court's decision. Thus, both the House and Senate prefer any point between S(C) (the point on the set of Pareto Optimals where the Senate is indifferent to the Court's decision) and H(C) (the point on the set of Pareto Optimals where the House is indifferent to the Court's decision) to a decision at C.

What, then, should a strategic Court do in this situation? If the Court rules at its ideal point, or indeed at any place off the set of Pareto Optimals, Congress will overturn the Court's decision and replace it with something that is necessarily worse from the Court's perspective. For example, if the Court rules at C, then Congress's result will be some place between S(C) and H(C). The trick for the Court is to find *the* point on the set of Pareto Optimals that is closest to its ideal point. By the Pythagorean Theorem, it accomplishes this by dropping a perpendicular onto the line. Thus, rather than voting sincerely at C and ending up with a policy someplace between S(C) and H(C), the Court rules at X*, the point between S(C) and H(C), indeed, the point between H and S, that it prefers the most.

The models of Ferejohn and Shipan (1990), Gely and Spiller (1990), and others vary in several details, such as the number of dimensions of the issues, the number of legislative chambers, the influence of committees, the existence of presidential veto, etc. But regardless of the specific assumptions made, these models (with the important exception of Marks) assume that the Court will push legislation as close to its ideal point as possible without getting overturned by Congress.

Theoretically, these models suffer from several problems: they almost always give Congress the last word, when the Supreme Court can readily review congressional overrides; they typically give the Supreme Court complete and perfect information over the preferences of Congress, such that the Court knows whether Congress would vote to override any decision the Court made; they generally force the Court to act in statutory mode when the Court can frequently switch to constitutional mode; and finally, these models underestimate the difficulty of passing override legislation, by ignoring factors such as transaction and opportunity costs. These real-world factors lead attitudinalists to argue that it might be completely rational for policy-minded justices to almost always vote their sincere policy preferences (see Segal 1997).

Empirically, most of the support for these models comes from case studies of decisions, often selected on the dependent variable, that appear to satisfy the expectations of the model. Yet as Epstein notes, "[T]he modus operandi of the theorem provers who have studied these questions will not suffice. The standards of social science simply require more than reading some cases (e.g., *Grove City* seems to be a favorite), developing a model, and then testing the model against the same cases used to develop it (again, *Grove City* comes to mind)" (quoted in Segal 1994:12).

Moreover, we must consider Baum's contention that an extraordinarily wide array of behavior can be interpreted consistently with strategic action (1995:4). Consider, for example, the Court's actions in *Ex parte Milligan* (1866), as discussed by Epstein and Walker (1995). In the case, the Supreme Court declared that "Milligan, a Confederate sympathizer living in Indiana, could not be arrested and tried by the military when civilian courts were in full operation and the area was not a combat zone" (1995:315–16). In April 1866, the Supreme Court issued a little noticed order, without an opinion, releasing Milligan. It was not until December of that year, after the Radical Republicans made monumental gains in the November elections, that the Court issued its opinion rendering Congress unable to create military tribunals remote from the actual theater of war. While April's order seems rational enough given the contemporary political environment, December's opinion does not. Moreover, the December opinion need not have been so harsh. The Court, for example, might have averted a crisis by adopting the more moderate opinion of Justice Chase. The Chase concurrence, and not the Davis majority, is arguably the action that the Court should have taken had it been behaving strategically. Indeed, had the Chase opinion been the majority, it would have been easy for Epstein and Walker to write that the Court readily and clearly saw what the results of the 1866 election meant.

More telling, perhaps, is Eskridge's (1991b) analysis of the Court's civil rights decisions. When the Court rules consistently with congressional preferences, it strategically defers to Congress. But when the Court rules inconsistently with congressional preferences, it is because the Court was "mistaken about the congressional median" (658), or was trying to shift Congressional preferences (659). With these saving maneuvers, the strategic model of behavior becomes completely unfalsifiable.

It may be useful to compare strategic and sincere models of Supreme Court decision-making during the three periods that Eskridge studies: 1962–72; 1972–81; and 1981–90. During the first period, there is no conflict between the two. Eskridge remarks that the Court was able to vote its sincere preferences because the legislative gatekeepers protected the Court from remedial legislation (646). During the second period, Eskridge argues that the Court voted more liberally than it otherwise would have due to fear of override by a liberal President and Congress. Needless to say, the characterization of Richard Nixon and Gerald Ford as civil rights liberals is just not supported by the evidence (Segal 1997). Moreover, a conservative Senate Judiciary Committee, chaired by James Eastland, undoubtedly would and could have protected the Court from whatever conservative decisions it might have wanted to make. A more likely explanation of the Court's moderate course is its composition. Through 1975 the Court consisted of three hard-core liberals (Douglas, Brennan, and Marshall) and three justices who had always been moderate on civil rights (White, who stayed moderate on civil rights even after he moved rightward on most other issues [Epstein et al. 1994:453–54]; Stewart, whom Southern conservatives strongly opposed during his nomination because of his progressive views on civil rights [Segal and Cover 1989]; and Blackmun, who was never as conservative on civil rights as he originally was on other issues [Epstein et al. 1994:442–43]). In 1975, Stevens replaced Douglas, but Stevens locates to the left of Stewart so this did not change the median (Epstein et al. 1994:449–51). Thus, I conclude that the Burger Court was moderate not because a liberal Congress and President pushed them in that direction, but because the moderate wing had a clear working majority. The fact that the early Burger Court was not constrained by Congress and the President in a liberal direction is proven by the fact that when the White House and Senate went Republican following the 1980 election, the justices on the Burger Court did not move to the right (Segal 1997).

Finally, in the 1987–90 period, following Democratic control of the Senate, the Court issued a series of hard-core conservative decisions. Eskridge readily admits that the Court was far more conservative than it should have been during this period. He argues that the Court was trying to inform Congress of the correctness of the Court's views, but another way of putting it is that the Court simply was voting sincerely in a manner that led to a large number of significant overrides. Thus, I believe, a clear case can be made that the Court voted sincerely throughout the period Eskridge studied.

Only one published work to date (Spiller and Gely 1992) provides any systematic support for the separation of powers model, though the conclusions to be drawn are mixed, as the authors recognize.[3] More recently, I found little support for the model (Segal 1997), though that work only looked at civil liberties decisions, and employed one (out of many possible) methodology. If my results are robust, they should apply to alternative issue areas (such as economics) and with alternative statistical tests. "It is high time that [Marksists] should openly, in the face of the whole world, systematically test their views" (Marx and Engels 1955:8),[4] for they are in dire need of greater systematic support.

Testing the Models

My basic strategy in testing the attitudinal and separation of powers models is to examine how the votes of U.S. Supreme Court justices

Table 11.1
Political Environment and Predicted Restraints, 1947–1993

Years	Era	Presidency	House	Senate	Predicted Shift
1947–48	1	Democrat	Republican	Republican	
1949–52	2	Democrat	Democrat	Democrat	Liberal
1953–54	3	Republican	Republican	Republican	Conservative
1955–60	4	Republican	Democrat	Democrat	Liberal
1961–68	5	Democrat	Democrat	Democrat	Liberal
1969–76	6	Republican	Democrat	Democrat	Conservative
1977–80	7	Democrat	Democrat	Democrat	Liberal
1981–86	8	Republican	Democrat	Republican	Conservative
1987–92	9	Republican	Democrat	Democrat	Liberal
1993	10	Democrat	Democrat	Democrat	Liberal

change as the political environment changes. Under my tests, justices can either be constrained by the political environment, such that voting their sincere preferences might potentially lead to override, or not constrained by the political environment, such that Congress and the President cannot or would not overturn their decisions. If the attitudinal model is correct, changes in the political environment should have little impact on the votes of the justices, regardless of whether the justices appear to be constrained or not. On the other hand, if the separation of powers model is correct, justices will defer to Congress when they might be constrained.

I conduct my tests by characterizing the 1947 through 1993 period as consisting of ten distinct political environments, as presented in table 11.1. If Congress and the President constrain the Court, we should observe changes in their voting behavior as the political environment shifts from Democratic to Republican to Democratic, etc. If the attitudinal model is correct, by and large we should see few such changes.

Data for the empirical tests consist of all statutory decisions in civil liberties and economic cases rendered by the Supreme Court between the beginning of the 1946 term and the end of the 1992 term. The data were derived from the U.S. Supreme Court Judicial Database, as backdated by Harold Spaeth to cover the Vinson Court era.[5] This selection procedure yielded 2,217 cases: 1,052 in civil liberties and 1,165 in economics. The Court voted liberally in 48.2 percent of the civil liberties cases and 60.2 percent of the economics cases.[6]

The next step is to determine which justices should be constrained in any given configuration of the political environment. Though there might be many ways of operationalizing the separation of powers models, I rely for this paper on broad, wholesale changes in the political environment described above. It is plausible, though not beyond dispute, that these changes in the political environment can adequately capture the spirit of the separation of powers models. On the one hand, these changes do not account for important institutional factors such as committee and leadership positions. Nevertheless, recent models of congressional law-making provide theoretical and empirical evidence that policy-making typically represents neither independent committee preferences nor independent leadership preferences, but the preferences of the majority party caucus (Cox and McCubbins 1993; Kiewiet and McCubbins 1991). Under such models, the type of legislation that can come to a vote and be approved by a chamber moves to the left when the chamber switches from Republican control to Democratic control and moves to the right when control passes from Democrats to Republicans. Thus, for example, the takeover of the Senate by Republicans, as in the 1980 elections, moves the balance of power in that chamber and in its Judiciary Committees to the right.

This model can be viewed as a reasonable approximation of Congressional outputs vis-à-vis Supreme Court decisions if

1) the committees are not made up of preference outliers, or
2) through institutional procedures such as discharge petitions and amendments, the Judiciary committees and party leaders cannot in fact act as *independent* agenda setters.

The scholarly literature on the preferences of committee members has not yielded consistent results. Weingast and Marshall (1988), for example, examined a number of committees and subcommittees in the House and found clear evidence of committees being constituted of preference outliers. Alternatively, Krehbiel's (1990) survey of House committees, including Judiciary, found almost no evidence of committee outliers. To be sure, Krehbiel's findings have been disputed. But even his critics find that committee bias is most likely to exist on committees whose jurisdiction is narrow and homogenous and who consider issues with concentrated benefits and dispersed costs (Hall and Grofman 1990:1163). This sounds much more like Agriculture and Armed Services than Judiciary and, perhaps, Commerce. For the House and Senate Judiciary Committees, at least, there is little empirical evidence of preference outliers (Cox and McCubbins 1993:chap. 3; Segal 1995).

Finally, even if the relevant committees consisted of preference out-liers, the party-caucus model would be reasonable if institutional de-signs enabled the floor to bypass committees that bottle up legislation. In the Senate, this is easily accomplished through amendments, which need not be germane. In the House, this can similarly be accomplished through a discharge petition, which requires no more than a simple majority. From a rational choice point of view, the fact that discharge petitions are almost never passed is hardly evidence for committee power, for, in equilibrium, committees would anticipate such action and approve legislation favored by the floor. Indeed, perhaps the only roll-call study to test whether committee votes are endogenous to floor outcomes clearly demonstrates that committees are significantly more likely to approve legislation if it is favored by the floor, even after con-trolling for the committees' preferences (VanDoren 1991). In sum, my goal is not to demonstrate the absolute validity of the operationaliza-tion, but merely to demonstrate its reasonableness. With the caveat that all tests, including these, are subject to alternative operationalizations, I continue.

Under the separation of powers model, not all shifts in the political environment should result in change for all of the justices. For example, a moderate Democrat on the Court should be uninfluenced by the shift to the Republican Party in 1981, as the Democratic House could block any attempts to override moderately liberal Court decisions. But if the Court is constrained by Congress, and if some of the justices do re-spond to such constraints, then some of these shifts should cause changes in the voting patterns of some of the justices in a manner con-sistent with the separation of powers model. Categorizing justices as liberals, moderate liberals, moderates, moderate conservatives, and conservatives, my assumptions are as follows:

1. Democratic (Republican) control of at least one chamber of Congress insulates liberals (conservatives) on the Court from being overruled. Under split control of Con-gress, all others are likewise unconstrained.
2. Control of the Presidency has a lesser effect: a Democratic (Republican) president facing a united Republican (Dem-ocratic) Congress insulates moderate liberals, but not pure liberals, from being overruled. Moderates, moderate conservatives (moderate liberals) and conservatives (lib-erals) are unconstrained.
3. When the government is completely unified by the Dem-ocrats (Republicans), moderate liberals (moderate con-

Table 11.2
The Justices' Constraints, 1947–1993

Years	Presidency	House	Senate	Constrained Justices	Direction
1947–48	Democrat	Republican	Republican	L	Conservative
1949–52	Democrat	Democrat	Democrat	M, MC, C	Liberal
1953–54	Republican	Republican	Republican	L, ML, M	Conservative
1955–60	Republican	Democrat	Democrat	C	Liberal
1961–68	Democrat	Democrat	Democrat	M, MC, C	Liberal
1969–76	Republican	Democrat	Democrat	C	Liberal
1977–80	Democrat	Democrat	Democrat	M, MC, C	Liberal
1981–86	Republican	Democrat	Republican	None	
1987–92	Republican	Democrat	Democrat	C	Liberal
1993	Democrat	Democrat	Democrat	M, MC, C	Liberal

Note. C = Conservative. L = Liberal. M = Moderate. MC = Moderate Conservative. ML = Moderate Liberal.

servatives) and liberals (conservatives) are insulated from being overruled. All others are constrained. Conservative (liberal) justices are more constrained facing a unified Democratic (Republican) government than they are facing a Democratic (Republican) Congress alone.

Table 11.3
Justices' Liberal Support Score in Constitutional Cases, 1946–1993 Terms

Justice	Civil Liberties	Economics	Justice	Civil Liberties	Economics
Black	75.1	85.7	White	43.1	60.4
Reed	37.5	56.3	Goldberg	93.1	41.7
Frankfurter	54.2	42.7	Fortas	85.0	71.4
Douglas	91.8	73.7	Marshall	84.2	72.1
Murphy	88.7	81.5	Burger	28.6	54.0
Jackson	37.6	30.9	Blackmun	50.9	60.3
Rutledge	85.9	72.4	Powell	39.4	59.0
Burton	40.0	53.5	Rehnquist	17.5	64.5
Clark	46.4	69.6	Stevens	64.0	49.0
Minton	42.1	55.6	O'Connor	30.9	47.1
Warren	83.0	73.1	Scalia	25.6	56.4
Harlan	43.3	53.3	Kennedy	38.8	51.5
Whitaker	44.2	47.1	Souter	54.3	40.0
Brennan	83.1	71.1	Thomas	23.8	41.2
Stewart	51.3	52.9	Ginsburg	63.2	33.3

Table 11.4
SOP-Derived Predictions for Changes in Economics Cases, 1946–1993

Justice (Eras)	Ideology	Political Eras								
		1–2	2–3	3–4	4–5	5–6	6–7	7–8	8–9	9–10
Black (1–6)	Liberal	+	−	+						
Reed (1–4)	Moderate	+	−	+						
Frankfurter (1–5)	Moderate	+	−	+	+					
Douglas (1–6)	Liberal	+	−	+						
Murphy (1–2)	Liberal	+								
Jackson (1–3)	Mod Con	+	−							
Rutledge (1–2)	Liberal	+								
Burton (1–4)	Moderate	+	−	+						
Vinson (1–3)	Moderate	+	−							
Clark (2–5)	Mod Lib		−	+						
Minton (2–4)	Moderate		−	+						
Warren (3–6)	Liberal			+						
Harlan (4–6)	Moderate				+	−				
Brennan (4–9)	Liberal									
Whittaker (4–5)	Moderate				+					
Stewart (4–8)	Moderate				+	−	+	−		
White (5–9)	Mod Lib									
Fortas (5–6)	Mod Lib									
Marshall (5–9)	Liberal									
Burger (6–8)	Moderate						+	−		
Blackmun (6–10)	Mod Lib									
Powell (6–9)	Moderate						+	−		
Rehnquist (6–10)	Mod Lib									
Stevens (6–10)	Moderate						+	−		+
O'Connor (8–10)	Moderate									+
Scalia (8–10)	Moderate									+
Kennedy (9–10)	Moderate									+
Souter (9–10)	Moderate									+
Thomas (9–10)	Moderate									+

These assumptions are all consistent with the separations of powers literature and will guide the tests that follow. The constraints on the justices are detailed in table 11.2.

I examine shifts by the justices, as above, using simple difference-of-means tests, examining the justices' votes for either statistically or substantively meaningful changes that are consistent with the separation of powers model. To derive specific predictions, I have labeled justices as liberal, moderate liberal, moderate, moderate conservative, and conservative based on what should be a relatively pure measure of their preferences: their liberal support scores in constitutional cases.[7] I code justices as liberal if their support scores are greater than 70 percent, moderately liberal if they are between 60 percent and 70 percent,

Table 11.5
SOP-Derived Predictions for Changes in Civil Liberties Cases, 1946–1993

Justice (Eras)	Ideology	Political Eras								
		1–2	2–3	3–4	4–5	5–6	6–7	7–8	8–9	9–10
Black (1–6)	Liberal	+	−	+						
Reed (1–4)	Mod Cons	+	−							
Frankfurter (1–5)	Moderate	+	−	+	+					
Douglas (1–6)	Liberal	+	−	+						
Murphy (1–2)	Liberal	+								
Jackson (1–3)	Mod Cons	+	−							
Rutledge (1–2)	Liberal	+								
Burton (1–4)	Moderate	+	−	+						
Vinson (1–3)	Mod Cons	+	−							
Clark (2–5)	Moderate		−	+	+					
Minton (2–4)	Moderate		−	+						
Warren (3–6)	Liberal			+						
Harlan (4–6)	Moderate				+	−				
Brennan (4–9)	Liberal									
Whittaker (4–5)	Moderate				+					
Stewart (4–8)	Moderate				+	−	+	−		
White (5–9)	Moderate					−	+	−		
Fortas (5–6)	Liberal									
Marshall (5–9)	Liberal									
Burger (6–8)	Conservative						+	−		
Blackmun (6–10)	Moderate						+	−		+
Powell (6–9)	Mod Cons						+	−		
Rehnquist (6–10)	Conservative						+	−	+	+
Stevens (6–10)	Mod Lib									
O'Connor (8–10)	Mod Con									+
Scalia (8–10)	Conservative								+	+
Kennedy (9–10)	Mod Con									+
Souter (9–10)	Moderate									+
Thomas (9–10)	Conservative									+

moderate if they are between 40 percent and 60 percent, moderate conservative if they are between 30 percent and 40 percent, and conservative if they are below 30 percent. The scores are presented in table 11.3. The predictions are presented in table 11.4 for economic cases and table 11.5 for civil liberties cases. These tables also contain the predictions, if any, for each justice as the political environment changed from one era to another. A "+" represents a predicted change in the liberal direction, while a "−" represents a predicted change in the conservative direction. A blank represents no predicted change.

The economics cases yielded forty-six predictions. Justices whose votes move significantly (p < .05, one tailed) in the direction of the political environment receive a "+"; those who move significantly in

Table 11.6
Accuracy of SOP-Derived Predictions, Economic Cases, 1946–1993

Justice (Eras)	Ideology	Political Eras								
		1–2	2–3	3–4	4–5	5–6	6–7	7–8	8–9	9–10
Black (1–6)	Liberal	xx	xx	x						
Reed (1–4)	Moderate	x	x	+						
Frankfurter (1–5)	Mod Cons	x	x	x	x					
Douglas (1–6)	Liberal	x	x	+						
Murphy (1–2)	Liberal	x								
Jackson (1–3)	Moderate	x	x							
Rutledge (1–2)	Liberal	x								
Burton (1–4)	Moderate	x	x	x						
Vinson (1–3)	Moderate	x	x							
Clark (2–5)	Mod Lib		x	+						
Minton (2–4)	Moderate		x	x						
Warren (3–6)	Liberal			+						
Harlan (4–6)	Moderate				x	x				
Brennan (4–9)	Liberal									
Whittaker (4–5)	Mod Cons				x					
Stewart (4–8)	Moderate				x	x	x	x		
White (5–9)	Moderate									
Fortas (5–6)	Mod Lib									
Marshall (5–9)	Liberal									
Burger (6–8)	Moderate						x	x		
Blackmun (6–10)	Mod Lib									
Powell (6–9)	Moderate						x	x		
Rehnquist (6–10)	Moderate									
Stevens (6–10)	Moderate						x	x		x
O'Connor (8–10)	Moderate									x
Scalia (8–10)	Moderate									x
Kennedy (9–10)	Moderate									x
Souter (9–10)	Moderate									x
Thomas (9–10)	Moderate									x

the opposite direction receive an "xx" (see table 11.6), while those who show no significant changes receive an "x."[8] Of these forty-six predictions, four are significant in the correct direction, while two are significant in the opposite direction (table 11.6). The remaining justices show no signs of constraint.

The civil liberties cases yielded fifty-three predictions. Of these, six are significant in the expected direction, while six more are significant in the opposite direction (see table 11.7). The remaining justices show no sign of constraint. The attitudinal model apparently survives this challenge as well.

While there obviously exist alternative methods of testing the separation of powers model, at the very least, these results should temper

Table 11.7
Accuracy of SOP-Dervied Predictions, Civil Liberties Cases, 1946–1993

Justice (Eras)	Ideology	Political Eras								
		1–2	2–3	3–4	4–5	5–6	6–7	7–8	8–9	9–10
Black (1–6)	Liberal	+	x	x						
Reed (1–4)	Mod Cons	x	x							
Frankfurter (1–5)	Moderate	x	x	xx	xx					
Douglas (1–6)	Liberal	x	x	+						
Murphy (1–2)	Liberal	+								
Jackson (1–3)	Mod Con	x	x							
Rutledge (1–2)	Liberal	+								
Burton (1–4)	Moderate	x	x	x						
Vinson (1–3)	Mod Cons	x	x							
Clark (2–5)	Moderate		x	x	x					
Minton (2–4)	Moderate		x	x						
Warren (3–6)	Liberal			+						
Harlan (4–6)	Moderate				x	x				
Brennan (4–9)	Liberal									
Whittaker (4–5)	Moderate				x					
Stewart (4–8)	Moderate				+	x	xx	x		
White (5–9)	Moderate					x	x	x		
Fortas (5–6)	Liberal									
Marshall (5–9)	Liberal									
Burger (6–8)	Conserv						xx	x		
Blackmun (6–10)	Moderate						x	xx		x
Powell (6–9)	Mod Cons						x	x		
Rehnquist (6–10)	Conserv						x	xx	x	x
Stevens (6–10)	Mod Lib									
O'Connor (8–10)	Mod Con									x
Scalia (8–10)	Conserv									x
Kennedy (9–10)	Mod Con									x
Souter (9–10)	Moderate									x
Thomas (9–10)	Conserv									x

those certain of the validity of them. With the exception of Spiller and Gely (1992), *systematic* evidence in support of these models at the Supreme Court level remains virtually nonexistent.

Discussion

I do not intend the arguments in this paper as evidence against rational-choice theory as applied to courts. The federal courts were designed to be independent; we should not be surprised that they are capable of actually being independent. Moreover, there exists a great deal of evidence that judges, including Supreme Court justices, can act in a sophisticated fashion when they need to (e.g., Brenner 1979; Boucher and Segal 1995; Epstein and Knight 1995b; Murphy 1964). Indeed, the separation of powers games may well prove useful in explaining the decisions of courts that are not as well insulated from political pressures as the Supreme Court is. Finally, the data presented herein do not in and of themselves refute these theories as applied to the Supreme Court. Rather, in the cumulative accretion of knowledge, they simply provide one set of tests that support the attitudinal model over this competitor. As they represent just a small subset of the ways in which these models can be tested, the door is wide open for those with appropriate alternative designs. At the same time, though, it is clear that those who have argued for the necessity of constrained decision-making vis-à-vis the Court's institutional environment might well be mistaken.

Justices of the Court unite! You have nothing to lose but your chains.

Notes

1. It is worth noting that while Wahlbeck et al. claim that the attitudinal model predicts unconstrained behavior on majority opinion coalitions, their primary example of strategic decision-making in that realm comes from Rohde and Spaeth (1976), one of the leading attitudinal works.

2. Specifically, Senate Judiciary Committee Chair Orrin Hatch (R., Utah) was able to keep override legislation bottled up in committee.

3. Martin (1996) provides some evidence for Court deference to Congress, but when he adds four variables representing Congressional preferences to a baseline attitudinal model, the percent of cases categorized correctly from the model actually worsens.

4. The original quote refers, of course, to Communists, not Marksists.

5. I chose all formally decided cases, whether *per curiam* or with signed opinions. For unit of analysis I originally included, in addition to the standard citation plus split votes, records in the data base corresponding to multiple legal provisions (or multiple issues/legal provisions), since numerous cases with statutory content could nevertheless show a constitutional issue in the first record. I then selected all records where the Court's stated authority for its decision was interpretation of a federal statute, treaty, court rule, executive order, regulation or rule. Finally, I deleted duplicate records from the same case dealing with the same value area, unless the direction of the decision differed from one record to the next. I then selected all cases Spaeth coded as dealing with civil liberties and economics.

6. See Epstein et al. (1994:168–69) for the definition of civil liberties cases, economics cases, and liberal decisions.

7. Using citation plus split votes as the unit of analysis, I chose all cases in which the authority the Court gave for its decision was judicial review at the national or state level.

8. Significance levels are based on the standard difference-of-means test.

12

External Pressure and the Supreme Court's Agenda

Charles R. Epp

The Supreme Court's agenda changed dramatically in this century from attention primarily to economic issues to a focus on civil liberties and civil rights (Pacelle 1991). Why did that transformation occur, why did it originate in the early decades of this century, and why did different clusters of rights claims—for instance freedom of speech and women's rights—gain a place on the agenda at very different points in this century? Proponents of the attitudinal model typically explain the transformation and these other variations by reference only to the justices' attitudes, particularly the replacement of conservatives with liberals in the late 1930s and early 1940s and again in the 1950s and early to mid-1960s (Segal and Spaeth 1993:97–118). In their view, judicial attitudes dominate the agenda-setting process because of the relative absence of institutional constraints on that process—the range of discretionary choice among the cases on the docket is unlimited, at least in any practical sense, and any issue that the justices might wish to decide is present among the cases on the docket. Some scholars (McGuire and Palmer 1995) go even further, suggesting that the justices not only have a wide array of choices in setting their agenda but also have the freedom to create issues they wish to decide.

The bare outlines of the agenda-setting process indeed at first may appear to fit those assumptions. Since the Judiciary Act of 1925, the justices have built their agenda largely by approving or denying petitions for *certiorari*, over which they have complete discretion.[1] In recent years the Court has received thousands of *certiorari* petitions annually, presenting a wide range of issues, out of which the Court typically grants *certiorari* to far less than two hundred. As the selection mechanism is discretionary and the available options so numerous, proponents of the attitudinal model have reasoned that changes in the Court's attitudinal composition have been the main influence on the development of the Court's agenda.

I shall suggest, however, that the transformation of the Court's agenda is best understood as the result of an interaction between the justices' policy preferences and two institutional constraints. The first consists of the justices' shared understanding of the Court's institutional responsibility to resolve particular kinds of issues, particularly those over which there is significant conflict in lower courts. The justices have developed an institutionalized reluctance to decide issues that have "percolated" little in lower courts (Perry 1991:230–34). Because of this, the available options for a place on the agenda are limited to those issues on which there is sustained litigation in lower courts. The second institutional constraint is related to the first. The political economy of litigation—particularly the availability of resources for litigation—determines the extent to which there is sustained litigation on any particular issue. On constitutional issues, in particular, the market does not supply those resources. Instead, constitutional litigation typically is dependent on a *support structure for legal mobilization,* consisting of lawyers, organizations, and sources of financing, that makes sustained litigation possible.

I hope to show in this chapter that the development of the support structure for civil liberties and civil rights litigation helps to explain the transformation of the Supreme Court's agenda in this century. My analysis is part of a growing body of scholarship on the interactive development between governmental institutions and nongovernmental organizations (the literature informed by this perspective is quite diverse; see, e.g., Chandler and Daems 1980; Powell and DiMaggio 1991; Griffin 1996; Murphy 1972; Putnam 1993; Sklar 1988; Walker 1991). The Court clearly contributed to the development of the support structure for legal mobilization at several key points in the last century. But my main contention is that attitudinally centered accounts of the development of the Court's civil liberties and rights agenda greatly underestimate that agenda's dependence on the development of institutions outside the Court. Changes in those institutions in this century democratized access to resources for constitutional litigation on noneconomic issues, which made possible the development of the Court's civil liberties and rights agenda.

The Development of the Supreme Court's Agenda

The history of the Court's agenda requires some initial consideration, because how it is described shapes analysis of the most important influences on it. Segal and Spaeth's description of the development of the Court's civil liberties and rights agenda is curiously threadbare, consisting primarily of a summary of landmark decisions (1993:97–118). Thus Segal and Spaeth characterize the civil liberties agenda as originating in the judicial revolution of 1937, with *Palko v. Connecticut* (1937) and footnote 4 of *U.S. v. Carolene Products* (1938) signaling the opening of the new agenda (1993:97, 102); they characterize *Mapp v. Ohio* (1961) as the origin of an agenda on criminal procedure (1993: 107), and so on. In each issue area covered by Segal and Spaeth in their historical chapter (1993:74–124), and particularly in their section on the civil liberties agenda (1993:97–118), they characterize the Court's agenda as a series of policy pronouncements flowing from landmark decisions.

That characterization leads to the inference that the source of the civil liberties agenda has been the Court's attitudinal composition, and that changes in the agenda have resulted only from the replacement of justices. Thus, in Segal and Spaeth's description, *Palko*, footnote 4, and the ensuing civil liberties agenda resulted from the "switch in time" in 1937 and the replacement of conservative justices by liberals beginning with Justice Van Devanter's resignation in May of 1937 (1993:97). This macro-level explanation of changes in the agenda, moreover, is consistent with the attitudinal model's emphasis on the wide latitude for judicial choice at the micro-level in the *certiorari* selection process (1993:191–94, and the literature cited there).

Although judicial policy preferences clearly influence the Court's agenda (meaningful agenda change undoubtedly consists of changes both in case outcomes and in the mix of cases decided), to characterize the agenda only as a creation of judicial preferences distorts the history of that agenda in systematic ways, particularly by ignoring substantial developments prior to landmark decisions as well as the often gradual, evolutionary nature of changes after landmark decisions. Richard Pacelle's research (1991) showed that the agenda space taken up by various issues typically has grown long before landmark decisions on those issues, and that agenda change after landmark decisions is often gradual rather than dramatic.

Those observations—substantial changes before landmark decisions and gradual changes after them—are anomalies for which a wholly attitudinal explanation cannot give a satisfactory account. But the anomalies are understandable if we consider the impact of the support structure for legal mobilization. I shall focus my analysis here on three such anomalies. First, by standard measures of judicial attitudes, most justices serving prior to 1937 (with some notable exceptions) were over-

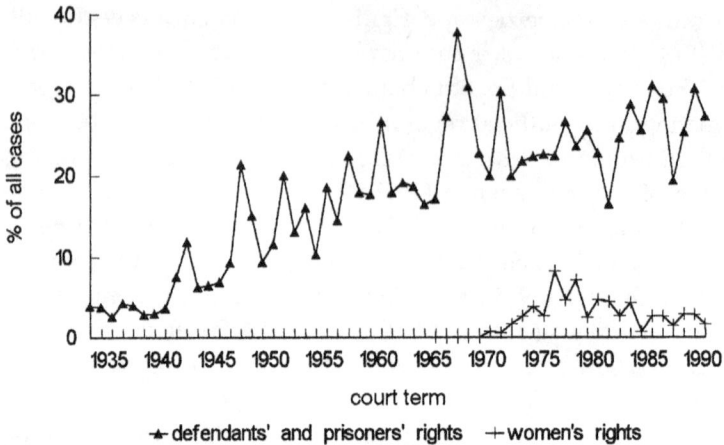

Figure 12.1 Rights Agenda of the Supreme Court.

whelmingly conservative and unsupportive of civil liberties claims (see, e.g., Murphy 1972; Pritchett 1948); yet the agenda space devoted to civil liberties issues began to grow at least two decades prior to the judicial revolution of 1937 in a small burst of litigation on freedom of speech and the press in 1917, 1918, and 1919, and in subsequent cases in the 1920s and early 1930s (Cortner 1981; Murphy 1972).

Second, until 1962 a majority of justices opposed extending to state trials the criminal procedure guarantees of the Bill of Rights; yet, as illustrated in figure 12.1, by that point almost two-thirds of the eventual growth in the agenda space devoted to criminal procedure had already occurred. Third, beginning in 1969 the Court's membership shifted sharply to the right; yet, as illustrated in figure 12.1, within two years the agenda space devoted to sex discrimination and other women's rights issues began to grow (Goldstein and Stech 1995). It is my contention that the development of the Supreme Court's agenda over the last century in these and other areas is best understood by considering not only judicial attitudes but also the justices' beliefs about the Court's institutional responsibilities and changes in the availability of resources for constitutional litigation.

INSTITUTIONAL CONSTRAINTS ON JUDICIAL CHOICE IN THE AGENDA-SETTING PROCESS

THE JUSTICES' BELIEFS ABOUT THE COURT'S INSTITUTIONAL RESPONSIBILITIES

The Judiciary Act of 1925 greatly expanded the Court's discretion over its docket, and the justices have used that discretion to shape their agenda. Individual justices tend to vote to grant *certiorari* more often to cases in which they disagree with the lower court's ruling, to cases in which they can expect their preferred outcome to win in the Supreme Court, and cases in which the justice is a member of a majority ideological position on the Court (Brenner 1979; Brenner and Krol 1989; Segal and Spaeth 1993:165–207). Moreover, recent research by Caldeira, Wright, and Zorn (1996) shows that the justices' decisions to place cases on the discuss list and their votes on cases on the discuss list exhibit patterns that are consistent with allowing a significant role for policy preferences and, concomitantly, for strategic decision-making. Agenda-setting decisions, then, clearly are influenced by preference-based strategies.

Nonetheless, the justices' beliefs about the Supreme Court's institutional role constrain the influence of raw preferences. First, as Epstein, Segal, and Johnson (1996) have argued, the justices are constrained by the *sua sponte* doctrine, of which one variant discourages courts from deciding substantive issues not raised by at least one of the parties to the case. Although the doctrine is not universally followed, it appears to be an important constraint on the justices' willingness to create their own agenda apart from the issues presented by litigants.

Second, the justices have developed an institutionalized reluctance to decide issues that have been the subject of little sustained litigation in lower courts; conversely, they share an institutionalized sense of responsibility to resolve important conflicts among lower courts, particularly among federal circuits. The likelihood that the Court will grant *certiorari* in any particular case is increased by the presence of indicators of important legal conflict in lower courts, particularly when the U.S. is a petitioner; when there is legal conflict *among* lower courts (conflict between federal appellate circuits is especially important); and when there is dissent in a lower court (Caldeira and Wright 1988, 1990; Caldeira, Wright, and Zorn 1996; Perry 1991; Provine 1980). In addition, Perry's interviews with justices and their clerks indicate that the justices are reluctant to take cases that have not "percolated" sufficiently in lower courts (Perry 1991:230–34).[2]

Third, in order for an issue to reach the agenda, the issue typically must be taken repeatedly to the Supreme Court itself. Because of the large number of *certiorari* petitions, as a clerk told Perry, "there is enormous pressure not to take a case" (1991:218). For this reason, early *certiorari* petitions on an issue are likely to be denied. The rationale, according to one of Perry's respondents, is that "it's going to come up again if it's really an important issue. In fact a test to see if an issue is really important is to see if it comes up again" (1991:221).

With some exceptions, cases must meet these threshold requirements—conflict among lower courts, dissent in a lower court, extensive
percolation, and repeated appearance on the docket—in order to be
considered seriously as candidates for a place on the agenda. Occasionally issues reach the agenda without having first percolated exten-
sively. Determined majorities on the Court may seize an issue for policy reasons, or aggressive action by a lower court virtually may force
the Supreme Court to take up an issue (as, for instance, when two federal appellate courts created a right to assisted suicide). Nonetheless,
most issues must meet the threshold requirements for serious consideration by the justices. The significance of these threshold requirements
is that the justices' discretion over their docket is not nearly as unconstrained, and the number of cases among which the justices may choose
is not nearly as large, as the attitudinal model assumes. In fact, Perry's
interviews suggest that the number of *certiorari* petitions open for serious consideration is typically only a small fraction of the total docket
(1991:218). Most petitions do not meet the threshold requirements and
are rejected from the start.

RESOURCE CONSTRAINTS ON THE ISSUES AVAILABLE FOR DECISION

The threshold requirements for access to the Court's agenda limit that
agenda, with some exceptions, to cases that emanate from broad legal
conflict in the lower courts. The attitudinal model's second assumption
is that any issue has been the subject of sufficient litigation to meet the
threshold requirements and gain the Court's attention. But that pre-
sumes a pluralism of litigating interests and an evenness of the litigation playing field that is unjustified in light of large bodies of research
on the structure of the legal profession, the mobilization of social movements and interest groups, and the mobilization of law. Not every issue
is now, nor has been in the past, the subject of extensive litigation in
lower courts, owing in part to limitations in the availability of resources
for legal mobilization.

Constitutional rights litigation, in particular, is greatly limited by the
availability of resources; only those cases supported by a substantial
resource base stand much chance of reaching the judicial agenda (see,
e.g., Lawrence 1990; Wasby 1995). In constitutional rights cases the possible monetary benefits to the litigant often are much less than the costs
of pursuing the case through multiple levels of the judicial system.
The principal benefits of constitutional rights are essentially "public
goods," legal guarantees that benefit a population much broader than

the immediate plaintiff seeking to create or expand the right. Undoubtedly winning a constitutional rights case also provides direct, pecuni-
ary benefits to the successful litigant; but often those benefits do not
cover the costs of the case. Moreover, in many cases the possible beneficiaries of a constitutional right have neither the resources nor any
other capacity necessary even to begin the process of litigating on the
issue, let alone to pursue it through multiple levels of the appeal process. Thus Linda Brown, the main named plaintiff in *Brown v. Board of
Education* (1954), hoped to create a constitutional right whose benefits
extended to a class far broader than herself and the other plaintiffs and
which far outweighed the costs of the case. But the economic returns
to the plaintiffs, in the event of victory, could not have outweighed
their costs and, in any event, it is highly unlikely that Linda Brown's
family had the resources to invest in the case even if assured a certain
victory. As Ruth Cowan observed regarding women's rights litigation,
"Success in the judicial arena, as in other political forums, hinges on
the organization and mobilization of resources" (1976:383). Similarly,
a civil rights litigator told Stephen Wasby (1995:96), "What there's
money for, you tend to do."

Constitutional litigation, then, depends on institutional mechanisms
that overcome cost barriers to individual plaintiffs. Histories of litigation before the Supreme Court provide a fairly clear picture of the nature of such mechanisms in the American context. They are interest
groups; law firms and a diverse legal profession; institutionalized
sources of financing for cases; and legal strategies of lawyers in the
Executive Branch. Organizations provide some resources for constitutional litigation; they coordinate strategies; and they facilitate the dis-
semination of information about cases and legal strategies. Lawyers
screen cases; they offer a variety of mechanisms, particularly the resources of law firms, for overcoming cost barriers to the judicial
agenda; and they form networks that facilitate communication and coordination of strategies. Institutional sources of financing, particularly
private foundations and government programs, help to underwrite the
costs of case development, research, legal fees, and the like. Finally,
the litigation policies of the Justice Department, by supporting the efforts of private litigants as well as initiating lawsuits in the government's name, have exerted a profound influence on the issues taken
to the Supreme Court. Taken together, these various sources form the
support structure for legal mobilization.

Much of the political economy of appellate litigation, it should be
noted, is shaped by government action. Changes in regulatory policy

or prosecutorial policy have provoked litigation by private actors. Thus, the rise of state and federal economic regulation in the late nineteenth century occasioned a growing wave of litigation by businesses, and prosecutions of radicals in the 1910s and 1920s occasioned litigation on free speech issues. Similarly, government support of various kinds, ranging from direct sponsorship to supportive use of *amicus* briefs, has been crucial to the development of the support structure for legal mobilization.

None of these observations about the political economy of constitutional litigation would be relevant if private resources flowed easily and naturally to new subjects of litigation in response to changes in the Supreme Court's attention. Certainly resources shift to some extent in response to the Court's policies. Thus, states began creating right to counsel policies in response to *Powell v. Alabama* (1932), and private foundations increased their contributions to rights-advocacy organizations in response to the Warren Court's civil liberties and rights decisions. But, as I shall show in the remainder of this chapter, the broadest changes in the support structure for legal mobilization in the U.S. were influenced not only by the Supreme Court but also by more broad-based transformations in American society and government.

The Support Structure for Legal Mobilization

The earliest developments in the support structure in the U.S. occurred between 1870 and 1910 in the organizational structures of businesses. Before 1870, most business enterprises were relatively small family-run operations with ad hoc, nonbureaucratic organizational structures and few professional managers. After 1870, in what business historians call the "managerial revolution," the American business sector began converting rapidly to large, bureaucratically structured, professionally managed organizations (Chandler 1977; Chandler and Daems 1980; Sklar 1988). In the United States, the managerial revolution began and flourished first in the railroad industry after 1870; in the 1880s, it spread to areas of the economy involving production of goods; in the late 1890s, it expanded into a merger revolution in which bureaucratic enterprises joined to form still larger organizations. By the middle of the second decade of this century, the managerial revolution had ended, having transformed organizational structures in many areas of the American economy.

The managerial revolution in American business produced the first nongovernmental organizations with the capacity and the interest to pursue long-term, strategic litigation. Their interest in strategic litigation grew out of the growth in government regulation. To influential political thinkers, as well as large sections of the population, the growth of large business organizations threatened traditional conceptions of the primacy of the individual and the importance of individual initiative in the economy (see, e.g., Croly 1965:105–17, 351–454). Legislatures responded by attempting to regulate the power of the new business organizations, leading to a massive change from previous conceptions of the limited constitutional powers of government (Gillman 1993:47–193). Business organizations, naturally, had an interest in manipulating the new regulations in their favor.

The new managerial structure, moreover, provided businesses with the capacity to plan strategically and to allocate resources for the implementation of long-term strategic plans (Chandler 1977, 1980). Additionally, the professional managers in the new organizational sector of the economy formed professional associations and networks of communication that allowed them to learn from each other and to coordinate political strategies (Chandler 1980:30–35). Many businesses, particularly the railroads, used their new-found capacity for coordinated action to pursue strategic litigation to influence state regulations. In the several decades after 1880, a number of the new business organizations devoted significant resources to strategic litigation campaigns intended to influence the path of government regulation.

The railroads, as Richard Cortner (1993) has observed, mounted the most extensive strategic litigation campaigns during the period. Several railroads challenged the so-called Granger Laws, state statutes that subjected railroads to rate regulation, but they lost their first important challenge in 1877, when the Court ruled that private property "affected with a public interest" may be subject to public regulation unhindered by judicial review (*Munn v. Illinois* 1877). In response, the railroads mounted a systematic, strategic litigation campaign intended to reverse that unfavorable decision. As Cortner observed (1993:xii), "[T]he litigation campaign of the roads exhibited a mastery of many of the tactics [test cases, careful development of supporting evidence, and pressure on the judicial appointment process] that have been characteristic of constitutional litigation conducted by interest groups during more recent times." During that campaign, the railroads won several landmark decisions that subjected state policies to judicial review under the Fourteenth Amendment (Cortner 1993). Nonetheless, there is clear evidence that the Supreme Court was not systematically biased in favor of particular business interests but instead, as several scholars have observed, ruled against constitutional challenges brought by business litigants far more often than it ruled in their favor (Gillman 1993; Urofsky 1983).

Although businesses could expect most of their constitutional challenges to fail in the Supreme Court, they continued to bring large numbers of cases. They dominated the field of constitutional litigation because they had the organizational and resource capacity to do so. Scholarship on the legal profession during the first several decades of the century amply demonstrates the new managerial businesses' capacity to control the field of legal resources. As one scholar observed, for instance, the list of lawyers serving the railroads in their strategic litigation campaign consisted of a "Who's Who" of the bar (Magrath, quoted in Cortner 1993:3). Similarly, Louis Brandeis, in a speech in 1905, declared that "lawyers have, to a large extent, allowed themselves to become adjuncts of great corporations. . . . The leading lawyers of the United States have been engaged mainly in supporting the claims of the corporations; often in endeavoring to evade or nullify the extremely crude laws by which legislators sought to regulate the power or curb the excesses of the corporations" (1914:337–38). Woodrow Wilson in a speech in 1910, too, declared that "we have witnessed in modern business the submergence of the individual within the organization," and that "in gaining new functions, in being drawn into modern business instead of standing outside of it . . . the lawyer has lost his old function"; therefore, the country "distrusts every 'corporation lawyer' " (1976:70, 79).

The alliance between leading lawyers and the leading managerial businesses of the day should not be especially surprising. Heinz and Laumann's (1982) path-breaking study on the social structure of the bar in Chicago revealed that the legal profession remains divided between an upper hemisphere of lawyers who serve large organizations, particularly corporate businesses, and a lower hemisphere of lawyers who serve individual clients. One of the more significant findings of the study is that lawyers who serve organizational clients have far less professional autonomy than other lawyers, largely because of the managerial power of their organizational clients. This pattern of the legal profession's subservience to managerial organizations dates to the emergence of such organizations in the 1870s and 1880s. Theron Strong, a prominent lawyer who experienced the organizational transformation, observed in 1914 that client relations "had undergone a complete and marvelous change. The advent of the captains of industry, the multi-millionaires, the mighty corporations and the tremendous business enterprises, with all the pride of wealth and luxury which have followed in their train, have reversed their relative positions, and the lawyer, with a more cultivated intellect than ever and as worthy of deference and respect as formerly, is not treated with the deference and respect of early days" (Strong 1914:378, quoted in Galanter and Palay 1991:16). The development of large organizations had transformed the legal world by dominating the work of lawyers and the development of litigation.

The extensive litigation campaigns mounted by businesses influenced the Supreme Court's agenda in profound ways, particularly by pushing the Court to address issues of interest to businesses. This is especially clear with regard to the Court's agenda under the new Fourteenth Amendment. As William Nelson observed (1988:8), "The Supreme Court began to elaborate doctrines resolving issues of priority [under the Fourteenth Amendment] only when a flood of cases in the closing decades of the nineteenth century made the inevitability of conflict fully apparent." The Court's evolving interpretation of the Fourteenth Amendment in the late nineteenth and early twentieth centuries, of course, encouraged businesses to continue to bring challenges to legislation and regulatory action—although many businesses lost their cases, leading decisions like *Adkins* (1923) clearly indicated the general direction of the Court's policies.

Yet even as managerial businesses dominated the field of constitutional litigation, several changes occurred in the availability of resources for legal mobilization that began to democratize access to the Supreme Court's agenda by transforming the capacity of nonbusiness interests to litigate on constitutional issues. The most important changes were the development of rights-advocacy organizations, the diversification and organizational development of the legal profession, and the gradual development of financial resources for civil liberties litigation.

RIGHTS-ADVOCACY ORGANIZATIONS

Between 1909 and 1920, the leading civil liberties and civil rights organizations—the American Civil Liberties Union (ACLU), the American Jewish Congress (AJC), and the National Association for the Advancement of Colored People (NAACP)—were created. In addition, in the 1910s and 1920s the Jehovah's Witnesses, a religious sect, became increasingly organized and began defending actions of its members in court, and the Communist party-affiliated International Labor Defense began defending radical labor organizers and others in court. Some important cause organizations formed somewhat later. Americans United, for instance, an organization that has supported litigation on the First Amendment's Establishment Clause, formed in 1947, and a number of civil liberties, civil rights, and women's rights organizations formed in the 1950s, 1960s, and 1970s. The development of such organizations is a principal explanation for the growing presence of civil liberties issues on the Court's agenda.

Of these organizations, the ACLU undoubtedly has had the greatest impact, both by pressing issues onto the Supreme Court's agenda and by developing an organizational model that has been widely followed by other groups (Walker 1990). Roger Baldwin, the ACLU's first leader, recognized the growing importance of organizations in American public life, and he became committed to institutionalizing the ACLU to increase its effectiveness. As Paul Murphy observed (1972:118), "It was no accident that the organization was referred to as a 'union' or that it sought to function on a national scale and implement centrally determined programs through a national organization." In 1922, the ACLU began to receive limited financial support for its activities from the American Fund for Public Service, of which Baldwin was director (Murphy 1972:163). Nonetheless, funding remained scarce, and the ACLU developed alternatives to the direct financing of cases, particularly the use of a network of "cooperating attorneys," lawyers who were not directly employed by the ACLU but who provided legal advice and representation for ACLU-supported court cases, often without charging a fee. Baldwin used the term "cooperating attorney" as early as 1920 (Walker 1990:47); since that time cooperating attorneys have proved to be one of the significant strengths of the organization. Additionally, state ACLU affiliate organizations grew out of the main organization over the years, significantly increasing the organization's reach throughout the country.

The ACLU's support for constitutional litigation profoundly affected the Supreme Court's agenda. The ACLU (or its predecessor, the National Civil Liberties Board) provided the primary support and coordination for the initial burst of civil liberties litigation between 1917 and the early 1930s. Although ACLU strategists had misgivings about financing litigation in the face of conservative courts (Murphy 1972:131–32; Walker 1990:47), the ACLU and its cooperating attorneys financed, provided legal counsel, or otherwise supported a remarkable number of important civil liberties cases in the 1920s and early 1930s. In fact, most of the Supreme Court's early civil liberties decisions were made in cases that were ACLU-supported and likely would not have reached the Court had not that organization or its cooperating attorneys supported the appeals. For instance, the organization sponsored *Gitlow v. New York* (1925), *Whitney v. California* (1927),[3] *Fiske v. Kansas* (1927), *DeJonge v. Oregon* (1937), *Everson v. Board of Education* (1947), and *Wolf v. Colorado* (1949); the organization jointly sponsored *Stromberg v. California* (1931) (along with the International Labor Defense); and ACLU lawyers argued *Powell v. Alabama* (1932), and filed an *amicus* brief in *Cantwell v. Connecticut* (1940). The organization offered to sponsor appeals in *Near v. Minnesota* (1931), but a wealthy publisher stepped in and took over financing (Walker 1990:91).

Several other organizations played similar foundational roles in the development of other areas of constitutional rights litigation. The NAACP, formed in 1909, supported test cases, and won them, in the Supreme Court in 1914 (striking down Oklahoma's grandfather clause for voting), in 1917 (striking down Louisville's exclusionary zoning law), and in 1926 (striking down Texas's white primary law).[4] In 1930, the organization received a $100,000 grant from the American Fund for Public Service that allowed it to develop its now well-known litigation strategy against racial segregation that led to the leading race discrimination cases before the Supreme Court (see, e.g., Kluger 1977; Tushnet 1987; Wasby 1995). The International Labor Defense (ILD) was formed by the Communist Party in 1925, and supported litigation campaigns on behalf of labor organizers and others. For instance, the ILD provided some of the support for the defense of the "Scottsboro Boys," which led to the Supreme Court's landmark decisions in *Powell v. Alabama* (1932), establishing a constitutional right to counsel in capital cases, and *Norris v. Alabama* (1937), barring exclusion of blacks from grand and trial juries (Carter 1979). The Jehovah's Witnesses, a religious sect, began supporting constitutional litigation in the 1920s and 1930s as the actions of its members increasingly clashed with official policies. By 1986, the Jehovah's Witnesses had sponsored thirty-six cases in the Supreme Court (McAninch 1987).

After the early 1950s, the number of organizations supporting constitutional rights litigation began to increase (Wasby 1995:46–75). This is especially clear in the area of women's rights. The women's movement of the 1960s and 1970s, unlike earlier women's movements, produced lasting organizations with professional staffs and substantial resources (Gelb 1989). Most of the growth in the movement and in the number of organizations occurred rapidly in the ten years following 1966 (see figure 12.2). Some of the organizations were dedicated specifically to financing and supporting women's rights litigation (O'Connor 1980;

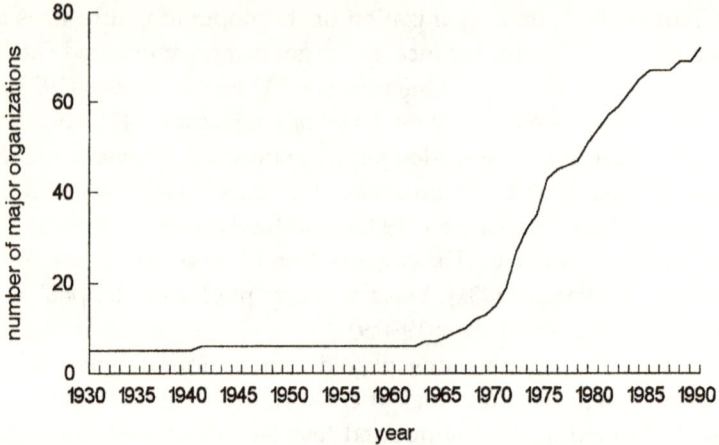

Figure 12.2 Women's Movement Organizations.

O'Connor and Epstein 1989). The ACLU's Women's Rights Project, for instance, played a leading role in directing the development of test case litigation both in lower courts and in the Supreme Court (Cowan 1976),[5] and the Center for Constitutional Rights, founded in 1966, developed the research behind privacy rights challenges to state abortion laws (Epstein 1993:137).

THE LEGAL PROFESSION

The legal profession, too, has changed profoundly in this century, and the changes have contributed greatly to the growing support for civil liberties and rights litigation. Lawyers began increasingly to practice in firms; the site of training shifted to law schools; the lawyer population diversified. I examine each of the changes in turn.

Law firms provide economies of scale and a capacity for specialization and long-term strategic planning, which are valuable assets in supporting strategic litigation campaigns (Galanter and Palay 1991:1–3). The widespread presence of law firms, like the other developments in the support structure, is a relatively new phenomenon. In 1872 there were only fifteen firms with four or more lawyers in the entire country; between 1892 and 1903 the number of firms jumped from eighty-seven to 210; by 1924 there were well over one thousand (Galanter and Palay 1991:14–15). As the number of firms grew, so did their size. In 1903, no firms consisted of ten or more lawyers; by 1914, there were six such larger firms; in the following years the number and size of large firms continued to grow. Various rights-advocacy organizations have drawn cooperating attorneys from law firms that free up their attorneys to do such work. In addition, liberal rights advocates in the 1960s and 1970s developed public interest law firms to gain the benefits of the firm structure. Development and spread of the law firm as a principal form of legal practice, then, contributed to the growing support structure for rights litigation.

Additionally, in the 1880s the site of legal training began to shift from apprenticeship under established lawyers to formal education in law schools. In the nineteenth century, most lawyers were trained in apprenticeships; by 1915, most lawyers were trained in law school (Abel 1989:40–44). That change had profound effects on the legal profession. First, the decline of apprenticeship and the rise of law schools disconnected training from the conservative interests of the practicing legal profession and provided the institutional basis for the development of theoretical study of law and reform-oriented political efforts (Auerbach 1976:74–101; Johnson 1978:164–70). For instance, the new law schools became the source for sociological jurisprudence and Legal Realism, two important movements in the study and practice of law that advanced the then novel theory that legal decision-making is policy-making in disguise, and that, therefore, judicial policies should be developed self-consciously for political ends.[6] The changes in legal education thus provided one of the foundations for the profound change in the justices' conception of their role as the defender of static constitutional limits on legislative power to a new role as guardian of evolving fundamental rights (Gillman 1993:147–93; 1994b). Moreover, the law schools also provided institutional support for clinical programs and legal research that supported some rights-advocacy litigation. The Court's decision in *Gideon v. Wainwright* (1963), for instance, was widely expected because of sustained litigation on the issue by, among others, several law professors from the University of Virginia (Meador 1967).

In addition, the growth of law schools enabled an increasingly diverse range of people who had difficulty getting apprenticeships under the old system to become lawyers. As late as 1910, the legal profession remained, as Abel writes (1988:201), "overwhelmingly Protestant and native born." The new law schools, however, were open to all, regardless of ethnic or religious background, and many of the schools offered night classes, which increased their accessibility to members of the lower classes. These changes led to a dramatic and substantial diversification of the lawyer population, as new Jewish and Catholic immigrants from eastern and southern Europe, among others, got law degrees (Abel 1989:78–80; Auerbach 1976:211–15; Bloomfield 1984). In New York City, for instance, between 1924 and 1929, 56 percent of new lawyers were Jewish; between 1930 and 1934 the percentage reached 80 percent (Abel 1989:86). Moreover, between 1920 and 1930, the number of lawyers grew rapidly, by 31 percent (Abel 1989:280).

The growing presence of Jewish, Catholic, and black lawyers in the U.S. in the late teens, 1920s and 1930s provided a growing base of legal representation for previously unrepresented groups. The new lawyers represented conscientious objectors, radical labor organizers, criminal defendants, communists, free speech advocates, and other unpopular figures and causes (Auerbach 1976; Bloomfield 1984; Carter 1979; Walker 1990). The significance of the change is revealed in part by its opponents' response. A prominent lawyer, for instance, railed against "the great flood of foreign blood . . . sweeping into the bar . . . [with] little sense of fairness, justice and honor as we understand them" (quoted in Auerbach 1976:107). Another (George Wickersham) wrote, "To think that those men, with their imperfect conception of our institutions, should have an influence upon the development of our constitution, and upon the growth of American institutions, is something that I shudder when I think of" (quoted in Auerbach 1976:115–16). In response, the established bar formed professional associations, worked to increase bar admission standards, and used character tests in an attempt to maintain the legal profession's allegiance to the fading traditional conception of the constitutional order (Abel 1989; Auerbach 1976). Moreover, some lawyers for the new interests faced disbarment proceedings; some even suffered beatings (Auerbach 1976:219). For instance, when a New York attorney presented evidence to J. Edgar Hoover of beatings and other repressive actions by federal agents against labor organizers in 1919, Hoover responded by urging that the attorney be disbarred for publicizing the evidence (Murphy 1972:79).

The changes in the legal profession in the years between the turn of the century and the advent of the New Deal, then, constituted the beginning of the powerful tradition of progressive "cause" lawyering that reached its peak during the Warren Court era and shortly after it. The growing diversity of the U.S. legal profession in the teens and 1920s thus provided an important source of support for the cases that transformed the Supreme Court's agenda after 1917.

The dramatic influx of women into the legal profession after 1965 produced a similar transformation of the base of support for women's rights litigation. The number of women entering the legal profession grew dramatically after the early 1960s and, by the mid-1970s, became

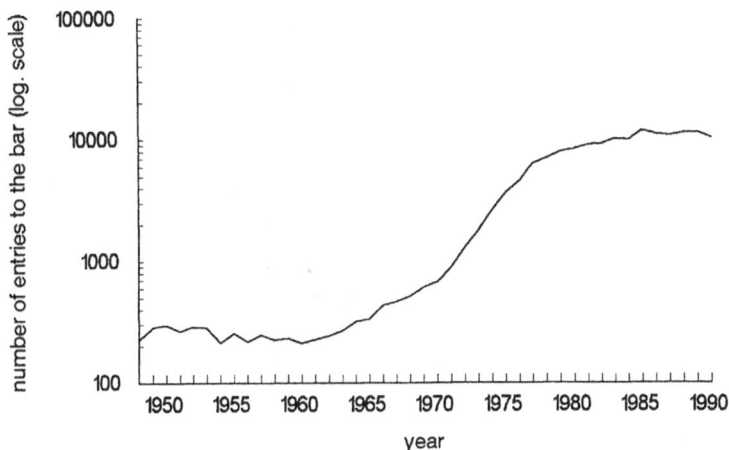

Figure 12.3 Women Lawyers.

a primary source for the very rapid growth in the total number of lawyers in the United States (Curran and Carson 1994). The growing number of women entering the legal profession is illustrated in figure 12.3.[7]

Many of these women lawyers supported the women's rights cause and women's rights litigation, and there is evidence that their efforts generated litigation campaigns that otherwise would not have existed. Early women's rights lawyers expressed frustration with what they regarded as male lawyers' lukewarm support of a narrow conception of women's rights; to fill the void, the new women lawyers vigorously pursued women's rights litigation on a number of fronts (Epstein 1993: 37–45, 130–61). Thus, a female attorney argued one of the first Supreme Court cases on women's rights, *Goesart v. Cleary* (1948), and two female women's rights lawyers who had just graduated from law school argued the landmark abortion rights case *Roe v. Wade* (1973). Ruth Bader Ginsburg, a prominent attorney appointed to the Supreme Court in 1993, directed the ACLU's Women's Rights Project in the 1970s and argued or otherwise supported many of the sex discrimination cases that reached the Supreme Court in the 1970s, among them the key early case *Reed v. Reed* (1971) (Markowitz 1989). The dramatic growth in the number of women lawyers beginning in the late 1960s, then, provided a new base of support for women's rights litigation.

Sources of Financing for Litigation Campaigns

Organized civil liberties groups provided the institutional direction and support for rights litigation after 1916, but they lacked sufficient resources to finance more than a few court cases. The financial support for court cases came from two main sources. The first was private philanthropy, in the early years donated by the American Fund for Public Service and some wealthy individuals, and in later years provided by major foundations, the Ford Foundation in particular.

The American Fund for Public Service (sometimes called the Garland Fund), a foundation dedicated to financing radical causes, was created in 1922 (Samson 1996; Walker 1990:70–71). Roger Baldwin, the director of the ACLU, became the director of the new fund, and the original board of directors consisted largely of members of the ACLU's national committee. The Fund provided the financing for several of the early civil liberties and rights organizations and it bankrolled the leading court challenges in the early years of the development of the rights agenda. The stock market crash of 1929 devastated the Fund, however, and, as a consequence, its support for litigation dropped dramatically in the 1930s.

Other foundations, particularly the Ford Foundation, provided major grants to organizations working in favor of civil liberties and civil rights. The Ford Foundation, for instance, gave $7.4 million to the National Legal Aid and Defender Association from 1953 to 1972, $15 million to create the pro–civil liberties Fund for the American Republic in 1952–53, $8.6 million to the Southern Regional Council from 1953 to 1977, $3.3 million to the NAACP–Legal Defense Fund from 1967 to 1976, and $13 million for the development of public interest law centers from 1970 to 1977 (Magat 1979:194–95).

In addition to donations from private sources, states developed right to counsel policies that provided support for legal defense and appellate litigation on behalf of the criminally accused. Undoubtedly the Supreme Court's *Powell* decision in 1932 (and the publicity in general around the Scottsboro case) encouraged some states to create policies guaranteeing counsel in capital cases. But many states soon went beyond the Court's requirements, providing counsel to indigent defendants not only in capital cases but in any felony case. The diffusion of state right to counsel policies covering felonies is illustrated in table 12.1. By the late 1950s, as the table shows, only six states limited their right to counsel policies to capital cases; most states guaranteed the right to counsel in felony cases, the standard that the Supreme Court eventually constitutionalized in 1963 in *Gideon v. Wainwright*. Clearly many of the state policies provided inadequate support for defendants. But, just as clearly, the spread of such policies propelled a growing number of criminal procedure cases onto the Supreme Court's agenda. As Casper (1972:89) showed, from 1957 through 1966 a significant pro-

Table 12.1
The Diffusion of State-level Right-to-Counsel Policies Covering Felonies

State	Year	State	Year
Nevada	1929	Utah	1943
Idaho	1932	West Virginia	1943
Washington	1932	Minnesota	1945
Indiana	1933	Iowa	1946
Tennessee	1934	Kentucky	1946
Colorado	1935	Arkansas	1947
Delaware	1935	Vermont	1947*
Georgia	1935	Wisconsin	1947
Illinois	1935	Wyoming	1947
Kansas	1935	Connecticut	1949
Montana	1935	Virginia	1950
New Jersey	1937	Michigan	1954
Oklahoma	1937	Texas	1954
Arizona	1939	New Hampshire	1955*
Missouri	1939	North Carolina	1955
Ohio	1939	Maine	1956**
South Dakota	1939	Rhode Island	1956
California	1941	Maryland	1957
New Mexico	1941*	Alabama	—
New York	1942	Florida	—
Louisiana	1943	Massachusetts	—
Nebraska	1943*	Mississippi	—
North Dakota	1943	Pennsylvania	—
Oregon	1943	South Carolina	—

* Includes only capital crimes and crimes punishable by three or more years imprisonment.
** By judicial decision.
Sources: Beaney (1955, 84–87), Special Committee (1959:Appendix).

portion of criminal defendants before the Supreme Court were represented by government-provided attorneys.

Finally, in 1965 the federal government launched a major initiative, the Legal Services Program, to provide financing for legal aid for the poor. In the late 1960s and early 1970s, 164 cases financed by the Legal Services Program reached the Supreme Court's agenda; in many of these cases, the Court announced landmark decisions that profoundly influenced the development of the due process revolution (Lawrence 1990). In the absence of the Legal Services Program it is highly unlikely that many of the cases would have reached the Court.

THE DEPARTMENT OF JUSTICE

The Department of Justice, and particularly the Solicitor General, the second-ranking Department official, also have profoundly influenced the Supreme Court's agenda. The Solicitor General screens cases lost by the federal government in lower courts, deciding which to petition the Supreme Court to hear. In 1984, for instance, then Solicitor General Rex Lee screened almost seven hundred government cases, taking only forty-three to the Court (Salokar 1992:114). Of those forty-three, the Court granted *certiorari* to thirty-three cases, a 76 percent success rate for the Solicitor General—far higher than the 4 percent success rate for other petitions in the same term (Salokar 1992:108). For the 1925–88 period, over 70 percent of petitions supported by the Justice Department were granted *certiorari* by the Court (Clayton 1992:67–68). Indeed, studies of the Court's *certiorari* process agree that the presence of the Solicitor General as petitioner greatly increases the likelihood that a case will be placed on the Court's agenda (Caldeira and Wright 1988; Perry 1991). Moreover, between 1959 and 1989, Solicitors General won over two-thirds of the Supreme Court cases in which they participated (Salokar 1992:29). The policies pushed by the federal government in its litigation before the Supreme Court, then, have a profound impact on the Court's agenda and policy decisions.

Beginning in the 1930s, the Justice Department increasingly advocated clear policy programs in the Supreme Court, and its strong support for civil rights in the late 1940s, 1950s, and 1960s greatly encouraged the Supreme Court to expand its civil rights agenda (Clayton 1992; Dixon 1968; Elliff 1987; Elman 1987). In 1939, Attorney General Frank Murphy created the Civil Rights Section of the Department's Criminal Division and charged it with enforcing long dormant Reconstruction-era federal civil rights laws. The new section worked primarily to bring cases against police and prison brutality in the South, many of which reached the Court in the 1940s and 1950s (Dixon 1968:110–12). In the late 1940s, Attorney General Tom Clark began pushing civil rights as part of an effort to shore up support for the Administration among northern blacks (Clayton 1992:128; Elman 1987: 818–19). As Clayton shows, the Justice Department's new commitment to civil rights led to its development of an *amicus* brief in support of the NAACP's case in *Shelley v. Kraemer* (1948), followed by similar briefs in a string of other NAACP cases. In the Eisenhower Administration, the Justice Department under Attorney General Herbert Brownell continued its support of civil rights, filing crucial briefs in *Brown* (1954) and other civil rights cases (Clayton 1992:129–31). Moreover, during the crucial period leading up to the Court's decision in *Brown*, Justice Frankfurter and Philip Elman, a lawyer in the Solicitor General's office (and former Frankfurter clerk), cooperated closely in developing strategies and counting votes in pursuit of a pro–civil rights decision on school segregation (Elman 1987:822–45).

After *Brown*, the Justice Department's influence over the Court's rights agenda deepened even further. The Department played a major role in the late 1950s and 1960s in pushing the civil rights agenda by supporting litigation against racial segregation and by pushing legislation that both expanded its own powers to fight segregation and broadened the scope of civil rights (Clayton 1992:131–37; Dixon 1968:114–17). As Robert Dixon (1968:114) observed, participation by the Justice Department in civil rights cases brought by private plaintiffs "strengthen[ed] their cases through the addition of federal legal resources." After the Department pushed for and gained the authority under the 1964 Civil Rights Act to bring suit in its own name in discrimination cases, its direct participation in civil rights litigation before the Court grew dramatically (Clayton 1992:126–27, 135). In addition, in the 1960s the Justice Department supported major expansions in the scope of statutory protection for civil rights, thereby providing the foundation for a new wave of litigation.

Thus, as Clayton (1992:126) argues, "The executive branch originally supported—even drove—the Supreme Court in its new political role" by pushing civil rights cases onto the Court's agenda and by urging the Court to broaden its support for civil rights.

The Impact of Judicial Policies on the Court's Support Structure

Although the most important changes in the support structure have sources that are broader than the Supreme Court's policies alone, the Court's policies, nonetheless, have influenced developments in the support structure. Wasby (1995:26–45) and McCann (1994) have explored in rich and nuanced detail the various effects of judicial policies on rights-advocacy organizations and movements. First, favorable judicial decisions typically have encouraged rights-advocacy organizations and lawyers to invest further resources in rights litigation. For instance, the Court's pro–civil liberties decisions in the early 1930s— *Near v. Minnesota* (1931), *Stromberg v. California* (1931), and *Powell v. Alabama* (1932)—encouraged the ACLU and its cooperating attorneys to continue their litigation campaigns (Murphy 1972; Walker 1990:79–92); similarly, *Brown v. Board of Education* (1954) and subsequent decisions encouraged civil rights organizations and private foundations to invest substantial resources in litigation campaigns (Wasby 1995:32).

Additionally, some judicial decisions have contributed directly to the

creation of resources for litigation. The Court's right to counsel decisions in *Gideon v. Wainwright* (1963) and subsequent cases contributed
directly to the deepening of institutional resources for criminal procedure litigation. The Court's decisions upholding the award of attorneys' fees under the Civil Rights Act of 1964 directly contributed to the
flow of resources to rights-advocacy organizations and lawyers (Wasby
1995:42–43). Similarly, the Court's various decisions loosening the
rules on standing and class actions broadened access by organized
group litigants to the judicial agenda.

Although favorable judicial decisions clearly have contributed to the
support structure, decisions against rights claims often have not diminished that structure. In the 1920s, the ACLU faced repeated negative
decisions from the Supreme Court, only to return to the Court with
additional cases. Had the ACLU's strategies been determined by the
Court's policies, *Stromberg*, a crucial case that opened the civil liberties
agenda in the 1930s, would never have reached the Court. Similarly,
as a civil rights litigator told Wasby (1995:31), "Many cases have gone
forward anyhow [in spite of apparent opposition from the Supreme
Court], or *Brown* wouldn't have happened." In short, although the Supreme Court's agenda-setting decisions matter, "litigators may attempt
to change such patterns" (Wasby 1995:28).

The Impact of the Support Structure on the Court's Agenda

Developments in the support structure for legal mobilization help to
explain why cases on freedom of speech and the press suddenly appeared on the Court's agenda beginning in the late 1910s, why criminal
procedure cases claimed an increasingly large share of the agenda after
the early 1930s, and why women's rights cases suddenly appeared on
the agenda in the early 1970s. In each era, the Court's agenda responded to litigants availing themselves of newly developed resources
for litigation.

The Supreme Court's agenda, then, is best understood in the context
of the support structure for legal mobilization. The support structure
has influenced the Court's agenda in two ways. First, the development
of external support for constitutional rights litigation has propelled
new issues onto the Court's agenda. In many instances of new issue
development, the justices have not clarified and solidified their attitudes on the issue prior to its appearance on their agenda and, therefore, preexisting policy preferences cannot fully explain the appearance
of the issue on the agenda. Particularly with the development of their

civil liberties agenda, the justices seem initially to have been unsure how best to resolve the vexing issues that reached the Court. Thus, as J. Woodford Howard (1968) showed, the *Everson v. Board of Education* (1947) case presented fundamentally new issues on which the justices had not yet developed their positions. "Ideological hardening came later," as Howard observed: "[T]ime and litigation may be necessary for implications to be perceived and attitudes to harden in a case-law system" (1968:54).

The second way in which the support structure for legal mobilization has influenced the judicial agenda is by supporting, after landmark decisions, continued litigation that capitalizes on openings offered by the justices. In the absence of a vibrant support structure, landmark decisions would remain isolated events, neither implemented nor developed through further litigation. For instance, since 1977 the Indian Supreme Court's decisions on due process have been as revolutionary as the leading decisions of the Warren Court, but the Indian Court's rights agenda has failed to develop because of the relative absence of a support structure for noneconomic litigation (Epp 1998:71–110).

The Supreme Court's agenda, then, has developed in interaction with changes in the support structure for legal mobilization. Broad changes in the support structure typically have preceded important developments in the Court's agenda. Thus the changes in the support structure after 1915—the development of liberal rights-advocacy organizations, the diversification and organizational development of the legal profession, the use of the Justice Department to promote a rights agenda, and the growth of financing—propelled new rights-based claims onto the Court's docket. Moreover, changes in the support structure typically have resulted from forces that are broader than the Court's policies alone. The major rights-advocacy organizations formed during the wave of institution-building in the Progressive Era, and the interest group system diversified tremendously as part of broader changes in American society in the post–World War II period; the legal profession diversified owing to the development of law schools and major demographic changes in American society; and the growth of foundation funding for rights advocacy reflected the rise of the foundations themselves. Nonetheless, the Court, in manipulating its agenda, has aided some developments in the support structure and not others, and thereby has influenced long-term developments in the agenda. Thus the Court's civil liberties decisions of the early 1930s, particularly *Near*, *Stromberg*, and *Powell*, encouraged ACLU lawyers to continue pursuing rights litigation; the *Brown* decision transformed the

entire field of civil rights litigation; and the Court's procedural decisions of the 1960s on standing, class actions, and the awarding of attorneys' fees provided significant support for liberal rights-advocacy organizations and lawyers.

Is this analysis mainly of historical interest? It might be argued that,
although in the 1930s the institutional support for some kinds of constitutional claims was undeveloped, now any issue has sufficient support
to gain a place on the Court's agenda. That is largely true, particularly
with the rise of conservative advocacy groups; nonetheless, some issues still gain little support. Allen Redlich recently lamented that "litigation on behalf of the poor community has disappeared" owing to
"years of fiscal neglect and political attacks" (1992:773, 776). Of course
an expansion of resources for litigation on behalf of the poor would
not automatically change the Court's agenda. Judicial hostility or indif-
ference to a claim generally precludes its development on the agenda
(which explains why some issues of interest to the well-resourced business community nonetheless rarely reach the Court's agenda). But, just
as surely, the justices will not attend to neglected issues unless there
is litigation on them. Moreover, sustained mobilization of resources for
litigation and legal research occasionally produces surprises, even in
the 1990s. After the Court's decision in *Bowers v. Hardwick* in 1986, few
observers would have predicted that the Court soon would accept an
equal protection claim based on sexual preference. Yet in *Romer v. Evans* (1996), during a sustained litigation campaign by several rights-
advocacy organizations, a far more conservative Court appeared to do
just that.

The Supreme Court's agenda on civil liberties and civil rights, then,
cannot be understood apart from its institutional context. The justices'
attitudes clearly influence the agenda, but they do so in the context of
the political economy of appellate litigation. That political economy
changed dramatically in this century as the system of rights-advocacy
organizations developed; as the legal profession grew, diversified, and
became managerially organized; and as sources of financing for litigation increased and the Justice Department came down on the side of
civil rights. Those changes contributed to the democratization of access
to the Supreme Court and the development of the Court's agenda on
civil liberties and civil rights.

Notes

I gratefully acknowledge helpful comments and suggestions from Cornell
Clayton, Howard Gillman, Joel Grossman, and Bert Kritzer.

1. Until 1988, some cases also reached the Court as appeals, which the jus-

tices technically were required to hear but which they treated as discretionary matters.

2. These indicators of legal conflict at the very least fit uncomfortably with the attitudinal model; more plausibly, they are deeply inconsistent with it. Caldeira and Wright (1988) suggest that the justices seek cases involving legal conflict in lower courts because such cases enhance their own policy-making power. Perry (1991:246–60), however, argues that these factors are important because the justices believe it to be their institutional responsibility to decide such cases in order to maintain coherence and consistency in the interpretation of federal law. At the very least, the indicators (presence of legal conflict, inter-circuit disagreement) more directly measure *legal* factors than attitudinal factors, because they are not direct measures of the *policy* importance of cases but instead are measures of the presence of legal conflict. Segal and Spaeth seem to concur: "[T]he justices . . . refuse to decide . . . meritless cases" (1993:70); they acknowledge the importance of legal conflict in lower courts as virtually a prerequisite for a case to reach the Court's agenda (1993:195–99).

3. In addition, the ACLU sponsored *Ruthenberg v. Michigan* (1927), for which Justice Brandeis had drafted a dissent that he turned into his famous concurrence in *Whitney* when Ruthenberg died, mooting the case.

4. *Guinn v. United States* (1915), *Buchanan v. Warley* (1917), and *Nixon v. Herndon* (1926), respectively.

5. Although women's rights organizations contributed significantly to the Supreme Court's women's rights agenda, many of the Supreme Court cases involving women's rights were not brought directly by such organizations. O'Connor and Epstein (1989:139) reported that only 29 percent of a total of sixty-three gender discrimination cases from the Court's 1969 to 1980 terms were brought by interest groups (and most of those were supported by the ACLU's Women's Rights Project).

6. American legal scholars may have been influenced by similar theories advanced by a German, Rudolf von Jhering (1913).

7. Data are from Curran and Carson, *The Lawyer Statistical Report* (1994), and letter from Curran and Carson on file with author. It is nearly impossible to construct an annual series of data on the total lawyer population (the lawyer population is available in three-year intervals from the mid-1950s to 1970, but then there is a ten-year gap until 1980, followed by a five-year gap until 1985, followed by a three-year gap until 1988, and a two-year gap until 1990). Admittedly the estimates presented in the figure do not provide a measure of the growth of the female legal profession as a whole; rather, they provide a measure of the pace of female entrance into the legal profession. That pace was roughly constant through the 1950s and early 1960s but quickened significantly after about 1965.

13

State Supreme Courts and Their Environments: Avenues to General Theories of Judicial Choice

Melinda Gann Hall and Paul Brace

Judicial politics scholarship is beginning to take an exciting new turn. Increasingly, scholars are utilizing a variety of innovative theoretical perspectives and methodological techniques to address fundamental issues about judicial processes and behavior in a manner that transcends the relatively simplistic approaches of the past. The either/or approach, where scholars focused exclusively on the impact of either law or politics to the virtual exclusion of the other, is being replaced by much more sophisticated models that encompass a wider range of forces influencing the activities of judges and courts. Also, the nature of the questions are changing, with scholars beginning to attack a much broader array of issues than ever before. One of the most noted scholars of judicial politics recently described these dramatic changes as "something of a renaissance," or a trend representative of an "extraordinary rebirth of our field" (Epstein 1996:575).

This growing interest in utilizing a broader range of theoretical and methodological tools to study judicial politics holds tremendous promise for advancing our knowledge well beyond the current bounds. From a purely theoretical perspective, however, any advances will fall substantially short of a renaissance unless scholars demonstrate a shift in focus to institutions and context, with the corresponding use of comparative research designs, and away from the almost singular focus on the United States Supreme Court. For while studies of single courts, such as the United States Supreme Court, are enormously important in their own right and are appropriate for developing theories of particular institutions, case studies necessarily generate a body of findings and theories that are highly circumscribed by time and place. Moreover, except with longitudinal designs capable of addressing a limited range of contextual and institutional hypotheses, case studies reduce discussions concerning the likely effects of institutional arrangements largely to speculation, a serious deficiency given the critical role played by these forces in the politics of the judiciary. To achieve the primary scientific goal of developing general theory that takes into account the complete range of forces affecting the politics of courts, comparative analysis is essential.

In fact, we prefer to view recent developments in judicial politics research with guarded optimism. Instead of a renaissance, these trends reasonably could be described as more akin to the end of a Thirty Years War, where the fundamental tenets of Walter Murphy's *Elements of Judicial Strategy* (1964), based solidly on the principles of rational choice theory, essentially were set aside to explore social-psychological models of judicial decision-making and to clash with the legalists. Merely replacing these old debates between the attitudinalists and the legalists with yet another debate directed solely at the United States Supreme Court will not advance the study of judicial choice to the optimal threshold.

In the following pages, we elaborate on these essential points by outlining an approach to the study of courts, and particularly to the study of judicial decision-making, that will substantially advance our understanding of the complex process of judging. In our estimation, research that rests squarely upon the premises of rational choice theory and that capitalizes on the analytical advantages of comparative research designs will allow scholars of the judiciary to make extraordinary gains in understanding the judicial calculus. We incorporate into this discussion some of the most convincing empirical evidence generated to date in order to demonstrate the utility of comparative approaches to studying judicial decision-making, the importance of the rational choice perspective as a theoretical foundation from which to deduce hypotheses about judicial choice, and the critical need to take institutions and context into account when evaluating the judicial vote. Finally, we describe how theoretically based comparative designs with a focus on institutions and context can resolve some of the most perplexing problems in judicial politics scholarship, including fundamental issues relevant to the United States Supreme Court. More specifically, we consider how institutional arrangements shape the willingness of courts to engage in the counter-majoritarian function, or, stated at the microlevel, the extent to which judges remain impervious to pressures in the external environment when casting votes in the cases before their courts.

Our central point, clearly supported theoretically by the tenets of

rational choice theory, as well as empirically by state comparative judicial politics scholarship, is that institutions and context matter. Courts
inextricably are tied to their external environments by various institutional arrangements. Any theory or model of judicial decision-making
that does not include these critical forces falls substantially short of
offering a satisfactory representation of the judicial calculus, and any
overall direction in scholarship that fails to embrace comparative research designs is quite circumscribed.

Rational Choice Theory, Comparative Designs, and the Politics of Judicial Choice

Deducing and testing hypotheses from the assumption that judges are
instrumentally rational—the most fundamental assumption of rational
choice theory—is an excellent means to advance the study of judicial
decision-making. Although Green and Shapiro (1994) recently have
challenged the contributions of rational choice theory to the study of
politics, the fact remains that some of the most path-breaking research
on judicial behavior has proceeded from the rationality assumption.[1]
Perhaps the best example is Walter Murphy's *Elements of Judicial Strategy* (1964), the now classic statement on the full range of behavior available to the Supreme Court justice seeking to maximize influence on
public policy within the context of the nation's highest court.

Neo-institutionalism, a component of rational choice theory, is particularly relevant for advancing the study of judicial choice. Neo-
institutionalism embraces rational choice assumptions about human
behavior but with a particular focus on the effects of institutional arrangements on purposive behavior. More precisely, neo-institutionalism considers "how the institutional rules of the game affect individual
behavior and collective outcomes" (Rohde and Shepsle 1978:2) and
how behavior, motivated by various goals, "is channeled by extant institutional practices" (*ibid.*).

Central to the concept of purposive behavior are goals. Instrumentally rational judges, by definition, act strategically to achieve a desired
goal or set of goals. In our judgment, judicial politics research would
progress substantially by accepting the rationality assumption as a basis for formulating predictions about what judges actually do, and by
proceeding in accordance with the following neo-institutional propositions about the inextricable linkages between goals, institutions, and
context.

FIRST, judges pursue multiple goals, including those related exclusively to basic self-interest. As Schlesinger (1966:2) noted, "[P]olitical institutions simplify motives." Judicial behavior is largely a function of the systematic pursuit of several fundamental goals.[2] Arguably the most significant are the electoral incentive,[3] progressive ambition,[4] and maximizing influence on public policy, with the policy motive being of primary importance. All things being equal, judges prefer to cast votes in the cases before their courts in accordance with their individual political preferences (see, e.g., Rohde and Spaeth 1976; Segal and Spaeth 1993). However, as discussed below, alternative goals, such as progressive ambition and the desire to retain office, supplant the policy motive under the right conditions and produce behavior that is inconsistent with judges' ideological preferences, though still quite rational.

SECOND, some goals are institutionally dependent. Goals do not exist universally in abstract space. The goals pursued by judges depend, to some extent, upon the institution within which the judge operates. Both the electoral incentive and progressive ambition are relevant only in certain institutions and under certain circumstances.

With regard to the electoral incentive, except for the small percentage of judges who occupy the federal bench or who serve in the handful of states that provide lifetime tenure to their judges, the desire to continue in office is a primary goal for structuring judicial behavior in the United States. Usually, the goal involves appeasing voters who have the ability to oust sitting judges through partisan, nonpartisan, or retention elections. Where judges are elected for specific terms of office and must regularly face voters in order to retain their seats, not alienating or antagonizing the voters with decisions that conflict with voter preferences becomes crucial.

In some cases, however, the strategy of retaining a seat is directed at legislatures, governors, or committees accountable to these state political elites, who pose a threat to the goal of retaining office. In several states, judges are initially appointed for a specific term of office but must be reappointed for subsequent terms by one of the other branches of state government. Judges required to win reappointment pursue strategies to enhance their chances for reappointment, such as not taking on the other branches of government in the game of separation of powers and being far more attentive to elite political preferences than judges selected under different institutional arrangements.

Alternatively, judges who are not required to seek reelection or reappointment have different parameters on their calculations as rational decision makers. Soothing public preferences or not challenging the other branches should not be a significant part of the judicial calculus in settings where judges are not elected or reappointed and therefore are not subject to any kind of direct, personal retaliation or retribution for unpopular rulings. Quite obviously, the concern for reappointment, and engaging in purposive behavior designed to insure it, are totally irrelevant for judges with lifetime tenure.

Similar arguments can be made about progressive ambition, or the goal of "aspiring to attain an office more important than the one [s/he] now seeks or is holding" (Schlesinger 1966:10). The overwhelming proportion of judges should have ambition for higher office. As Schlesinger observed, "[A]mbition lies at the heart of politics. Politics thrive on the hope of preferment and the drive for office" (1966:1). Only members of the United States Supreme Court lack opportunities for career advancement and therefore are not motivated by a goal that requires strategic behavior, such as amassing voting records that will be acceptable to future constituencies.

THIRD, and closely related to the second proposition, judges' goals are pursued strategically in response to context and to institutional arrangements that link the two. This proposition lies at the heart of our argument and is critical in developing a realistic understanding of the politics of judging. Institutions and context matter, not only in determining goals, but also in establishing the conditions under which goals are pursued and in establishing which goals emerge as paramount. Generally, one might expect the nature of a court's or a judge's response to context to depend, in part, upon institutional features that create, to greater or lesser degrees, linkages to the political environment.[5] Courts vary widely in their internal operating rules, docket types, recruitment and retention methods, and other important features. We have every reason to expect that these variations will influence the decisions of judges by affecting the manner in which pressures are filtered to the individual and by creating incentives or disincentives for individuals to manifest their personal preferences. In the process of deciding cases, judges can be expected to respond to a host of stimuli, including their own preferences, case facts, and forces generated in the external political arena. However, these influences are modified by structural characteristics of courts that inhibit or enhance their importance.[6]

In the scientific literature on judicial choice, there is substantial empirical evidence at both aggregate and individual levels of analysis and for multiple types of judicial behavior that the above propositions regarding linkages between goals, contexts, and institutional arrangements are sound. To demonstrate our point more directly, however, we present data in table 13.1 and table 13.2 that provide compelling evidence of the vital importance of institutional arrangements in shaping the way in which judges respond to external stimuli.[7]

First, table 13.1 reports three separate probit models that analyze various forms of individual dissent in six state supreme courts (California, Kentucky, Louisiana, New Jersey, North Carolina, and Ohio) from 1980 through 1988 in the death penalty decisions issued by these courts. From the perspective of judicial politics scholarship, examining dissent is crucial; the willingness of judges to express disagreement openly with their court majorities presents a striking challenge to the notion that legal doctrines adequately explain the judicial vote and also provides important opportunities to assess the motivations and influences underlying judicial choice.

The three models reported in table 13.1 test the basic hypothesis that institutional arrangements condition the effects of the other major categories of variables (attitudinal, jurisprudential, and contextual) affecting judicial choice. Stated differently, the models examine whether the effects of attitudinal, jurisprudential, and contextual variables differ in alternative institutional settings. The specific variables, which are described fully in appendix A, include several personal attribute variables (partisan affiliation, majority party status on the court, and seniority) that serve as surrogates for ideological preferences, two case-related variables (the presence of aggravating circumstances and victim characteristics), two institutional arrangements (ballot type and seniority-based voting rules), and one state environmental feature (partisan competition). Additionally, time-point dummy variables distinguish between forces affecting specific courts and those affecting all courts simultaneously over time. With the inclusion of these variables and the use of interaction terms to examine conditional effects, we can examine whether institutional arrangements are, in fact, crucial forces in judicial decision-making, as posited by the neo-institutionalists.

The first model presented in table 13.1 evaluates the decisions of state supreme court justices to join court majorities, irrespective of ideological direction of the court's decisions. The performance of two of three interaction terms provides strong evidence of the importance of institutional features in conditioning the effects of other forces on judicial decision-making. As the estimates in table 13.1 indicate, in states that do not accord senior members advantages in decision-making, the effects of seniority are positive (see Seniority). In these courts, senior members are more supportive of court majorities. However, in the

Table 13.1
Pooled Probit Analysis of State Supreme Court Justices' Votes in Death Penalty Cases in Six States,[a] 1980–1988

	Join Majority MLE	MLE/s.e. (t)	Liberal Dissent MLE	MLE/s.e. (t)	Conservative Dissent MLE	MLE/s.e. (t)
Case Characteristics	-0.05	-0.34	0.56	1.65	0.0004	0.002
Democrat	-0.17	-1.29	1.33	7.09	-1.38	-6.57
Majority Party	1.07	8.74	-1.41	-6.89	-0.29	-1.69
Seniority	0.02	2.30	-0.03	-1.78	-0.03	-2.13
Competition	0.01	1.88	-0.05	-1.10	-0.01	-1.82
Ballot	2.61	4.33	-3.89	-1.74	-3.84	-4.55
Seniority Rules	0.31	1.47	1.93	1.19	-1.79	-5.52
Ballot × Case	-0.002	-1.03	-0.005	-1.17	0.005	1.97
Char. × Competition						
Ballot × Competition	-0.03	-3.90	0.07	1.64	0.03	3.31
Seniority Rules × Seniority	-0.05	-3.55	-0.01	-0.47	0.11	4.92
Intercept	-0.99	-1.80	0.76	0.34	2.98	3.92
1980–1982	0.16	1.32	0.09	0.36	-0.17	-1.05
1983–1985	0.39	3.19	-0.07	-0.30	-0.86	-4.97
N	1988		1070		918	
% in Modal Category	86.47		90.60		86.82	
% Predicted Correctly	85.86		90.56		87.15	
Chi-square (significance)	1376.36 (.01)		928.92 (.01)		668.04 (.01)	
Estimated R^2	0.41		0.46		0.42	

t ≥ 1.28 significant at the .10 level (one-tailed test).

t ≥ 1.64 significant at the .05 level (one-tailed test).

t ≥ 2.34 significant at the .01 level (one-tailed test).

[a] California, Kentucky, Louisiana, New Jersey, North Carolina, and Ohio.

presence of institutional rules that provide a seniority advantage, the effects of seniority are reversed (see Seniority Rules × Seniority). Senior justices actually are significantly more likely to dissent in states that recognize seniority in their voting rules. Stated another way, in states that provide a seniority advantage in voting, junior justices are less likely to dissent than are their more senior counterparts. Because of institutional incentives, junior justices in these states are encouraged to endorse the decisions of the court, or to acquiesce to their court majorities.

Similarly, the effects of political competition vary according to the type of ballot used to select judges. In states that do not utilize partisan ballots, partisan competition promotes votes with majorities in death penalty decisions in the states (see Competition). However, when partisan ballots are used, partisan competition actually promotes dissent (see Ballot × Competition).

The second model reported in table 13.1 evaluates the factors associated with the casting of liberal dissents, or on the issue of capital punishment, going out on a perilous limb with voters by opposing majority decisions to uphold death sentences.[8] As in the previous model, the effects of institutional rules are pronounced.

While the interaction term of case characteristics, ballot, and partisan competition falls just short of statistical significance, the direction of the coefficient is opposite that of the case variable alone. In politically competitive environments where justices are elected on partisan ballots, justices are less likely to cast liberal dissents in cases that contain aggravating circumstances. Consistent with Hall's studies of constituency influence (1987, 1992, 1995), the direction of the interaction term provides additional evidence that the probability of a justice voicing disagreement with a conservative decision of the court is a function of electoral politics and a concern with constituency preferences.

Similarly, while seniority is negatively related to the propensity to dissent from decisions upholding the death penalty in states that do not utilize seniority-based rules (see Seniority), seniority does not exert a significant influence on liberal dissents in states where internal operating rules recognize seniority (see Seniority Rules × Seniority). Finally, competition does not reach an acceptable level of statistical significance but does have a negative sign. However, in states using partisan ballots, the effects of competition are positive and significant (see Ballot × Competition). The joint effect of partisan ballots and electoral competition promotes division on courts.

As in the two previous models, institutional effects are striking in the third model reported in table 13.1, which examines decisions to dissent from liberal court decisions, or to oppose majority decisions overturning the imposition of death sentences in capital murder cases. Seniority and partisan competition have significantly different effects on decisions to cast conservative dissents when the influence of institutional structure is controlled. In states with rules that afford greater influence to more senior members, seniority is positively related to these conservative dissents rather than negatively related (see Seniority Rules × Seniority). Stated another way, in states with rules recognizing seniority, senior members are more inclined to dissent than to seek consensus. Similarly, competition works to increase the likelihood of dissents favoring the death penalty in states with partisan judicial ballots (see Ballot × Competition) but decreases the probability of conservative dissents in states where partisan ballots are not used (see Competition). Finally, case characteristics representing aggravating circumstances in murders are not related to the likelihood of justices casting conservative dissents in states not utilizing partisan judicial ballots (see Case Characteristics). However, aggravating factors increase the probability of such votes in states using partisan ballots and where there are higher levels of partisan competition (see Ballot × Case Characteristics × Competition).

Overall, these data clearly demonstrate that the performance of attitudinal/attribute variables, jurisprudential forces, and contextual factors is conditioned by institutional arrangements. In these three models of judicial dissent, there are observable significant interactions between institutional features and other forces affecting the politics of courts. Stated simply, institutional arrangements serve to induce individual judges to cast votes differently than if acting in isolation from institutional structures.

Are these dramatic institutional effects also evident in decisions on the merits of cases? Table 13.2 addresses this issue by evaluating the decisions to overturn or uphold the imposition of death sentences by the justices in eight state supreme courts (California, Illinois, Kentucky, Louisiana, New Jersey, North Carolina, Ohio, and Texas) from 1986 through 1988. Like the models of dissent just discussed, this model of decision-making on the merits is fully specified; all major categories of variables operating on the judicial decision-making process are included in the analysis. Specifically, the model contains two case-related variables (both crime and victim characteristics variables), attitudinal/attribute variables (partisan affiliation), environmental forces (state partisan competition), and institutional forces (selection system, term

Table 13.2
Pooled Probit Analysis of Supreme Court Justices' Votes in Death Penalty Cases
in Eight States,[a] 1986–1988

	MLE	MLE/s.e. (t)
Competition	−15.59***	2.89
Democrat	.89**	.07
Victim Characteristics	−.19**	.08
Crime Characteristics	.20*	.13
Elected Judges	−4.20***	1.00
Term Length	.27***	.06
Victim Statute	−1.23***	.18
Crime Statute	.10	.15
Competition × Elected Judges	14.65***	2.93
Democrat × Term Length	−.16***	.04
Victim Characteristics × Victim Statute	.52***	.11
Crime Characteristics × Crime Statute	.058	.16
N = 2345		
% Modal Category	64.35	
% Predicted Correctly	70.23	
Chi Square	455.6	
R^2 (corrected)[b]	.283	
% ROE	16.99	

* Significant at p < .10 (two-tailed test).
** Significant at p < .05 (two-tailed test).
*** Significant at p < .01 (two-tailed test).
[a] California, Illinois, Kentucky, Louisiana, New Jersey, North Carolina, Ohio, Texas.
[b] The Aldrich-Nelson R^2 is corrected using the procedure described by Hagle and Mitchell (1992).

length, and statutory content). A complete description of these variables is contained in appendix B.

Like table 13.1, table 13.2 gives testimony to the importance of institutions.[9] As the results clearly indicate, the effects of case characteristics, personal attributes, and environmental forces are contingent upon institutional features. First, the impact of state partisan competition is conditioned by method of judicial selection. State partisan competition is associated with votes opposing the death penalty in states that do not elect judges (see Competition). However, where judges must face voters to retain their positions, state partisan competition exerts a positive influence on support for the death penalty (see Competition × Elected Judges). Votes to uphold death sentences are more likely in politically competitive states with elected judges.

Second, the effects of the justices' partisan affiliations are contingent upon term length. Justices with longer terms of office are more willing to manifest their partisanship than justices serving shorter terms. Specifically, Democrats with long terms are least likely to support the death penalty (see Democrat × Term Length), and Republicans with long terms are most likely to support the death penalty (see Term Length). In essence, term length serves as a linkage between judges and the external political context by influencing the willingness of individual judges to express their partisanship, or to act strictly in accordance with their personal preferences.

Third, the impact of victim characteristics on justices' support for the death penalty is contingent upon specific statutory provisions. In states without statutory provisions that specifically list "heinous" action as an aggravating circumstance, cases involving female or elderly victims actually are less likely to result in death sentences (see Victim Characteristics). However, in states with such statutory provisions, cases with female or elderly victims are more likely to result in sentences of death rather than life imprisonment (see Victim Characteristics × Victim Statute).

The same cannot be said for crime characteristics. Directionally, it appears that crime characteristics (i.e., commission of a robbery, sexual assault, or multiple victims) promote capital punishment in states with statutory provisions denoting such crime factors as aggravating circumstances (see Crime × Crime Statute). However, the result is not statistically significant. Based on the estimates in table 13.2, it seems quite likely that judges respond to crime characteristics irrespective of statutory language (see Crime Characteristics).

To summarize, models of both dissent behavior and decision-making on the merits provide clear and convincing evidence that institutional arrangements play a crucial role in the politics of judicial choice, at least on the issue of the death penalty. Any explanation of judicial decision-making must consider carefully the importance of both institutional context and strategic calculations to the judicial vote.

Unfortunately, we have very little work that attempts to disentangle the interactive effects of institutional arrangements with other forces affecting judicial behavior. It is with this line of inquiry that rational-choice theory holds great promise. While judges can be assumed to be rational, utility-maximizing individuals who wish to see their personal preferences translated into public policy, they are constrained in pursuing their own agendas by external forces emanating from at least two sources: 1) the social and political context within which the court operates, and 2) the power of the other institutions. Moreover, the effects of both sets of these constraints undoubtedly are mediated by institutional arrangements. A host of exogenous forces impinge upon the calculations of judges under the right circumstances, and institutional arrangements serve to structure these circumstances.

Broadly stated, judicial choice is best conceptualized as a nested game, as defined by George Tsebelis (1990). In such games, what may appear to be irrational or erratic when narrowly considered actually becomes plausible when one takes into account the external arenas constraining behavior. We may know, for example, that a judge is very liberal yet votes consistently to uphold death sentences in capital murder cases. At first glance, this behavior seems counterproductive or irrational but it may be entirely consistent with an external game dominated by the potential threat of a conservative legislature or electoral defeat.[10] Formulating propositions about what purposive actors do under alternative sets of constraints, or across contexts, and in different types of institutional configurations will serve to integrate macrolevel and microlevel explanations of judicial choice and move beyond theories that are institution-specific.

FOURTH, judges' goals and their subsequent behavior must be studied in a comparative context in order to construct a general theory of judicial choice. Comparative research is essential for developing general theories capable of unifying contextual and individual explanations of judicial choice. Research designs that facilitate both cross-sectional and longitudinal comparisons, and that integrate attitudinal, case-related, institutional, and contextual variables into single models, will hasten the development of theory that connects judges to their institutional, political, and social contexts. We will make extraordinary strides toward understanding the intricacies of the American judiciary by modeling judicial behavior across contexts, and interactively across contextual and individual levels of analysis. Otherwise, general theory will continue to be elusive.

Ideally suited for this task are the American states, which stand as diverse comparative laboratories offering analytical leverage for addressing a wide range of institutional and contextual hypotheses.[11] The states provide fifty laboratories at once, and the variance in these diverse settings provides much more leverage on significant political variables than anything at the national level. In other words, state courts, particularly state supreme courts, present special opportunities to test important general hypotheses about judicial processes and behavior.

Within state supreme courts are individual decision makers with highly diverse backgrounds, experiences, and values. Moreover, because of the sheer volume of cases, these courts address virtually every legal issue and fact pattern likely to arise at the appellate level. Similarly, in resolving these issues, state supreme court justices interpret and apply a variety of constitutional provisions, statutes, and other types of law. State supreme courts also present a wide array of institutional features and configurations, both in terms of structures and in terms of external and internal rules and procedures. Finally, the American states, the environments within which state supreme courts operate, are diverse politically, economically, and culturally. Therefore, within the context of state supreme courts, the influence of all major forces on judicial politics and behavior identified to date can be evaluated comparatively.

By capitalizing on the analytical advantages of the states, we will have the capability of building models that are not institution-specific. We also will enhance significantly our knowledge of the role of institutions and context in shaping judicial processes and behavior. Stated another way, comparative state judicial politics scholarship presents scholars with the opportunity to transcend the compartmentalization of findings and the disjunction between microlevel and macrolevel explanations of judicial behavior that typify the existing body of work.

An excellent example of how comparative designs with a focus on institutions and context can resolve some of the most perplexing problems of judicial politics, including fundamental issues relevant to the United States Supreme Court, is the debate currently raging between attitudinalists and positive political theorists over the extent to which the United States Supreme Court exercises the counter-majoritarian function by overturning acts of Congress.[12] Essentially two different conceptualizations of courts as institutions, and justices as individual decision makers, have emerged in this discussion.

First, scholars working within the framework of attitudinal theory (e.g., Rohde and Spaeth 1976; Segal and Spaeth 1993) have posited that the Supreme Court is a highly autonomous institution whose judgments essentially reflect the aggregation of preferences of its members. Because various institutional arrangements (e.g., lifetime tenure) insulate the Court from sanctions, it lacks incentives to respond to forces in the external environment, including Congress, "except on the rarest of occasions" (Segal 1995:25). Given the highly insular nature of the Court, individual justices are free to cast votes in the cases in accordance with their preferences on issues of public policy. Therefore, the Supreme Court overturns statutes under conditions where the preferences of the court majority and Congress merely conflict, without reference to exogenous factors.[13]

Alternatively, scholars working within the rational choice frame-work have offered another conceptualization of the relationship be-tween the Supreme Court and Congress that poses a serious challenge to the widely accepted principle of judicial autonomy and purely attitu-dinal voting. Positive theorists have argued that even when preferences conflict, the Supreme Court frequently will acquiesce to the legislative majority when the Court anticipates some possible reprisal or sanction for its actions (Gely and Spiller 1990, 1992; Spiller and Gely 1992; Spiller and Spitzer 1992). One particularly important reprisal is subsequent statutory revision. Stated differently, rational-choice theorists model the preferences of Congress as a significant constraint on judicial choice in the nation's highest court, and the power of Congress as a limit on the autonomy of the Supreme Court.

While these two alternative perspectives on the status of the United States Supreme Court will continue to be debated as new evidence is brought to bear on the issue, some very recent research raises serious doubts about the utility of models derived from rational choice theory for explaining the Supreme Court's interaction with Congress. In a highly thought-provoking paper, Jeffrey Segal (1995) presents a con-vincing case that assumptions about the insularity of courts are theoret-ically sound and empirically correct for the Supreme Court, even in matters of statutory interpretation. As Segal demonstrates, very much in accordance with the voluminous literature on attitudinal theory, in-dividual justices cast votes on the basis of their personal preferences, displaying little evidence of deference to Congress. In other words, the Supreme Court's decisions are not constrained by anticipated reactions from Congress. As mentioned, Segal attributes the failure to find em-pirical support for separation of powers models to the institutional ar-rangements that define the Court and free its members from the need to engage in strategic voting.

The matter of the United States Supreme Court's insularity from Congress appears to be resolved, at least for the moment. However, arguments about the effects of institutional arrangements on judicial choice actually are untested, though highly plausible hypotheses. Moreover, studies of the Supreme Court leave unaddressed the issue of how alternative rules and structures generally might affect the au-tonomy of courts. While Segal (1995) argues and demonstrates convinc-ingly that United States Supreme Court justices fail to act strategically vis-à-vis external political conditions, this begs the question of whether judges act strategically if operating within a less insular environment.

Are positive theorists dead wrong? Or are they simply wrong about the types of courts to which their arguments best apply?

In order to test hypotheses about the effects of alternative institutional arrangements on judicial choice and to transcend theories that are institution-specific, comparative analysis is essential. In fact, it is most reasonable to observe that if scholars had first studied courts comparatively instead of relying so heavily on the case study approach seemingly endemic to judicial politics scholarship, the preceding debate between the attitudinalists and positive theorists probably would have been avoided. By studying single institutions, assertions about the effects of institutional arrangements remain hypotheses rather than validated propositions.

By extending our focus beyond the United States Supreme Court, we have the ability to assess the extent to which courts in alternative contexts and with different institutional features respond to their external environments. With regard to the above example, if the judicial process is, in fact, a single arena game, the extent to which decisions of courts comport with the external political environment will be shaped largely by the recruitment process. Congruity between judicial and legislative majorities will occur because of a coincidence of preferences and goals promoted by selection processes affecting both institutions. Alternatively, if external arenas affect judicial voting strategies, then judicial outcomes are brought in line with legislative preferences through mechanisms in addition to, or other than, recruitment. Most basically, if judicial responses to legislatures vary systematically in alternative settings and under different institutional structures and rule configurations, we reasonably can infer that the autonomy of courts is conditional, and that rational choice theory has merit for understanding judicial-legislative interaction broadly considered.

Conclusion

Research premised on the rationality assumption, with a focus on the interaction of goals, institutions, and context, offers an important avenue for tackling a number of major debates about the essential functions of courts and for broadening our understanding of the role of institutions and context in judicial processes and behavior. Such theoretically based research, using the American states as a comparative laboratory, would serve as the point of departure for rigorous, multivariate analysis of complex causal relationships that include diverse contextual and institutional influences. Stated plainly, it simply does not make sense to continue to examine judicial decision-making without considering the importance of institutions and context, or to continue to construct theories of decision-making that apply only to one court.

Further, the focus in judicial politics research should be on generating hypotheses about what purposive actors do, given particular goals, institutional settings, and external environments, rather than on trying to figure out what a judge's goal or motivation may have been, given a particular behavior. While such scholars as Gillman (1997) have raised issues about the approach advocated in this chapter, we think it highly problematic to adopt the perspective of the "post-positivists" that intensive assessments of judicial motivations will be fruitful. Instead, we should begin with assumptions about goals and then test hypotheses derived from those assumptions, rather than testing the assumptions themselves.

More than anything else, scholars of judicial politics should broaden their focus beyond the United States Supreme Court and begin to ask the fundamental question "compared to what?" For through comparative analysis, hypotheses deduced from theory, including rational choice theory and neo-institutionalism, about the effects of rules and structures on behavior and outcomes actually can be tested. Courts can be studied as institutions, and assertions about the extent to which exogenous forces penetrate courts, and how institutional arrangements condition those forces, can achieve the status of confirmed propositions rather than educated speculation. More importantly, we can move beyond theories that are particularistic and instead begin to understand the politics of courts comprehensively.

Appendix A: Variable Descriptions for Table 1

Ballot	= 1 for states using partisan ballots in supreme court elections (Louisiana, North Carolina, Ohio)
	= 0 otherwise (California, Kentucky, New Jersey)
Case Characteristics	= 1 if the victim was female, elderly, a child less than 12 years of age, or a law enforcement officer; or if a robbery or rape occurred during the murder
	= 0 otherwise

Competition	= 100—the average net difference between Republican and Democratic candidates for statewide offices lagged one year
Conservative Dissent	= 1 if the vote is a dissent favoring the death penalty (i.e., a dissent from a liberal court decision)
	= 0 otherwise (i.e., a vote with a liberal majority)
Majority Party	= 1 if the justice casting the vote is a member of the party composing the majority on the court
	= 0 otherwise
Liberal Dissent	= 1 if the vote is a dissent opposing the death penalty (i.e., a dissent from a conservative court decision)
	= 0 otherwise (i.e., a vote with the conservative majority)
Democrat	= 1 if the justice casting the vote is a Democrat
	= 0 otherwise
1980–1982	= 1 if the vote was cast in 1980, 1981, 1982
	= 0 otherwise
1983–1985	= 1 if the vote was cast in 1983, 1984, 1985
	= 0 otherwise
Seniority	= Number of years served on the court by the justice casting the vote
Seniority Rules	= 1 for states in which supreme court justices vote by seniority (California, New Jersey)
	= 0 otherwise (Kentucky, Louisiana, North Carolina, Ohio)
Join Majority	= 1 if the vote is part of the majority decision coalition
	= 0 otherwise

Appendix B: Variable Descriptions for Table 2

CASE CHARACTERISTICS

Crime Characteristics	= 1 if capital crime involved robbery or sexual assault, or multiple victims
	= 0 otherwise

Victim Characteristics   = 1 if the victim was female, or over age 65,
                            or less than 12
                          = 0 otherwise

PERSONAL ATTRIBUTES

Democrat   = 1 if judge identified as a Democrat
                          = 0 otherwise

ENVIRONMENTAL
  INFLUENCES

Competition   = Index of interparty competition (Bibby et
                            al. 1990). This measure was computed
                            using 1980–88 data. In the current analy-
                            sis the index was "folded" to remove
                            partisan direction.

INSTITUTIONAL STRUC-
  TURE AND RULES

Elected Judges   = 1 if state uses partisan or nonpartisan
                            elections to select state supreme court
                            justices (Illinois, Kentucky, Louisiana,
                            North Carolina, Ohio, Texas)
                          = 0 otherwise (California, New Jersey)

Victim Statute   = 1 if state lists as an aggravating circum-
                            stance "heinous" or "vile" action (Cali-
                            fornia, Illinois, Louisiana, North Caro-
                            lina, New Jersey)
                          = 0 otherwise (Kentucky, Ohio, Texas)

Crime Statute   = 1 if state lists as an aggravating circum-
                            stance robbery or sexual assault, or mul-
                            tiple victims (California, Kentucky, Loui-
                            siana, New Jersey, North Carolina, Ohio)
                          = 0 otherwise (Illinois, Texas)

Term Length   = Length of term for state supreme court
                            justices, in years.

Notes

This work was truly collaborative. Order of authorship was assigned randomly.

1. Fiorina (1995a:87) notes that "the only thing all rational choice people
would agree upon is that individuals behave purposively." Obviously, this
literature is quite diverse and very complex.

2. Baum (1994b) does an excellent job of cataloging the wide range of goals relevant to judges.

3. See Mayhew (1974) for a thorough discussion of the electoral incentive for Congress.

4. See Schlesinger (1966) for a comprehensive discussion of ambition theory.

5. Research on nonjudicial institutions clearly suggests that rules affect the aggregation of preferences within an institution and the responsiveness of public officials to their external environment (e.g., Cox and Tutt 1984; Niou and Ordeshook 1984; Weingast 1979).

6. Without question, researchers have made significant strides in understanding the complex phenomenon of judging. Studies representing decades of effort have produced a wealth of knowledge about the myriad forces affecting the exercise of judicial discretion. But in spite of the important contributions of past research, and the recent attention to integrated models of judicial choice (e.g., Brace and Hall 1993, 1995; Emmert 1992; George and Epstein 1992; Hall and Brace 1992, 1994; Songer and Haire 1992), we have only begun to recognize the complex interactions that take place among the major categories of forces affecting judicial choice.

7. The following discussion is taken from Brace and Hall (1993).

8. In death penalty cases, liberal decisions generally are defined as decisions to overturn death sentences while conservative decisions uphold death sentences.

9. The following discussion is taken from Brace and Hall (1995).

10. To elaborate, legislatures generally pose a threat to courts by having the power to undermine judicial rulings through subsequent statutory or constitutional revision. Therefore, in the interest of coming as close to their preferred policy position as possible, courts should defer to legislatures when some sort of reprisal is likely. Not voting strictly in accordance with one's personal ideological preferences is a rational way to avoid further defeat in the future. However, courts (and judges) should be less concerned with confronting legislatures when judges are shielded by lifetime tenure or when party control of government is divided and the likelihood of a legislative response to judicial action is lessened.

11. The newly created United States Supreme Court and the United States Courts of Appeals data bases, and corresponding work on these institutions, are not appropriate for a comprehensive examination of institutional and contextual hypotheses. While research on the federal appellate courts current stands on the threshold of extraordinary advancement because of the existence of systematic data bases that now will facilitate lines of inquiry that heretofore were impossible to pursue, the fact remains that the range of inquiry possible with either data base or institution is limited. Neither allows a consideration of the total array of forces affecting judicial processes and behavior, since neither setting presents variation in institutional rules and structures. The Courts of Appeals do not vary, for instance, in such basic institutional arrangements as selection/retention procedures for the bench, internal operating rules, and docket control. Moreover, assessing the influences of various contextual features is problematic using the Courts of Appeals data base, since the federal circuits are artificial boundaries that include several states (e.g., the Ninth Cir-

cuit contains nine states, Guam, and the Northern Mariana Islands!). To understand comprehensively the politics of courts and to achieve a level of theoretical understanding that transcends particular institutions, comparative state research is essential.

12. This example is taken from Brace, Hall, and Langer (1996).

13. Both macrolevel and microlevel approaches have been utilized to address fundamental questions about the exercise of judicial review. At the macrolevel, scholars generally have focused on conditions under which the United States Supreme Court finds itself at odds with Congress. These studies call attention to the role of recruitment and retention processes that shape both judicial and legislative institutions and affect their interaction. Principally, the Supreme Court invalidates statutes when the partisan majority of the Court is incompatible with the partisan majority of Congress, largely as a consequence of lags in membership replacement during periods of electoral change (Dahl 1957; Funston 1975). These seminal studies are highly consistent with the attitudinal model, which posits that justices' votes primarily are a reflection of their personal policy preferences (e.g., Rohde and Spaeth 1976; Segal and Spaeth 1993).

REFERENCES

Abel, Richard L. 1989. *American Lawyers.* New York: Oxford University Press.
————. 1988. "United States: The Contradictions of Professionalism." In *Lawyers in Society, vol. I: The Common Law World,* ed. Richard L. Abel and Philip S. C. Lewis. Berkeley: University of California Press.
Abraham, Henry J. 1992. *Justices and Presidents: A Political History of Appointments to the Supreme Court.* 3rd ed. New York: Oxford University Press.
Abramson, Paul R., John H. Aldrich, and David W. Rohde. 1987. "Progressive Ambition among United States Senators: 1972–1988." *Journal of Politics* 49: 3–35.
Ackerman, Bruce. 1991. *We the People.* Cambridge, Mass.: Harvard University Press.
Adamany, David. 1980. "The Supreme Court's Role in Critical Elections." In *Realignment in American Politics,* ed. Richard J. Trilling. Austin: University of Texas Press.
Aldrich, John. 1994. "Rational Choice Theory and the Study of American Politics." In *The Dynamics of American Politics: Approaches and Interpretations,* ed. Larry Dodd and Calvin Jillson. Boulder: Westview Press.
Aldrich, John H. 1995. *Why Parties? The Origin and Transformation of Political Parties in America.* Chicago: University of Chicago Press.
Aliotta, Jilda M. 1988. "Social Backgrounds, Social Motives and Participation on the U.S. Supreme Court." *Political Behavior* 10:267–84.
Alt, James E., and Kenneth A. Shepsle, eds. 1990. *Perspectives on Positive Political Economy.* Cambridge: Cambridge University Press.
Atkins, Burton M. 1972. "Decision-Making Rules and Judicial Strategy on the United States Courts of Appeals." *Western Political Quarterly* 25:626–42.
————. 1970. "Some Theoretical Effects of the Decision-Making Rules on the United States Courts of Appeals." *Jurimetrics Journal* 11:13–23.
Atkins, Burton M., and William Zavoina. 1974. "Judicial Leadership on the Court of Appeals: A Probability Analysis of Panel Assignment in Race Relations Cases on the Fifth Circuit." *American Journal of Political Science* 18:701–11.
Auerbach, Jerold. 1976. *Unequal Justice: Lawyers and Social Change in Modern America.* New York: Oxford University Press.

Austin-Smith, David. 1987. "Sophisticated Sincerity: Voting over Endogenous Agendas." *American Political Science Review* 81:1323–29.

Austin-Smith, David, and John R. Wright. 1992. "Competitive Lobbying for a Legislator's Vote." *Social Choice and Welfare* 9:231.

Axelrod, Robert. 1984. *The Evolution of Cooperation.* New York: Basic Books.

Bach, Stanley, and Steven S. Smith. 1988. *Managing Uncertainty in the House of Representatives: Adaptation and Innovation in Special Rules.* Washington, D.C.: Brookings Institution.

Ball, Howard. 1990. *"We Have a Duty": The Supreme Court and the Watergate Tapes Litigation.* New York: Greenwood Press.

Barber, James David. 1992 [1972]. *The Presidential Character: Predicting Performance in the White House.* 3rd ed. Englewood Cliffs, N.J.: Prentice-Hall.

———. 1965. *The Lawmakers: Recruitment and Adaptation to Legislative Life.* New Haven, Conn.: Yale University Press.

Barber, Satirious A. 1989. "Normative Theory, the New Institutuionalism, and the Future of Public Law." *Studies in American Political Development* 3:56–73.

Baum, Lawrence. 1997. *The Puzzle of Judicial Behavior.* Ann Arbor, MI: University of Michigan Press.

———. 1996. "How Strategic Are Judges?" Paper presented at the annual meeting of the Midwest Political Science Association, Chicago.

———. 1995. "What Motivates Supreme Court Justices? Assessing the Evidence on Justices' Goals." Paper presented at the annual meeting of the Midwest Political Science Association, Chicago.

———. 1994a. "Symposium: The Supreme Court and the Attitudinal Model." *Law and Courts Newsletter* 4:3–5

———. 1994b. "What Judges Want: Judges' Goals and Judicial Behavior." *Political Research Quarterly* 47:749–68.

———. 1988. "Measuring Policy Change in the U.S. Supreme Court." *American Political Science Review* 82:905–21.

Bawn, Kathleen, and Charles R. Shipan. 1997. "Congressional Responses to Supreme Court Decisions: Imperfect Anticipation and Institutional Constraints." Unpublished manuscript.

Beaney, William M. 1955. *The Right to Counsel in American Courts.* Ann Arbor, Mich.: University of Michigan Press.

Belknap, Michael R. 1977. *Cold War Political Justice: The Smith Act, the Communist Party, and American Civil Liberties.* Westport, Conn.: Greenwood Press.

Berelson, Bernard R., Paul F. Lazarsfeld, and William N. McPhee. 1954. *Voting.* Chicago: University of Chicago Press.

Bibby, John F., Cornelius P. Cotter, James L. Gibson, and Robert Huckshorn. 1990. "Parties in State Politics." In *Politics in the American States.* 5th ed., ed. Virginia Gray, Herbert Jacob, and Robert B. Albritton. Glenview, Ill.: Scott, Foresman.

Binder, Sarah A. 1997. *Minority Rights, Majority Rule: Partisanship and the Development of Congress.* New York: Cambridge University Press.

Biskupic, Joan. 1994a. "The Mysterious Mr. Rehnquist: Where Is the Chief Justice Going and Who Will Follow?" *Washington Post,* 25 September 1994, sect. C.

———. 1994b. " 'I Am Not an Uncle Tom,' Thomas Says at Meeting," *Washington Post,* October 28, sect. A.

Bickel, Alexander. 1967. *The Unpublished Opinions of Mr. Justice Brandeis.* Chicago: University of Chicago Press.

Black, Gordon S. 1972. "A Theory of Political Ambition: Career Choices and the Role of Structural Incentives." *American Political Science Review* 66:144–59.

Bloomfield, Maxwell. 1984. "From Deference to Confrontation: The Early Black Lawyers of Galveston, Texas, 1895–1920." In *The New High Priests: Lawyers in Post-Civil War America,* ed. Gerard W. Gawalt. Westport, Conn.: Greenwood Press.

Bogue, Allan G., Jerome M. Clubb, Carroll R. McKibbin, and Santa A. Traugott. 1976. "Members of the House of Representatives and the Processes of Modernization, 1789–1960." *Journal of American History* 63:275–302.

Bohman, James F. 1991. *New Philosophy of Social Science.* Cambridge: Polity Press.

Boucher, Robert, and Jeffrey A. Segal. 1995. "Supreme Court Justices as Strategic Decision Makers: Offensive Grants and Defensive Denials on the Vinson Court." *Journal of Politics* 57:824–37.

Bork, Robert H. 1990. *The Tempting of America: The Political Seduction of Law.* New York: Simon and Schuster.

Brace, Paul, and Melinda Gann Hall. 1995. "Studying Courts Comparatively: The View from the American States." *Political Research Quarterly* 48:5–29.

———. 1993. "Integrated Models of Judicial Dissent." *Journal of Politics* 55:914–935.

———. 1990. "Neo-Institutionalism and Dissent in State Supreme Courts." *Journal of Politics* 52:54–70.

Brace, Paul, Melinda Gann Hall, and Laura Langer. 1996. "Judicial Choice and the Politics of Abortion: Institutions, Context, and the Autonomy of Courts." Paper presented at the annual meeting of the American Political Science Association, San Francisco.

Brady, David, and Edward Schwartz. 1995. "Ideology and Interests in Congressional Voting: The Politics of Abortion in the U.S. Senate." *Public Choice* 84: 25–48.

Brandeis, Louis. 1914. "The Opportunity in the Law." In *Business—A Profession.* Boston: Small, Maynard.

Brennan, William Jr. 1986. "In Defense of Dissents." *Hastings Law Journal* 37: 427–38.

Brenner, Saul. 1984. "Issue Specialization as a Variable in Opinion Assignment on the U.S. Supreme Court." *Journal of Politics* 45:1217–25.

———. 1982. "Strategic Choice and Opinion Assignment on the U.S. Supreme Court: A Reexamination." *Western Political Quarterly* 35:204–11.

———. 1979. "The New Certiorari Game." *Journal of Politics* 41:649–55.

Brenner, Saul, Timothy M. Hagle, and Harold J. Spaeth. 1990. "Increasing the Size of Minimum Winning Original Coalitions on the Warren Court." *Polity* 23:309–18.

Brenner, Saul, and John F. Krol. 1989. "Strategies in Certiorari Voting on the United States Supreme Court." *Journal of Politics* 51:828.

Brenner, Saul, and Jan Palmer. 1988. "The Time Taken to Write Opinions as a Determinant of Opinion Assignments." *Judicature* 72:179–84.

Brenner, Saul, and Harold J. Spaeth. 1988. "Majority Opinion Assignments and the Maintenance of the Original Coalition on the Warren Court." *American Journal of Political Science* 32:72–81.

———. 1986. "Issue Specialization in Majority Opinion Assignment on the Burger Court." *Western Political Quarterly* 39:520–27.

Brenner, Saul, and Marc Stier. 1995. "Does Stare Decisions Influence the Justices' Voting on the Supreme Court?" Paper presented at the annual meeting of the American Political Science Association, Chicago.

Brigham, John. 1987a. *The Cult of the Court.* Philadelphia: Temple University Press.

———. 1987b. "Rights, Rage, and Remedy: Forms of Law in Political Discourse." *Studies in American Political Development* 2: 303–17.

———. 1978. *Constitutional Language: An Interpretation of Judicial Decisions.* Westport, Conn.: Greenwood Press.

Brigham, John, and Diana R. Gordon. 1996. "Law in Politics: Struggles over Property and Public Space on New York City's Lower East Side." *Law and Social Inquiry* 21:265–83.

Brisbin, Richard A. 1996. "Slaying the Dragon: Segal, Spaeth and the Function of Law in Supreme Court Decisionmaking." *American Journal of Political Science* 40:1004–17.

Buchanon, James M., and Gordon Tullock. 1962. *The Calculus of Consent: Logical Foundations of Constitutional Democracy.* Ann Arborm, Mich.: University of Michigan Press.

Burgess, Susan R. 1993. "Beyond Instrumental Politics: The New Institutionalism, Legal Rhetoric, and Judicial Supremacy." *Polity* 24:445–59.

Bussiere, Elizabeth. 1997. *(Dis)Entitling the Poor: The Warren Court, Welfare Rights, and the American Political Tradition.* University Park, Penn.: Pennsylvania State Press.

———. 1994. "The Failure of Constitutional Welfare Rights in the Warren Court." *Political Science Quarterly* 109:105–31.

Caldeira, Greg A. 1977. "Judicial Incentives: Some Evidence from Urban Trial Courts." *Justicia* 4(2):1–28.

Caldeira, Gregory A., and John R. Wright. 1995. "Lobbying for Justice: The Rise of Organized Conflict in the Politics of Federal Judgeships." In *Contemplating Courts,* ed. Lee Epstein. Washington, D.C.: CQ Press.

———. 1990. "The Discuss List: Agenda Building in the Supreme Court." *Law and Society Review* 24(3):807–36.

———. 1988. "Organized Interests and Agenda Setting in the U.S. Supreme Court." *American Political Science Review* 82:1109–27.

Caldeira, Gregory A., John R. Wright, and Christopher J. W. Zorn. 1996. "Strategic Voting and Gatekeeping in the Supreme Court." Paper presented at the annual meeting of the American Political Science Association, San Francisco.

Calvert, Randall L., and Richard F. Fenno, Jr. 1994. "Strategy and Sophisticated Voting in the Senate." *Journal of Politics* 56:349–76.

Cameron, Charles M. 1994. "Decision-Making and Positive Political Theory (Or, Using Game Theory to Study Judicial Politics)." Paper presented at the 1994 Columbus Conference, Columbus, Ohio.

Cameron, Charles, Jeffrey Segal, and Donald R. Songer. 1997. "Strategic Auditing in a Political Hierarchy: An Informational Model of the Supreme

Court's Certiorari Decisions." Paper presented at the annual meeting of the Law and Society Association, St. Louis.

Campbell, Angus, Philip E. Converse, Warren E. Miller, and Donald E. Stokes. 1960. *The American Voter*. New York: John Wiley and Sons.

Campbell, Colin. 1986. *Managing the Presidency: Carter, Reagan and the Search for Executive Harmony*. Pittsburgh, Penn.: University of Pittsburgh Press.

Campbell, J., III. 1983. "The Spirit of Dissent." *Judicature* 66:305–12.

Canon, David T. 1990. *Actors, Athletes, and Astronauts: Political Amateurs in the United States Congress*. Chicago: University of Chicago Press.

Caplan, Lincoln. 1987. *The Tenth Justice: The Solicitor General and the Rule of Law*. New York: Alfred A. Knopf.

Carrington, Paul D. 1976. *Justice On Appeal*. St. Paul, Minn.: West Publishing Company.

Carter, Dan T. 1979. *Scottsboro: A Tragedy of the American South*. Rev. ed. Baton Rouge, La.: Louisiana State University Press.

Casper, Jonathan. 1972. *Lawyers before the Warren Court: Civil Liberties and Civil Rights, 1957–1966*. Urbana, Ill.: University of Illinois Press.

Casto, William R. 1995. *The Supreme Court in the Early Republic: The Chief Justiceships of John Jay and Oliver Ellsworth*. Columbia, S.C. : University of South Carolina Press.

Chandler, Alfred D., Jr. 1980. "The United States: Seedbed of Managerial Capitalism." In *Managerial Hierarchies: Comparative Perspectives on the Rise of the Modern Industrial Enterprise*, ed. Alfred D. Chandler Jr. and Herman Daems. Cambridge, Mass.: Harvard University Press.

———. 1977. *The Visible Hand: The Managerial Revolution in American Business*. Cambridge, Mass.: Harvard University Press.

Chandler, Alfred D., Jr., and Herman Daems, eds. 1980. *Managerial Hierarchies: Comparative Perspectives on the Rise of the Modern Industrial Enterprise*. Cambridge, Mass.: Harvard University Press.

Clayton, Cornell W. 1994. "Separate Branches—Separate Politics: The Case for Judicial Enforcement of Congressional Intent." *Political Science Quarterly* 109: 843–72.

———. 1992. *The Politics of Justice: The Attorney General and the Making of Legal Policy*. Armonk, N.Y.: M. E. Sharpe.

Coffin, Frank M. 1994. *On Appeal: Courts, Lawyering and Judging*. New York: Norton.

Cohen, Linda R., and Matthew L. Spitzer. 1994. "Solving the *Chevron* Puzzle." *Law and Contemporary Problems* 57:65–110.

Congressional Quarterly. 1990. "101st Congress Leaves Behind Plenty of Laws, Criticisms." *Congressional Quarterly Weekly Report* 48:3683–3709.

Conkle, Daniel O. 1997. "The Second Death of Substantive Due Process." *Indiana Law Journal* 62:215–42.

Cook, Beverly Blair. 1995. "Justice Brennan and the Institutionalization of Dissent Assignment." *Judicature* 79:17–23.

———. 1992. "Testing a Model of Opinion Assignment: The Burger Court." Paper presented at the annual meeting of the American Political Science Association, San Francisco.

Cortner, Richard C. 1993. *The Iron Horse and the Constitution: The Railroads and the Transformation of the Fourteenth Amendment.* Westport, Conn.: Greenwood Press.

―――. 1981. *The Supreme Court and the Second Bill of Rights: The Fourteenth Amendment and the Nationalization of Civil Liberties.* Madison, Wisc.: University of Wisconsin Press.

Corwin, Edward S. 1940. *The President: Office and Powers.* New York: New York University Press.

―――. 1936. "The Constitution as Instrument and Symbol." *American Political Science Review* 30:1071–85.

―――. 1934. *The Twilight of the Supreme Court: A History of Our Constitutional Theory.* New Haven, Conn.: Yale University Press.

―――. 1929. "The Democratic Dogma and the Future of Political Science." *American Political Science Review* 23:569–92.

―――. 1928. "The Higher Law Background of the American Constitution." *Harvard Law Review* 42:149–85 and 365–409.

Cowan, Ruth B. 1976. "Women's Rights through Litigation: An Examination of the American Civil Liberties Union Women's Rights Project, 1971–1976." *Columbia Human Rights Law Review* 8:373–412.

Cox, Gary W., and Matthew D. McCubbins. 1993. *Legislative Leviathan: Party Government in the House.* Berkeley: University of California Press.

Cox, Gary W., and Timothy N. Tutt. 1984. "Universalism and Allocative in the Los Angeles County Board of Supervisors." *Journal of Politics* 46:546–55.

Croly, Herbert. 1965 [1909]. *The Promise of American Life.* Indianapolis, Ind.: Bobbs-Merrill.

Curran, Barbara, and Clara N. Carson. 1994. *The Lawyer Statistical Report: The U.S. Legal Profession in the 1990s.* Chicago: American Bar Foundation.

Curran, Barbara A., Clara N. Carson, Mark Puccetti, and Katherine J. Roshich. 1985. *The Lawyer Statistical Profile of the U.S. Legal Profession in the 1980's.* Chicago: American Bar Foundation.

Cushman, Robert E. 1925. *Leading Constitutional Decisions.* New York: F. S. Crofts.

Dahl, Robert. 1961. "The Behavioral Approach in Political Science." *American Political Science Review* 55:763–72.

―――. 1957. "Decision-Making in a Democracy: The Supreme Court as a National Policy-Maker." *Journal of Public Law* 6:279–95.

Danelski, David J. 1960. "The Influence of the Chief Justice in the Decisional Process of the Supreme Court." In *American Court Systems: Readings in Judicial Process and Behavior,* ed. Sheldon Goldman and Austin Sarat. San Francisco: W. H. Freeman and Company, 1978.

Danelski, David, and Joseph Tulchin, eds. 1973. *The Autobiographical Notes of Charles Evans Hughes.* Cambridge, Mass.: Harvard University Press.

Davis, J. F., and W. Reynolds. 1974. "Juridical Cripples: Plurality Opinions in the Supreme Court." *Duke Law Journal* 59–86.

Davis, Martha F. 1993. *Brutal Need: Lawyers and the Welfare Rights Movement, 1960–1973.* New Haven, Conn.: Yale University Press.

Davis, Richard. 1994. *Decisions and Images: The Supreme Court and the Press.* Englewood Cliffs, N.J.: Prentice Hall.

Davis, Sue. 1992. "Rehnquist and State Courts: Federalism Revisited." *Western Political Quarterly* 45:773–82.

———. 1990. "Power on the Court: Chief Justice Rehnquist's Opinion Assignments." *Judicature* 74:66–72.

De Figueiredo, John M., and Emerson H. Tiller. 1996. "Congressional Control of the Courts: A Theoretical and Empirical Analysis of Expansion of the Federal Judiciary." *Journal of Law and Economics* 39:435–62.

Dion, Douglas. 1997. *Turning the Legislative Thumbscrew: Minority Rights and Procedural Change in Legislative Politics.* Ann Arbor, Mich.: University of Michigan Press.

Dixon, Robert G. 1968. "The Attorney General and Civil Rights, 1870–1964." In *Roles of the Attorney General of the United States,* ed. Luther A. Huston, Arthur Selwyn Miller, Samuel Krislov, and Robert G. Dixon. Washington, D.C.: American Enterprise Institute.

Dorsen, Norman. 1993. "John Marshall Harlan and the Warren Court." In *The Warren Court in Historical and Political Perspective,* ed. Mark Tushnet. Charlottesville, Va.: University Press of Virginia.

Douglas, William O. 1980. *The Court Years, 1939–1975: The Autobiography of William O. Douglas.* New York: Random House.

———. 1972. "Memorandum." Available in Justice William O. Douglas's papers. Washington, D.C.: Library of Congress. June 2.

Eisner, Marc A., and Kenneth J. Meier. 1990. "Presidential Control Versus Bureaucratic Power: Explaining the Reagan Revolution in Antitrust." *American Journal of Political Science* 34:269–87.

Elliff, John T. 1987. *The United States Department of Justice and Individual Rights, 1937–1962.* New York: Garland.

Elman, Philip. 1987. "The Solicitor General's Office, Justice Frankfurter, and Civil Rights Litigation, 1946–1960: An Oral History." *Harvard Law Review* 100:817–52.

Elster, Jon. 1995. "Equal or Proportional? Arguing and Bargaining over the Senate at the Federal Convention." In *Explaining Social Institutions,* ed. Jack Knight and Itai Sened. Ann Arbor, Mich.: University of Michigan Press.

———. 1986. "Introduction." In *Rational Choice,* ed. Jon Elster. New York: New York University Press.

Ely, James W. 1992. "Rule of Four." Entry in *The Oxford Companion to the Supreme Court of the United States,* editor-in-chief Kermit L. Hall. New York: Oxford University Press.

Ely, John Hart. 1980. *Democracy and Distrust: A Theory of Judicial Review.* Cambridge, Mass.: Harvard University Press.

Emmert, Craig F. 1992. "An Integrated Case-Related Model of Judicial Decision Making: Explaining Supreme Court Decisions in Judicial Review Cases." *Journal of Politics* 54:543–52.

Epp, Charles R. 1998. *The Rights Revolution: Lawyers, Activists, and Supreme Courts in Comparative Perspective.* Chicago: University of Chicago Press.

Epstein, Cynthia Fuchs. 1993. *Women in Law.* 2nd ed. Urbana, Ill.: University of Illinois Press.

Epstein, Lee. 1996. Call for Papers: Law and Courts Section. *PS: Political Science & Politics* 29:575–76.

————. 1993. "Interest Group Litigation during the Rehnquist Court Era." *Journal of Law and Politics* 9:639–717.

Epstein, Lee, and Jack Knight. 1998. *The Choices Justices Make.* Washington, D.C.: CQ Press.

————. 1997. "The New Institutionalism, Part II." *Law and Courts* 7:4–9.

————. 1996. "On the Struggle for Judicial Supremacy." *Law and Society Review* 30:87–120.

————. 1995a. "Documenting Strategic Interaction on the U.S. Supreme Court." Paper presented at the annual meeting of the American Political Science Association, Chicago.

————. 1995b. "Positive Approaches to Supreme Court Decision-Making." Paper presented at the annual meeting of the American Political Science Association, Chicago.

Epstein, Lee, and Joseph F. Kobylka. 1992. *The Supreme Court and Legal Change: Abortion and the Death Penalty.* Chapel Hill, N.C.: University of North Carolina Press.

Epstein, Lee, and Carol Mershon. 1996. "Measuring Political Preferences." *American Journal of Political Science* 40:261–94.

Epstein, Lee, Jeffrey A. Segal, and Timothy Johnson. 1996. "The Claim of Issue Creation on the U.S. Supreme Court." *American Political Science Review* 90: 845–52.

Epstein, Lee, Jeffrey A. Segal, Harold J. Spaeth, and Thomas G. Walker. 1996. *The Supreme Court Compendium: Data, Decisions, and Developments.* 2nd ed. Washington, D.C. CQ Press.

————. 1994. *The Supreme Court Compendium: Data Decisions and Developments.* Washington, D.C.: CQ Press.

Epstein, Lee and Thomas G. Walker. 1995. "The Role of the Supreme Court in American Society: Playing the Reconstruction Game." In *Contemplating Courts,* ed. Lee Epstein. Washington, D.C.: CQ Press.

Epstein, Lee, Thomas Walker, and William J. Dixon. 1989. "The Supreme Court and Criminal Justice Disputes: A Neo-Institutional Perspective." *American Journal of Political Science* 33:825–41.

Epstein, Richard A. 1990. "The Independence of Judges: The Uses and Limitations of Public Choice Theory." *Brigham Young University Law Review* 1990: 827–55.

Eskridge, William N., Jr. 1991a. "Overriding Supreme Court Statutory Interpretation Decisions." *Yale Law Journal* 101:331–417.

————. 1991b. "Reneging on History? Playing the Court/Congress/President Civil Rights Game." *California Law Review* 79:613–84.

Ethington, Philip J., and Eileen L. McDonagh. 1995. "The Common Space of Social Science Inquiry." *Polity* 28:85–90.

Evans, Peter R., Dietrick Rueschemeyer, and Theda Skocpol. 1985. *Bringing the State Back In.* New York: Cambridge University Press.

Farber, Daniel A., and Philip P. Frickey. 1991. *Law and Public Choice: A Critical Introduction.* Chicago: University of Chicago Press.

Farquarson, Robin. 1969. *Theory of Voting.* New Haven, Conn.: Yale University Press.

Fenno, Richard, Jr. 1966. *Power of the Purse.* Boston: Little, Brown.

———. 1962. "The House Appropriations Committee as a Political System: The Problem of Integration." *American Political Science Review* 56:310–24.

Ferejohn, John. 1995. "Law, Legislation, and Positive Political Theory." In *Modern Political Economy: Old Topics, New Directions,* ed. Jeffrey S. Banks and Eric A. Hanushek. New York: Cambridge University Press.

———. 1991. "Rationality and Interpretation: Parliamentary Elections in Early Stuart England." In *The Economic Approach to Politics: A Critical Reassessment of the Theory of Rational Action,* ed. Kristen Renwick Monroe. New York: HarperCollins.

Ferejohn, John, and Charles Shipan. 1990. "Congressional Influence on Bureaucracy." *Journal of Law Economics and Organization* 6:1–20.

Ferejohn, John, and Barry Weingast. 1992. "Strategic Statutory Interpretation." *Georgetown Law Journal* 80:565.

Fish, Peter. 1984. "The Office of the Chief Justice of the United States: Into the Federal Judiciary's Bicentennial Decade." In *The Office of the Chief Justice.* Charlottesville, Va.: University of Virginia.

Fisher, Louis. 1990. "Is the Solicitor General an Executive or a Judicial Agent? Caplan's *Tenth Justice.*" *Law and Social Inquiry* 15:305–20.

———. 1988. *Constitutional Dialogues.* Princeton, N.J.: Princeton University Press.

Fisher, Marc. "The Private World of Justice Thomas." *Washington Post,* 11 September 1995, sect. B.

Fisher, William, Morton J. Horwitz, and Thomas Reed, eds. 1993. *American Legal Realism.* New York: Oxford University Press.

Fiske, Susan T. 1993. "Cognitive Theory and the Presidency." In *Researching the Presidency: Vital Questions, New Approaches,* ed. George C. Edwards III, John H. Kessel, and Bert A. Rockman. Pittsburgh, Pa.: University of Pittsburgh Press.

Fiorina, Morris P. 1995a. "Rational Choice, Empirical Contributions, and the Scientific Enterprise." *Critical Review* 9:85–94.

———. 1995b. "Rational Choice and the New(?) Institutionalism." *Polity* 28:107–16.

Fortas, Abe. 1975. "Chief Justice Warren: The Enigma of Leadership." *Yale Law Journal* 84:405–12.

Fowler, Linda L. 1993. *Candidates, Congress, and the American Democracy.* Ann Arbor, Mich.: University of Michigan Press.

Fuld, Stanley H. 1962. "The Voices of Dissent." *Columbia Law Review* 62:926–29.

Funston, Richard. 1975. "The Supreme Court and Critical Elections." *American Political Science Review* 69:795–811.

Fried, Charles. 1988. "Jurisprudential Responses to Legal Realism." *Cornell Law Review* 73:331.

Galanter, Marc, and Thomas Palay. 1991. *Tournament of Lawyers: The Transformation of the Big Law Firm.* Chicago: University of Chicago Press.

Garbus, Martin. 1971. *Ready for the Defense.* New York: Farrar, Straus, and Giroux.

Garner, Bryan A. 1992. "Opinions, Style of." In *The Oxford Companion to the Supreme Court of the United States,* ed. Kermit Hall. New York: Oxford University Press.

Garrow, David J. 1996. "The Rehnquist Reins." *New York Times Magazine,* October 6.

Gates, John B. 1991. "Theory, Methods, and the New Institutionalism in Judicial Research." In *The American Courts: A Critical Assessment,* ed. John B. Gates and Charles Johnson. Washington D.C.: CQ Press.

Gelb, Joyce. 1989. *Feminism and Politics: A Comparative Perspective.* Berkeley: University of California Press.

Gely, Rafael, and Pablo T. Spiller. 1992. "The Political Economy of Supreme Court Constitutional Decisions: The Case of Roosevelt's Court-Packing Plan." *International Review of Law and Economics* 12:45–67.

———. 1990. "A Rational Choice Theory of Supreme Court with Applications to the *State Farm* and *Grove City* Cases." *Journal of Law, Economics, and Organizations* 6:263–300.

George, Alexander L. 1980. *Presidential Decisionmaking in Foreign Policy: The Effective Use of Information and Advice.* Boulder, Colo.: Westview Press.

George, Tracey E., and Lee Epstein. 1992. "On the Nature of Supreme Court Decision Making." *American Political Science Review* 86:323–37.

Gibson, James L. 1986. "The Social Science of Judicial Politics." In *Political Science: The Science of Politics,* ed. Herbert Weisberg. New York: Agathon Press.

———. 1983. "From Simplicity to Complexity: The Development of Theory in the Study of Judicial Behavior." *Political Behavior* 5:7–49.

———. 1978. "Judges' Role Orientation, Attitudes and Decisions: An Interactive Model." *American Political Science Review* 72:911–24.

Gillman, Howard. 1997. "The New Institutionalism, Part I." *Law and Courts Newsletter* 7:6–11.

———. 1996. "More on the Origins of the Fuller Court's Jurisprudence: The Scope of Federal Power Over Commerce and Manufacturing in Nineteenth-Century Constitutional Law." *Political Research Quarterly* 49:415–37.

———. 1994a. "On Constructing a Science of Judicial Politics." *Law and Society Review* 28:355–76.

———. 1994b. "Preferred Freedoms: The Progressive Expansion of State Power and the Rise of Modern Civil Liberties Jurisprudence." *Political Research Quarterly* 47:623–53.

———. 1993. *The Constitution Besieged: The Rise and Demise of Lochner Era Police Powers Jurisprudence.* Durham, N.C.: Duke University Press.

Goldman, Sheldon. 1991. "Federal Judicial Recruitment." In *The American Courts: A Critical Assessment,* ed. John B. Gates and Charles A. Johnson. Washington, D.C.: CQ Press.

———. 1982. *Constitutional Law and Supreme Court Decisionmaking.* New York: Harper and Row.

Goldman, Sheldon, and Charles Lamb, eds. 1986. *Judicial Conflict and Consensus:*

Behavior Studies of American Appellate Courts. Lexington, Ky.: University Press of Kentucky.

Goldstein, Leslie Friedman, and Diana Stech. 1995. "Explaining Transformation in Supreme Court Policy." *Judicature* 79:80–85.

Gordon, Linda. 1994. *Pitied but Not Entitled: Single Mothers and the History of Welfare.* New York: Free Press.

Gordon, Robert W. 1984. "Critical Legal Histories." *Stanford Law Review* 36:57–125.

Graber, Mark A. 1995. "The Passive-Aggressive Virtues: Cohens v. Virginia and the Problematic Establishment of Judicial Power." *Constitutional Commentary* 12:67–92.

———. 1993. "The Nonmajoritarian Difficulty: Legislative Deference to the Judiciary." *Studies in American Political Development* 7:35–73.

Grafstein, Robert. 1992. *Institutional Realism.* New Haven, Conn.: Yale University Press.

Graham, Jean Ann, Michael Argyle, and Adrian Furnham. 1980. "The Goal Structure of Situations." *European Journal of Social Psychology* 10:345–66.

Granovetter, Mark, and Richard Swedberg, eds. 1992. *The Sociology of Economic Life.* Boulder, Colo.: Westview Press.

Green, Donald P., and Ian Shapiro. 1994. *Pathologies of Rational Choice Theory: A Critique of Applications in Political Science.* New Haven, Conn.: Yale University Press.

Greenhouse, Linda. 1992a. "Slim Margin; Moderates on Court Defy Predictions." *New York Times,* July 5, Week in Review, page 1.

———. 1992b. "At the Supreme Court, A Pendulum Stops." *New York Times,* November 8, Week in Review, page 6.

Griffin, Stephen M. 1996. *American Constitutionalism: From Theory to Politics.* Princeton, N.J.: Princeton University Press.

Grossman, Joel B. 1965. *Lawyers and Judges: The ABA and the Politics of Judicial Selection.* New York: John Wiley and Sons.

Hagle, Timothy M., and Glenn E. Mitchell II. 1992. "Goodness-of-Fit Measures for Probit and Logic." *American Journal of Political Science* 36:762–84.

Hagle, Timothy M., and Harold J. Spaeth. 1993. "Ideological Patterns in the Justices' Voting in the Burger Court's Business Cases." *Journal of Politics* 55:492–505.

———. 1992. "The Emergence of a New Ideology: The Business Decisions of the Burger Court." *Journal of Politics* 54:120–34.

Haines, Charles Grove. 1944. *The Role of the Supreme Court in American Government and Politics, 1789–1835.* Berkeley: University of California Press.

———. 1922. "General Observations on the Effects of Personal, Political, and Economic Influences in the Decisions of Judges." Reprinted in *Judicial Behavior: A Reader in Theory and Research,* ed. Glendon A. Schubert. Chicago: Rand McNally.

Hakman, Nathan. 1969. "The Supreme Court's Political Environment: The Processing of Non-Commercial Litigation." In *Frontiers of Judicial Research,* ed. Joel B. Grossman and Joseph Tanenhaus. New York: John Wiley and Sons.

Hall, Kermit. 1996. "The Warren Court in Historical Perspective." In *The Warren*

Court: Retrospective, ed. Bernard Schwartz. New York: Oxford University Press.

Hall, Melinda Gann. 1995. "Justices as Representatives: Elections and Judicial Politics in the American States." *American Politics Quarterly* 23:485–503.

———. 1992. "Electoral Politics and Strategic Voting in State Supreme Courts." *Journal of Politics* 54:427–46.

———. 1987. "Constituent Influence in State Supreme Courts: Conceptual Notes and a Case Study." *Journal of Politics* 49:1117–24.

Hall, Melinda Gann, and Paul Brace. 1994. "The Vicissitudes of Death by Decree: Forces Influencing Capital Punishment in State Supreme Courts." *Social Science Quarterly* 75:136–51.

———. 1993. "Integrated Models of Judicial Dissent." *Journal of Politics* 55:914–35.

———. 1992. "Toward an Integrated Model of Judicial Voting Behavior." *American Politics Quarterly* 20:147–68.

———. 1989. "Order in the Courts: A Neo-Institutional Approach to Judicial Consensus." *Western Political Quarterly* 42:391–407.

Hall, Richard L., and Bernard Grofman. 1990. "The Committee Assignment Process and the Conditional Nature of Committee Bias." *American Political Science Review* 84:1149–66.

Hand, Learned. 1962. *The Bill of Rights*. Cambridge, Mass.: Harvard University Press.

Hansen, Mark J. 1991. *Gaining Access: Congress and the Farm Lobby*. Chicago: University of Chicago Press.

Harris, William F., III. 1982. "Bonding Word and Polity: The Logic of American Constitutionalism." *American Political Science Review* 76:34–45.

Hart, Henry. 1959. "The Time Chart of the Justices." *Harvard Law Review* 73: 84–129.

Haynie, Stacia L. 1992. "Leadership and Consensus on the U.S. Supreme Court." *Journal of Politics* 54:1158–69.

Heclo, Hugh. 1994. "Ideas, Interests, and Institutions." In *The Dynamics of American Politics: Approaches and Interpretations*, ed. Larry Dodd and Calvin Jillson. Boulder, Colo.: Westview Press.

Heinz, John P., and Edward O. Laumann. 1982. *Chicago Lawyers: The Social Structure of the Bar*. New York: Russell Sage Foundation.

Hess, Stephen. 1988. *Organizing the Presidency*. Washington, D.C.: Brookings Institution.

Hiley, David R., James F. Bohman, and Richard Shusterman, eds. 1991. *The Interpretive Turn*. Ithaca, N.Y.: Cornell University Press.

Howard, J. Woodford, Jr. 1977. "Role Perceptions and Behavior in Three U.S. Courts of Appeals." *Journal of Politics* 39:916–38.

———. 1971. "Judicial Biography and the Behavioral Persuasion." *American Political Science Review* 65:704–15.

———. 1968. "On the Fluidity of Judicial Choice." *American Political Science Review* 62:43–56.

Hughes, Charles E. 1936 [1928]. *The Supreme Court of the United States*. New York: Garden City [1928:Columbia University Press].

Hughes, David F. 1965. "Salmon P. Chase: Chief Justice." *Vanderbilt Law Review* 18:589–614.

Hurst, James Willard. 1956. *Law and the Conditions of Freedom in the Nineteenth-Century United States.* Madison, Wisc.: University of Wisconsin Press.

Ignagni, Joseph, and James Meernik. 1994. "Explaining Congressional Attempts to Reverse Supreme Court Decisions." *Political Research Quarterly* 47: 353–71.

Ignatieff, Michael. 1983. "State Civil Society and Total Institutions: A Critique of Recent Social Histories of Punishment." In *Legality, Ideology, and the State,* ed. David Sugarman. New York: Academic Press.

Jackson, Robert H. 1951. "Advocacy Before the Supreme Court: Suggestions for Effective Case Presentation." *A.B.A. Journal* 37:801.

Jackson, Percival. 1969. *Dissent in the Supreme Court.* Norman, Okla.: University of Oklahoma Press.

Jenkins, John A. 1985. "The Partisan: A Talk with Justice Rehnquist." *New York Times Magazine,* March 3, pp. 28–35.

Johnson, Charles A., and Bradley C. Canon. 1984. *Judicial Policies: Implementation and Impact.* Washington, D.C.: CQ Press.

Johnson, William R. 1978. *Schooled Lawyers: A Study in the Clash of Professional Cultures.* New York: New York University Press.

Jones, Bryan D. 1994. *Reconceiving Decision-Making in Democratic Politics: Attention, Choice, and Public Policy.* Chicago: University of Chicago Press.

Jost, Kenneth. 1995. *The Supreme Court Yearbook 1994–1995.* Washington, D.C.: CQ Press.

Kahn, Ronald. 1996a. "Constitutive Supreme Court , Social Facts, and the 'New' or 'Historical' Institutionalism." Paper to the annual meeting of the American Political Science Association, San Francisco.

———. 1996b. "Social Science, Social Facts, and the Rights of Subordinated Groups." Paper presented at the Joint International Conference of the Law and Society Association and the Research Committee on the Sociology of Law of the International Sociological Association, University of Strathclyde, Glasgow, Scotland.

———. 1994. *The Supreme Court and Constitutional Theory.* Lawrence, Kans.: University Press of Kansas.

———. 1993. "God Save Us From the Coercion Test: Constitutive Decisionmaking, Polity Principles, and Religious Freedom." *Case-Western Reserve Law Review* 43: 983–1020.

Kahn, Ronald, ed. 1994. "Symposium on Social Facts, Constitutional Theory, and Doctrinal Change." *Law and Courts* 5:3–15.

Kalman, Laura. 1996. *The Strange Career of Legal Liberalism.* New Haven, Conn.: Yale University Press.

Katzmann, Robert A. 1997. *Courts and Congress.* Washington, D.C.: Brookings Institution.

Kearns, Doris. 1976. *Lyndon Johnson and the American Dream.* New York: Harper and Row.

Kenrick, Douglas T., and David C. Funder. 1988. "Profiting from Controversy: Lessons from the Person-Situation Debate." *American Psychologist* 43:23–34.

Kens, Paul. 1991. "The Source of a Myth: Police Powers of the States and Laissez Faire Constitutionalism, 1900–37." *American Journal of Legal History* 35:70–98.

Keynes, Edward. 1996. *Liberty, Property, and Privacy: Toward a Jurisprudence of Substantive Due Process.* University Park, Penn.: Pennsylvania State University Press.

Kiewiet, D. Roderick, and Matthew D. McCubbins. 1991. *The Logic of Delegation: Congressional Parties and the Appropriations Process.* Chicago: University of Chicago Press.

Kloppenberg, James T. 1995. "Institutionalism, Rational Choice, and Historical Analysis." *Polity* 28:125–28.

Kluger, Richard. 1977. *Simple Justice.* New York: Vintage.

Knight, Jack. 1994. "Symposium: The Supreme Court and the Attitudinal Model." *Law and Courts Newsletter* 4:5–6.

———. 1993. "Interpretation as Social Interaction." Paper presented at the Political Economy of the Law Conference, Wallis Institute, University of Rochester.

———. 1992. *Institutions and Social Conflict.* New York: Cambridge University Press.

Knight, Jack, and Lee Epstein. 1996a. "On the Struggle for Judicial Supremacy." *Law and Society Review* 30:87–120.

———. 1996b. "The Norm of Stare Decisis." *American Journal of Political Science* 40:1018–35.

Knight, Jack, and Itai Sened, eds. 1995. *Explaining Social Institutions.* Ann Arbor, Mich.: University of Michigan Press.

Kobylka, Joseph F. 1989. "Leadership on the Supreme Court of the United States: Chief Justice Burger and the Establishment Clause." *Western Political Quarterly* 42:545–68.

Koelble, Thomas A. 1995. "The New Institutionalism in Political Science and Sociology." *Comparative Politics* 231–43.

Krehbiel, Keith. 1998. *Pivotal Politics.* Chicago: University of Chicago Press.

———. 1990. "Are Congressional Committees Composed of Preference Outliers." *American Political Science Review* 84:149–64.

Krislov, Samuel. 1963. "The Amicus Curiae: From Friendship to Advocacy." *Yale Law Journal* 72:694–721.

Krol, John F., and Saul Brenner. 1990. "Strategies in Certiorari Voting on the United States Supreme Court: A Reevaluation." *Western Political Quarterly* 43:335–42.

Kunda, Ziva. 1990. "The Case for Motivated Reasoning." *Psychological Bulletin* 108:480–98.

Kurland, Philip B., and Gerhard Casper. 1975. *Landmark Briefs and Arguments before the Supreme Court of the United States: Constitutional Law,* vol. 68. Arlington, Va.: University Publications of America.

Kutler, Stanley I. 1968. *Judicial Power and Reconstruction Politics.* Chicago: University of Chicago Press.

Lamb, Charles M., and Stephen C. Halpern, eds. 1991. *The Burger Court: Political and Judicial Profiles.* Urbana, Ill.: University of Illinois Press.

Landes, William M., and Richard A. Posner. 1975. "The Independent Judiciary in an Interest-Group Perspective." *Journal of Law and Economics* 18:875–901.

Lasser, William. 1985. "The Supreme Court and Periods of Critical Realignment." *Journal of Politics* 47:1124–87.

Lasswell, Harold Dwight. 1948. *Power and Personality*. New York: Norton.

Lawrence, Susan E. 1990. *The Poor in Court: The Legal Services Program and Supreme Court* . Princeton, N.J.: Princeton University Press.

Levi, Edward. 1949. *An Introduction to Legal Reasoning*. Chicago: University of Chicago Press.

Leyh, Gregory. 1992. *Legal Hermeneutics: History, Theory, and Practice*. Berkeley, Calif.: University of California Press.

Llewellyn, Karl N. 1930. "A Realistic Jurisprudence—The Next Step." *Columbia Law Review* 30:431–65.

Magat, Richard. 1979. *The Ford Foundation at Work: Philanthropic Choices, Methods and Styles*. New York: Plenum.

Maltzman, Forrest, and Paul J. Wahlbeck. 1996a. "May It Please the Chief? Opinion Assignments in the Rehnquist Court." *American Journal of Political Science* 40:421–43.

———. 1996b. "Strategic Policy Considerations and Voting Fluidity on the Burger Court." *American Political Science Review* 90:581–592.

———. 1995. "Hail to the Chief: Opinion Assignment on the Supreme Court." Paper presented at the annual meeting of the American Political Science Association, Chicago.

Manley, John F. 1970. *The Politics of Finance: The House Committee on Ways and Means*. Boston: Little, Brown.

March, James G., and Johan P. Olsen. 1989. *Rediscovering Institutions: The Organizational Basis of Politics*. New York: Free Press.

———. 1984. "The New Institutionalism: Organizational Factors in Political Life." *American Political Science Review* 78:734–49.

Markowitz, Deborah L. 1989. "In Pursuit of Equality: One Woman's Work to Change the Law." *Women's Rights Law Reporter* 11:2–73.

Marks, Brian A. 1988. *A Model of Judicial Influence on Congressional Policymaking: Grove City College v. Bell*. Working Papers in Political Science, P-88-7, The Hoover Institution, Stanford University.

Martin, Andrew D. 1996. "The Separation of Powers and Strategic on the Supreme Court: An Empirical Test." Paper presented at the Conference on the Scientific Study of Law and Courts, St. Louis.

Marvick, Dwaine. 1976. "Continuities in Recruitment Theory and Research: Toward a New Model." In *Elite Recruitment in Democratic Polities: Comparative Studies Across Nations*, ed. Heinz Eulau and Moshe M. Czudnowski, 29–44. New York: John Wiley and Sons.

Marx, Karl, and Friedrich Engels. 1955. *The Communist Manifesto*. Northbrook, Ill.: AHM Publishing.

Mason, Alpheus Thomas. 1956. *Harlan Fiske Stone: Pillar of the Law*. New York: Viking Press.

Mason, Alpheus T., and William M. Beaney. 1959. *The Supreme Court in a Free Society*. Englewood Cliffs, N.J.: Prentice-Hall.

Matthews, Donald R. 1960. *U.S. Senators and Their World*. Chapel Hill, N.C.: University of North Carolina Press.

Mayhew, David R. 1974. *Congress: The Electoral Connection*. New Haven, Conn.: Yale University Press.

McAninch, William Shepard. 1987. "A Catalyst for the Evolution of Constitutional Law: Jehovah's Witnesses in the Supreme Court." *Cincinnati Law Review* 55:997–1077.

McCann, Michael W. 1996. "Causal versus Constitutive Explanations (or, On the Difficulty of Being So Positive . . .)." *Law and Social Inquiry* 21:457–82.

———. 1994. *Rights at Work: Pay Equity and the Politics of Legal Mobilization*. Chicago: University of Chicago Press.

———. 1989. "Equal Protection for Social Inequality: Race and Clas in Constitutional Ideology." In *Judging the Constitution: Critical Essays on Judicial Lawmaking*, ed. Michael W. McCann and Gerald L. Houseman. Boston: Scott, Foresman.

McCloskey, Robert G. 1960. *The American Supreme Court*. Chicago: University of Chicago Press.

McCubbins, Mathew D., Roger G. Noll, and Barry R. Weingast. 1989. "Structure and Process, Politics and Policy: Administrative Arrangements and the Political Control of Agencies." *Virginia Law Review* 75:431–82.

McGuire, Kevin, and Gregory Caldeira. 1993. "Lawyers, Organized Interests, and the Law of Obscenity: Agenda Setting in the Supreme Court." *American Political Science Review* 87:717–26.

McGuire, Kevin T., and Barbara Palmer. 1995. "Issue Fluidity on the Supreme Court." *American Political Science Review* 89:691–702.

McIntosh, Wayne V. 1990. *The Appeal of Civil Law: A Political-Economic Analysis of Litigation*. Urbana, Ill.: University of Illinois Press.

McLauchlan, William P. 1972. "Research Note: Ideology and Conflict in Supreme Court Opinion Assignment, 1946–1962." *Western Political Quarterly* 25:16–27.

Meader, Paul, A. Carrington, and G. Rosenberg. 1976. *Justice on Appeal*. St. Paul, Minn.: West Publishing.

Meador, Daniel John. 1967. *Preludes to Gideon: Notes on Appellate Advocacy, Habeas Corpus, and Constitutional Litigation*. Charlottesville, Va.: Michie Press.

Meernik, James, and Joseph Ignagni. 1997. "Judicial Review and Coordinate Construction of the Constitution." *American Journal of Political Science* 41:447–67.

Melnick, R. Shep. 1994. *Between the Lines: Interpreting Welfare Rights*. Washington, D.C.: Brookings Institution.

Mendelson, Wallace. 1964. "The Untroubled World of Jurimetrics." *Journal of Politics* 26:914–22.

Mendelson, Wallace. 1963. "The Neo-Behavioral Approach to the Judicial Process: A Critique." *American Political Science Review* 57:593–603.

Milkis, Sidney M. 1993. *The President and the Parties: The Transformation of the American Party System since the New Deal*. New York: Oxford University Press.

Miller, Arthur Selwyn. 1968. *The Supreme Court and American Capitalism*. New York: Free Press.

Miller, Mark C. 1995. *The High Priests of American Politics: The Role of Lawyers in American Political Institutions*. Knoxville, Tenn.: University of Tennessee Press.

Moe, Terry M. 1987. "Interests, Institutions, and Positive Theory: The Politics of the NLRB." *Studies in American Political Development* 2:236–99.

———. 1985. "Control and Feedback in Economic Regulation: The Case of the NLRB." *American Political Science Review* 79:1094–1116.

Montgomery, David. 1967. *Beyond Equality: Labor and the Radical Republicans, 1862–1872*. New York: Alfred A. Knopf.

Morgan, D. 1944. "Mr. Justice William Johnson and the Constitution." *Harvard Law Review* 57:328.

Murphy, Paul L. 1972. *The Meaning of Freedom of Speech: First Amendment Freedoms from Wilson to FDR*. Westport, Conn.: Greenwood Press.

Murphy, Walter F. 1964. *Elements of Judicial Strategy*. Chicago: University of Chicago Press.

Murphy, Walter F., and Tanenhaus, Joseph. 1972. *The Study of Public Law*. New York: Random House.

Nagel, Stuart. 1962. "Ethnic Affiliations and Judicial Propensities." *Journal of Politics* 24:94–110.

———. 1961. "Political Party Affiliation and Judges' Decisions." *American Political Science Review* 55:843.

Nathan, Richard. 1983. *The Administrative Presidency*. New York: John Wiley and Sons.

Neiman, Donald G. 1992. "Mississippi v. Johnson." In *The Oxford Companion to the Supreme Court of the United States*, ed. Kermit Hall. New York: Oxford University Press.

Nelson, William E. 1988. *The Fourteenth Amendment: From Political Principle to Judicial Doctrine*. Cambridge, Mass.: Harvard University Press.

Niou, Emerson, and Peter C. Ordeshook. 1984. "Universalism in Congress." *American Journal of Political Science* 28:247–58.

Niven, John, ed. 1993. *The Salmon P. Chase Papers*. Kent, Ohio: Kent State University Press.

North, Douglass C. 1990. *Institutions, Institutional Change and Economic Performance*. New York: Cambridge University Press.

O'Brien, David M. 1996. *Storm Center: The Supreme Court in American Politics*. 4th ed. New York: Norton.

———. 1993. *Storm Center: The Supreme Court in American Politics*. 3rd ed. New York: Norton.

O'Connor, Karen. 1980. *Women's Organizations' Use of the Courts*. Lexington, Mass.: Lexington Books.

O'Connor, Karen, and Lee Epstein. 1989. "Beyond Legislative Lobbying: Women's Rights Groups and the Supreme Court." *Judicature* 67:134–43.

———. 1983. "Court Rules and Workload." *Justice System Journal* 8:40–41.

Ordeshook. 1992. *A Political Theory Primer*. New York: Routledge.

Orren, Karen. 1995a. "Ideas and Institutions." *Polity* 28:97–102.

———. 1995b. "The Primacy of Labor in American Constitutional Development." *American Political Science Review* 89:377–88.

Orren, Karen, and Stephen Skowronek. 1994. "Beyond the Iconography of Order: Notes for a "New" Institutionalism." In *The Dynamics of American Poli-*

tics: Approaches and Interpretations, ed. Larry Dodd and Calvin Jillson. Boulder, Colo.: Westview Press.

———. 1986. *Studies in American Political Development,* vol. 1. New Haven, Conn.: Yale University Press.

Ostrom, Elinor. 1995. "New Horizons in Institutional Analysis." *American Political Science Review* 89:174–78.

Pacelle, Richard L., Jr. 1991. *The Transformation of the Supreme Court's Agenda from the New Deal to the Reagan Administration.* Boulder, Colo.: Westview Press.

Palmer, Jan. 1982. "An Econometric Analysis of the U.S. Supreme Court's Certiorari Decisions." *Public Choice* 39:387.

Patry, Jean-Luc. 1989. "Contradictory Goals, Different Expectations: Towards an Explanation of Cross-Situational Specificity in Social Behavior." *Psychological Reports* 65:1331–39.

Payne, James L., Oliver H. Woshinsky, Eric P. Veblen, William H. Coogan, and Gene E. Bigler. 1984. *The Motivation of Politicians.* Chicago: Nelson Hall.

Peabody, Robert L., Norman J. Ornstein, and David W. Rohde. 1976. "The United States Senate as a Presidential Incubator: Many Are Called but Few Are Chosen." *Political Science Quarterly* 91:237–58.

Pear, Robert. 1996. "Clinton Considers Move to Soften Cuts in Welfare." *New York Times,* November 27, sect. A.

Perry, H. W., Jr. 1991. *Deciding to Decide: Agenda Setting in the United States Supreme Court.* Cambridge, Mass.: Harvard University Press.

Pfiffner, James P. 1991. *The Managerial Presidency.* Belmont, Calif.: Wadsworth, Inc.

———. 1988. *The Strategic Presidency: Hitting the Ground Running.* Chicago: Dorsey Press.

Polsby, Nelson W., Robert A. Dentler, and Paul A. Smith. 1963. "A Brief Introduction to the Scientific Study of Political Behavior." In *Politics and Social Life: An Introduction to Political Behavior,* ed. Nelson W. Polsby, Robert A. Dentler, and Paul A. Smith. Boston: Houghton Mifflin Company.

Poole, Keith, and Howard Rosenthal. 1991. "Patterns of Congressional Voting." *American Journal of Political Science.* 35:228–78.

Posner, Richard A. 1995. *Overcoming Law.* Cambridge, Mass.: Harvard University Press.

———. 1994. "What do Judges Maximize? (The Same Thing Everybody Else Does)." *Supreme Court Economics Review* 3:1.

———. 1990. *The Problems of Jurisprudence.* Cambridge, Mass.: Harvard University Press.

———. 1987. "The Decline of Law as an Autonomous Discipline: 1962–1987." *Harvard Law Review* 100(1987):761–80.

———. 1985. *The Federal Courts.* Cambridge, Mass.: Harvard University Press.

Powell, Walter W., and Paul J. DiMaggio, eds. 1991. *The New Institutionalism in Organizational Analysis.* Chicago: University of Chicago Press.

Prewitt, Kenneth. 1970. *The Recruitment of Political Leaders: A Study of Citizen-Politicians.* Indianapolis, Ind.: Bobbs-Merrill.

Pritchett, C. Herman. 1961. *Congress versus the Supreme Court, 1957–1960.* Minneapolish: University of Minnesota Press.

————. 1954. *Civil Liberties and the Vinson Court*. Chicago: University of Chicago Press.

————. 1948. *The Roosevelt Court*. New York: Macmillan.

————. 1945. "Dissent on the Supreme Court, 1943–1944." *American Political Science Review* 39:42–54.

————. 1941. "Divisions of Opinion among Justices of the U.S. Supreme Court." *American Political Science Review* 35:890–98.

Prinz, Timothy S. 1993. "The Career Paths of Elected Politicians: A Review and Prospectus." In *Ambition and Beyond: Career Paths of American Politicians*, ed. Shirley Williams and Edward L. Lascher, Jr. Berkeley: Institute of Governmental Studies Press, University of California.

Provine, Doris Marie. 1980. *Case Selection in the United States Supreme Court*. Chicago: University of Chicago Press.

Puro, Steven. 1971. "The Role of Amicus Curiae in the United States Supreme Court." Ph.D. dissertation, State University of New York at Buffalo.

Putnam, Robert D. 1993. *Making Democracy Work: Civic Traditions in Modern Italy*. Princeton, N.J.: Princeton University Press.

Rand, Ayn. 1965. *The Virtue of Selfishness: A New Concept of Egoism*. New York: New American Library.

Rathjen, Gregory. 1974. "Policy Goals, Strategic Choices, and Majority Opinion Assignments in the U.S. Supreme Court: A Replication." *American Journal of Political Science* 18:713–24.

"Reagan's Mr. Right." 1986. *Time*, June 30.

Redlich, Allen. 1992. "Who Will Litigate Constitutional Issues for the Poor?" *Hastings Constitutional Law Quarterly* 19:745–82.

Rehnquist, William H. 1987. *The Supreme Court: How It Was, How It Is*. New York: Morrow.

————. 1982. "Are the True Old Times Dead?" MacSwinford Lecture, University of Kentucky, September 23, 1982.

Reich, Charles. 1964. "The New Property." *Yale Law Journal* 73:733–87.

————. 1965. "Individual Rights and Social Welfare: The Emerging Legal Issues." *Yale Law Journal* 74:1245–57.

Riker, William H. 1986. *The Art of Political Manipulation*. New Haven, Conn.: Yale University Press.

————. 1982. *Liberalism against Populism*. San Francisco: W. H. Freeman.

————. 1980. "Implications from the Disequilibrium of Majority Rule for the Study of Institutions." *American Political Science Review* 74:432–46.

————. 1962. *Theory of Coalition Formation*. New Haven, Conn.: Yale University Press.

Riker, William H., and Donald Niemi. 1962. "The Stability of Coalitions on Roll Calls in the House of Representatives." *American Political Science Review* 56: 58–65.

Roberts, Owen. 1946. Address, Meeting of the Association of the Bar of the City of New York and the New York County Lawyers' Association, December 12.

Rodriguez, Daniel B. 1994. "The Positive Political Dimensions of Regulatory Reform." *Washington University Law Quarterly* 72:1–150.

Rohde, David W. 1979. "Risk-Bearing and Progressive Ambition: The Case of

Members of the United States House of Representatives." *American Journal of Political Science* 23:1–26.

———. 1972a. "Policy Goals and Opinion Coalitions in the Supreme Court." *Midwest Journal of Political Science* 16:208–24.

———. 1972b. "A Theory of the Formation of Opinion Coalitions in the U.S. Supreme Court." In *Probability Models of Collective Decision Making,* ed. Richard G. Niemi and Herbert F. Weisberg. Columbus, Ohio: Charles E. Merrill.

———. 1972c. "Policy Goals, Strategic Choice and Majority Opinion Assignments in the U.S. Supreme Court." *Midwest Journal of Political Science* 16:653–82.

Rohde, David W., and Kenneth A. Shepsle. 1978. "Taking Stock of Congressional Research: The New Institutionalism." Paper presented at the annual meeting of the Midwest Political Science Association, Chicago.

Rohde, David W., and Harold J. Spaeth. 1976. *Supreme Court.* San Francisco: W. H. Freeman.

Rosen, Jeffrey. 1993. "Court Marshall." *The New Republic,* June 21.

Rosenberg, Gerald N. 1994. "Symposium: The Supreme Court and the Attitudinal Model." *Law and Courts Newsletter* 4:6–8.

———. 1991. *The Hollow Hope: Can Courts Bring about Social Change?* Chicago: University of Chicago Press.

Ross, Lee, and Richard F. Nisbett. 1991. *The Person and the Situation: Perspectives of Social Psychology.* New York: McGraw-Hill.

Rumble, Wilfred. 1968. *American Legal Realism: Skepticism, Reform, and the Judicial Process.* Ithaca: Cornell University Press.

Salokar, Rebecca Mae. 1995. "Politics, Law, and the Office of the Solicitor General." In *Government Lawyers: The Federal Legal Bureaucracy and Presidential Politics,* ed. Cornell W. Clayton. Lawrence, Kans.: University Press of Kansas.

———. 1992. *The Solicitor General: The Politics of Law.* Philadelphia: Temple University Press.

Samson, Gloria Garrett. 1996. *The American Fund for Public Service: Charles Garland and Radical Philanthropy, 1922–1941.* Westport, Conn.: Greenwood Press.

Sandel, Michael J. 1995. *Democracy and Its Discontents.* Cambridge, Mass.: Harvard University Press.

———. 1984. "The Procedural Republic and the Unencumbered Self." *Political Theory* 12:81–96.

Sanders, Joe W. 1963. "The Role of Dissenting Opinions in Louisiana." *Louisiana Law Review* 23:676.

Sarat, Austin. 1977. "Judging in Trial Courts: An Exploratory Study." *Journal of Politics* 39:368–98.

Sarat, Austin, and Thomas R. Kearns. 1993. *The Fate of Law.* Ann Arbor, Mich.: University of Michigan Press.

Savage, David G. 1996a. "Mixed Record Marks 10 Years of Rehnquist Supreme Court." *Los Angeles Times,* June 18, sect. A.

———. 1996b. "Stormy Sessions." *ABA Journal,* March 1.

———. 1995. "Supreme Court Rulings Herald Rehnquist Era." *Los Angeles Times,* July 2, sect. A.

Scalia, Antonin. 1994. "The Dissenting Opinion." *Journal of Supreme Court History* 1994:33–44.

Scheingold, Stuart. 1974. *The Politics of Rights*. New Haven, Conn.: Yale University Press.

Schelling, Thomas C. 1980. *The Strategy of Conflict*. Cambridge, Mass.: Harvard University Press.

Scheppele, Kim Lane. 1996. "Political Science and Legal Studies: The Case for Dualism." *Law and Courts Newsletter*. Spring.

Schlesinger, Joseph A. 1966. *Ambition and Politics: Political Careers in the United States*. Chicago: Rand McNally.

Schmidhauser, John R. 1979. *Judges and Justices: The Federal Appellate Judiciary*. Boston, Mass.: Little, Brown.

———. 1961. "Judicial Behavior and the Sectional Crisis of 1837–1860." *Journal of Politics* 23:615–640.

———. 1959. "The Justices of the Supreme Court: A Collective Portrait." *Midwest Journal of Political Science* 3:1–57.

Schmidt, Benno C., Jr. 1986. "The Rehnquist Court: A Watershed." *New York Times*, June 22.

Schubert, Glendon. 1974. *The Judicial Mind Revisited: A Psychometric Analysis of Supreme Court Ideology*. New York: Free Press.

———. 1965. *The Judicial Mind: The Attitudes and Ideologies of Supreme Court Justices, 1946–1963*. Evanston, Ill.: Northwestern University Press.

———. 1964. "The Power of Organized Minorities in a Small Group." *Administrative Science Quarterly* 9:133–153.

———. 1962a. "The 1960 Term of the Supreme Court." *American Political Science Review* 56:90.

———. 1962b. "Policy without Law: An Extension of the Certiorari Game." *Stanford Law Review* 14:284–327.

———. 1959. *Quantitative Analysis of Judicial Behavior*. Glencoe, Ill.: Free Press.

Schubert, Glendon, ed. 1964. *Judicial Behavior: A Reader in Theory and Research*. Chicago: Rand McNally.

———. 1963. *Judicial Decision-Making*. New York: Free Press.

Schwartz, Bernard. 1996. *Decision: How the Supreme Court Decides Cases*. New York: Oxford University Press.

———. 1993. *A History of the Supreme Court*. New York: Oxford University Press.

———. 1988. *The Unpublished Opinions of the Burger Court*. New York: Oxford University Press.

———. 1985. *The Unpublished Opinions of the Warren Court*. New York: Oxford University Press.

———. 1983. *Super Chief: Earl Warren and His Supreme Court—A Judicial Biography*. New York: Oxford University Press.

Schwartz, Edward P. 1996. "The Proliferation of Concurring Opinions on the U.S. Supreme Court: Politics Killed the Norm." Paper presented at the annual meeting of the Midwest Political Science Association, Chicago.

Schwartz, Louis. 1989. "Rebels with a Cause, But without a Leader." *New Jersey Law Journal*, August 10.

Scigliano, Robert. 1971. *The Supreme Court and the Presidency*. New York: Free Press.

Searing, Donald D. 1991. "Roles, Rules, and Rationality in the New Institutionalism." *American Political Science Review* 85:1239–60.

Segal, Jeffrey A. 1997. "Separation-of-Powers Games in the Positive Theory of Law and Courts." *American Political Science Review* 91:28–44.

———. 1995. "Marksist (and Neo-Marksist) Models of Supreme Court: Separation-of-Powers Games in the Positive Theory of Law and Courts." Paper presented at the annual meeting of the American Political Science Association, Chicago.

———. 1994. "Symposium: The Supreme Court and the Attitudinal Model." *Law and Courts Newsletter*. Spring:10–12.

———. 1991. "Courts, Legislatures, and Executives." In *The American Courts*, ed. Gates, John B., and Charles A. Johnson. Washington D.C.: CQ Press.

Segal, Jeffrey A., and Albert D. Cover. 1989. "Ideological Values and the Votes of U.S. Supreme Court Justices." *American Political Science Review* 83:557–65.

Segal, Jeffrey A., Lee Epstein, Charles M. Cameron, and Harold J. Spaeth. 1995. "Ideological Values and the Votes of U.S. Supreme Court Justices Revisited." *Journal of Politics* 57:812–23.

Segal, Jeffrey A., and Cheryl D. Reedy. 1988. "The Supreme Court and Sex Discrimination: The Role of the Solicitor General." *Western Political Quarterly* 41:553–68.

Segal, Jeffrey, D. Songer, and C. Cameron. 1995. "Decision-making on the U.S. Courts of Appeals." In *Contemplating Courts*, ed. Lee Epstein. Washington, D.C.: CQ Press.

Segal, Jeffrey A., and Harold J. Spaeth. 1996. "The Influence of Stare Decisis on the Votes of U.S. Supreme Court Justices." *American Journal of Political Science* 40:971–1003.

———. 1993. *The Supreme Court and the Attitudinal Model*. New York: Cambridge University Press.

Seidman, Michael Louis, and Tushnet, Mark V. 1996. *Remnants of Belief: Contemporary Constitutional Issues*. New York: Oxford University Press.

Selznick, Philip. 1996. "Institutionalism 'Old' and 'New.' " *Administrative Science Quarterly* 41: 270–77.

Shapiro, Martin. 1990. "The Supreme Court: From Warren to Burger." In *The New American Political System*, 2nd ed., ed. Anthony King. Washington, D.C.: American Enterprise Institute.

———. 1989. "Political Jurisprudence, Public Law, and Post-Consequentialist Ethics: Comment on Professors Barber and Smith." *Studies in American Political Development* 3:88–102.

———. 1986. "The Supreme Court's Return to Economic Regulation." In *Studies in American Political Development*, ed. Karen Orren and Stephen Skowronek. New Haven: Yale University Press.

———. 1984. "Whither Political Jurisprudence: A Symposium." *Western Political Quarterly* 36:533–70.

———. 1983. "Fathers and Sons: The Court, the Commentators, and the Search for Values." In *The Burger Court: The Counter-Revolution That Wasn't*, ed. Vincent Blasi. New Haven, Conn.: Yale University Press.

———. 1981. *Courts: A Comparative and Political Analysis*. Chicago: University of Chicago Press.

———. 1978. "The Supreme Court from Warren to Burger." In *The New American Political System*, ed. Anthony King. Washington, D.C.: American Enterprise Institute.

———. 1964a. *Law and Politics in the Supreme Court: New Approaches to Political Jurisprudence*. New York: Free Press.

———. 1964b. "Political Jurisprudence." *Kentucky Law Review* 52:294–345.

Sheldon, Charles H. 1988/89. "The Evolution of Law Clerking with the Washington Supreme Court: From 'Elbow Clerks' to 'Puisne Judges'." *Gonzaga Law Review* 24:45.

———. 1988. *A Century of Judging: A Political History of the Washington Supreme Court*. Seattle, Wash.: University of Washington Press.

———. 1986. "The Recruitment of Judges to the Washington Supreme Court: Past and Present." *Willamette Law Review* 22:85–128.

———. 1981. "Law Clerking with a State Supreme Court: Views from the Perspective of the Personal Assistants to the Judges." *Justice System Journal* 8:346.

Sheldon, Charles H., and Nicholas P. Lovrich, Jr. 1991. "State Judicial Recruitment." In *The American Courts: A Critical Assessment*, ed. John B. Gates and Charles A. Johnson. Washington, D.C.: CQ Press.

Sheldon, Charles H., and Linda Maule. 1997. *Choosing Justice: The Recruitment of State and Federal Judges*. Pullman, Wash.: Washington State University Press.

Shepsle, Kenneth A. 1989. "Studying Institutions: Some Lessons from the Rational Choice Approach." *Journal of Theoretical Politics* 1:131–47.

———. 1986. "Institutional Equilibrium and Equilibrium Institutions." In *Political Science: The Science of Politics*, ed. Herbert F. Weisberg. New York: Agathon Press.

———. 1979. "Institutional Arrangements and Equilibrium in Multi-Dimensional Voting Models." *American Journal of Political Science* 23:27–59.

Shepsle, Kenneth A., and Barry R. Weingast. 1995. "Positive Theories of Congressional Institutions." In *Positive Theories of Congressional Institutions*, ed. Kenneth A. Shepsle and Barry R. Weingast. Ann Arbor, Mich.: University of Michigan Press.

———. 1987. "The Institutional Foundations of Committee Power." *American Political Science Review* 81:85–104.

———. 1984. "Uncovered Sets and Sophisticated Voting Outcomes with Implications for Agenda Institutions." *American Journal of Political Science* 29:49–74.

Silverstein, Mark. 1994. *Judicious Choices: The New Politics of Supreme Court Confirmations*. New York: W. W. Norton.

Silverstein, Mark, and Benjamin Ginsberg. 1987. "The Supreme Court and the New Politics of Judicial Power." *Political Science Quarterly* 102:371–88.

Simon, Herbert A. 1985. "Human Nature in Politics: The Dialogue of Psychology with Political Science." *American Political Science Review* 79:293–304.

Simon, James F. 1995. *The Center Holds: The Power Struggle inside the Rehnquist Court*. New York: Simon and Schuster.

Sinclair, Barbara. 1995. "House Special Rules and the Institutional Design Controversy." In *Positive Theories of Congressional Institutions*, ed. Kenneth A. Shepsle and Barry R. Weingast. Ann Arbor, Mich.: University of Michigan Press.

Sklar, Martin. 1988. *The Corporate Reconstruction of American Capitalism, 1890–1916: The Market, the Law, and Politics*. Cambridge: Cambridge University Press.

Skocpol, Theda. 1995. "Why I Am an Historical Institutionalist." *Polity* 28:103–6.

Skowronek, Stephen. 1995. "Order and Change." *Polity* 28:91–96.

Slotnick, Elliot E. 1979. "Who Speaks for the Court? Majority Opinion Assignment from Taft to Burger." *American Journal of Political Science* 23:60–77.

———. 1978. "The Chief Justices and Self-Assignment of Majority Opinions: A Research Note." *Western Political Quarterly* 31:219–25.

Smith, Rogers M. 1996. "Science, Non-Science and Politics." In *The Historic Turn in Human Science*, ed. Terrence J. McDonald. Ann Arbor, Mich.: University of Michigan Press.

———. 1995. "Ideas, Institutions, and Strategic Choices." *Polity* 28:135–40.

———. 1994. "Symposium: The Supreme Court and the Attitudinal Model." *Law and Courts Newsletter* 4:8–9.

———. 1992. "If Politics Matters: Implications for a 'New Institutionalism.' " *Studies in American Political Development* 6:1–36.

———. 1989. "The New Institutionalism and Normative Theory: Reply to Professor Barber." *Studies in American Political Development* 3:74–87.

———. 1988. "Political Jurisprudence, the 'New Institutionalism,' and the Future of Public Law." *American Political Science Review* 82:89–108.

———. 1985. *Liberalism and American Constitutional Law*. Cambridge Mass.: Harvard University Press.

Smith, Steven S. 1989. *Call to Order: Floor Politics in the House and Senate*. Washington, D.C.: Brookings Institution.

Snyder, Mark, and William Ickes. 1985. "Personality and Social Behavior." In *Handbook of Social Psychology*. 3rd ed., ed. Gardner, Lindzey and Elliot Aronson. New York: Random House.

Solimine, Michael E., and James L. Walker. 1992. "The Next Word: Congressional Response to Supreme Court Statutory Decisions." *Temple Law Review* 65:425–58.

Songer, Donald R., Sue Davis, and Susan Haire. 1994. "A Reappraisal of Diversification in the Federal Courts: Gender Effects in the Courts of Appeals." *Journal of Politics* 56:425–39.

Songer, Donald R., and Susan Haire. 1992. "Integrating Alternative Approaches to the Study of Judicial Voting: Obscenity Cases in the U.S. Courts of Appeals." *American Journal of Political Science* 36:963–82.

Songer, Donald R., and Stefanie Lindquist. 1996. "Not the Whole Story: The Impact of Justices' Values on Supreme Court." *American Journal of Political Science* 40:1049–63.

Songer, Donald R, Jeff Segal, and C. Cameron. 1994. "The Hierarchy of Justice: Testing a Principal-Agent Model of Supreme Court-Circuit Court Interactions." *American Journal of Political Science* 38:673–96.

Songer, Donald R., and Reginald S. Sheehan. 1993. "Interest Group Success in the Courts: Amicus Participation in the Supreme Court." *Political Research Quarterly* 46:339–54.

Spaeth, Harold J. 1996. "Different Strokes for Different Folks: A Reply to Professor Shapiro's Assessment of the Subfield." *Law and Courts Newsletter.* Spring.

———. 1995. "The Attitudinal Model." In *Contemplating Courts,* ed. Lee Epstein. Washington, D.C.: CQ Press.

———. 1984. "Distributive Justice: Majority Opinion Assignments in the Burger Court." *Judicature* 67:299–304.

———. 1963. "An Analysis of Judicial Attitudes in the Labor Relations Decisions of the Warren Court." *Journal of Politics* 25:290–311.

———. 1961. "An Approach to the Study of Attitudinal Differences as an Aspect of Judicial Behavior." *Midwest Journal of Political Science* 5:180.

Special Committee of the Association of the Bar of the City of New York. 1959. *Equal Justice for the Accused.* Garden City, N.Y.: Doubleday.

Spiller, Pablo T., and Rafael Gely. 1992. "Congressional Control or Judicial Independence: The Determinants of U.S. Supreme Court Labor-Relations Decisions, 1949–1988." *RAND Journal of Economics,* 23:463–92.

Spiller, Pablo T., and Matthew L. Spitzer. 1992. "Judicial Choice of Legal Doctrines." *Journal of Law, Economics and Organizations* 8:8–46.

Spriggs, James F., II. 1997. "Explaining Bureaucratic Compliance with Supreme Court Opinions." *Political Research Quarterly* 50:567–593.

———. 1996. "The Supreme Court and Federal Administrative Agencies: A Resource-Based Theory and Analysis of Judicial Impact." *American Journal of Political Science* 40:1122–1151.

Spriggs, James F., II, Forrest Maltzman, and Paul J. Wahlbeck. Forthcoming. "Bargaining on the U.S. Supreme Court: Justices' Responses to Majority Opinion Drafts." *Journal of Politics.*

Spriggs, James F., II, and Paul J. Wahlbeck. Forthcoming. "Amicus Curiae and the Role of Information at the Supreme Court." *Political Research Quarterly.*

Spriggs, James F., II, Paul J. Wahlbeck, and Forrest Maltzman. 1997. "The Process of Bargaining and Accommodation on the U.S. Supreme Court." Paper presented at the annual meeting of the Law and Society Association, St. Louis.

Steamer, Robert J. 1986. *Chief Justice: Leadership and the Supreme Court.* Columbia, S.C.: University of South Carolina Press.

Steinmo, Sven, Kathleen Thelen, and Frank Longstreth, eds. 1992. *Structuring Politics: Historical Institutionalism in Comparative Analysis.* New York: Cambridge University Press.

Stevens, John Paul. 1982. "Some Thoughts on Judicial Restraint." *Judicature* 66: 177–83.

Stimson, James A., Michael B. MacKuen, and Robert S. Erickson. 1995. "Dynamic Representation. *American Political Science Review* 89:543–65.

Stone, Harlan. 1942. "Dissenting Opinions Are Not without Value." *Journal of the American Judicature Society* 26:78.

Strong, Theron. 1914. *Landmarks of a Lawyer's Lifetime.* New York: Dodd, Mead.

Tamanaka, Brian Z. 1996. "The Internal/External Distinction and the Notion of a 'Practice' in Legal Theory and Sociolegal Studies." *Law and Society Review* 30:163–204.

Tanenhaus, Joseph, Marvin Schick, Matthew Muraskin, and Daniel Rosen. 1963. "The Supreme Court's Certiorari Jurisdiction: Cue Theory." In *Judicial Decision-Making*, ed. Glendon Schubert. New York: Free Press.

Tate, C. Neal. 1981. "Personal Attribute Models of the Voting Behavior of U.S. Supreme Court Justices: Liberalism in Civil Liberties and Economics Decisions, 1946–1978." *American Political Science Review* 75:355–67.

Tate, C. Neal, and Roger Handberg. 1991. "Time Binding and Theory Building in Personal Attribute Models of Supreme Court Voting Behavior, 1916–88." *American Journal of Political Science* 35:460–80.

Taylor, Charles. 1985. *Philosophy and the Human Sciences*. New York: Cambridge University Press.

Tsebelis, George. 1990. *Nested Games: Rational Choice in Comparative Politics*. Berkeley: University of California Press.

Tushnet, Mark. 1993. "The Warren Court as History: An Interpretation." In *The Warren Court in Historical and Political Perspective*, ed. Mark Tushnet. Charlottesville, Va.: University Press of Virginia.

———. 1987. *The NAACP's Legal Strategy against Segregated Education, 1925–1950*. Chapel Hill, N.C.: University of North Carolina Press.

Ulmer, S. Sidney. 1984. "The Supreme Court's Certiorari Decisions: Conflict as a Predictive Variable." *American Political Science Review* 78:901–11.

———. 1983. "Conflict with Supreme Court Precedents and the Granting of Plenary Review." *Journal of Politics* 45:474–78.

———. 1978. "Selecting Cases for Supreme Court Review: An Underdog Model." *American Political Science Review* 72:902–10.

———. 1973. "Social Background as an Indicator to the Votes of Supreme Court Justices in Criminal Cases: 1947–1956 Terms." *American Journal of Political Science* 17:622–30.

———. 1972. "The Decision to Grant Certiorari as an Indicator to Decision 'On the Merits.' " *Polity* 4:429–47.

———. 1970a. "Dissent Behavior and the Social Background of Supreme Court Justices." *Journal of Politics* 32:580–98.

———. 1970b. "The Use of Power in the Supreme Court: The Opinion Assignments of Earl Warren, 1953–1960." *Journal of Public Law* 19:49–67.

———. 1970c. "The Use of Power in the Supreme Court." *Western Political Quarterly* 25:16–27.

———. 1965. "Toward a Theory of Sub-Group Formation in the United States Supreme Court." *Journal of Politics* 27:133–52.

———. 1961. "Introduction to Political Behavior." In *Readings in Political Behavior*, ed. Sidney Ulmer. Chicago: Rand McNally.

———. 1960. "The Analysis of Behavior Patterns on the United States Supreme Court." *Journal of Politics* 22:629–53.

Urofsky, Melvin I. 1983. "Myth and Reality: The Supreme Court and Protective Legislation in the Progressive Era." *Yearbook—Supreme Court Historical Society* 53–72.

VanDoren, Peter M. 1991. *Politics, Markets, and Congressional Policy Choices*. Ann Arbor, Mich.: University of Michigan Press.

Vines, Kenneth N. 1964. "Federal District Judges and Race Relations Cases in the South." *Journal of Politics* 26:337–57.

Von Jhering, Rudof. 1913. *Law as a Means to an End*. Boston: Boston Book Co.

Wahlbeck, Paul J. 1997. "The Life of the Law: Judicial Politics and Legal Change." *Journal of Politics* 59:778–802.

Wahlbeck, Paul J., Forrest Maltzman, and James F. Spriggs II. 1996. "Strategic Choices and the Decision to Join the Majority Opinion." Paper presented at the Conference on the Scientific Study of Judicial Politics, St. Louis.

Wahlbeck, Paul J., James F. Spriggs II, and Forrest Maltzman. 1998. "Marshalling the Court: Bargaining and Accommodation on the Supreme Court." *American Journal of Political Science* 42:294–315.

———. 1997. "The Politics of Dissents and Concurrences on the U.S. Supreme Court." Paper presented at the annual meeting of the American Political Science Association, Washington, D.C.

Walker, Jack. 1991. *Mobilizing Interest Groups in America: Patrons, Professions, and Social Movements*. Ann Arbor, Mich.: University of Michigan Press.

Walker, Samuel. 1990. *In Defense of American Liberties: A History of the ACLU*. New York: Oxford University Press.

Walker, Thomas G., Lee Epstein, and William J. Dixon. 1988. "On the Mysterious Demise of Consensual Norms in the United States Supreme Court." *Journal of Politics* 50:362–89.

Waller, Niels G., Veronica Benet, and Darrell L. Farney. 1994. "Modeling Person-Situation Correspondence over Time: A Study of 103 Evangelical Disciple-Makers." *Journal of Personality* 62:177–97.

Warren, Charles. 1913. "The Progressiveness of the United States Supreme Court." *Columbia Law Review* 13:294.

Wasby, Stephen L. 1995. *Race Relations Litigation in an Age of Complexity*. Charlottesville, Va.: University Press of Virginia.

Waterman, Richard W. 1989. *Presidential Influence and the Administrative State*. Knoxville, Tenn.: University of Tennessee Press.

Watson, Richard A., and Rondal G. Downing. 1969. *The Politics of the Bench and the Bar: Judicial Selection under the Missouri Nonpartisan Court Plan*. New York: John Wiley and Sons.

Wechsler, Herbert. 1961. *Principles, Politics and Fundamental Law*. Chicago: University of Chicago Press.

Weingast, Barry R. 1992. "Fighting Fire with Fire." In *The Postreform Congress*, ed. Roger Davidson. New York: St. Martin's Press.

———. 1979. "A Rational Choice Perspective on Congressional Norms." *American Journal of Political Science* 23:245–62.

Weingast, Barry R., and William J. Marshall. 1988. "The Industrial Organization of Congress." *Journal of Political Economy* 96:132–63.

Weingast, Barry R., and Mark J. Moran. 1984. "Bureaucratic Discretion or Congressional Control: Regulatory Policymaking by the FTC." *Journal of Political Economy* 91:765–800.

Westin, Alan F. 1958. *The Anatomy of a Constitutional Law Case*. New York: Macmillan.

White, Morton. 1957. *Social Thought in America: The Revolt Against Formalism*. Boston: Beacon Press.

Wiggins, G. Stephen. 1976. "Quasi-Party in the Guise of Amicus Curiae." *Cumberland Law Review* 7:293–305.

Wildavsky, Aaron. 1994. "Why Self-Interest Means Less Outside of a Social Context." *Journal of Theoretical Politics* 6:131–59.

Williams, Shirley. 1993. "Introduction." In *Ambition and Beyond: Career Paths of American Politicians,* ed. Shirley Williams and Edward L. Lascher, Jr. Berkeley: Institute of Governmental Studies Press, University of California.

Wilson, Woodrow. 1976. *The Papers of Woodrow Wilson,* vol. 21 (1910). Ed. Arthur S. Link. Princeton, N.J.: Princeton University Press.

Winter, David G. 1987. "Leader Appeal, Leader Performance, and the Motive Profiles of Leaders and Followers: A Study of American Presidents and Elections." *Journal of Personality and Political Psychology* 52:196–202.

Witt, Elder. 1990. *Congressional Quarterly's Guide to the U.S. Supreme Court.* 2nd ed. Washington, D.C.: CQ Press.

Wood, B. Dan. 1988. "Principals, Bureaucrats, and Responsiveness in Clean Air Enforcement." *American Political Science Review* 82:213–34.

Wood, B. Dan, and James E. Anderson. 1993. "The Politics of U.S. Antitrust Regulation." *American Journal of Political Science* 37:1–39.

Wood, Sandra L. 1996. "Bargaining and Negotiation on the Burger Court." Paper presented at the annual meeting of the American Political Science Association Meeting, San Francisco.

Woodward, Bob, and Scott Armstrong. 1979. *The Brethren: Inside the Supreme Court.* New York: Simon and Schuster.

Zobell, Karl M. 1959. "Division of Opinion in the Supreme Court: A History of Judicial Disintegration," *Cornell Law Quarterly* 44:186–214.

Zorn, Christopher. 1995. "Congress and the Supreme Court: Reevaluating the 'Interest Group Perspective.' " Paper presented at the annual meeting of the Midwest Political Science Association, Chicago.

CASES CITED

Adkins v. Children's Hospital. 1923. 261 U.S. 525.

Agostini v. Felton. 1997. 117 S.Ct. 2000.

Aguilar v. Felton. 1985. 473 U.S. 402.

Akron v. Akron Center for Reproductive Health. 1983. 462 US 416.

American Trucking Assns. v. Smith. 1990. 110 L Ed 2d 148.

Arizona v. Fulminante. 1991. 499 U.S. 279.

Baker v. Carr. 1962. 369 U.S. 186.

Barnes v. Glen Theatre, Inc. 1991. 111 S.Ct. 2456.

Batson v. Kentucky. 1986. 476 U.S. 79.

Board of Education v. Vail. 1984. 466 U.S. 377.

Bowers v. Hardwick. 1986. 478 U.S. 186.

Brotton v. Langert. 1890. 1 Wash. 73.

Brown v. Allen. 1953. 344 U.S. 443, 535.

Brown v. Board of Education of Topeka, Kansas. 1954. 347 U.S. 483.

Buchanan v. Warley. 1917. 245 U.S. 60.

Bush v. Vera. 1996. 116 S.Ct. 1941.

Cantwell v. Connecticut. 1940. 310 US 296.

Chevron v. National Resources Defense Council. 1984. 467 U.S. 837.

Church of Lukumi Babalu Aye v. City of Hialeah. 1993. 113 S.Ct. 2217.

City of Boerne v. Flores, Archbishop of San Antonio, et Al. 1997. 95 U.S. S.Ct.: 2074.

Cohens v. Virginia. 1821. 6 Wheat. 264.

Coleman v. Balkcom. 1981. 451 U.S. 949.

Coleman v. Thompson. 1991. 501 U.S. 722.

Cooper v. Aaron. 1958. 358 U.S. 1.

Cruzan by Cruzan v. Director, Missouri Dept. of Health. 1990. 497 U.S. 261.

Dandridge v. Williams. 1970. 397 U.S. 471.

Davis v. United States. 1973. 411 U.S. 23.

DeJonge v. Oregon. 1937. 299 U.S. 353.

DeShaney v. Winnebago County Dept. of Social Services. 1989. 489 U.S. 872.

Douglas v. California. 1963. 372 U.S. 353.

Dred Scott v. Sandford. 1857. 19 How. 393.

Edwards v. California. 1941. 314 U.S. 160.

Eisenstadt v. Baird. 1972. 405 U.S. 438.

Employment Division, Department of Human Resources of Oregon v. Smith. 1990. 494 U.S. 189.

Seminole Tribe v. Florida. 1996. 116 S.Ct. 1114.
Shapiro v. Thompson. 1969. 394 U.S. 618.
Shelley v. Kraemer. 1948. 334 U.S. 1.
Sherbert v. Verner. 1963. 374 U.S. 398.
Simms & Wise v. Slacum. 1806. 3 CRANCH 300.
State Farm Mutual Automobile Insurance v. Motor Vehicle Manufacturers Association of the United States. 1983. 463 U.S. 29.
Strader v. Graham. 1851. 51 U.S. (10 HOW.) 82.
Stromberg v. California. 1931. 283 U.S. 359.
Sumner v. Mata. 1981. 449 U.S. 539.
Texas v. Johnson. 1989. 491 U.S. 397.
Thornburgh v. American College of Obstreticians and Gynecologists. 1986. 476 U.S. 747.
Townsend v. Swank. 1971. 404 U.S. 282.
U.S. v. Carolene Products. 1938. 304 U.S. 144.
U.S. v. Eichman. 1990. 496 U.S. 310.

U.S. v. Fordice. 1992. 505 U.S. 717.
U.S. v. Guest. 1966. 383 U.S. 745.
U.S. v. Leon. 1984. 468 U.S. 1250.
U.S. v. Lopez. 1995. 115 S.Ct. 1624.
U.S. v. New York. 1992. 112 S.Ct. 2408.
U.S. v. Nixon. 1974. 418 U.S. 683.
Wadman v. Immigration and Naturalization Service. 1964. 329 F.2d 812.
Wainwright v. Sykes. 1977. 443 U.S. 72.
Webster v. Reproductive Health Services. 1989. 492 U.S. 490.
Whitney v. California. 1927. 274 U.S. 357.
Wisconsin v. Yoder. 1972. 406 U.S. 208.
Witters v. Washington Department of Services for the Blind. 1986. 474 U.S. 481.
Wolf v. Colorado. 1949. 338 U.S. 25.
Youngstown Sheet and Tube Co. v. Sawyer. 1952. 343 U.S. 579.
Zobrest v. Catalina Foothills School District. 1993. 509 U.S. 1.

CONTRIBUTORS

Lawrence Baum is Professor of Political Science at Ohio State University. He is author of *The Supreme Court* (1998), *American Courts* (1998), and *The Puzzle of Judicial Behavior* (1997). Subjects of his research include sources of change in Supreme Court policy and interactions between the Supreme Court and lower courts.

Paul Brace is Clarence Carter Professor of Political Science at Rice University. He has published *State Government and Economic Performance* (1993) and *Follow the Leader: Opinion Polls and the Modern Presidents* (1992; with Barbara Hinckley). The latter book won the Neustadt Prize from the Presidency Research Section of the American Political Science Association in 1993. His research has appeared in *American Political Science Review, Journal of Politics, Political Research Quarterly, Polity, Social Science Quarterly, American Politics Quarterly, Legislative Studies Quarterly*, and elsewhere. He has served, or is serving, on the editorial boards of the *American Political Science Review, Journal of Politics, Political Research Quarterly*, and *American Politics Quarterly*.

Elizabeth Bussiere is an Associate Professor of Political Science at the University of Massachusetts at Boston. She is the author of *(Dis)Entitling the Poor: The Warren Court, Welfare, Rights, and the American Political Tradition* (1997). Her articles on constitutional law have appeared in several journals, including *Political Science Quarterly*, and her current research focuses on the American jury system.

Cornell W. Clayton is Associate Professor in the Political Science Department at Washington State University. He is author of *The Politics of Justice: The Attorney General and the Making of Legal Policy* (1992) and recently edited *Government Lawyers: The Federal Legal Bureaucracy and*

Presidential Politics (1995). He is currently working on a book that examines institutional structures and the Court.

Sue Davis is Professor of Political Science at the University of Delaware. She is the author of *Justice Rehnquist and the Constitution* (1989) and a number of articles examining his decision-making that have appeared in journals including *Western Political Quarterly, Polity,* and *Judicature.* She has also published work examining judicial behavior on the United States Courts of Appeal. Her most recent work is *American Political Thought: Four Hundred Years of Ideas and Ideologies* (1997).

Charles R. Epp is an Assistant Professor of Government at the University of Kansas. His articles on civil rights litigation, the legal profession, and the judicial rights agenda have appeared in several journals, including the *American Political Science Review, Law and Society Review,* and *Law and Social Inquiry.* He is the author of *The Rights Revolution: Lawyers, Activists, and Supreme Courts in Comparative Perspective* (1998). His current research examines the effects of the rights revolution on policy and the administrative process in city governments.

Lee Epstein is the Edward Mallinckrodt Distinguished University Professor of Political Science and Chair of the Department of Political Science at Washington University in St. Louis. She is the author, co-author, and editor of numerous books on constitutional law and judicial politics, including *The Supreme Court and Legal Change* (1992; with Joseph F. Kobylka), *The Supreme Court of the United States: An Introduction* (1993; with Thomas G. Walker), *Constitutional Law For a Changing America,* 2nd edition (1995; with Thomas G. Walker), and *The Supreme Court Compendium* (1994; with Jeffrey A. Segal, Harold Spaeth, and Thomas G. Walker). Her articles on judicial politics, interest group litigation and social science methodology have appeared in many social science journals and law reviews. Most recently, she is the author of *The Choices Justices Make* (1998; with Jack Knight).

Howard Gillman is an Associate Professor of Political Science at the University of Southern California. He is the author of *The Constitution Besieged: The Rise and Demise of Lochner Era Police Powers Jurisprudence* (1993), which was the recipient of the C. Herman Pritchett Award for the best book in the field of Law and Courts by a political scientist. His articles on judicial politics and American constitutional development have appeared in a number of journals, including *Law and Social Inquiry, Law and Society Review, Political Research Quarterly,* and *Studies in American Political Development.* He is currently finishing a book on the rise of civil liberties jurisprudence in the Supreme Court during the twentieth century.

Melinda Gann Hall is Professor of Political Science at Michigan State University. Her research on judicial politics and behavior has appeared in the *Journal of Politics, Political Research Quarterly, Social Science Quarterly, American Politics Quarterly,* and a variety of other scholarly journals and edited volumes. Currently she is completing *Judicial Elections in the American States,* an examination of all state supreme court elections from 1980 to 1995.

Ronald Kahn is James Monroe Professor of Politics and Law and Chair of the Law and Society Program, Oberlin College. He is author of *The Supreme Court and Constitutional Theory, 1953–1993* (1994) and numerous articles on Supreme Court decision-making, constitutional law, and legal theory. He is presently working on a book entitled *Social Facts and the Rights of Subordinated Groups in Post-Pluralist America.* He has been elected to the Executive Committee of the American Political Science Association (1988–90) and its organized section on Law and Courts (1995–97).

Jack Knight is an Associate Professor in the Department of Political Science at Washington University in St. Louis. His books include *Explaining Social Institutions* (1995; edited with Itai Sened) and *Institutions and Social Conflict* (1992). He has written numerous articles and book chapters on constitutionalism, institutional change, interpretation, political philosophy, and social science methodology. His most recent book is *The Choices Justices Make* (1998; with Lee Epstein) and he has already turned his attention to projects that assess the strengths and weakness of nonfoundationalist or pragmatist justifications of democracy.

Forrest Maltzman is an Associate Professor of Political Science at George Washington University. He received his Ph.D. from the University of Minnesota in 1993. He has published articles in the *American Political Science Review,* the *American Journal of Political Science,* the *Journal of Politics,* and *Legislative Studies Quarterly.* He is also the author of *Competing Principals: Committees, Parties, and the Organization of Congress* (1997).

David M. O'Brien is The Leone Reeves and George W. Spicer Professor of Government at the University of Virginia. He has also been a Research Associate and Judicial Fellow at the Supreme Court of the

United States, a visiting Fellow at the Russell Sage Foundation, a Fulbright Lecturer in Constitutional Studies at Oxford University, and a Fulbright Researcher in Japan. He has authored numerous articles and thirteen books, including *Constitutional Law and Politics* (3d ed., 1997), an annual *Supreme Court Watch, To Dream of Dreams: Religious Freedom and Constitutional Politics in Postwar Japan* (1996), and *Storm Center: The Supreme Court in American Politics* (4th ed., 1996), which received the American Bar Association's Silver Gavel Award.

Jeffrey A. Segal is Professor of Political Science at the State University of New York at Stony Brook. He received his Ph.D. from Michigan State University. His books include *The Supreme Court and the Attitudinal Model* (1993; with Harold Spaeth) and *The Supreme Court Compendium* (1994; with Lee Epstein, Harold J. Spaeth, and Thomas G. Walker). His articles on the Supreme Court have appeared in many political science journals, including the *American Political Science Review, American Journal of Political Science,* and *Journal of Politics.*

Charles H. Sheldon is the Claudius O. Johnson Distinguished Professor in the Department of Political Science at Washington State University. His articles on state judicial politics have been published in numerous journals, including: *Judicature, Publius, Political Research Quarterly,* and the *Georgetown Law Journal.* He is the author or editor of more than ten books, including; *The High Bench: A Biographical History of the Washington Supreme Court* (1992), *A Century Of Judging: A Political History of the Washington Supreme Court* (1988) and *The American Judicial Process: Models and Approaches* (1970).

James F. Spriggs II is an Assistant Professor of Political Science at the University of California, Davis. He received his Ph.D. from Washington University in St. Louis in 1994. His research on judicial decision-making and judicial impact has been published in the *American Journal of Political Science, Journal of Politics,* and *Political Research Quarterly.*

Paul J. Wahlbeck is an Assistant Professor of Political Science at George Washington University. He received his Ph.D. from Washington University in St. Louis. He has published articles in the *American Political Science Review, American Journal of Political Science, Journal of Politics,* and *Political Research Quarterly.* His research focuses on legal change and argumentation, strategic interaction among justices, and judicial appointments and retirements.

INDEX

Abel, Richard, 269
abortion, 177–85
Ackerman, Bruce, 18, 27–29, 41n. 8
Adams, John, 220–21
Adkins v. Children's Hospital, 265
agenda-setting process: Department of Justice, 273–75; in general, 255–56; historical background, 256–58; institutional constraints, 258–60; legal mobilization, 262–78; resource constraints, 260–62
Agostini v. Felton, 187–90
Aguilar Court, 189–95
Aguilar v. Felton, 187–88
Aid to Families with Dependent Children (AFDC), 155, 161, 162, 166–69
Akron v. Akron Center for Reproductive Health, 181
American Civil Liberties Union (ACLU), 265–68, 275–76
American Fund for Public Service, 272
American Trucking Assns. v. Smith, 18
amicus curiae, 11, 38, 215–16, 221–31, 234n. 23
Antiterrorism and Effective Death Penalty Act, 143
appellate courts: consensus, 124–28; dissensus, 116–19, 128–33; dissent, 115, 123–24; institutional change and dissent, 119–23
Arizona v. Fulminante, 111, 154n. 11
attitudinal model: agenda-setting, 255–56, 257; individual preferences, 60, 65–66, 237; institutional

constraints, 258–60; overview, 1–3, 22–30, 44–46, 238–40; problems with, 3–5, 25–26; vs. rational choice approach, 293–95; resource constraints, 260–62; static quality, 52; tested vs. separation of powers model, 244–53

Baer, Harold, Jr., 152
Baldwin, Roger, 266, 272
bargaining among justices. *See* opinion-writing process
Barnes v. Glen Theatre, Inc., 154n. 6
Baum, Lawrence, 11, 25, 49, 242
Beard, Charles, 16
behavioralism (*see also* attitudinal model): 22–23, 28–30, 65
Bentley, Arthur, 35
Black, Hugo L.: appointment of, 96; debates with Jackson, 98; dissent, 93, 100, 105, 180; *Griffin v. Illinois*, 160; liberal judicial activism, 102; Marble Temple, 103; political ambition, 204
Blackmun, Harry, 179, 182, 187, 191, 244
Board of Education v. Vail, 228
Bork, Robert H., 29
Boucher, Robert, 53
Bowers v. Hardwick, 278
Brace, Paul, 12
Brandeis, Louis D., 93, 95–96, 101–2, 264
Brennan, William: articles, 220; attention to Congress, 230–31; and Burger, 110; circulation records,

www.ingramcontent.com/pod-product-compliance
Lightning Source LLC
Chambersburg PA
CBHW022134020426
42334CB00015B/895